"James Reston, Jr., paints a vivid yet sensitive p[...]
effervescent friendships in the rich intellectual [...]
Republic, the brew of excitement and egoistic par[...]
his astronomical discoveries with the telescope [...]
derelict brother and the lawsuit over his sister's dowry, the ag[...],
trip to Rome to face the Inquisition. It is a dramatic story, often told, but
never as compellingly as this."   —Owen Gingerich,
Harvard-Smithsonian Center for Astrophysics

"This is a spectacular feat of both scholarship and writing. James Reston
brings Galileo out of the pantheon of scientists and makes him walk,
breathe—and suffer—among us. One needs constantly to be reminded of
how enlightenment can suffer at the hands of the powerful and unen-
lightened."   —Daniel Schorr, Senior News Analyst,
National Public Radio

"*Galileo: A Life* is the best biography I have read in years. James Reston,
Jr. brilliantly recreates the life of a scientific genius, whose prolific inventions and innovations made him virtually a reincarnation of Leonardo da
Vinci. The author stunningly portrays the world of the late Renaissance,
cogently arguing that the suppression of Galileo was not only a terrible
scandal and embarrassment for the Roman Catholic Church but also
marked the decline of Italy as the center of European culture. . . . Like a
breath of fresh air in a monastery, Reston's scintillating biography of
Galileo exhilarates the spirit."   —*Nashville Banner*

"Author James Reston, Jr., a prolific novelist, historian and journalist,
narrates Galileo's tragic yet triumphant life with insight and compassion."
—*Minneapolis Star Tribune*

"A sharply focused biography of a heroic figure in the history of science."
—*Cleveland Plain Dealer*

"At once a man deeply embedded in and polarized by his milieu and its
surrounding force fields. Reston delineates the personal and institutional
storms that Galileo endured and seemed unerringly to seek out. . . . He
recreates the era with immediacy by mining Galileo's journals and letters
for dialogue."   —*Publishers Weekly*

"A well-rounded portrait, convincing the reader to appreciate Galileo's
mood swings, his intellectual arrogance, and his final capitulation as
behavior to be expected from the man portrayed. . . . An interesting character study and political biography of the great scientist."
—*Kirkus Reviews*

GALILEO

A
Life

JAMES RESTON, JR.

HarperPerennial
A Division of HarperCollins*Publishers*

A hardcover edition of this book was published in 1994 by HarperCollins Publishers.

GALILEO. Copyright © 1994 by James Reston, Jr. All rights reserved. Printed in the United States of America. No part of this book may be used or reproduced in any manner whatsoever except in the case of brief quotations embodied in critical articles and reviews. For information address HarperCollins Publishers, Inc., 10 East 53rd Street, New York, NY 10022.

HarperCollins books may be purchased for educational, business, or sales promotional use. For information please write: Special Markets Department, HarperCollins Publishers, Inc., 10 East 53rd Street, New York, NY 10022.

First HarperPerennial edition published 1995.

Designed by George J. McKeon

The Library of Congress has catalogued the hardcover edition as follows:
Reston, James, 1941–
  Galileo : a life / James Reston, Jr.
    p. cm.
  Includes index.
   ISBN 0-06-016378-X
   1. Galilei, Galileo, 1564–1642—Biography. 2. Astronomers—Italy—Biography. I. Title.
QB36.G2R27 1994
520'.92—dc20
[B]   93-29221

ISBN 0-06-092607-4 (pbk.)
95 96 97 98 99 ❖/RRD 10 9 8 7 6 5 4 3 2 1

For Edward Burlingame

CONTENTS

PRELUDE

During 1992, 350 years after his death, Galileo Galilei was much in the news. In his native land, the entire year had been set aside for him. Seminars dissected him. Exhibitions celebrated him. Artists sought to capture his essence. In Padua, where he had taught for eighteen years and spent the happiest time of his life, they commemorated the 400th anniversary of his first lecture at the university. In Pisa, where he was born and schooled and first became a teacher, physicists prepared to drop balls from the Tower of Pisa, just as Galileo supposedly had done in 1589. The modern scientists, dressed fetchingly in Renaissance garb, mugged for the television cameras as they used Galileo's legendary gravity experiment to publicize their own proposal to test the same "equivalence principle" in outer space.

In Venice, where Galileo had frolicked with a street wench (who eventually bore him three children and where he had presented his invention of a spyglass to an amazed doge) the Galileistas—that small cult of scholars devoted solely to the study of Galileo's life—gathered to applaud one another's papers on such topics as the role of Simplicio in Galileo's famous *Dialogue* or the musical culture of Venice in Galileo's time. At the Palazzo Vecchio in Florence, where Galileo had been the first philosopher of the Medici grand duke, a stormy conclave with Jesuit astronomers and Apache Indians took place, in which the Apaches lam-

basted the Vatican for defiling sacred ground by building a modern observatory on Indian burial lands in Arizona, and a Florentine city council-
man, an environmentalist by persuasion and a marquis by birth, tried to
mediate in the name of Galileo between the two warring sides.

In Rome there were more important doings. For thirteen years, since
1979, when Pope John Paul II had requested a commission "serenely" to
reconsider the Galileo case, the Vatican had struggled to come to grips
with the most enduring embarrassment of the church's history. For the
church, the name Galileo was generally coupled with the word *affair*, like
the Dreyfus affair or the Watergate affair, and the implication was to cast
aspersions on the personality of Galileo and to distract attention from the
actions of the church. During the thirteen-year reprise of the case, papers
and books were generated by the stack, conclaves were held around
Europe, and commissions were empaneled. But the work was deflective
and tentative, for it was not known what the pope really wanted in his
reconsideration. What was their mandate? How far could the church
depart from its authorized version of the story that Galileo had been disciplined merely for disobedience? Would the pope authorize a formal
apology? Did he really want to "purify" church history, or did he want to
whitewash it? How could the church bear the embarrassment of an apology, and what ramifications would a real apology have for issues of science
and morals in modern times?

In the end, it was a papal decision, and at last, on October 31, 1992,
John Paul acted. In his formal announcement, he acknowledged the suffering of Galileo at the hands of churchmen and acknowledged in general
terms that errors were made. Never again! he seemed to be saying. The
case of Galileo had finally been "resolved," the official Vatican paper,
L'Osservatore Romano, declared. But had it?

On December 8, 1992, meanwhile, I ventured down to the headquar-
ters of NASA in Washington. There, in governmental and scientific
precincts, sanitized versions of Galileo flourished as well. NASA's Galileo
affair was technological and financial rather than moral or historical. The
"case" involved a noble project gone awry. In 1977, with some trepida-
tion—for it feared questions about the church and the Inquisition—the
American space agency had named the most ambitious interplanetary
mission of the space-shuttle era after Galileo. It was to be a glorious mission to Jupiter, the most exotic and fascinating of the outer planets, and
to the planet's moons, which Galileo had been the first to observe and

which he had named after his Medici patrons. For the first time, the Galileo mission proposed to penetrate, indeed to "taste," the Jovian atmosphere with a bell-shaped ballistic until the probe burned up in the red clouds and hydrogen.

As planning proceeded, it was clear that the mission was well named. Its grandiose intention was beset by delay, detour, and catastrophe. Its design was rethought; its dangerous nuclear dynamo was removed after the *Challenger* disaster, and inquiries, sometimes rising to the level of inquisition, took place over its $1.4 billion price tag. Skirting between the few narrow-launch "windows" available for its interplanetary trajectory, *Galileo* finally blasted into space in October 1989, seven years late. It streaked in the wrong direction, toward the sun rather than Jupiter, because without its powerful nuclear heart it had to depend on the benign laws of physics to propel it. Over the next three years, it made two detours around Venus until now, on December 8, 1992, it was passing by our moon and our earth for the last time, before at last it headed directly for Jupiter.

Like Galileo the man, *Galileo* the machine was crippled. This too had its symbolic perfection. The spacecraft's umbrellalike antenna was stuck, and no amount of electronic hammering had succeeded in freeing the mechanism from its stubborn immobility. As a result, its scientific payload was jeopardized. Bravely, the NASA managers spoke of salvaging 70 percent of the data from a smaller antenna on the spacecraft, but they did not emphasize that 30 percent of a $1.4 billion budget equals a $420 million loss. Galileo seemed to be a curse. In all things connected with him, genius and embarrassment seemed to come in equal parts. The other extravagant space mission of the shuttle era was the Hubble Space Telescope, the modern equivalent of Galileo's first telescope. But it was suffering from optical cataracts, and its $1.5 billion vision was blurred. (The mission to correct this flawed vision, successful as it was in December 1993, cost NASA nearly another billion dollars.)

Still, on December 8, 1992, the space engineers were upbeat. Not given to spiritual or emotional lapses, they were men in love with machines. They spoke in acronyms and mathematical formulas, and in that narrow sense they were true successors to Galileo. For he had been the first to say that the universe had a language, and it was the language of mathematics. If one did not understand its geometric figures, Galileo had said, it was humanly impossible to understand the universe, and one wandered about in a dark labyrinth. These modern astronomers knew their way around the universe very well. They simply lacked Galileo's awe and wonder and humility. I was accustomed to their dry, bloodless discourses when they presented the most astonishing and inspiring celestial discoveries. And I knew that this very dryness was the reason that their wondrous discoveries had ceased to move the general public.

It came, therefore, as a mild surprise when an engineer at the Jet Propulsion Laboratory prefaced his presentation on the "trajectory change maneuver" and "solid-state imagining" with a personal note. He had lived with *Galileo* for fifteen years, he declared with evident emotion, and the night before, when the "great, big, beautiful" moon was full for the first time after days of rain, and he knew that *Galileo* was, at that moment, hurtling by the moon and about to pass the earth only twelve hours later on its way to Jupiter, "I said a quiet goodbye to *Galileo*, and Jupiter said a long-distance hello."

When the time for questions came, I seized upon this brief and uncharacteristic glimpse into a modern scientist's spiritual side. Perhaps there was more poetry there.

"Mr. Inman," I will call him. "In those fifteen years of preoccupation with this mission, did you ever see the face of Galileo Galilei hovering over your efforts?" I asked.

Nervous twitters filled the hall in Pasadena and could be heard clearly over the wire to my perch in Washington. Apparently, I had trespassed some forbidden ground and had created embarrassment. Mr. Inman paused for the snickers of his fellow scientists to subside.

"No," he said cryptically, and that was all.

The following day a full eclipse covered Mr. Inman's moon. In its mysterious, upsetting appearance, the apparition was so strange that it caused dark forebodings even in the modern world—but nothing like the terror of Pope Urban VIII, Galileo's persecutor, who considered such eclipses to be harbingers of his own death. That suspicious and paranoid pope had resorted to astrology to defeat their evil influences.

At the rate of 31,000 miles per hour, the *Galileo* spacecraft was receding rapidly from Earth. In a week's time, its camera was turned on again to reveal our world and its moon together in a fragile, vulnerable dance, suspended precariously in space just as Galileo had imagined it. "I have never doubted," he had written in 1610, "that if our globe were seen from afar when it was flooded with sunlight, the land regions would appear brighter and the watery regions darker." Before the mission to Jupiter ends, that Earth will be a mere point of light, one among billions.

With that perspective, as if on a moving platform, I will view Galileo in this work. His life is a brilliant, colorful star receding steadily in time and distance and yet forever with us in a near or a far orbit, sparkling with the brightness of the first magnitude. As a biographer, I propose to borrow a principle of astronomy: to turn his telescope around on him and look back in time, to see how he was formed, and to portray the hot gases through which he passed before he arrived in his permanent place in our cosmos, just as the modern astronomer can see back in time, even to the very moment when the universe was created.

With this life, however, I will be looking for the precise moment when modern history was born.

Part 1

PISA

THE WRANGLER

In the summer of 1579, high in the sylvan meadows of Vallombrosa, the young man of fifteen declared his intention to become a monk. For four years, at an abbey famous for its discipline and charity, the monks had groomed the youth for this passionate moment of commitment. His declaration was the fulfillment of their attentions. They had schooled him in Latin and Greek, drilled him in mathematics and rudimentary science, and nurtured his interests in literature and drawing, as they guided his religious exercises. The welcoming of a novice was to be celebrated whenever it happened, but this strapping red-haired lad was special. He was a child of the grand duke's court, the son of a well-known musician, and a youth of evident promise whose mother was even related to an important cardinal in Rome. The order was honored. The abbot was pleased. The young man could rise high within their ranks.

The distinguished father was coming for a visit. He was said to be a favorite of the grand duchess of Tuscany, a beautiful Venetian about whom there was always such interesting talk. The musician had even written madrigals in honor of the Lady Bianca and was said to be part of a fashionable circle of artists who were experimenting with combining music and myth into a single stage performance. But the monks already knew their novice's father to be difficult. He was abrasive and opinionated, altogether quite full of himself. It was easy to see the father's reflection in the son. The monks were eager for this holy, happy passage to be appreciated by the family, but they were apprehensive.

For centuries the climb up the mountain from Pontassieve had been the torment of the pilgrim. To Vallombrosa to pay homage to Saint John Gualberto they trudged, and then over the mountain into the upper valley of the Arno, to the sacred hermitage of the Camaldoli and on to La Verna and the bare rock where Saint Francis had received his stigmata. For the less devout, the carriage ride from Florence along the tortuous roads, along the sharp and dangerous spine of the Apennines, and through the dark fir forests could put a person in bad humor.

Perhaps that explained the rudeness of the court maestro when he arrived at the abbey and began to criticize the behavior of the monks. Abrupt and disrespectful, he waved aside their talk about the novitiate. The joy of the monks about the accomplishments of his son or about the solemn ceremony of initiation did not interest him. Instead, to their shock, he accused them of inattention to his son's health. The boy had a serious eye infection. Could they not see that? In their preoccupation with the next world, the monks had shirked their duty in this world, he exclaimed. Besides, they were ill equipped to treat his son's condition.

He proposed to take the boy away to Florence at once for medical attention. The boy, still in his hooded habit, climbed reluctantly into his father's carriage, and it moved off swiftly down the narrow *viale*, beneath the bower of beech branches, east toward Florence and liberation. The youth turned back for one last, wistful glance. He was leaving behind a career in the church—and a different course for history.

When the carriage reached Saltino, the vista opened up over the wide Arno valley, and in the far distance, through the summer haze, the lovely domes and spires of the city were barely visible. The monks and their piety and their iron grip receded into the distance and in memory, and Vincenzo Galilei could relax. For him there was no backward glance. They could talk of God and the tonsure later. For now, he wished to talk to his son about the wool trade.

That was in 1579. But the life of the young man had begun fifteen years before, far to the west. For decades his town of nine thousand poor and beleaguered citizens had been a dank, uninviting, deserted place. Situated upon a soggy plain, surrounded by malarial swamps, hemmed in by the white Alps of Carrara to the north and the Tyrrhenian Sea six miles to the west, it was fit only for ragged fishermen, Muslim slaves, and a few dissipated noblemen. Its river was clogged with seaweed and tamarisk. Its stagnant canals stank with sewage. Its water was foul, its air heavy, and its populace hostile and vulgar. The depleted place seemed destined to be visited forever by war, pestilence, and famine.

But in 1564, Pisa was a town on the rise. The duke of Florence, Cosimo de' Medici, still flushed from his victory over the French at Siena several years before, had worked miracles in the town during the preceding decade. Although his terrible dungeons were full and his secret police terrifying to the Tuscan people elsewhere, he had drained the swamps around Pisa, and this had improved sanitation and purified the air. He had dredged the fetid canals and created a board of public works. He had reconstructed the crenellated brick walls, improving the gates and invigorating the trades. Along the Lung'Arno, the thoroughfare bordering the bow-shaped river bend in the center of the town, handsome new docks were built, and soon the river was filled with colorful boats laden with goods. In the town itself he had established a botanical garden, the first in all of Europe. And as a great supporter of the arts and music, he had reestablished the university as the preeminent place of learning in Tuscany. He could do everything, it seemed to his subjects, except straighten the towers.

By his public works and his continued presence, Cosimo was a popular ruler in Pisa, whatever his reputation for brutality may have been in Florence or in subjugated Siena. He had made himself all the more so by establishing the Order of Saint Stephen, a fraternity of Pisan knights whose mission was to rid the shores of dusky pirates and to liberate good Christians who had been captured by Turkish and Moorish infidels. To the delight of the populace, these Christian soldiers trained and paraded in the Piazza dei Cavalieri. When he came to Pisa, the duke held court in his palace across the river from the fortress. Occasionally, he ventured to the baths of Pisa across the plain in the foothills, Nero's Bath, as it was called, there to bathe and be rubbed down with a salve made of lye, lime, and arsenic-laced orpiment, which made body hair fall out in ten minutes. And the duke and his sons, one of whom at the age of nineteen had been made a cardinal and the archbishop of Pisa, were partial to the hunt. Over the muddy fields and rolling hills of Maremma to the south they often galloped in pursuit of rabbit and boar.

It had been on one of these hunting expeditions several years before that Cosimo's two sons had contracted malaria and died within days of each other. This had spawned the sensational rumor that they had died not of fever but in hot-blooded combat during a quarrel over whose hound had killed the hare. In the streets and in the printed bulletin called *Avviso* the story was broadcast widely that the younger brother had killed the elder, and then the bodyguard of the youthful cardinal had killed him. The death of his sons put Cosimo into a dangerous melancholy for his remaining years, even when he went to Rome in 1570 to be coronated—a reward for his campaign against the infidels—as the first grand duke of Tuscany. The title was conferred by the pope of the new Roman Catholic church, reinvigorated by the decrees of the Council of Trent.

A short walk east along the Lung'Arno from the royal palace of Cosimo, outside the ancient wall of the city, past the plaza of the cauliflower and past the synagogue, lay the quarter known as San Francesco. It was an undistinguished neighborhood of artisans and shopkeepers, with streets designated for butchers and flaskmakers, which in centuries past were subject to the unpredictable floods of the river. A warren of narrow alleys and low-slung houses, it was situated not far from the local garrison, set around a lively market, and graced by only the small, ancient chapel of Saint Andrew.

The musician Vincenzo Galilei had rented a narrow, four-story row house there along the Via del Cuore, overlooking the market. Galilei was an accomplished lutinist and singer, a composer and teacher who had studied contrapuntal music with a Venetian master. He had settled in Pisa only the year before, establishing a small and not very successful school of music in the nearby house of a noble family named Bocca. There he taught the lute and the organ, arranged compositions that he could accompany with his fine tenor voice, and composed his madrigals and fugues.

His wife, Giulia Ammananti, was a bitter and shrill woman. She came from a higher social station, and she never let her husband forget the disparity between them. She hailed from the Ammananti family of Pescia and Pistoia and could claim to be the distant cousin of an important cardinal in Rome. Since music was scarcely a lucrative calling in this remote backwater, Vincenzo made his living largely as a trader in wool. There was never enough money, not now, not when Giulia began to have children, not even when Vincenzo gained a measure of recognition in the

Tuscan court. Giulia felt that her noble birth entitled her to a better standard of living than this struggling musician and sometime wool trader was providing. Hectoring her husband from morning till night to do more trading and less composing, she was never satisfied. To appease her, Vincenzo had to be nimble and enterprising.

On February 15, 1564, three days before Michelangelo died in Rome in his ninetieth year, their first son, Galileo, was born. Six more children would follow until the house of Galilei was an ongoing explosion of cacophony and contention. Somehow, amid the chaos of his family, the complaints of his wife, the clatter of the market, and the revelry of the intoxicated soldiers, Vincenzo Galilei continued to pursue his music. More and more he turned from performance to theory. With ideological fervor, he began to reject the complicated and inaccessible modes of the Venetian tradition in which he had been trained. Four-part counterpoint had developed from the perfect acoustics of the four domes of the Cathedral of Saint Mark, where choruses could answer and combine with one another in magical harmony. In other churches, in other places, the voices clashed, and the music seemed esoteric, pleasing only to the professional musician whose pleasure lay in the craftsmanship. The music failed to stir the passions of the common man. And why did the church have to dominate music, anyway? Vincenzo Galilei longed for music to recapture the power of ancient Greece.

Four years after the birth of his first son, Vincenzo published his first written work. In it he touted the lute as a loftier instrument than the organ, because it mirrored basic human emotion. The lute expressed "the affections of harmonies, such as hardness and softness, harshness and sweetness," he wrote. His favorite instrument could wondrously reflect human shrieks, laments, complaints, and weeping with superior grace, he argued. Given the discord of his own household, he knew what he was talking about.

In 1572 Vincenzo left his growing family behind in Pisa to return to his native Florence, the thriving heart of Tuscany, and there to join the circle of a Florentine count named Giovanni de Bardi. Count Bardi had encouraged Galilei in his early Venetian studies and now presided over a well-known circle of musicians and dilettantes who were experimenting with new musical forms. Vincenzo was especially taken with the idea that music could be combined with classical Greek myth and thereby an ancient union might be recaptured.

He began to study classical texts. During 1572 he started to correspond with a Florentine humanist living in Rome named Girolamo Mei, who was regarded as Italy's most knowledgeable man in ancient music. The power of Greek music, Mei announced to Galilei, derived from a single melody for the voice. Its rhythms were based on the meter of Greek poetry, and Greek modes were different from church modes. In ancient times the text came before the music, and the music served the text. "Almost contemptuous of nature where man is given a voice, so that he can understand the thoughts of others and make himself understood," Mei wrote to Galilei, "musicians today imitate the warbling and lowing of beasts." The scholar challenged his new disciple to recapture the Greek ideal for contemporary music.

In 1574, when Galileo was ten years old, the Galilei family was reunited in Florence. They settled in a modest home upstream from the city center in what today is called Piazza de Mozzi. Under the eye of his father, young Galileo became proficient in the lute and on the organ, and indeed, Vincenzo's eye was needed for more than that. Already the extraordinary intelligence of his child was evident, yet he was being schooled in grammar by a teacher who was "extremely vulgar." In disgust, Vincenzo took over the instruction of his son, tutoring him in Latin and Greek and the classics. Still the struggle to make ends meet was unrelenting, and it created great tension between the ethereal musician and his demanding wife. For Vincenzo Galilei, music came first. He was a part of more than a circle now. He was caught up in a revolution.

Revolutionary thoughts and esoteric discussions put no bread on the table. Giulia Ammananti berated her husband continuously for his inattention to the family's well-being. As young Galileo learned the lute and Latin, so he knew deprivation. As he admired his father's art, so he knew his mother's contempt. The duties of the firstborn son were heaped upon him, and he learned to be cunning. Deep within him was the determination never to live this way when he was older.

Vincenzo Galilei seemed to transcend the annoyances of everyday life. In his written work he had turned against his Venetian training with increasing ferocity. Even though he had composed many polyphonous madrigals in his early career, he now called contrapuntal music an impertinence. It was decadent and sterile, he declared. Such music could never stir the emotions. Emphasis on technique could never achieve the ideal.

His father's revolt against authority was not lost on young Galileo.

Skepticism permeated the Galilei household. Vincenzo's tongue was increasingly sharp and uncontrolled, and Galileo soon adopted his father's confrontational style. "It appears to me," Vincenzo Galileo remarked, "that they who rely simply on the weight of authority to prove any assertion, without searching out the arguments to support it, act absurdly. I wish to question freely and to answer freely without any sort of adulation. That well becomes any who are sincere in the search for truth."

To be liberated from authority became the longing of the son as well.

Galilei's first experiment with the Greek ideal was performed in the house of his patron. For his text, he chose a horrendous episode in Pisa's history: the imprisonment of Count Ugolino three hundred years before for treason. During a conflict between the Guelphs and the Ghibellines the count, his sons, and grandsons were betrayed by a cardinal and imprisoned in the Tower of Hunger, where they starved to death. The words of the libretto were taken from Dante's "Inferno," where Count Ugolino's lament comprises some seventy lines of the *Divine Comedy*. In Vincenzo Galilei's adaptation, a solo tenor is accompanied by a consort of viols. And the operatic lament ends with the sentiment of contempt for Galilei's old city.

> O Pisa, blot of shame upon the people
> of that fair land where the sound of "si" is heard!
> Since your neighbors hesitate to punish you
> Let Capraia and Gorgona move and join,
> damming up the river Arno at its mouth,
> and let every Pisan perish in its flood!
> For if Count Ugolino was accused
> of turning traitor, trading in your castles,
> you had no right to make his children suffer.

Vincenzo's experiment in sung speech was not well received. But originality was in the air, and Count Bardi's rebels could feel that they were serving the human spirit of their age. It fell to Vincenzo to commit the new musical credo to paper. He did so in the form of an imagined dialogue between Count Bardi and another Florentine patrician on the purpose of music, the shortcomings of modern music, and the new wave. His barbs were petulant, polemical, categorical. He spoke of how modern music aroused only laughter and contempt in its listeners, with its syncopated notes that sounded like hiccups. In his low notes, the modern singer sounded like someone groaning to frighten small children, and in his high notes, like someone shrieking from excessive pain.

"There is not heard today the slightest sign of modern music accomplishing what ancient music accomplished," Vincenzo wrote in his Dialogue. "Neither its novelty nor its excellence has ever had the power of producing any of the virtuous effects that ancient music produced," his character says. At another point he attacks the tradition that spawned him. "Consider the rule of the contrapuntists. They aim at nothing but the delight of the ear, if it can truly be called delight. The last thing the moderns think of is the expression of words with the passion that these words require, excepting in a ridiculous way."

With Vincenzo Galilei, there could be no middle ground.

In 1575 Galileo's potential was evident to Vincenzo. In lessons on the lute his son had developed so quickly that "in charm of style and delicacy of touch" he seemed the equal of the father. After a year of intense personal tutoring, Vincenzo had taken his son's instruction as far as he could; the time had come for formal education in the humanities. After the fashion of the Tuscan court, Vincenzo chose the mysterious, mountaintop abbey of Vallombrosa, twenty miles east of Florence, high above the confluence of the Arno and Sieve rivers. The monks were well known for their strictness and their austerity.

For the gifted and expansive eleven-year-old boy, accustomed to the effulgence of family life, the scene at Vallombrosa seemed hostile and forbidding at first. With its fortresslike bell tower and its imposing walls, the stone abbey was situated in an alpine glade of fir and beech trees more than three thousand feet high, where the fog and snow enshrouded the place in a wild and lonely seclusion. The ascetic, tonsured monks emerged from their silent cells in the morning to dispense their stern lessons in Greek and Latin, to test the boys in logic, to expose them to philosophy, and to cultivate their religious education, before retreating again to their private studies.

The howling of the wintry wind made the myths of Vallombrosa more terrifying and profound: Five hundred years before, the son of a Florentine noble had witnessed the passionate killing of his brother and had vowed revenge. He met his brother's murderer on a narrow path bordered by high rocks and raised his sword of vengeance, only to have the villain drop to his knees, extend his arms like Christ, and beg forgiveness. After a moment of doubt, the avenger lowered his weapon, raised his brother's killer from his knees, and forgave him. Afterward, praying to his God at San Miniato al Monte, the young noble lifted his eyes to the crucifix to see the Christ figure on the altar nod his head in approval of this act of forgiveness.

Thus a saint was born. Saint John Gualberto founded the Vallombrosian order on this mountaintop. His brothers committed themselves to obedience, poverty, community, harmony, and love of neighbor. Over the centuries, they planted the fir and beech forests on the steep mountain slopes, and they tended their sheep in the lupin-filled meadows. They took their motto from their patron saint: "He who cannot forgive others destroys a bridge over which he must pass himself. For every man has need to be forgiven." Later, as legend had it, on a knoll not far from young Galileo's window, the devil chased down Saint John, grasped his habit with his claws, and threw the abbot off a precipice known as Masso del Diavolo into the boulders of the cascading stream below. But somehow, the saint landed safely, miraculously unhurt. For a youth with a rich imagination, the ghosts of Vallombrosa were real. And the name Vallombrosa, "valley of mist," could denote mistrust and fear as well as harmony and forgiveness. To John Milton, in the fir forests and the fog, the valley of shadow was the place where Satan mobilized his legions.

Over time, the ambience of the abbey appealed to young Galileo. Among the monks there were men of substance, scholars who recognized their student's intellect, teachers who encouraged his interest in mathematics and science, and artists who nurtured him in drawing and literature. Carefully, they laid the groundwork for a literary style that would become luminous. The monks could even laugh at themselves—occasionally. In the lore of Vallombrosa was the story of the poet and practical joker who stole the monks' hoods off their clothesline, put them on his donkeys, and paraded the braying beasts beneath the windows of the abbey.

Into his fourth year at the monastery and now fifteen years old, full of piety and indoctrination, Galileo declared his desire to become a monk. His father was appalled at this turn of events and seized on his son's severe eye infection as a ruse to remove him from the influence of the monks. They in turn reacted with dismay. In the annals of Vallombrosa, the young man was branded with an ugly word: *Sfratato!*

Defrocked! The slur wounded the boy deeply.

*   *   *

In the ensuing months, Galileo became reconciled to the tactic of his father, and he gave up his ambition for the priesthood. The year before, his mother had given birth to her sixth child, and the house near the Piazza de Mozzi was stretched beyond limit. It had been decided that Galileo would return to Pisa and live there with his cousin, a generous man who possessed the additional virtue of being associated with Vincenzo Galilei in several wool ventures. The plan was clear. While Galileo pursued his education, his cousin would train him to be a wool merchant. It was not a lofty calling, perhaps, but it was an honest living and paid a decent wage. This proved a satisfactory arrangement, and several years later the young man prepared to enter the University of Pisa.

In the summer of 1581, only a month before Galileo entered the university, Pisa was abuzz with reports of a clerical scandal. Priests were once again at one another's throats and had become the butt of ridicule. The most recent episode had taken place in a particularly holy place, the Church of Saint Peter at Grado. There, according to legend, Saint Peter had built his first church in Italy, when his boat washed ashore after the journey from Judea. As he converted many, Simon Peter had commanded that a simple church of brown brick be built before he set off for Babylon, known later as Rome, to build a more elaborate church. Later the simple structure at Grado had been expanded and decorated in the Romanesque style.

Its high altar was a holy relic, a marble slab where Peter's successor, Saint Clement, had celebrated a mass. As he consecrated the church, miraculously three drops of blood had fallen from the saint's nose onto the marble slab, and fifteen centuries later the blood still appeared luminous and fresh, as if it had been spilled minutes before. Through the centuries pilgrims flocked to the place, and once a fleet of Genoese tartans landed in an attempt to steal the relic. The pirates were able only to break off one piece of the marble table containing one of the drops, but once they had their booty on board, their ship sank, as if by divine provenance. Every year in late June on the day of Saint Peter, a solemn procession from the town wound its way to the church, where the priests dispensed indulgences before the pilgrims continued on to the seashore.

Two weeks after Saint Peter's day in 1581, a distinguished gentleman of Pisa had died and been buried by the monks at the famous church. The following morning, as the monks stood reverently over the casket, priests from Pisa arrived to celebrate mass, but the monks were insistent on protecting the serenity of the dead. The town priests forced their way forward to the high altar, despite the protests of the angry monks. The dispute continued around the marble table, when suddenly a priest slapped the face of a monk. "This was a signal for hostilities, which then began in good style on both sides," wrote Montaigne, who was in Pisa at the time. "From slaps on the face, they got to fisticuffs, and from fisticuffs to fighting with sticks, candlesticks, tapers, and anything else they could lay hands upon." Before long, Saint Clement's blood was diluted by that of less pious men. The unholy spectacle so amused Montaigne that he rushed to the scene to hear the testimonials of the adversaries.

In the late summer of 1581, Galileo entered the University of Pisa and embarked on a course of medicine. In this path, he was acquiescing once again in the wishes of his father, for it had finally dawned on Vincenzo that the wool trade was beneath the talent of his son. Still, the musician was determined to direct Galileo toward a practical and well-paying occupation. In Vincenzo himself, the family had enough of the struggling artist.

Ironically, medicine came under the heading of the arts, and this was apt since the profession still contained a large element of faith and hocus-pocus. During the first year, theory was stressed. Galileo got a heavy dose of Aristotle's natural philosophy, Galen's physiology, and Avicenna's theory of recovery, along with further grounding in Greek, Latin, and Hebrew. Mathematics was considered an adjunct and an abstract intellectual exercise, and the sciences, such as botany, came later, before the student moved into practical medicine, anatomy, and the principles of surgery.

Soon enough, Galileo's likes and dislikes were evident. The tedious emphasis on outdated classical authors annoyed him, and in certain disquisitions he could see that the Greeks were not only irrelevant but wrong. When hail fell on Pisa, Aristotle commanded the student to believe that the larger pellets fell faster than the smaller pellets, since under the Aristotelian system, larger, heavier objects were supposed to accelerate more quickly than smaller, lighter ones as they fell from high places. Therefore, the smaller pellets must have originated in a lower heaven. Galileo guffawed at this claptrap and confronted his professors with its absurdity.

Mathematics drew him. Increasingly, he slighted his standard medical lectures so that he could focus on this tangential subject. When the Tuscan court shifted its traditional venue to Pisa between Christmas and Easter and the whole town was galvanized, Galileo learned that an official mathematician of the court, Ostilio Ricci, was lecturing to the wards of the grand duke, and Galileo managed to slip in to listen. Ever the outsider, he repeated this secret practice on a number of occasions. His inquisitiveness, outspokenness, and obvious fascination captivated Ricci.

Ricci was a progressive thinker. He had a wide range of interests, from hydraulic engineering to military defense to cosmology. To him, mathematics was no idle preoccupation but a way of looking at the world and the cosmos. Mathematical principles might well replace the logic of Aristotle in explaining the planets and the stars, Ricci thought, and he pointed to the original work that was then going on in Padua and Bologna. Galileo listened intently.

At the university his indifference to his medical studies rather than his curiosity was getting the attention. His regular professors did not appreciate his outspokenness but regarded it as disrespect. They tagged the medical student with the unflattering label of "the wrangler," as if he delighted in arguing about anything simply for the fun of it and in the secret hope of making the distinguished professors look ridiculous. In his own defense, Galileo was to invoke the wisdom of Horace:

> Perhaps they think it's a weakness
> To yield to your juniors,
> To admit when you're old
> That what you learned, while beardless,
>   Was a waste.

His absence from core lectures became a serious problem. In due course the university informed his family that their son was in danger of flunking out, and his father could see his hopes for his son vanishing. During the summer of 1583, back in Florence, Galileo sought out Ricci and persuaded the court mathematician to meet his father and plead the case of mathematics. Ricci undertook the mission gladly. Galileo should abandon medicine and take up mathematics full time, Ricci told Vincenzo, and Ricci offered personally to manage Galileo's education.

Vincenzo Galilei was ambivalent. The dream of seeing his son become a doctor did not die easily, for in medicine lay security and comfort. To Vincenzo, mathematics remained an esoteric calling, perhaps a little too much like music, with few opportunities, low pay, and great uncertainty. And yet he prized the advice of his colleague in the Tuscan court and knew that Ricci's interest in his son could be useful. For a year Galileo lived in limbo, still enrolled officially in the medical program at Pisa while he privately and secretly took his instruction from Ricci. It was not an arrangement that could last.

Splendid teacher that he was, Ostilio Ricci led Galileo carefully from Euclid to Archimedes to Leon Battista Alberti, from pure geometry to theories of perspective and techniques of abstract measurement. In Ricci's own career Galileo could see the profit of applied mathematics, particularly in the area of military engineering, for Ricci was consulted on problems of fortication, a field Galileo was soon to adopt. After Galileo left his tutelage, Ricci was put in charge of building the defenses off the island of If, just off Marseilles (whose ramparts came thrillingly alive later in Alexandre Dumas's *The Count of Monte Cristo*). His own mentor was the living example of how royalty would pay big fees for the advice of mathematicians. The impressionable Galileo took note.

Unquestionably, the secret instruction of the grand duke's mathematician played to Galileo's arrogance as well as his genius. Around the Piazza dei Cavalieri, where the students gathered to gossip and frolic and where the brave soldiers trained for combat with the infidels, he became more insufferable than ever. He infuriated his teachers with his insolence and patronized his fellow medical students. In his sense of his own superiority, however, he did not lose his humility about religion. He took pleasure in the churches of his town, from the humble Saint Andrew near his birthplace to the great cathedral in the Plaza of Miracles. Especially the cathedral. Situated upon the ground of Hadrian's palace, constructed from the ruins of ancient Rome, embellished by the spoils of ancient Greece and Egypt, appointed with the earth of Jerusalem, which had been brought from the Holy Land by Pisan crusaders, the great church abounded with fascinating lore.

And in 1583 Galileo was to contribute to that lore and to his own. As the story goes, the student was attending services one Sunday in the cathedral when his mind drifted from the drone of the vespers and his gaze fell upon a decorative oil lamp that hung by a long wire from the lacunar ceiling in the center of the nave. The flames of the lamps flickered with the draft inside the great church, and the lamp oscillated steadily, back and forth, with such regularity that it was like, well, the beating of the pulse. *Ecco!* With that inspired connection, Galileo rushed back to his cousin's house in the street of the merchants. There he began to experiment with different lengths of string and different weights, until he arrived at a rudimentary device that could measure the rate and variation of a patient's pulse, simply by varying the length of the string. The idea was simple, elegant, and ingenious. And the concept was generalized: the pendulum was the best marker for small intervals of time.

This device put Galileo temporarily back into the good graces of the university. His professors congratulated him and promptly stole his idea. With some work, they constructed a doctor's tool called a *pulsilogia* upon the pendulum concept, and the instrument would stay in use for many years, credited to the distinguished medical faculty of Pisa.

This was the first of the Galileo legends. Wherever the truth of this story lies, it presents a central theme of Galileo's life: an act of inspiration, born in a religious setting, led to an abstract principle that could be tested through experiment and adapted into an invention for the lasting benefit of mankind.

2

LUCIFER'S ARM

Vincenzo Galilei saw one last hope for his eldest son to become a doctor. The grand duke of Tuscany was offering forty scholarships to needy students, and Galileo appeared to fit the prescription. Few impecunious students could boast Galileo's advantages. As a twenty-one-year-old, he already could boast of having invented a significant medical implement, and he had a father who was a noteworthy figure in the Tuscan court of the beautiful grand duchess, the auburn-haired Venetian named Bianca Capello.

Galileo was reluctant to apply, for as mathematics had fascinated him increasingly, he had lost his interest in medicine. But for a while longer he acquiesced in his father's ambition. Galileo's record spoke loudly for itself, but loud boasting was precisely the young man's problem. His detractors on the faculty were already significant in number. When his application came before the professors of medicine, they complained of his insolence and his trouble-making, and the request was turned down. Vincenzo was heartsick, for he could no longer pay for his son's education, and he saw his dreams of family security disappearing. Covered with shame, Galileo was forced to leave the University of Pisa without a degree. He returned to Florence and reentered his overtaxed family household.

For the next four years, from 1585 to 1589, the young scholar did what he could to pull his own weight. He began a practice that would endure for twenty-five years: privately tutoring students in mathematics. In Siena as well as in Florence he pursued this avocation, living in the humble fashion of an itinerant schoolmaster and scraping in what *julios* he could. In 1588, he returned to the abbey at Vallombrosa to teach the novices about mathematical perspective. Where he found interest, he gave public lectures. But the invitations were infrequent.

Meanwhile, he turned his mind to another icon of antiquity who was being rediscovered by the mathematicians of the time. Perhaps, given his penchant for self-promotion, Galileo was drawn as much to the myths as to the substance of science, since debunking a popular myth could do more for one's fame than amending an obscure theorem. Now he was attracted by the target of Archimedes and, especially, the Greek's famous test for the purity of the king's crown. (This was the experiment that prompted the man of Syracuse to forget himself and run naked through the streets shouting "Eureka!") The quandary had arisen when King Hiero suspected his royal milliner of cheating him by debasing the gold of his new crown with a lesser metal. But how to discover the theft, without melting down the crown? Shortly after he stepped into his bath and noted the overflow of water, Archimedes had arrived at the solution. If they were weighed in water as well as air, an alloyed crown would reveal a different density from an identical crown of pure gold. This had led to the Archimedes principle, which holds that a body in water is buoyed by a force equal to the weight of the displaced fluid.

Young Galileo worshipped the "divine" Archimedes. "Those who read his works realize only too clearly how inferior all other minds are compared to Archimedes," he was to say, "and what small hope is left to anyone of ever discovering things similar to one he discovered." Still, when it came to precise measurement and experiment, Galileo thought he could improve upon the methods of his ancient rival.

He conceived a small, delicate scale, whose wand was suspended at its center by a thin wire. At the center point the wire was wrapped tightly around the wand, and these revolutions doubled as the ticks of measurement. So fine was the wire that the calibrations could not be made visually. "To count them easily," Galileo explained, "take a very sharp stiletto and pass it very slowly over the wires. Partly through hearing, partly through your hand feeling an obstacle at each turn of wire, you will easily count the number of turns." On one end of the wand was a receptacle that could contain fluid, into which various metals could be placed, and on the other end was the counterweight.

Galileo called his device La Bilanchetta, or "little balance." Eventually, it would be rendered into glass, producing a scientific instrument that was also a lovely object of art. His invention prompted his first piece of scientific writing, a pamphlet that accompanied his device and promoted the instrument's capability to measure the density of metals and fluids. The precision of his method, by contrast to Archimedes, he argued, was exquisite.

As he tutored his students and taunted Archimedes, Galileo's grand ambition was to land a chair of mathematics in a major university. But he was young, his credentials were meager, and his champions few. In 1587 the University of Bologna tantalized him with its chair of mathematics, after its holder, the priest Ignazio Danti, had died. Galileo mounted a spirited campaign to capture it.

His quest took him to Rome for the first time, for he hoped to solicit the recommendations of well-known mathematicians and churchmen, including the famous Jesuit mathematician at the Collegio Romano, Christopher Clavius. Known as the "Euclid of the Sixteenth Century," Clavius's fame was widespread. Not only were his mathematics textbooks the standard across the continent, but he also was given credit for the reform of the Christian calendar into the famous Gregorian calendar five years before.

Clavius had presided over a committee of reformers in a chamber atop the Tower of Winds in the Vatican, the chamber that had been designed by the very mathematician, the late Ignazio Danti, whose chair Galileo now sought. Friar Danti had been the pontifical cosmographer. In the Tower of Winds, high above the Vatican Library, he had constructed a brick meridian in the stone floor upon a north-south axis and then cut a corresponding hole in the ceiling, so that the ray of sunlight could fall on the meridian at the appropriate change in the seasons. By church decree at the Council of Trent twenty-five years before, at which Pope Gregory XIII had been a jurist and a papal deputy, the spring equinox was decreed to be March 21. But in Danti's chamber in the Tower of Winds the ray of sunlight fell on the meridian not on March 21 but on March 11 under the old Julian calendar, and it was this ungodly discrepancy that convinced Gregory XIII that reform was needed. The Gregorian calendar, with ten days fewer than the Julian calendar, went into effect in January 1582.

With this historic reform, the Vatican began its interest in the science of the heavens. Religion had joined with science in an accomplishment that would guide the affairs of humankind for the next four centuries. For Galileo to visit the best-known mathematician of the century was a high honor. When the young man met the impressive Jesuit, the chamber atop the Tower of Winds was being frescoed with scenes depicting the winds of time and good fortune, making this room of scientific inquiry into a monument of the Catholic faith. The hole in the ceiling became the mouth of an angel, blowing the north wind in a quiet storm, as below, Christ and his disciples navigated in a windblown dhow. Science and faith were united in a work of Vatican art.

The pretext for Galileo's visit to Clavius was his focus on the gravitational center for solids, an area in which his mentor, Archimedes, still reigned supreme and about which the young Galileo had developed original theorems. As he went to Rome, armed with an introduction from Ostilio Ricci, Galileo's ostensible mission was to invite Clavius to analyze and, he hoped, to bless his postulations. His real hope, of course, was that Clavius would discern in him great scientific promise and recommend him for the post in Bologna.

When Galileo came face-to-face with the famous Jesuit, he found a startling figure. The young scientist was ushered into a cluttered office, books piled one upon another, astrolabes, compasses, and quadrants strewn about, and in the center, a short, stout Bavarian with a heavy accent, a close-cropped snowy goatee, and a four-pointed beret above his ruddy, round face. Clavius greeted Galileo warmly. To Galileo's surprise, he seemed to have none of the pretensions of a great man. More important, he treated his visitor as a scholar, taking Galileo's theorems seriously and encouraging him to attend lectures at the Collegio Romano. (At one such lecture a Jesuit astronomer, using biblical epochs, asserted that the universe had begun 5,748 years before.) Galileo's theorems genuinely intrigued Clavius, but he found the demonstrations of them unconvincing. As yet, the Euclid of his time did not see a budding Archimedes before him. In succeeding months the two men engaged in a correct mathematical correspondence.

"If you are satisfied, then I will be too," Galileo wrote insecurely to Clavius soon after their first meeting. "But if you are still dissatisfied, then I will be also and will continue to search for other proofs."

So far as is known, Father Clavius wrote no recommendation to the

University of Bologna for Galileo. He did, however, introduce his visitor to a powerful churchman, a cardinal named Enrico Caetani, who was the treasurer of the Holy See. Cardinal Caetani did write a pro forma recommendation to Bologna, but this tepid support from the Vatican did not sway the search committee.

To Galileo's disappointment, the Bologna post was conferred instead on Antonio Magini, a Paduan nine years older than he, who had already published several mathematical books and who was better qualified as an astronomer and geographer as well as a mathematician. In this first academic competition, Galileo learned an important lesson. When he got a second chance to compete with Magini five years later, he was better prepared.

As Galileo fretted about his future, fascinating events were taking place around him in Florence. If he were to get ahead, he would need to capture the attention of the Tuscan court, where his father was a familiar figure but without influence. The atmosphere of the court gave Galileo hope. The grand duke, Francis I, fancied himself a scientist as well as a patron of the arts in the grand tradition of the Medici. For years in his private laboratory he had been conducting chemical experiments, which ranged from the ridiculous to the brilliant. He experimented with quack medicines, but he could claim to be the first to melt rock crystal. As he imagined new medical palliatives, so he was an accomplished potter who made lovely porcelain vases in the oriental style. In 1582 he had founded a literary society known as the Accademia della Crusca—*crusca* means the wheat separated from the chaff—and dedicated his society to studies in the pure Tuscan language. In stature the Accademia della Crusca, which Galileo later joined, was meant to equal the Accademia Fiorentina, or the Academy of Florence, which the dukes of Tuscany had used for decades to influence Florentine culture.

In 1587, the year Galileo lost the competition for the mathematics chair at Bologna, Francis I had been married for nine years to the romantic and controversial Bianca Capello. She was an exquisite beauty, who hailed from Venice and had been Francis's mistress for many years before his first wife, Johanna, died, embittered and alone, having born six children, of whom only two daughters had survived. Of Bianca, the French writer Montaigne would remark, "She is beautiful by Italian notions, an agreeable and imperious face, big bust, and breasts the way they like them. She certainly seems clever enough to have bewitched this prince and to keep him devoted to her for a long time." The duke, by contrast, was nothing special to the envious Montaigne. Dark and stout, Bianca's husband merely had large limbs and a healthy bearing.

The affair of Francis and Bianca was a delectable scandal, for it was widely known that when Francis was not tinkering in his laboratory, he was passing through the secret tunnel from the Pitti Palace to Bianca's house on the Via Maggio. Francis's brother, Ferdinand, a cardinal who had stayed in Rome throughout Francis's thirteen-year reign, disapproved bitterly of Bianca, and the brothers were estranged. By 1587, however, Bianca had presided over nine tranquil years as the grand duchess. Within her lively court, full of ceremony and Vincenzo Galilei's music, she set the Florentine standard for beauty and feminine devotion. She was the object of many a young man's dreams and longings, including those of Galileo Galilei.

As Galileo plotted what to do after his Bologna rejection, a terrible event took place. During the early fall, the grand duke and duchess had retreated to their country estate at Poggio a Caiano eleven miles northwest of Florence, where Ferdinand joined them in yet another of Bianca's attempts to effect a reconciliation between the brothers. After some days of peace, a hunting expedition through the ducal park was organized, and the brothers set off happily. Suddenly, the grand duke became overheated, sat down by a lakeside, and was soon overcome by a violent chill, followed by a high fever. Back at Poggio a Caiano, the duke insisted on taking his own chemical concoctions, mainly an Arabic remedy known as Bezzuar, which was extracted from the ducts of the crocodile and mixed with secretions from the porcupine, the Peruvian goat, and the Indian gazelle. The Arabic masters swore that the potion cured all ailments.

Independently, Bianca became ill as well. After five days of Bezzuar, Francis's condition grew critical, and Bianca, desperate over her husband, grew worse too. In separate rooms, delirious and without knowledge of the details of the other's condition, the duke and the duchess failed rapidly and then expired within twelve hours of each other. In the romantic lore of Bianca Capello, her last words were said to have been: "Give my farewell to my Lord, Francesco de' Medici. Say to him that I have always been most faithful and most loving toward him. Tell him that my illness is made so great because of his. And beg him to pardon me if I ever offended him in anything."

In Galileo's Florence, the predictable rumors swept the streets. One story was that the ruthless brother, Ferdinand, had poisoned the beautiful duchess. The counterrumor held that the wicked foreign beauty had botched an attempt to poison her brother-in-law. The gossip became lurid when the fishwives whispered about a poisonous tart that Bianca supposedly had intended for Ferdinand but that her beloved Francis had consumed by mistake; when Bianca saw what had happened, she ate the remainder of the tart. Galileo and all of Florence hotly debated these rumors back and forth, with Galileo siding sentimentally with the lovely Bianca.

Delicious as the rumors were, the death of the grand duke and duchess had an adverse consequence for Galileo. The new grand duke was the suspect, Ferdinand, who during his long absence in Rome was a stranger to all of Florence. For a time, at least, Galileo would have to look to lesser angels.

Still, a year after these events, in 1588, the young man had learned a few lessons. He was now pursuing the chair of mathematics at Pisa and lobbying for the defunct chair of mathematics to be revived in Florence. From his Bologna experience, he had appreciated the importance of allies. He had befriended the marquis Guidobaldo del Monte, an accomplished mathematician and a nobleman of high standing. That year the marquis had published a tract on mechanics that was to become the definitive work on the subject in the sixteenth century. With questions about the gravity of solids as their common ground, Galileo shared his propositions with the marquis, as he had done with Clavius. This led to a friendship and a patronage that lasted until the marquis's death eighteen years later.

The del Monte family served Galileo well. The marquis introduced him to the grand duke Ferdinand, whose cardinal's hat had now been conferred on del Monte's brother. The marquis's cousin was a commander in the Venetian army, a piece of good fortune that would prove useful.

On July 16, 1588, Galileo wrote to the marquis at his palace in Pesaro to report on his various campaigns. "My wish regarding Pisa, about which I wrote your Lordship, will not work out. A certain monk, who lectured there formerly and who gave up the post to become general of his Order, has resigned his generalship and has taken to lecturing once again. His Highness, the Grand Duke, has already appointed him to be lecturer.

"But here in Florence, there was in times past a professorship of mathematics, which was instituted by the Grand Duke Cosimo I, and which many nobles would willingly see revived. I have petititioned for it and hope to obtain it through your illustrious brother, to whom I have entrusted my petition. As there have been foreigners here with whom His Highness has been engaged, I have not been able to speak on the subject to him myself. Therefore, I beg you to write again and mention my name."

Through these struggling years Galileo's relationship with his father had mellowed and deepened. Vincenzo Galilei was approaching seventy and coming to the end of a hard but productive life. The accession to power of Ferdinand I as the new grand duke of Tuscany had had an even greater consequence for Vincenzo. For he had dedicated an entire book of madrigals to Bianca Capello thirteen years before, and this compromised his position with the new grand duke, who despised anything and everything that was associated with the wicked Venetian. Vincenzo's standing in the Medici court declined rapidly after 1587, and he was not commissioned further to contribute any new work for the celebrations of the court. Especially disappointing was his exile from the wedding of the new grand duke to Christine of Lorraine in 1589. Vincenzo could teach his son well about the joy and the caprice of patronage.

As his own career was dawning and his father's waned, Galileo derived great pleasure in accompanying his father on the lute or the organ. The marriage of music and science became a subject for animated conversation between them. Galileo's mathematics and physics advanced Vincenzo's thinking about such technical problems as acoustics, which preoccupied the old man in 1588. Vincenzo struggled to understand how the various stringing of instruments could produce different effects within different confined spaces. These problems lent themselves to mathematical formulation, such as the ratio of vibration to string length. Here Galileo could help his father immensely. Just as Galileo's scientific thinking was useful to Vincenzo in his musical theory, so Vincenzo's instruments provided Galileo a ready tool for experiment on certain physical hypotheses.

Galileo remained emotionally tied to these problems for life and would return to them in his last days. Under house arrest, prohibited from seeing friends, and going blind, he turned to the lute as his sole source of joy. As his father had done, he committed to paper his reflections on the sensations of music and showed yet again his literary and his sensual sides. Upon scraping a brass plate with a chisel, he took note of the marks his tool made when the action produced a shrill sound. And when he thought about octaves and fifths, he also thought about the body. "The effect of the fifth is to produce a tickling of the eardrum, so that its gentleness is modified by sprightliness, giving the impression simultaneously of a gentle kiss and of a bite."

In due course, the young Galileo got his break. At the fabled Academy of Florence, where the city's cultivated men had gathered for nearly fifty years to consider the work of Boccaccio and Dante, to compose poetry, to hone the elegance of their elocution, and to celebrate the purity of the Tuscan language, there was a passionate and enduring controversy. The question, about which there could be no clear resolution and about which anyone could have a strong opinion, went back one hundred years: What were the location, shape, and dimensions of Dante's Inferno?

There was nothing frivolous about the question in Florence. This was Tuscany, where Dante was the icon of Florentine culture, and Dante's language was the standard for eloquence. The refined members of the academy came from all professions and threw themselves into the affairs of the institution, striving toward a model of human perfection, which they defined as the "universal man." In this universal man, knowledge was vast and the spirit was deep. There was no such thing as a specialist.

The president of the academy, a prominent senator named Baccio Valori, had an excellent idea: If literary men could not resolve this dispute over the Inferno, let them turn to a man of science. Let him apply scientific techniques of measurement to the greatest epic in Italian literature and see if insights emerged.

How Galileo was chosen for this sporting event is not clear. Perhaps only he among the Florentine scientists had the youth and the wit, the daring and the foolhardiness to undertake such an assignment. As yet he had no dignity or reputation to risk. He approached this honor with deadly seriousness. This was his chance. He was appearing before the most distinguished literary society in Florence, a forum inaugurated by the first Medici grand duke of Tuscany, Cosimo I, to guide the cultural life of his revitalized and much expanded state. And Galileo believed what he was going to say. Perhaps he believed it too deeply, for it showed him to be still the product of the Middle Ages rather than the Renaissance.

As the audience gathered in the Medici palace in the Via Larga,

Galileo stepped confidently to the platform, graciously paying tribute to previous commentators who had addressed the question before the academy. He began by pointing to the difficulty of the problem, for it was hard enough to understand what one could see above earth, much less to understand what is underground. He proceeded to describe the appearance of Dante's Hell. It was shaped like a cone, he said, consisting of a sector about one-twelfth the total mass of the earth. Its vortex was the home of Lucifer, where the fallen angel stood locked in ice halfway up his gigantic chest, with his belly button forming the very center of the earth. From Lucifer, the sectoral lines extended to Jerusalem on the surface of the earth and east to some unknown point. The Inferno itself was like an amphitheater, divided into eight levels. He took special note of the fifth level, with its foul-smelling swamp called Styx and its wicked City of Dis, where the heretics suffer in the presence of Lucifer himself. The lot of heretics seemed the worst of all fates for the damned.

Then he came to the nub of the question. "Let us speculate on the size of Lucifer," he said solemnly. "There is a relation between the size of Dante and the size of the giant, Nimrod, in the pit of hell, and in turn, between Nimrod and the arm of Lucifer. Therefore, if we know Dante's size, and Nimrod's size, we can deduce the size of Lucifer."

Dante was of average size, shorter than Galileo himself, he imagined, something like "three arm-lengths." Of Nimrod, Dante had written,

> His face was about as long
> And just as wide as St. Peter's cone in Rome.

Therein lay a mathematical clue. Galileo seized upon the passage, for it gave the scientist something specific to measure. The massive pinecone dominating the Vatican City courtyard behind the Belvedere provided a point of reference. "If the face of the giant is the size of Saint Peter's cone," Galileo proclaimed triumphantly, "it will be five arm-lengths and a half. Since men are usually eight heads tall, the giant's face will be eight times as large. Therefore, he will be forty-four arm-lengths tall."

From this, he extrapolated a formula. "Dante, the man, is to the giant as three is to forty-four. The relation of a giant to the arm of Lucifer is the same as the man is to the giant. The formula then must be three is to forty-four, as forty-four is to X. Therefore, the arm of Lucifer is 645 meters. Since the length of an arm is generally one-third of the entire height, we can say that Lucifer's height will be 1,935 arm-lengths."

He paused. "Let's round it off to the height of two thousand arm-lengths," he said. "And the interval from the belly button to the middle of the chest should be five hundred arms, since it is one-fourth of the entire body."

This lecture before the Academy of Florence marked the one bright spot in four years of frustration for Galileo. It enabled him to present himself as an important literary figure rather than a struggling schoolmaster, and the lecture would be remembered favorably. Moreover, he learned a lesson from it: If science could provide insight into literature, so literature was useful to the scientist.

But his central difficulty was neither scientific nor literary. It was how to secure gainful employment as a mathematician. Rebuffed at every turn, in Padua, Pisa, Florence, Rome, and Bologna, he had come close to despair. It was time to give up the quest. Together with a young Florentine friend named Ricasoli Baroni, he began to look to distant shores, to the Middle East and beyond. Perhaps there, among the heathen Turks, he could find his place as a scientist.

In Marquis Guidobaldo del Monte, however, he had a true admirer. To the marquis this talk of flight to distant lands was abhorrent. He wanted to help his young colleague. "With the greatest satisfaction," the marquis wrote in December 1588, "I've heard that you wish to publish your thoughts on the center of gravity, which confer much honor upon you. As you well know, if I can serve you, I am yours to command."

Command Galileo did.

In the summer of 1589, as unpredictably as his failures had become predictable, a new post of mathematics came open at the University of Pisa. Now Galileo was a seasoned campaigner, and he had powerful allies. Quickly he enlisted Marquis del Monte and Cardinal del Monte in his campaign. This time he found success.

His appointment was for three years.

Galileo's salary at the University of Pisa was a paltry sixty crowns per year. But the junior lecturer was scarcely in a position to complain. The stipend was in line with the nominal amounts that mathematicians generally were paid at the time. The hard truth was that mathematics was not a valued occupation. It was considered a marginal aid to the study of medicine, which stood at the center of the "arts," and its chair was relegated to the fringe of real work, somewhere near the astrology chair. Professors of mathematics traditionally had been priests, who cared nothing about salary. As Galileo assumed his post, another professor of mathematics was about to retire at the salary of 125 crowns after thirty years of teaching.

The university was spread among a series of low-slung buildings on the north side of the Arno only a few blocks from the Tower and the Plaza of Miracles. The first Medici grand dukes, Cosimo I and Francis I, had tried to build the university into one of the finest in Italy. Cosimo had drained the marshes around the town to make Pisa a healthier place to live and teach, while Francis had tried to attract eminent faculty with large salaries and had attempted (without success) to build aqueducts from the mountains to improve the quality of the water.

But the Medici princes had achieved only mixed results. In 1589, as Galileo assumed his post, there were about six hundred students at the university, two-thirds of whom read law. Many of those never pursued their studies diligently to a degree. Only about thirty to forty degrees were conferred in a given year. So dominant were the priests on the faculty in Pisa that a slogan about universities in Italy had gained credence, doing Pisa no favors: "In Bologna, there are lovers; in Padua, scholars; in Pavia, soldiers; and at Pisa, friars." No wonder Bologna could boast more than twice the faculty and far brighter students.

The eminent scholars who came to Pisa with big salaries generally did not stay long, for the town was a backwater, despite the abundance of its holy relics and its marble masterpieces. If a scholar stayed long in Pisa, it was considered a mark of mediocrity—or a duty to Christ.

It did not take Galileo long to develop contempt for the pompous eminences on the faculty. He nodded appreciatively when the old saw about the Pisan professors was invoked: "The doctors are like watermelons in the grass." Among the largest watermelons in the patch was a balding conservative philosopher named Girolamo Borro. For Galileo, Borro was the perfect fruit to be sliced up, for his Aristotelian positions were the epitome of conventional wisdom. Yet he possessed a vaulted reputation for wisdom and eloquence. When distinguished visitors such as Montaigne came to Pisa, it was Borro they sought out.

"I met an excellent man at Pisa," Montaigne essayed, "but such an Aristotelian that his strongest opinion is that the touchstone of all truth is conformity to the teachings of Aristotle. Outside of these there is nothing but chimeras and inanities to him. Because this position of his was interpreted a little too broadly and maliciously, it put him for a long while in great danger from the Inquisition in Rome." To Galileo at this early stage, Borro's troubles with the Inquisition were a mark in his favor.

Beneath Galileo's contempt for the professors of Borro's stripe there was a touch of envy. Borro had written on the tides and on motion, subjects that keenly interested the lecturer, even though they were the province not of mathematics but of natural philosophy. Galileo was quick to debunk, and eager to displace his former professors. Among Borro's works was a book entitled *On the Flux and Reflux of the Sea*—the very title, word for word, that Galileo would adopt for a work of his own twenty-five years later—and also a book entitled *De Motu gravium et levium*. Galileo was equally interested in the fact that the Aristotelian had written in vernacular Italian to enlarge his audience.

In his discourses on motion, Professor Borro believed in testing hypotheses with experiment. This represented a radical departure from the blind followers of Aristotle's law and proof that not all Aristotelians were alike. Specifically, Borro tested Aristotle's principle on falling bodies to see if objects of equal weight but different materials really did fall at the same speed. "We threw two pieces of equal weight from a rather high window of our house at the same time and with the same force," Professor Borro wrote. "The lead ball descended more slowly, that is, it descended above the wood ball, which had fallen to the ground first. We tried this experiment not once but many times with the same results."

Other eminent professors of an anti-Aristotelian stripe had treated the subject of motion differently, addressing questions not only of free-fall but of motion in a void, acceleration, and the path of projectiles. Among them was a philosopher named Jacopo Mazzoni, who had come to Pisa the year before Galileo (at a salary eleven times higher) and to whom Galileo was drawn. Mazzoni had a great breadth of interest. Best known for his defense of Dante, Mazzoni was a great raconteur, and many, including Galileo, had gathered at his house in 1589 to listen to the philosopher's thoughts on a new stellar nova that had appeared in the sky that year. But there was an additional curiosity about Mazzoni. Twenty years before he had won a championship memory contest by rattling off 5,193 maxims in rapid succession, and this peculiar form of athletics impressed Galileo. In the field of dynamics, Mazzoni embraced the notion that large and small bodies of the same material would fall not with different speeds, as Aristotle argued, but with the same speed. That too appealed to Galileo, for if it was true, it would undermine the foundation of Aristotelian physics.

The young Galileo yearned to enter this debate, for he longed to prove the maxim, "Ignorance of motion is ignorance of nature." That these questions were not the province of mathematics as it was then practiced did not deter Galileo, for instinctively, he wanted to change the role of mathematics. During his first year at Pisa, as he taught the First Book of Euclid to his classes, he began to write about motion. As other authors at Pisa had done, Galileo entitled his work "De Motu," and he borrowed much from the ideas of his contemporaries. Writing alone did not satisfy him. Taking a leaf from Girolamo Borro, he wished to base his thought on experiment, which Borro had called the "teacher of all things." And he wished to improve upon Borro's absurd high-window method.

He climbed atop the Tower of Pisa. The boldness of the idea was its obviousness, but no one before him had thought of it, or had dared to attempt it. The problem was to measure the rate of free-fall. What better place was there to conduct the experiment than this nearby monument to man's imperfections? If Aristotle argued that "a one hundred pound ball falling from a height of one hundred cubits reaches the ground before another of one pound has descended a distance of one cubit," how easy it was to confirm or shatter that assertion. (One hundred cubits is the equivalent of 58.4 meters; the Tower of Pisa measures 54 meters.)

Up the winding staircase he carried balls of different weights and sizes, of lead and ebony, perhaps even of gold and porphyry and copper. Later he would imagine the difference in the flight of a hen's egg versus that of a marble egg. As legend has it, he advertised his demonstration widely, bringing out an excited throng of students and professors. Emerging expansively at the top amid the pilasters and precarious open arcades, he played to his crowd. He was greeted by a roar. The odd catcall punctuated the amused cheers, for most of the crowd undoubtedly hoped to witness a fiasco. There was something about the tower that seemed to attract freaks and exhibitionists. Who was this junior genius, this radical, to challenge not only the senior experts in this field but Aristotle himself? Perhaps he was like the hunchback who had supposedly built the tower to lean this way to flaunt his own deformity!

Galileo was unintimidated by the gaze of the experts below. He reveled in his boldness and scorned their pedantry. "These grand personages who set out to discover the great truth and never quite find it give me a pain," he scoffed. "They can't find it, because they're always looking in the wrong place." His contempt for the pedestrians was profound. "A good doctor needs to be accompanied by at least thirty scholars," he jeered. "If unaccompanied, others will say, 'This is an ignorant man. Better that he be a friar. At least they go about in pairs like spinach and brooms.'"

He had entered into a world of his own, exhibiting the enormous confidence of an original mind. "If you're going to find the truth, you have to employ fantasy," he mused. "You have to play at invention and guess a little. When I'm looking for the truth, I always look for the opposite, because great good and great evil are always there together like chickens at the market." As the balls thudded simultaneously at the base of the tower, Aristotle's formula made a thud as well.

The rate of fall was not a function of weight or mass. If the resistance of air were removed (or if the balls descended in a vacuum), Galileo postulated, they would fall at precisely the same rate. (Astronaut Neil Armstrong would test this "equivalence principle" on the moon, as he dropped a hammer and a feather and watched them reach the surface at the same time. "You see," Armstrong remarked happily, "Galileo was right!") "Aristotle Debunked!" the headline of the *Avviso* might have read. Some could see the dawning of a new age, others only the long arm of Lucifer.

Curiously, Galileo did not write about this experiment at the time, nor did any of his contemporaries, and this has cast doubt in the minds of some as to whether the experiment ever took place. His first biographer, Vincenzo Viviani, began the legend by transcribing Galileo's recollections at the end of his life. By his demonstration at the tower, Viviani wrote, "he upheld the dignity of his professorial chair with so great fame and reputation, before judges well disposed then and since that many of his rivals, stirred with envy, were aroused against him." Undoubtedly, Viviani heard that analysis as well from Galileo. Did Viviani make up this story? Was the old Galileo merely imagining youthful heroics?

Though Galileo did not describe his experiment directly at the time, he did so tangentially later. Sprinkled through his writings on motion over the years are ample references to objects dropped from towers. In his most famous work, the *Dialogue Concerning the Two Chief Systems of the World*, written thirty years later, the experiment from the Leaning Tower resounds in his discussion of falling bodies. And in his later pure work of science, his *Discourses on Two New Sciences*, published at the end of his life, he answers Aristotle's proposition directly. "I say, that the balls reach the ground at the same time. In doing the experiment, you find that when the heavier mass touches the ground the lighter is two fingers away. Now you are stressing my minor mistake while forgetting about the big one of 99 cubits by Aristotle." Later in the work he would assert that in dropping balls from towers, only minuscule differences in the time of arrival existed between balls of gold, lead, copper, and porphyry, when they were of equal weight.

Drawing upon the results of his experiments in dynamics, Galileo produced his first significant piece of writing. Called "De Motu," this discourse on motion was dry, incomplete, and unpersuasive. It groped toward a theory of free-fall but never quite articulated one. It addressed the parabolic flight path of projectiles, but his ballistics needed greater exposition. The tract tied the specific weight of falling objects to their rate of acceleration but did not arrive at a basic law.

Still, there were flashes of brilliance, promise of true breakthroughs to come, an air of originality. In "De Motu" the contours of later revolutionary discovery could be seen on the horizon, discovery that would be central to the evolution of modern physics: the law of inertial motion, the basic laws of falling bodies, the equivalence principle that started with Galileo, evolved with Isaac Newton, was perfected by Albert Einstein, and is now to be tested in outer space. In opposition to Aristotle's view that the speed of downward motion was directly proportional to the total weight of the object, Galileo asked a simple question: "If two stones were flung at the same moment from a high tower, one stone twice the size of the other, who would believe that, when the smaller was halfway down, the larger had already struck the ground?" And then he answered: "If one takes two different bodies, which have such properties that the first should fall twice as fast as the second, and if one then lets them fall from a tower, the first will not reach the ground appreciably faster nor twice as fast."

For all his natural boldness, for all his congenital skepticism of conventional wisdom, the young Galileo had a sudden and unexpected failure of courage. He decided not to publish "De Motu." It would languish, to be revisited years later by a mature Galileo, borrowed from piecemeal, retooled and polished. But in 1590, still in the early stage of a career, he seemed to realize that his ideas were raw and inchoate. He had not yet squared theory with experiment. His treatise, he knew instinctively, was plagued with contradiction. In these early jottings he had set for himself a high standard of logical and experimental accuracy: "In this treatise the method we shall follow will be always to make what is said depend on what is said before, and never, if possible, to assume as true that which requires proof. My teachers of mathematics taught me that." He knew he could not meet his own standard. He knew he had not achieved proof.

If in this youthful concentration he was to have his first failure of courage, so he was to demonstrate his first real paranoia about criticism. This paranoia began as a cloud and grew into a tempest later in his life, and it would mar his judgment. "There will be many," he wrote in a marginal note to "De Motu," "who, after reading my writings, will turn their mind not to consider what I have said as true, but only to seek means of impugning my arguments, whether justly or unjustly." Thus, his basic instinct was to assume bad faith and malicious intent in anyone who disagreed with him.

Besides the promise of future discovery, his early dynamics produced another surprising harbinger of future work. For the first time he turned to literary artifice. His father, along with the Vallombrosan friars, had early brought him to literature, and it had gotten into his blood along with music. The great epic poem of his day, Ariosto's *Orlando Furioso*, was his favorite work, and by the time he assumed his professorship at Pisa, he could recite vast chunks of it from memory. "When I enter into *Orlando Furioso*, it is as if a treasure room opens up before me, a regal gallery adorned with a hundred classical statues by the most renowned masters, with countless historical pictures—the very best ones by the most excellent painters—with a great number of vases, crystals, agates, and other jewels, a festive hall full of everything that is rare, precious, admirable, and perfect."

Against this joy in Ariosto, he contrasted the poetry of the greatest living poet in Italy, Torquato Tasso. To compare the two was a popular diversion of cultured men, but Galileo brought to the comparison an acid tongue. When he read Tasso, he entered a different sort of place, "the study of some little man with a taste for curios who has taken delight in fitting it out with things that have something strange about them, either because of age or because of rarity, but are, as a matter of fact, nothing but bric-a-brac: a petrified crayfish, a dried-up chameleon, a fly and a spider embedded in a piece of amber, some of those little clay figures which are said to be found in the ancient tombs of Egypt."

To read Tasso after you read Ariosto, Galileo remarked, was like eating a cucumber after you have had a fine melon.

In his lecture on Dante to the Academy of Florence, Galileo had discovered how science could bring insight into literary questions, and now he wished to reverse the favor. A literary approach might strengthen the weakness in his scientific argument as it would widen his audience. Unsatisfied with his formal treatise, he devised the story of two old friends, Alexander and Dominicus, who meet outside Pisa on a wintry morning and walk along the Arno to the seashore six miles away to buy some fish for lunch. Their gaze falls upon a boatman, rowing upstream against the current, and this triggers an interchange on the nature of motion. Before they are finished, they progress from boats moving upstream to balls dropping from towers to cannonballs bouncing off castle walls. Alexander is the voice of Galileo, and Alexander dispenses the wisdom.

Regrettably, he is also Galileo without his wit or sense of humor. The dialogue contained the same dry phraseology as Galileo had used in his treatise. Moreover, he wrote the interchange in turgid Latin. But his dialogue on motion is just the first foray into literary pastures. Far better sojourns lay ahead.

During his three years at Pisa, Galileo floated in a limbo between the establishment and the counterculture. At times he longed to excel within the rules, but more often he bridled against them. He still wrote in Latin; he hoped for recognition; and he dutifully taught his courses in Euclid. At the same time, he attacked Professor Borro, partly because Borro treated him paternalistically as an obstreperous student rather than as a colleague. Galileo's tongue was loose. His sting was hornetlike, and he feared no one. He strode commandingly through the Piazza della Berlina and the Piazza dei Cavalieri, his large frame lumbering forward and his red hair flowing, ready to stop and argue almost any proposition as if it were an invitation to a fight. He did nothing to hide his contempt for the lazy and pretentious dromedaries around him and for their prosaic braying. Instead of wearing the long, flowing toga of a professor, he dressed haphazardly. His disheveled look was a metaphor for his contempt and an emblem of his radicalism.

The toga, he proclaimed, was the disguise of the empty-headed. He would rather go naked, like the animals, who knew the evil of clothes. If you wear a toga, he told his students, you have to follow certain rules. You can't go to a brothel, for example, because the dignity of the professor's gown would not allow it. The uniform was not for busy people like him. "I often have to run, so the bailiff won't catch me," he spoofed. "I'm always afraid that the man after me is a messenger from my boss."

Not surprisingly, his colleagues were not amused by these bawdy remarks. His satire had crossed the line beyond bad manners into outright revolt. His impertinence became a pretext that masked their resentment at his originality. To his masters, Galileo's behavior had become boorish and unacceptable, and they looked for a way to get rid of him.

Galileo continued to laugh at them. He was twenty-nine years old, as sure of himself as the professors were full of themselves. He was too young to be diplomatic, yet old enough to do real damage.

He went too far. To an audience of twittering students, he expressed a fantasy. "Men are like wine flasks," he professed. "Go to a tavern. Look at the flasks, before you drink red wine. Some bottles don't have much decoration on them. They're dusty and naked to the bone. . . . But full of such wine that people rhapsodize upon it, calling it glorious and divine. Then look at the other bottles with the handsome labels. When you taste them, they are full of air or perfume or rouge. These are bottles fit only to pee into!"

His three-year contract at the University of Pisa was not renewed.

Part II

Padua and Venice

3

THE GOLDEN OX

Late in the summer of 1592 Galileo launched a campaign to capture the chair of mathematics at the University of Padua. The Ox, "Il Bo," as the university was affectionately known (after the insignia of the hotel across the street), was the college of Dante and Copernicus and the second oldest university in Italy after Bologna. It competed with Oxford and Salamanca, Paris and Heidelberg as a center of Europe's highest learning. Its students were diverse and international, with a particularly large component of Germans, who had their own courses and societies and even called themselves, in absentia, the German nation. The students congregated boisterously in the cafes near their library on San Biagio and in squares and narrow streets around the Palazzo della Ragione, where they kept a wary eye out for the Venetian police, the *sbirri*, who came to spy on them.

For two centuries Il Bo had been divided into two faculties: jurisprudence and the arts. The arts included philosophy, medicine, and theology. Under the wide umbrella of philosophy, the chair of mathematics was among the university's most prestigious posts. The professorship had been vacant for four years, since the death of Giuseppe Moletti. This mathematician, geographer, and astronomer was a much beloved figure in Padua. Moletti's reputation had rested largely upon his participation in the reform of the Julian calendar, but he also was famous for his openness to new ideas, especially challenges to conventional Aristotelian thinking.

Accordingly, he set the stage for bolder iconoclasts to come. The university did not want to rush into a replacement for such an admired member of the mathematical studio.

Padua, of course, was located in the Serene Republic of Venice. As a Tuscan native, Galileo was competing as an outsider, and this put him at a decided disadvantage. If the post were offered by the Venetian senate, he would need the permission of Grand Duke Ferdinand of Tuscany to take the foreign post. Able competitors were likely to present themselves, men who were as well qualified, with Venetian roots and none of Galileo's controversial baggage. This probability became a reality soon enough in the person of an old nemesis. Giovanni Antonio Magini, who had bested Galileo four years before in capturing the chair of mathematics at Bologna, now put himself forward for the chair at Il Bo. A Padua native, Magini wanted to return to his hometown. To make matters worse for Galileo, Magini was considered the most brilliant disciple of the much mourned Moletti.

Packing all his possessions in a box weighing less than one hundred pounds, young Galileo struck out for Venice, as if it were the Hollywood of his day and he had impossible dreams of stardom. Along the way he tarried briefly in Padua. There he met and charmed the gregarious and influential Gianvincenzio Pinelli. Pinelli cut a wide swath in the vibrant Paduan culture. For several decades since he came to Padua from his native Naples, he had presided over a salon of writers and scientists in his sandy palazzo on the Via del Santo. His private library was said to contain more than eighty thousand volumes, along with a splendid collection of paintings, mathematical and astronomical instruments, bronzes, and maps. His role, as he saw it, was not as an artist but as an inspirer of art, and thus he perceived in this bold young visitor a rambunctious addition to his circle.

Pinelli offered Galileo a battle plan to win over the Venetian senate. The plan included introductions to such worthies in Venice as Friar Paolo Sarpi, the Servite priest who was already a dominant figure in Venetian politics, and General Francesco del Monte, a bona fide war hero and the commander of the Venetian infantry who had authority over the fortresses of the expansive Venetian republic.

Once in Venice, the Tuscan ambassador to the Serene Republic took Galileo in tow. Pinelli and del Monte had laid the groundwork with the three examiners. As Galileo put forward a confident face, displaying his grasp and range and speaking with his irresistible ironic wit, two of the three reformers were quickly won over. Three weeks later the Venetian senate met and approved the examiners' recommendation, 149 for, 8 against, with 3 abstentions. The formal senate resolution spoke of Domino Galileo Galilei, "who lectured at Pisa with very great honor and success, and of whom it can be said, he is the most outstanding person in this field." He had won on personality and influence. His contract was guaranteed for four years, with two additional option years at the discretion of His Serenity, the doge. The salary was a humble 180 gold crowns a year. The native Paduan, Magini, retreated to Bologna, bitter and resentful. His relationship with Galileo was cordial until eighteen years later, when Magini became a deceitful opponent following Galileo's first telescopic discoveries.

The semester was due to begin on October 18, the day of Saint Luke in the Christian calendar, but The Ox and the doge granted Galileo time to return to Tuscany to put his affairs in order. Most important, he needed to solicit the permission of Grand Duke Ferdinand I to take the foreign post. In the five years of his reign, Ferdinand had surprised many by proving himself a decent and worthy successor to his brother, Francis, although he did not have Francis's interest in science. He had quickly overcome the apparent scandal of his accession to the throne by ordering immediate autopsies of his brother and sister-in-law after their strange and suspicious deaths. The autopsies showed that Bianca had died not of a poisoned tart but of dropsy, and Francis from his bizarre elixir of crocodile and porcupine juice. Although the rumors persisted—for they were irresistible—the findings of the autopsies were generally accepted, and Ferdinand was able to get on with the business of governing.

Galileo had no special sway with Ferdinand, for the grand duke's passion was art. Under these circumstances, the request of young Galileo to take a university post in the Venetian republic was a trifling matter, a mere clerical decision. At the Pitti Palace the grand duke sanctioned the move without apparent regret or even much thought. Eighteen years later the loss of Galileo to Padua was considered one of the great mistakes of the Medici family, and Ferdinand's successor, Cosimo II, set out to correct the error.

On December 7, 1592, Galileo assumed the podium of the Great Hall, the Aula Magna, to deliver his inaugural lecture before a skeptical audience of his peers. By ancient Paduan tradition, the new professor was required to present himself before the university community and, surrounded by the resplendent velvet and the shields of the great families of the Veneto, to deliver an oration upon the fundamental principles of his field. The formal lecture was to be given in Latin, as befitted the solemnity of the occasion. For weeks Galileo had worked on his lecture, crafting its ornate and important phrases, committing the text to memory, practicing its delivery with grandiose gestures. Because the style of the declamation was as important as the substance, Galileo did not read from a text, and no transcript of the lecture has survived.

Whatever its content, word of this speech spread quickly through the scientific world. The German students in the audience carried the news to the most famous astronomer of the day, Tycho Brahe. Brahe took note of it and remarked that a new star had appeared in their firmament. Closer at hand, Galileo's new friend, Count Marc Antonio Bissaro, announced that Padua was the perfect "theater" for Galileo's forceful personality. And from Pisa, the famous doctor, Girolamo Mercuriale, declared Padua to be "the natural home for your genius."

Galileo settled into the exuberant life of his adopted city with his usual zest. For some time he lived with Pinelli, entering the social swirl of that fascinating household. Pinelli's table was famous for its outspoken guests. Among them were Enrico Van de Putte, the Dutch transplant and humanist historian, and Paolo Gualdo, who had renounced his canonship in the church two years before yet remained a great supporter of the Jesuits and was famous for his compositions in the Paduan vernacular. Occasionally, the poet Torquato Tasso passed through Padua, on his last, half-mad wanderings through Italy before his death. Even though Galileo found him a "mean, poor, and miserable" old man, Galileo held a lifelong love of his poetry. Most important, there was the charismatic friar Paolo Sarpi, later called the Machiavelli of Venice, who was already planning his critical history of the Council of Trent.

Given his love for debate and controversy, it is likely that Pinelli invited dangerous discussions of religion, for the hand of the Vatican rested heavily on science and art, politics and music, foreign affairs and university matters. Forty years before, the Council of Trent initiated the Counter-Reformation as a response to the challenges of Luther and Calvin. At Trent from 1546 to 1563, the authority of the Catholic church over secular matters was reaffirmed and strengthened. Theology was purified and revitalized. The question of how Holy Scripture should be interpreted, and by whom, was defined. The correct view of such doctrines as transubstantiation was promulgated, while the procedure for dealing with heresy was laid out. The Index of Prohibited Books was revised, and the power of Inquisition sanctioned.

At Pinelli's house the artists and intellectuals bridled under this strict authority, but they criticized Rome without tempering their faith in Christ. Rebels bold enough to challenge Rome openly were, however, figures of great curiosity. Besides Sarpi, it is likely that Pinelli entertained three other religious rebels who were in Padua during the year Galileo arrived and who were confronting the issue of science and faith. They were Tommaso Campanella, a Dominican from Calabria who espoused a philosophy of observation and who would, two years later, be imprisoned in Naples by the Inquisition because of his views; the former Jesuit, Mark Antony de Dominis, once the archbishop of Split in Dalmatia, who briefly was a professor of mathematics and philosophy at Padua before he joined with Sarpi in anti-Roman views and was eventually forced to renounce them; and finally, the dark and mysterious Giordano Bruno. Bruno, however, was not long for Padua. After three months of lecturing to German scholars at Il Bo, Bruno was seized by the Venetian Inquisition and turned over to Rome on a capital charge of heresy.

At Pinelli's table they discussed literature and science, politics and religion, and when they grew tired of that they turned to music. In that sphere, Galileo basked in the reflected glory of his father, for the work of the late Vincenzo Galilei was very well known. His innovative juxtaposition of music and poetry was about to have its first full realization in a Florentine production based on the myth of Daphne. It would be a few years yet before this new form was called opera. Pinelli's evenings often ended when he brought out his lyre and Galileo his lute and they accompanied each other in madrigal and fugue, sometimes those of Vincenzo Galilei.

During his first months in Padua Galileo's mind ranged broadly, as if his brain was searching for the area worthy of its power. He wrote a tract on mechanics, an interest to which he would return repeatedly and with great distinction throughout his life. He also wrote an unlikely treatise on military fortification. This was undoubtedly undertaken at the insistence of General Francesco del Monte, the commander of the Venetian infantry whose castles dotted the landscape from Brescia to the new fortress at Palmanova in Friuli. He had been helpful in securing the chair of mathematics for Galileo and now wished to call in the favor.

There is nothing new about a relationship between a general and a mathematician. Then as now, there was money to be made in military contracts. But, given his reputation for other work, to find Galileo, in his first months in Padua thinking about large towers and half-moon rivetments, about the angles of military walls and flanking movements, about soldiers scaling forts with ladders is surprising, unless one appreciates the obligation he felt to General del Monte. Here is Galileo on bulwarks: "For the bulwark to be strong, the side walls must be large and the angle between the two side walls must be the least acute as it can possibly be. The less acute the angle, the more difficult it will be for the enemy to attack it successfully."

He was still a medieval man, but he had already adapted the depersonalized language of modern military theorists.

"Defense can be achieved in two ways, and the commander must decide which is more useful, either the thrusting type of shot or the grazing type. The grazing shot follows a line parallel to the wall. Its advantage is clear. When ladders are resting on the curtain walls, one shot can remove many ladders, while the thrusting shot can remove only one ladder at a time. But the thrusting shot has the advantage of neutralizing a man with a pickaxe, which is the most important assault weapon."

Besides the problem of fortification, a number of military problems cried out for the attention of a clever practical scientist, and the Venetian authorities were ready to pay well for solutions. Of enduring concern was the defense of the only ship channel into the lagoon of Venice, the channel of San Nicolo to the east of the Lido, for this was the knife pointed at a fragile and vulnerable heart. It was defended by a fort on either side, the Castel San Andrea and the Castel Vecchio, and by a cumbersome iron chain that could be winched up and tightened across the channel at the first sign of an approaching enemy ship. The chain would then be joined with a huge, turtle-shaped barge packed with cannons. For centuries these defenses had been adequate, but their effectiveness depended on considerable advance notice. In the age of faster ships and night attacks, could a scientist suggest a greater measure of security and preparedness? Galileo put his mind to the problem.

The great industry of Venice remained shipbuilding at the Arsenale, where oceangoing galleys could be constructed in a matter of hours in a Renaissance version of an assembly line that employed more than five thousand workers. The efficiency of the Arsenale was the stuff of legend and the reason the Maritime Republic was the commercial power of the Occident. It is said that once, to impress the visiting king of France with the capabilities of the shipyard, an entire warship was constructed over the course of a state banquet. Dante, in his "Inferno," cited the Arsenale, comparing the hot, sticky, viscous substance on the riverbank in Lower Hell to the tar used for ship repair.

Not long after he came to Padua, Galileo had his first contact with the *grandi* of Venice. It came in the person of Giacomo Contarini, a senator and the new superintendent of the Arsenale, whom Galileo encountered at Pinelli's house. Among Contarini's first tasks at the shipyard was to launch a crash program to build one hundred galleons. He was pondering the design for the new ships, particularly the placement of the oars. To Galileo, he put a number of questions: Could the rowers be put outside the hull of the ship? Would it make a difference? What was the proper height for the oar ports above the level of the water? And how long should the oars be in relation to the size of the hull? To Contarini's delight, Galileo studied these questions as problems of physics and wrote a formal reply. As a result, certain design changes were made. It was not long before practical questions from all quarters were being put to him. For example, the superintendent of the new fortress at Palmanova in Friuli, Alvise Mocenigo, wrote Galileo about the design of an oil lamp to illuminate the fortress, and Galileo promptly suggested a better design.

His financial situation took a desperate turn in May 1593, the month he wrote his reflections on fortification. He needed some fortification of his own, as his modest university stipend was insufficient now that he was the head of the Galilei family after the death of his father. He was falling badly behind in his debts, the most pressing the dowry of his sister Virginia, who two years before had married a strong-willed plodder named Benedetto Landucci. The dowry was akin to a mortgage payment, amounting to thousands of crowns over several decades. Woe to him who missed a payment. On May 29, as he prepared to return to Florence for his first summer holiday, Galileo had missed more than one installment and received an urgent letter from his mother: "Come, but you should know that Benedetto wants his money now and is threatening to have you forcibly arrested immediately when you arrive here," Giulia wrote. "He is just the man to do it, so I warn you: it would grieve me much if anything of the kind were to happen."

Galileo bravely went to Florence anyway and avoided the indignity of debtors prison only by borrowing two hundred crowns. The persistent Landucci cosigned the note and then pocketed the money.

Within a year of coming to Padua, Galileo had moved out of Pinelli's home and into a modest house in the shadow of Santa Giustina, a great battleship of a church with thick, unadorned earthen walls, domes like turrets, and rose windows like cannon ports. To supplement his income, the twenty-eight-year-old Galileo took on a hectic schedule of private tutorials, which captured his interest far more than his formal lectures on Euclidian mathematics. In the second year, however, he turned to a new area, the cosmology of Ptolemy.

At first he did not question the conventional belief that a stationary earth was at the center of the universe, while the sun and the planets revolved around it, nor did he dispute the church-sanctioned myth of a great winch system of stars called the *primum mobile*, which was cranked around the earth every twenty-four hours by an angel of God, but he had not yet thought deeply about astronomy. In his early lectures on astronomy there are references to "the earth in the center of the celestial sphere" and to the earth being immobile.

Giordano Bruno, by contrast, had leapt to a radical intuition about the cosmos: The sun, not the earth, was the center of the universe, and beyond that there were many universes, made up of stars and galaxies too infinite to count, which were unlimited in space and time. To this determined mystic and visionary, Christianity was more majestic with his view than with the orthodox, earth-centered view, since the infinity of God pointed to the infinity of the heavens. That soaring, prophetic vision came from Bruno's soul rather than from any scientific instinct. For it Bruno had been snatched from Venice and now sat in chains in Castel Sant'Angelo in Rome, where the Inquisition interrogated him ruthlessly and unceasingly. Such treatment did not encourage Galileo to leap into dangerous areas.

In 1593 Galileo was casting about in other areas to invent useful and money-making devices. Remembering his first success ten years before with the instrument to measure the pulse, he now experimented with another glass device that could measure the temperature of the body. He devised a simple glass bulb, the size of a small egg, at the end of a glass stem two palms in length (twenty-two inches) and inserted it into a beaker of water. Grasping the bulb with his hand to impart heat, he found that when he withdrew the hand, the water rose uniformly in the stem to the height of one palm. Nineteen years later he returned to this device, replaced the water with wine, and got headier results. (Mercury was not tried until 1670, but Galileo's early experiments lay his claim to being the inventor of the thermometer.)

This invention was interesting, but there was no money in it. So he turned to agriculture. There the problem—and the opportunity—was irrigation, so Galileo devised a new method of raising large amounts of water from aquifers. Operating on Archimedean principles, the machine made ingenious use of a heavy underground pendulum to power the rachets of a dynamo, which in turn raised water in buckets on a pulley system and disgorged the water through specially constructed spouts. In his first letter to the Venetian senate about it in December 1593, he announced: "I have invented a device for raising water from the earth most easily, at little expense and great accommodation, which from the motion of one horse can spout water continuously through twenty mouths." He asked for a patent,* and nine months later the senate granted it to him for a period of twenty years. Galileo might have hoped that farmers throughout Italy would rush to order the equipment and make him rich. Instead, only one wealthy patron ordered the contraption. The famous Contarinis, the family of doges and senators, had a miniature version of Galileo's device installed in the garden of their Paduan palace in 1598.

Galileo never gave up hope that his invention would catch on. He even wrote promotionally about it, adopting the popular literary artifice of the dialogue. These dialogues had two interlocutors, named Salviati and Sagredo, who discussed the principle and the merits of his irrigation machine. Salviati was really Galileo, and Sagredo was his witty and doting foil. Salviati began with uncharacteristic modesty.

"I don't know if I have understood well the principle of this new instrument, which will lift very heavy weights with little work. But I will tell you what I understand, and you can add whatever I miss." Very quickly, the protagonist dropped this false humility. "With a very subtle trick, the author of this machine has made the arm of the lever much heavier, weighing more than four hundred pounds, and has changed it into a pendulum. When the pendulum is pointed straight down, any minimum strength can make it move from its perpendicular state."

"I understand very well," Sagredo, the sidekick, said. "What do you say of an invention so bizarre?"

"I say that it looks like one of the most ingenious inventions which ever have fallen on the most enlightened intellect."

---

*In the histories of patent law, it is often noted that with this request to protect his screw device, Galileo became one of the first persons ever to claim a patent.

The Sagredo of this exchange was a literary invention, but inspired by a real personality. Indeed, that person had been as dear to Galileo as any friend in his entire life. His name was Gianfrancesco Sagredo. That Galileo would select Sagredo as his literary foil after Sagredo's death is testimony to the intimacy of their vibrant friendship. Sagredo was a Venetian nobleman, nine years younger than Galileo, whose family could claim a cardinal, an ambassador to Paris, a doge, and even a saint. He lived splendidly and eccentrically in a palace on the arm of San Sofia along the Grand Canal. Located hard by the Ca' d' Oro (the golden house that was the most elegant palace in Venice) and the Rialto Bridge, his pink Gothic palace had Byzantine lancet-and-rosette windows, a grand staircase, marble floors covered with oriental rugs, high-ceilinged ballrooms, and tiny, hidden rooms on the top floor for assignations with the most famous courtesans of Venice. The palace was often compared to Noah's ark, not only for its floating square shape, but also for its zoolike denizens.

Sagredo was a confirmed bachelor, who seemed to have been exhausted by the dissipation of his early life. Rumor had it that he had killed nine men in duels. But as he grew older he turned to tamer pursuits, including wild parties at his country estate on the river Brenta. He filled his palace with rare dogs, cats, and exotic domestic birds of all varieties. These were to keep him company but also to display his lively scientific curiosities, to show his sensitivities, and to amuse his equally exotic guests. Good-natured, extravagant, religious (but with a keen Venetian distaste for Jesuits), sarcastic, and a bit frumpy, this libertine made several brief forays into government service, as a treasurer at a Veneto fortress and later as diplomat for the Venetian republic in the Middle East. By his station in life, he was a member of the Supreme Council of the Republic at the age of twenty-five. But he found public service too unsettling and confining, and he was eager to retreat into the serenity of his study or into the erudite company he gathered around him.

Once, in a letter, Sagredo wrote of himself:

I am a Venetian gentleman. I have never called myself one of the literati, but hold dear the protection of the literati. Never have I intended to take advantage of my fortune. My studies always concern those things which,
as a Christian, I owe to God,
as a citizen I owe to my country,
as a nobleman, I owe to my house,

as a man of society, I owe to my friends,
and as a gallant man and true philosopher, I owe to myself.

My palace in Venice has often been compared to Noah's Ark, partly because of its shape, partly because inside I keep all manner of beasts. As a bachelor, I spend my time in conversation. If occasionally I speculate on science, don't believe, dear sir, that I presume to be equal to the professors. I investigate freely the truth of those propositions which give me pleasure.

When they met through Galileo's university activities, Sagredo and Galileo took to each other instantly. In Galileo, Sagredo found a mentor, a big brother, a cause célèbre, a brilliant conversationalist and savant who imparted importance and splendor to his ark. In Sagredo, Galileo found an amusing and loyal sidekick, a wit, a keen mind, a political agent, an eager party-giver, and a playmate.

Trips to Venice for pleasure and relaxation soon became a regular feature of Galileo's. When his university lectures were finished and his responsibilities to his private students had a lull, he would hire a coach at his house near Santa Giustina for three lire ten and wind through the narrow cobblestone streets to the Piovego canal, where the barge to Venetian delights awaited him.

In the last years of the sixteenth century, Venice was moving into a period of decline, but Galileo was not aware of it. The city of 150,000 was poised between two terrible spasms of plague: the epidemics of 1576–1577 and of 1630–1631, the latter of which would take 46,000 lives. The city remained the commercial heart of the European Occident and a buffer state against Spanish influence for the German states to the north. With a keen sense of its unique relationship with the sea, "married" as it were to the water, it was accustomed to visitors and welcomed them. Its silk shops along the Mercerie drew customers from all over Europe, and its endless games and spectacles made it a perpetual stage. It boasted more professional courtesans than Rome, and it consumed 40 million bottles of wine in a year. Upon its narrow *calle* and wide canals, comedies, regattas, dog fights, and battles for the bridges by wrestlers and swordsmen went on without pause. In February, before Lent, Carnival invited the population to recede behind masks, to drop class lines, to set aside marriage bonds, and to license all debauchery with the mere lighting of a domestic candle. With this huge appetite for fun and naughtiness, the gulf between the social classes narrowed, as noble families lived closely together with their vassals and merchants.

This leveling was much to Galileo's liking. In the floating city he was free to indulge his enormous appetites for food and women, free to express any unconventional thought that came into his head, free in his associations across social class. He and Sagredo brainstormed and skylarked and argued on a wide range of subjects, from birds to magnets, bronzes to the theory of light. They could imagine the most outlandish things together. During a discussion of magnets they visualized a device that could enable a person to talk to another person who was as far away as two or three miles!

They also delighted in games, music, and practical jokes. Once, indulging Sagredo's prejudices against the Jesuit order, they composed a series of fictitious letters, as if they were written by a rich and noble widow with questions about her personal scruples and with religious doubts. These missives were sent to a Venetian Jesuit. Over a four-month period the priest replied promptly with earnest counsel and, no doubt, a sincere hope that his exertions would result in a contribution to the church. On another occasion, indulging Galileo's prejudice against pompous professors, they composed a letter as if from an amateur mathematician who was confused about a particularly difficult equation, and sent it to one of Galileo's colleagues at the University of Padua. The professor also replied promptly—with a gross miscalculation, and the ark in Venice reverberated with wicked laughter.

If the conversation was grand, the contacts were useful. In Sagredo's circle Galileo met the future doges, Niccolò Contarini and Leonardo Donà. The former would commission work from him, and the latter would hire him for life. At the pink palace he also encountered Girolamo Magagnati, the acerbic playwright, burlesque poet, and glass manufacturer in Murano, who later was to become Galileo's supplier of optical lenses. Along with his bills, Magagnati passed on the gossip of Venice in the raw Paduan dialect that he so fancied. They shared a love of food and of cooking and traded fish and sausages. "Come here soon for the vintage and stay till polenta time and even turnip time, if you want to see me become fat like a pig . . . or like you." They often traded jokes—one was a bet about an excommunication in a synagogue. Their correspondence was spiced with their newest recipes for peasant soups or their latest taste in *barolo*.

In one letter, after he commiserated with Galileo about his indisposition—"I heard that you had eaten so many turnips that you became ill, because the frost didn't cook them so well"—the poet became chatty.

Today the mills are closed, and I wander freely, because the priest doesn't want people to work, so I tell you that I have had your letter with a piece of meat. My dear fellow, you must send me weekly a piece of meat, with a pair of chops that I like very well. You started this, and now I'm accustomed to it and can't do without. For my part, I will prepare something for you on Thursday evening, so don't buy anything there, because on Friday you will take back the net with so many fish as you need. I will bring the shepherd's staff, and we'll make a good broth and many good soups. As the man said, we make like asses: we'll scratch each other where we itch . . . that is, in the throat.

"Take it easy, dear friend," Magagnati closed his letter, "and long live love! Because even if you're old, you don't have to be stupid!"

With this happy escape, the seven years in Padua that brought him up to the seventeenth century were among the most pleasurable of Galileo's life. Those years formed the heart of his vital thirties, when he was well established, vigorous, and reasonably carefree. He loved this city, which Shakespeare memorialized as "fair Padua, nursery of the arts." With evident pleasure, he walked the city's narrow cobblestone streets and porticoed sidewalks, strolled along the riviera of the languorous Bacchiglione, tarried by its canals and in its circular botanical garden representing the Ptolemaic cosmos, and in its greens like the oval-shaped, moated Prato della Valle. He prayed in its Moorish basilicas, gazed upon Donatello's statues and Giotto's frescoes, and shopped the markets around the Palazzo della Ragione, the town center whose great salon was a mammoth upside-down wooden ark. With his students, he conversed in the cafes around the Piazza dei Signori or upon the marble steps of the Loggia della Gran Guardia.

But Galileo was not an enthusiastic lecturer. It should have been otherwise, for the rules of lecturing at Il Bo suited his style. As he began his professorship, students decried boring professors who merely read their timeworn lectures from yellowed parchment—the paper doctors, they were called—instead of speaking to them conversationally. By the order of the Venetian senate, a fine of twenty crowns was levied for such a crime against intellectual liveliness. Galileo should have adored that command, for it played to his showy side. He was duty-bound to perform, to be dramatic in the lecture hall: *Commedia della scienza*. But he disliked the impersonality of the lecture and preferred the quiet absorption of private lessons.

The university teemed with life and controversy. As the radical stu-

dents fought the snooping police in San Biagio, the professors fought the
Jesuits in more bloodless combat. During Galileo's first years in Padua, the
Jesuits had persisted in an effort to establish a second, competing university in the city. Public opinion was sharply divided. The faculty of Il Bo
resisted vigorously. The conflict became known as the battle between the
bovisti and the *gesuiti,* and it began with a sophomoric raid of the Jesuit
house by rowdy young Venetian noblemen who turned the priests out of
their beds and into the streets, naked as babies. Galileo did his best to
stay out of this dangerous controversy, for he valued his relationship with
the Jesuits.

At the university there were national figures in law, the arts, and philosophy, but the medical faculty stood above all others. In 1587, Girolamo Mercuriale, the best-known physician in Italy, who had written a
famous book on the benefits of physical exercise, had relinquished his
chair to Dr. Alessandro Massaria, who was the best doctor of practical
medicine in northern Italy. Among the more junior faculty members, a
debate raged over the efficacy of bloodletting. The first chair of surgery
and anatomy was held by Girolamo Fabricio of Acquapendente, who was
known as the "Columbus of the human body," partly for having discovered the valves in human veins. He had designed the intimate, anatomical arena at Il Bo in the shape of a human eye, with balustraded balconies
banked above the surgical table. Upon the table, special emphasis was
given to remedies for the typical acts of violence: dagger wounds and poi-
sonings. The arena gave an operation the air of sport.

That so many good doctors were close at hand was a plus for Galileo.
In the summer of 1593, together with three friends, he set out on a long
excursion into the countryside. The party went as far as Verona, back-
tracked to Vicenza, and ended up one hot night in the small village of
Costozza, where a well-known lawyer and patron of the arts had his summer villa. There they were welcomed grandly, and after a long night of
indulgence, complete with pitchers of the full-bodied rosso di Costozza,
Galileo lay down naked in the heat next to an aperture from which emit-
ted a natural draft chilled by a nearby rock-encased spring. He contracted
a terrible cold, which lasted several days, and eventually had to be transported back to Padua in a litter. This ailment was soon compounded by a
nagging and persistent arthritis, which was complicated in due course by
a host of other maladies that tormented him for the rest of his life. In
Padua, Girolamo Fabricio became his personal doctor. Like other important people in Galileo's life, Fabricio inevitably found his way into

Galileo's writings. Fifteen years later, when Galileo was making the point that mathematics could not be separated from philosophy, he made an analogy to the relation between medicine and surgery:

> Such separation is no less foolish than to suggest that the great surgeon of Acquapendente [Fabricio] should content himself to remain among his scalpels and ointments without trying to effect cures by medicine, as if knowledge of surgery destroyed a knowledge of medicine. Many times I recovered my health through the ministrations of Signor Acquapendente. And I can attest that he never gave me any compound of threads, bandages, probes and razors to drink, nor did he ever, instead of feeling my pulse, cauterize me or pull a tooth from my mouth.

Galileo maintained an interest in medical science, especially anatomy, throughout his life. The debates in the medical school connected with a number of philosophical questions that interested him: the nature of pain, the origin of the nerves, the circulation of the blood. He was an eager celebrant at the dedication of Fabricio's Anatomical Arena in 1594.

His course on Ptolemy in 1594 and 1595 at the university had established astronomy as one of his many fields, and there, as everywhere, he could be counted upon to have definite opinions. People wrote to him for his views on a wide assortment of subjects. In 1597 he heard from his old friend at the University of Pisa, Jacopo Mazzoni, the man with the incredible memory. Mazzoni had turned his mind from Dante to Aristotle and wanted Galileo's opinion about his new book, in which he compared Aristotle and Plato. Galileo felt that a passage relating to the Copernican theory was befuddled, and he was ready to set his friend straight. After praising certain aspects of the book, he criticized the way Mazzoni had debunked Copernicus's theory about the diurnal motion of the earth. To Galileo, the view of Copernicus had become far more plausible than the time-worn opinions of Aristotle and Ptolemy, which fixed the earth in the center of the universe. This is Galileo's first known expression of support for the Copernican theory.

Several months later he would do so again. Now he asserted that he had held Copernicus's view for many years. Yet another book came to his attention. Written in the universal language of Latin, it came from a twenty-six-year-old teacher at a Protestant school in Graz, in the Holy Roman Empire, who had learned of Galileo through the German tie to

Padua. Its author was Johannes Kepler, and the book's title was *Mysterium Cosmographicum*. A soaring mixture of science and mysticism, it held the young Kepler's intuitive "proof" that the sun, not the earth, was the center of the universe. He imagined a divine arrangement of the planets that could be explained by the sacred number five: five perfect solids and five intervals between the planets. It was as if he had perceived a connection between the motion of the planets and the gospel of Matthew, which likened the kingdom of heaven to ten virgins, five who were wise, five who were foolish.

I believe Divine Providence arranged matters in such a way that what I could not obtain with all my efforts was given to me through chance. I believe all the more that this is so as I have always prayed to God that he should make my plan succeed, if what Copernicus has said was the truth.

Such a methodology should have engendered contempt in Galileo, for it was hocus-pocus and entirely wrongheaded, even if a few years later its intuition led to Kepler's brilliant laws of planetary motion. Galileo, it seems, was drawn to anyone bold enough to espouse Copernicanism, for he saw it as a dangerous and exciting act. His reply to Kepler was enthusiastic and revealing. At last he had found a worthy ally with whom he could commiserate in private. For now he was willing to let Kepler lead the public charge.

"It is really pitiful that so few seek truth," Galileo wrote to his new confidant, "but this is not the place to mourn over the miseries of our times. I shall read your book with special pleasure, because I have been an adherent of the Copernican system for many years. It explains to me the causes of many appearances of nature which are quite unintelligible within the commonly accepted hypothesis."

Galileo's letter to Kepler, however, was not so much a declaration of belief as a confession of cowardice.

"I have collected many arguments to refute the [Aristotelian] theory, but I do not publish them, for fear of sharing the fate of our master, Copernicus.* Although he has earned immortal fame with some, with

---

*Copernicus's book, *De Revolutionibus*, was published in 1543 as the author lay on his deathbed. Unknown to Copernicus, the book was published with a preface intended to disarm prejudice against its radical view by insisting on the purely hypothetical nature of Copernicus's conjectures.

many others (so great is the number of fools) he has become an object of ridicule and scorn. If there were more people like you, I would publish my speculations. This not being the case, I refrain."

The struggle within Galileo between private belief and public expression, between the brave and the cowardly man, between the leader and the follower, between the idealistic and the practical was evident in this important interchange. In October Kepler cheered him on. Publish! Kepler urged. And if it be too dangerous to do so in Italy, publish in Germany. Kepler exulted in his new friendship and trumpeted a call to arms. "Have confidence! Galileo, and proceed!" he exclaimed. "I do not think that Europe's famous mathematicians will oppose us. The truth must be all-convincing!"

But Galileo did not proceed. There was little to gain and much to lose by doing so. By instinct, he was more interested in proofs and demonstrations than speculations, and he was still preoccupied with ways to make money, not trouble, on the side.

In the summer of 1597 he began his ten-year collaboration with a toolmaker named Marc'antonio Mazzoleni, who had learned his craft at the Arsenale in Venice. Their first venture was a return to the old well of military hardware. Again, the relationship with the del Monte clan, Marquis del Monte in Florence and General del Monte in Padua, prompted the undertaking. Artillery, in this day of castle walls and heavy cannons, remained as much an art as a science. The marquis wondered if it were possible to devise a lightweight military compass that could replace the bulky and inexact instruments used by his brother's cannoneers: to gauge the distance and the height of a target, to measure the accurate angle of elevation for the cannon barrel, and to track the trajectory of the projectile. In 1596 Galileo put his mind to the problem.

The result was his military and geometric compass. It was a lightweight, bronze drafting instrument with two adjustable arms bound together by a floral hinge and beautifully engraved with four pairs of lines. Lower on the instrument a quadrant, scored with transversal lines to measure height, was attached to the arms. The compass could be placed in the barrel and read on the side without the gunner having to stand in front of the bore, a useful safety measure.

In 1597 Galileo added more scales to its measurements, so that the instrument could be adapted to civilian uses such as surveying. While Galileo wrote a manual for his instrument, Mazzoleni produced them by the score in his workshop. At last Galileo had invented a practical tool that could be manufactured in quantity and for which there was a ready market. He further supplemented his income by giving practical laboratories in its use, charging his students 120 lire for their instruction. (For good business and political reasons, he presented gifts of his compass to such important and helpful personages as Pinelli and Friar Sarpi.) This business began to go so well that in 1599 Mazzoleni moved into Galileo's house, along with his wife (who became the cook and housekeeper) and his child. In addition to his lodging, Mazzoleni was paid a miserly six crowns a year by his master. Their compass factory was opened on the ground floor. Before the venture ended, Mazzoleni would produce more than a hundred instruments, for which Galileo charged fifty lire, more than three times the cost of production, not including the one Mazzoleni made of silver to present to Grand Duke Ferdinand of Austria.

In scholarly Padua, Galileo's entrepreneurial spirit was both envied and resented. From the start of his tenure at The Ox, a cadre of detractors had gossiped about him and searched diligently for a way to bring him down to size. Instead of assuaging them, Galileo taunted them, and thus the situation raced toward a confrontation. It would come a few years later, when Galileo printed his manual on the use of his military compass. To his horror, a young Milanese named Baldassare Capra published a book of his own on a military compass and claimed priority for the invention. Galileo stood charged with plagiarism.

This was a serious accusation, and Galileo had to marshal his forces quickly. Sagredo, Mazzoleni, and even Friar Paolo Sarpi gave depositions in Galileo's defense, stating that in 1597 they were among the fortunate whom Galileo had instructed on the instrument's use. Galileo had even given Sarpi one of the compasses, which the friar happily produced for the judges. Among the others who had been instructed on its operation, it turned out, was the accuser, Baldassare Capra, who was then only seventeen years old. As the university officials looked into the matter, they found Capra's book to be little more than a Latin translation of Galileo's book. The accuser became the accused and found himself charged with plagiarism. Copies of his book were seized, and Capra was drummed out of Padua.

Then and later, Galileo seemed unable to rise above such transparent slanders. Even though Capra was disgraced by the authorities, Galileo felt compelled to write an entire tract about the affair on the pretext that thirty copies of Capra's book remained unaccounted for and to have the pamphlet published in Venice. Twenty years after that, when he was arguably the most famous man in the world and Capra lurked in some back-alley shadow, Galileo returned to the grim subject with renewed passion in his book, *The Assayer*. Capra became the symbol of the usurpers and imposters who with "admirable dexterity" had tried to steal his discoveries and his glory.

"May I be pardoned if on this occasion—against my nature, my custom and my present purpose—I show resentment and protest (perhaps too bitterly) about something I have kept to myself all these years." His revelation? That a dark German conspiracy had been behind the plagiarism scandal of 1607. Capra's teacher, a German called Simon Mayr, had inspired Capra's long-since forgotten plagiarism.

Who cared? Galileo did.

As the turn of the century approached, Galileo had good reason for satisfaction. At thirty-five years of age, he had become a man of means. From his modest cottage near the bastion of Santa Giustina, he had moved into an expansive three-story house behind the lovely domed Basilica of San Antonio and around the corner from Pinelli's dusky palazzo. There, on a street named Via Vignali del Santo, "vineyard of the saint," his house could accommodate a score of boarders, a staff of servants, his workshop, and the family of Marc'antonio Mazzoleni, as well as a large suite of rooms on the first floor for the master of the house himself.

The large walled garden behind gave him particular pleasure, and there for years he would tend its trellised vines and flowers and walkways. For his private students, young scholars from Italy and noblemen from abroad, the memory of Galileo in his garden remained vivid. It was a place of gathering, of music and poetry, of philosophy and laughter, especially in the summer when they took their meals under the trees with the contours of moonlit domes of Saint Anthony barely visible above the wall.

His first tenure at the university expired in 1599. The pleasure of the doge was that he continue for another seven years. The Venetian senate obliged with a new contract, nearly doubling his salary to 320 crowns a year.

At this moment Galileo was relaxed and carefree. It was the happiest time of his life.

4

FROGS AND MICE

Far away in Rome, the advent of a new century was a time of celebration and renewal. With a sigh of good riddance, the authorities of the Catholic church bade farewell to the most disastrous century in its history, the century of Luther and Calvin and Henry VIII. Tortured though he was by terrible gout in his hands and feet, the Florentine pope, Clement VIII, was intent that the new century begin happily. He had declared 1600 to be a Year of Jubilee, full of festivals and marathon preachings in Rome, when the best sermonizers in the Catholic world would be brought to the great cathedrals of Catholicism—Cardinal Bellarmine would hold forth in the Jesuit church, the Gesu—when over a million pilgrims were expected to swell the city and the ailing pope himself would personally receive the confessions of protestants and heretics in the courtyard of the Belvedere. Clement dragged himself from his sickbed on the last day of December to discharge the sixteenth century and to herald the new age with a stirring message of counter-reformation and with the *urbi et orbi*, the universal blessing to the city of Rome and to the world.

The diplomatic successes of Clement VIII in the previous few years had engendered great hope. Henry IV of France had disavowed his Protestantism and had submitted to the power of the Vatican. Spain was exhausted externally by fighting across Europe as well as by the defeat of its Armada, while the excesses of the Inquisition had exhausted the country internally. Its influence in Rome and across northern Italy was in decline . . . temporarily. In 1598 Spain experienced a renewal as Philip III was crowned. Although the Edict of Nantes was signed, and thereby the freedom of worship was assured for the French Huguenots, France and Spain had made peace. And heretical Elizabethan England had been isolated. A giddiness seized the Eternal City as visitors filled the streets.

The new century also began with a terrible event, a harbinger of what was to come for Galileo. Early in the morning of Saturday, February 19, 1600, several hooded members of a group known as the Company of Mercy and Pity (also known as the Company of Saint John the Beheaded) went to the Nona Tower, the secular prison across the Tiber from the holy prison of Castel Sant'Angelo, and there they took charge of a man. Placing him in a simple wagon, they set off to the Campo dei Fiori, the Square of Flowers, down the cramped streets and through the square that had housed Domitian's stadium.

During the slow ride over the stones, Jesuit and Dominican priests mumbled their imprecations to the prisoner for a last-minute recantation of his awful beliefs, inviting him to express contrition for his sins, lest he be lost forever in eternal damnation as a heretic. They offered him icons to kiss and presented him with tablets, painted with images of Christ and the Holy Virgin and even the pope, whom the prisoner had called a triumphant beast. But the heretic's jaw was clamped shut with an iron gag, a long spike piercing his tongue, and another spike stuck in his palate. He would not be able to say to these minions or excite the crowd with the words he had uttered to the greatest intellectual of the Catholic church, Cardinal Robert Bellarmine: "I neither ought to recant, nor will I. I have nothing to recant, nor do I know what I should recant."

The prisoner had only contempt for his accusers and his judges. When they prepared to deliver their judgment, he leveled his gaze at them and exclaimed, "In pronouncing my sentence, *your* fear is greater than mine in hearing it."

Along the way, bystanders asked who the man was. He was "a Lutheran," the priests answered with the generic slur for any heretic. In fact, he was a Dominican, once a member in high standing of the very order of spiritual police—"Dominican" is translated as "dogs of God"— that had now condemned him. He had been in jail for eight years, an inordinately long time, precisely because the Dominicans had hoped for a recantation and an escape from this final, awful duty. And the culprit had toyed with abjuration, making promises that now seemed like a tactic of delay. They had charged him with error in eight propositions, and upon several he had wavered. About one, however, he stood firm. He believed in the infinity of the cosmos. Just as God was infinite, so was the universe he had created. Moreover, he believed that the earth traveled around the sun, and that in the cosmos there were many earths, which also contained the living creations of God.

When they arrived at their terrible destination, the throng quivered with anticipation. The sentence was vague and encoded on a "Day of Justice." The prisoner should be punished "with as great a clemency as possible and without effusion of blood." Mumbling appeals, reciting his errors, mouthing prayers about deliverance and charity, the hooded friars guided him to the stake. They stripped him naked and pressed a crucifix toward his face, but he turned away in disgust, sending excited shrieks through the crowd.

Then Giordano Bruno was burned, bloodlessly, as the priests chanted their litanies.

"Thus, it is our custom to proceed against such men," wrote one well-satisfied witness, "or against such monsters. In short, I would never end, were I to pass in review all the monstrosities he has advanced, whether in his books or by word of mouth. There is not an error of the pagan philosophers or of our heretics, ancient or modern, that he did not sustain."

In the *Avvisi* and the *Ritorni*, the Roman tabloids of the day, the reports of Bruno's death varied. One reported that he had died with his tongue tied to prevent him from uttering blasphemies to the mob. The other cast him as a martyr whose soul would rise with the smoke of Paradise. "Now he knows whether he spoke the truth," one account wrote drolly. And in the report of the brothers of Mercy and Pity, it was stated that the culprit "remained to the end in his accursed obstinacy, his brain and intellect seething with a thousand errors and vanities."

Thus, Giordano Bruno showed the way of the pure martyr. To the end he was faithful to his wild and brilliant convictions.

In 1600, the Year of Jubilee, Galileo entered a period of his life where messy personal matters preoccupied him. He was the head of his large family and its only breadwinner. His extravagant younger brother, Michelangelo, expected Galileo to support his uncertain ambitions to become a professional musician. There had been a series of false starts, where Michelangelo went off, with Galileo's crowns, to pursue promising leads, only to return downcast and penniless soon after. At last in the summer of 1600 he secured a post as the court musician to the noble Radziwill family in Poland. This enabled Michelangelo to play the *gran signor*, for he would be seated dressed in satin and velvet at the elegant table of the prince, be pampered by two servants and a coach at the ready, and would pull down a salary of three hundred crowns a year. Galileo should have been pleased, except for the fact that the Polish court expected his brother to turn up well outfitted and to have a number of fine musical instruments with him. It fell to Galileo to support these preparations at the cost of two hundred crowns.

Meanwhile, the sixth Galilei sibling, his sister Livia, had tired of the nun's life. Perhaps marriage would be preferable, she surmised, and it had better happen soon, since she was nearing thirty. So a search got under way for a suitable bridegroom. The first candidate had the impressive name of Pompeo but made a salary of less than one hundred crowns per year. Thus Galileo faced the unpleasant prospect of paying for a dowry and underpinning an impecunious household for years to come, in addition to supporting Michelangelo's extravagant court life.

"It is impossible for me to consent to this arrangement just at present," he wrote to his mother on August 7, 1600. Perhaps when Michelangelo got settled in his new post and could contribute a portion of his new salary to a dowry, Livia's marriage might be possible, "since she is determined to come out and partake of the miseries of the world." She should be patient, he thought. "Tell her that there have been queens and great ladies who have not married till they were old enough to be her mother."

Galileo himself came up with a more suitable candidate who would cost him no less, even though he was a gentleman from Pisa. From Poland, Michelangelo promised to contribute to the dowry of eighteen hundred crowns, of which two hundred would be needed immediately for a trousseau, six hundred more in cash, and the rest to be paid over a five-year period. A year into Livia's marriage, Michelangelo had still not contributed a single *julio*. "If I had imagined that things were going to turn out in this manner," Galileo wrote him resentfully, "I would not have given the child in marriage, or else I would have given her only such a dowry as I was able to pay myself. I seem destined to bear every burden alone."

Four years later Michelangelo lost his post at the Polish court and was back in Padua, sponging off his brother. Again, through Galileo's efforts, Michelangelo got an appointment as the court musician to the duke of Bavaria. With Michelangelo back on salary, Galileo renewed his request for assistance in paying various dowries amounting to more than fourteen hundred crowns, especially after he heard reports of his brother's extravagance in Bavaria.

"You complain of me having spent such a large sum on one feast," Michelangelo replied coolly. "The sum was large, yes, but it was my wedding. There were more than eighty persons present, among whom were many gentlemen of importance. Present were no less than four ambassadors! If I had not followed the custom of this country, I should have been put to shame."

Galileo might have been able to accept this whining, had not Michelangelo followed with this insolence: "I know you will say that I should have waited and thought of our sisters before taking a wife. But good heavens! The idea of toiling all one's life just to save a few farthings for one's sisters! This joke is too heavy and bitter." Michelangelo ended his letter with an expression of annoyance. "I understand that you are going to send the case of lutes shortly. I have been expecting their arrival with some impatience. I will need them for concerts this Lent and would not mind paying a little extra for the carriage."

Meanwhile, the new century brought a new entanglement for Galileo. Upon one of the many nights of pleasure at Sagredo's palace in Venice, he had encountered a fiery beauty from the back streets of San Sofia named Marina Gamba. She was only twenty-one years old, fourteen years younger than he, but she was precocious, just as Galileo was unpracticed in giving himself emotionally. The hot-tempered, strapping, lusty, and probably illiterate woman was well known to Sagredo and many on the Nuova Strada and the Ramo d'Oca, the alley of the goose. Her reputation was as a woman of *facile costume*, of easy habits. The attraction between her and the effusive scientist was immediate. Their passion was robust, and it would last for ten years.

They were never to live together under one roof, but their union soon bore fruit. In the summer of 1600 Gamba had a child. In admirably straightforward language, the registry in the parish of San Lorenzo in Padua announced the event. "Virginia, daughter of Marina of Venice, born of fornication, August 13, 1600." When a second child came almost exactly a year later, the language of the notice was only slightly more stately. "Livia Antonia, daughter of Madonna Marina de Antonio Gamba and of . . ." Galileo's paternity was covered up when a third child came five years later. "Father uncertain," read the notice. From fornication to fatherhood, a local dignitary must be protected. So Marina and her children were deposited in cramped quarters in the Ponte Corvo, the noisy commercial street around the corner from Galileo's quiet mansion.

To have children by a common woman was scarcely a disgrace in Renaissance Italy, especially in the easygoing Serene Republic of Venice, but neither was it something to flaunt. Marina Gamba was kept from the view of the dignitaries who passed through the house on Via Vignali. To keep the class lines perfectly clear, Galileo made his servants godparents to his children. Padua was a small town, and the relationship was well known. In Galileo's own family, his passion for Gamba was a source of contention. His once noble, now shrewish mother, Giulia, was especially offended by the presence of this common woman in the family. As she depended on Galileo for financial support, so was she incessant in her disapproval of his personal life.

The low point came in a visit to Padua after Galileo's second child was born, when Giulia had come to confirm her worst suspicions. The visit commenced with loud arguments between Galileo's mistress and his mother and quickly disintegrated into a hair-pulling brawl, whose screams filled the Vineyard of the Saint. Thereafter, Giulia recruited Galileo's servant to spy on the lovers. Particularly offensive to Galileo's mother was the worry that this loose woman would take possession of her fine linens. Her spy was to write to her secretly about what the lovers said behind closed doors. If this wasn't enough, Giulia prevailed on her secret agent to steal a few lenses from her son, once he began to construct his telescopes.

By 1602, under these circumstances, it is no surprise that Galileo was getting restless. During the summer of that year, he was engaged in an interesting colloquy with Sagredo and Friar Sarpi about the properties of magnets, but he was torn between mounting family responsibilities, great ambitions for new work, and his annoying duties at the university. In 1603 his request for an increase in salary was denied. The distraction of his private lessons was increasingly resented. To the Tuscan secretary of state, Belasario Vinta, he expressed his hope to shed his private students.

But how?

From an unexpected quarter, an answer presented itself. In March 1604, the duke of Mantua, Vincenzo Gonzaga, invited Galileo to his small duchy a hundred miles southwest of Padua for business discussions. Mantua was a center of the arts and the birthplace of Virgil. Leon Battista Alberti, the prototype of the Renaissance man, had designed its buildings; Montegna had decorated its palaces; and Monteverdi was soon to fill their ballrooms with the strains of his first two operas and his incomparable Magnificat.

Galileo's friend Fra Paolo Sarpi had been attached to the court of Mantua as a young man, and he had stories to tell about serving the bizarre Gonzaga of Mantua. The hunchback duke was a famous practical joker. Once, after a mule was foaled at the castle, the duke solemnly asked his young court theologian to prepare a horoscope on the event. Though Sarpi did not approve of astrology, he did his master's bidding. Gonzaga promptly sent the horoscope to the famous astrologers throughout Italy, announcing a blessed palace birth and asking them to interpret the signs. The enthusiastic responses came back rapidly. The newborn was destined to be a great warrior or a cardinal, a noted philosopher, maybe even a pope. Gonzaga was well pleased. But Sarpi was not amused at being duped by the duke and soon left Mantua in a huff. Very likely, this story would have appealed to Galileo's sense of humor.

Mantua was also a fortress town, a marshy place on the banks of the Mincio River just west of its confluence with the Po. And the duke himself was an eccentric, with a cripple's acute sense of inferiority and a visceral need to prove his manhood. Galileo's principal attraction to the prince was not as a mathematician but as a military engineer. For Gonzaga was a warlord, tormented by a passionate hatred of Spain and seized with grandiose military aspirations. To recruit Galileo as his chief military adviser would be a grand coup and something of a threat to his enemies.

Given his financial distress, Galileo was ready to listen. As he demonstrated his military compass and charmed the Mantuan court, he was presented with a tempting offer: double his present salary and liberation, at long last, from his private students. The duke flattered and cajoled, presenting Galileo with a necklace of gold and a medal bearing his image, while his son, Carlo Gonzaga, offered the visitor two saucers of pure silver.

Galileo bowed servilely and offered his thanks, but when he was home, the offer began to seem less attractive. Mantua under the strange Gonzaga was severe and dangerous. Its spartan ways paled before the pleasures of Venice and the vibrancy of Padua. Galileo demurred.

As he pondered less radical ways to escape his dilemma, he amused himself in the summer of 1604 in translating the mock Homeric epic "War of the Mice and the Frogs" from the original Greek.

In September 1604, as he was experimenting with his irrigation device in the garden of the Contarinis in Padua, Galileo received an excited communication. It came from one Ilario Altobelli, yet another independent-minded priest, who was skilled in scientific observation. Altobelli announced that he had observed a new star in the constellation Sagittarius. Any new star in the firmament was cause for tremendous interest, since conventional Aristotelian thinking held that the heavens were fixed for the enjoyment of man. Stars were jewels, cold, beautiful, and perfect, which could not appear or disappear frivolously. In 1572, when a bright nova had appeared in the sky and then disappeared, it caused consternation in the Catholic church, for it suggested a heaven not fixed but fluid and dynamic, and this affronted Catholic theology. Soon enough others, including the Paduan astronomers, even the fraud Baldassare Capra, observed the new star. In Germany the great teacher in Tübingen, Michael Maestlin, saw it together with his pupil, Johannes Kepler.

Kepler was soon to claim it for his own. It was, he argued, a transitory star, which existed deep and high in the Milky Way. This radical thought was fiercely disputed by the conventional thinkers who for theological as well as scientific reasons put the star somewhere in the dross beneath the moon rather than within the fixed stars. By Kepler's writings on the phenomena, the new star of 1604 became known as Kepler's Nova.

On October 10 the sky was interesting enough to astronomers without any new apparition, since Jupiter and Mars were in conjunction in the southern sky and Saturn was only eight and a half degrees opposite them. This triple conjunction of the three planets was also of interest to superstitious doctors, for the Black Death had begun in Europe two and a half centuries earlier after a similar alignment in Aquarius.

At sunset, in the vicinity of Jupiter and Mars, the new light appeared. At first it was dim, but in succeeding days it grew into a huge mass, brighter than any other star except Venus. It was reddish in hue and flashed mysteriously and ominously. Galileo finally saw the star with his own eyes in late October.

"At one point, it would contrast its rays with a sudden and faint extinction, paling before Mars's reddish glow," Galileo observed. "Then straightaway, it would shed even more fulsome rays as if coming back to life, holding forth its own splendor with Jupiter's brilliance. Anyone might believe with good reason that this new light was an offspring of Jupiter and Mars, most especially because it appeared to be born both in the same general location and at the same time as a predicted planetary conjunction."

In these days of superstition when Hell and Lucifer were real and lived in the form of witches, plagues, and ghosts, this flickering light was terrifying. It put the intellectual, the spiritual, and the scientific communities into turmoil, as excited explanations about the meaning of the star were put forward and debated. The apparition fueled fantastic opinions, but the most widely held was that this was a sign of the wrath of God and the star itself was God's angry eye. It was an omen of terrible disasters in the offing: famine, earthquakes, floods, pestilence, and war. To impart a sexual connotation to the apparition as the offspring of Jupiter and Mars, as Galileo did, could lead to wild, pagan imaginings.

Because of his reputation for independent thought, Galileo's opinion was eagerly awaited. In December 1604 and January 1605, the Great Hall of Il Bo was reserved for his three lectures on the subject. The crowds were enormous, more than three hundred crammed into the small space. To his students, the occasions were a lasting memory. To history, they mark the first public appearance of Galileo as an astronomer.

Speaking in Latin, he played first, like any good teacher, to the emotions of the audience and then appealed to knowledge over superstition. "You are the witnesses, all of you young people who flock here to hear me discourse on this marvelous apparition. Some of you are terrified and excited by vain superstition. You came to learn whether some outstanding portent of ill omen was being foretold. Others wonder whether a true constellation of stars exists in the heavens or whether this new star is merely vapor near the earth. By Hercules! That splendid desire of yours is worthy of the most superior intellects! Ah, would that my slight intellect could serve the magnitude of the question and of your expectations! I despair of doing so."

This was not necessarily false humility. Galileo knew better what to criticize than what to assert. The Aristotelian nonsense of some strange happening "beneath the moon" was absurd, and he discarded it contemptuously. With Kepler he was sure that the light existed in the most distant stars. But what was it? A meteor? A delusion of celestial vapors? In his lectures he was struggling for the first time with a big new problem: Copernicus's theory concerning the rotation of the earth around the sun. Two months after the strange light appeared, when Galileo made his pronouncements from the lectern, the star was changing. As its brightness lessened, Galileo deduced that the star was moving away from the earth. As it gradually appeared at a different angle from the earth, he was onto the idea of parallax. The logic of his argument was clear: The earth, as well as the mysterious star, was moving!

He did not say so in so many words. Instead he was oblique and poetic, almost as if he wanted to mislead his audience about what he was thinking. "Blood red and saffron orange vapors often rise from the Earth and reflect the light of the sun. Occasionally in the middle of the night, they light up the sky so much that more light is shed on the Earth than at twilight. I have seen this many times in Venice, when the air is so much brighter to the North. This produces a marvelous effect where the northerly roads are illumined on both sides, while houses were not even casting shadows on the ground. This great light comes from nearly a quarter part of the heaven."

Galileo's three lectures were a triumph. They cemented his unique position of fame within Padua. No one else could command such audiences and hold them rapt with his combination of insight, wit, and eloquence, and it would not be long before his normal lectures had to be moved outside in order to accommodate the curious. He made his competitors appear to be frogs and mice battling at his feet. Envy of him rose to a new level. The Aristotelians in particular were upset, for Galileo was promoting the virtues of observation over dogma. This argument aimed at their very foundations.

An imposing adversary stepped forward to defend traditional values. He was Cesare Cremonini, a thin-faced and strong-willed Peripatetic, fourteen years older than Galileo, who exercised great influence at Il Bo from his perch atop the highest chair of natural philosophy. He had real presence, with huge doe's eyes peering wearily out beneath an expansive forehead dominated by a huge protuberance that seemed to be the volcanic remnant of some especially profound thought. Cremonini lived grandly in a palazzo not far from the university, and his salon, with its complement of Roman cardinals, Venetian senators, and opinionated German students, rivaled Pinelli's. (He had been elected the protector of the "German nation" in 1593.)

Cremonini was no stranger to controversy. Arriving in Padua from Ferrara the year before Galileo, he quickly became embroiled in the Jesuit controversy, taking up the banner of suppression and heading a commission of academics to the Venetian senate to block the Jesuit university in Padua. This campaign soured the Catholic church on him, and it began to look at his work. In his commentaries on Aristotle, he had insisted, even more fiercely and publicly than Galileo would later, on a separation between natural philosophy and theology, between reason and faith, between the mind and the soul. He was suspected of being a "mortalist" who did not believe in the immortality of the soul, just as his work seemed to dispute the church doctrine on creation and divine providence. The Inquisition soon focused on him. But in Padua—as Galileo should have taken note—Cremonini was safe from the grasp of the Catholic church. The Venetian senate passed a resolution to protect him and eventually raised his salary, at the end of his career, to two thousand crowns, double Galileo's salary after his invention of the telescope.

Ironically, the two adversaries, Cremonini and Galileo, enjoyed the intimacy of rivals. They both relished a good duel of wits for its own sake. As Galileo's elder, Cremonini tolerated the iconoclasm of his colleague with a combination of condescension and amusement, while Galileo saw in Cremonini the perfect symbol of the pompous and hidebound Aristotelian. Cremonini was not only older but richer, and this too bound them together. On separate occasions they owed each other money. Four years later Cremonini put up the security as Galileo was granted a full year's salary in advance.

But Galileo's argument in his notorious lectures in the Great Hall threatened the philosopher's hold on science. Cremonini understood the seriousness of the challenge, for at issue were not only facts but also a fundamental approach to natural phenomena. For the six months after the first appearance of the new star, Galileo thought about almost nothing else. As many correspondents wrote to him about the star, Cremonini prepared a written counterattack, while he and Galileo jousted in public. It was a great moment for Galileo, and as usual, he would file it away in his memory, to be retrieved later. In his famous *Dialogue* twenty-five years later, his character would say of Cremonini: "Oh, what a Doctor is this! I am his to command, for he will not let himself be imposed on by Aristotle, but will lead him by the nose and make him speak to his purpose." With a certain grudging admiration, Galileo would describe Cremonini as a man who could change his mind to suit any situation. If Cremonini had trouble in publishing controversial opinions, there was no problem. By Galileo's wicked insight, the doctor would merely change a few statements to arrive at the opposite opinion. But Cremonini had something that Galileo desperately wanted: respect as a philosopher.

The debate between Cremonini and Galileo was really a debate between philosophy and science, between first principles of Aristotle and the evidence of the senses. As such their argument prefigured the later conflict between the church and Galileo, for Galileo's complaint with his distinguished elder colleague now, like his later complaint with the elders of the Catholic church, was over literal-mindedness and blind faith.

"If we abandon Aristotle, who will be our guide in philosophy!" Galileo has his Aristotelian exclaim in his great book.

"Only the blind need a guide," was his reply. "Those with eyes and those with a mind must use these faculties to discern for themselves."

Still, for all their public dueling in the corridors of The Ox and the salons of Padua, both Galileo and Cremonini chose to attack each other obliquely in print. Cremonini opened by contributing to a tract of obscure authorship called "Discourse on the New Star," in which "the mathematicians" were lumped together as having nothing to say about matters their senses could not confirm.

"If we were close to the Star, there would be no difficulty," exclaimed Cremonini's cipher, "but since opinion is unclear in such distant things, know that you Mathematicians do not start from the senses any more than we Philosophers do."

Galileo replied incognito, but his signature was unmistakable. He crafted a sprightly dialogue between a farmer and a surveyor and wrote it in the earthy Paduan dialect. (Soft and pleasing in tone and sprinkled with Greek and Spanish words, the Paduan dialect had become high fashion for intellectuals since the poetry of Ruzzante.) Its title was "Dialogue Concerning the New Star," and Galileo's pseudonym for the work was Cecco di Ronchitti. To set the tone for the work, the author dedicated it to Antonio Querengo, the canon of Padua, a Latin poet and a diplomat who had replaced Pinelli as the most learned man in Padua after Pinelli's death in 1601.

"What would you say, Reverend Patron, if you saw a poor servant of yours, never occupied with anything but herds and fields, in a quarrel with one of the Doctors of Padua? Wouldn't it make you laugh?"

He was saying that any common field hand could know as much from his senses as the most elevated doctor of Padua (that is, Cremonini). And thus commenced his dialogue as his surveyor, Natale, came upon his worried farmer, Matteo, looking sadly at his drought-dried river.

"It's said, Matteo, that whenever a rain cloud shows up, it goes away again without wetting the sand as much as a pissing frog." Natale says, "If things go on this way, I think we're near the end of the world."

"Let's take it easy under this walnut tree," Matteo replies. "Do you have any idea what's causing this drought?"

"Why, didn't you see that star three months ago, shining at night like a skunk's eye? The real bright one. Why, that's what's causing these freaks of nature. That's what a Doctor at Padua says."

"A pox on those goat turds at Padua. Maybe just because that fellow never saw it before, he wants everybody to believe it wasn't there. Me? . . . I've never been to Germany, but it's there just the same."

"All the same, we've got to admit the star was new."

"Sure, but so far away, he can't know what the hell it is."

"Far? Bull. It's not even as far as the moon, from what that book says."

"Who is this fellow anyway, the one who wrote that book? Is he a land surveyor?"

"No, he's a philosopher."

"A philosopher, is he? What has philosophy got to do with measuring? You know that a cobbler's helper can't figure out buckles. It's the mathematicians you've got to believe. They are the surveyors of empty air, just like I survey fields and can tell you how long and how wide they are."

"You know what he says about the mathematicians?"

"What?"

"He says they imagine that the sky can be destroyed or created a bit at a time!"

"If mathematicians would just stick to measuring! What do they care if something can be created or not? If the heavens were made of polenta, they could still see it, couldn't they? The boners of this doctor in Padua make me laugh."

"But the doctor says, if this new star was in the heavens, all natural philosophy would be a joke. If one more star is added, the sky could not move at all."

"A pox on this star then. It did wrong to ruin the philosophy of those fellows like that. If I were those philosophers, I would have the star hauled before the Mayor and charged with illegal possession. I'd put up a tough fight, I would. Get a public order against that star for causing the sky not to move. Still . . . there are a lot of people . . . and good ones too . . . who believe the sky doesn't move."

"You know what else he says?"

"What?"

"That the sky couldn't go around, because the elements go up and down, not around."

"What if I contradict him? I say they also go around. He leaves out the writers who say that the earth goes around like a windmill."

The earth goes around like a windmill. In an entertainment such as Galileo had composed, this reference to the Copernicans might escape the notice of most readers. Since Galileo obscured his authorship, he could not be held to account in any case. Ironically, in a second edition, published in Verona several months after the original Paduan edition, he added an important qualifying adjective that changed the whole thrust of the text. In the second edition, the line read: "He leaves out the cross-eyed writers who say that the earth goes around like a windmill." To muddy his meaning still further, Galileo ended his dialogue with a poem about the mysterious nova:

> *No lower than the other stars it lies*
> *And does not move in other ways around*
> *Than all fixed stars—nor change in sign or size.*
> *All this is proved on purest reason's ground;*
> *It has no parallax for us on earth*
> *By reason of the sky's enormous girth.*

Was he trying to protect himself? Was he afraid? Had he suddenly become disenchanted with the Copernicans? Had the behavior of the new star itself—as its brightness diminished and its parallax remained fixed—changed his mind about the Copernican theory?

During the summer of 1605, Galileo returned to Florence as was his custom, to visit his family and to mind his political garden. He had to be nimble in case his in-laws sent the police to arrest him. No payment to his sister Livia's dowry had been made for the preceding two years. He had had no help from his brother, Michelangelo, and the entire balance of eight hundred crowns was now due by default. In the previous March, Livia's husband had sued Galileo in the Venetian courts for the money, and this insult had so upset Galileo that he fell ill for weeks. Unable to pay and unable to appear in court, he had prevailed upon Sagredo to carry the court costs and to stand in as his proxy. Seeing a good thing, his other brother-in-law, Benedetto Landucci, the husband of his sister Virginia, had rushed into court in Florence to demand the payment of his incomplete dowry.

With the legal process tightening around him, it appeared as if all avenues of escape were cut off. But then he had a stroke of luck. Through the chief of her wardrobe, Grand Duchess Christine of Tuscany had sent word of her interest in having Galileo instruct her son, Prince Cosimo, in the uses of the military compass. Now Galileo had something to work with.

To gain the affection of parents through their children is a time-honored ploy, and with Galileo the results were excellent. Soon enough he was invited by the duchess to broaden his instruction and become the general tutor for the crown prince through the summer. By some mysterious process, the litigation against Galileo in the Tuscan courts was quietly dropped.

That was not all Galileo wanted from the grand duchess. As he prepared to return to Padua, he solicited letters of support from the Tuscan court to the Venetian court for an increase in his salary.

Back in Padua he would need all the assistance he could get. The news of his public bickering with the respected Cremonini over the new star had reached Venice and had raised eyebrows. Doubts were expressed about him personally. For a brief time he seemed in jeopardy of receiving no increase, and, worse, of not having his contract renewed at all when it came up again in 1606. These worries led Galileo to make further overtures to the Tuscan court about returning to Florence and permanently entering the service of the Medici. Toward this end, he dedicated his handbook on the operation of his military compass (which was to be published the following summer in Italian rather than Latin) to Cosimo II. This flattery was not enough, however. The Medici court did not respond to Galileo's hints.

Elsewhere, the world began to turn with great events. In January 1606, his acquaintance Leonardo Donà was elected the doge of the Venetian republic. Donà had made a career of opposing Vatican influence in Venice and was the leader of the anti-Romanist party. His election was the culmination of fifteen years of political defiance in which tensions had risen steadily between this free-spirited temporal state and the spiritual authority of the Roman Curia. If Donà was an extremist, so was his election the response to the election of Paul V the year before. Pope Paul was a lawyer by training, an expert in canon law. No sooner had he received the tiara than he sought to enforce existing church law to the letter and to expand its hold over Catholic states. As free expression flourished in Venice, so in Rome, under Paul, more and more books were banned.

"God has given us power over all," the pope proclaimed categorically.

"We are able to depose kings and to set up others, and we are over those things which tend to a supernatural end."

Quarrels between the two powers broke out regarding taxes and tithes, boundaries and sovereignty over islands. When Rome sought to build churches in Venice, the republic exercised a veto and sought to impose taxes on those that were built. Perhaps most provocative, two priests, an abbot from Friuli and a canon from Vicenza, had been charged with a series of crimes, including murder and unnatural acts. The republic had thrown the scoundrels into the ducal dungeons across the Bridge of Sighs and insisted that they be tried by temporal rather than ecclesiastical courts. The pope reacted angrily and demanded the immediate release of the priests. The republic refused.

Thus, the doge and the pope faced off. On the Vatican side, the power behind the faith was Giordano Bruno's executioner and Galileo's eventual inquisitor, Cardinal Robert Bellarmine. In his literary work, Bellarmine had written voluminously about heretics. In his work is the fundamental thinking of the Holy See on the supremacy of the church and even on the infallibility of the pope. Now, as Venice challenged the pope, Bellarmine argued that Vatican authority was to temporal authority as the spirit was to the flesh. Just as the spirit must govern the flesh, so secular power could not put itself above spiritual power, nor attempt to restrain it. To Bellarmine, that constituted "heretical rebellion." To equate secular affairs with carnal pleasure was an interesting point of departure for a priest, but it did not afford much leeway for negotiation.

On the Venetian side, the power behind the doge was Galileo's friend, the remarkable Friar Paolo Sarpi. As the confrontation with the Vatican grew desperate, he had been appointed theological counselor to the doge. The son of a failed merchant and a blonde Venetian beauty, square-faced, wiry, and handsome, Sarpi matched Bellarmine's sober cast of mind. He had entered religious life at the age of fifteen. He was a vegetarian. And he hated vulgar behavior. With Galileo, who was twelve years younger, Sarpi maintained a spirited, vibrant relationship, and Galileo would refer to Sarpi as "my father and my master." When they got together and Galileo lapsed into coarse language or vulgar ways, the dismayed Sarpi had a standard rebuke. "There comes the virgin. Let us talk of something else."

But Sarpi's curiosity in worldly matters was far greater than Bellarmine's, for the friar became a politician, a philosopher, a historian, and a scientist. In his studies of physical science, he was credited with discovering the valves in the veins, the oscillations in the pupil of the eye, and the polar attraction of magnets. He had worked with Galileo's doctor, Fabricio d'Acquapendente, on blood circulation and with Galileo himself on the military compass, the laws of physics, and, later, telescopic discoveries. He also had mastered optics, chemistry, and metallurgy. Devout though he was, Sarpi was a passionate critic of the Holy See, partly, one suspects, because three times he had been turned down for a bishopric. He despised the Vatican's interference in secular affairs and hated the clammy reach of the Inquisition. With his ravenous curiosity, he had to be careful, since iconoclasts of all stripes were forever sending him incendiary books that were banned on the Index. He would call that index of banned books "the first secret device religion ever invented to make men stupid." The true Christian religion, Sarpi wrote, proceeds along the road to heaven, and it should not interfere with political government, which proceeds along the roads of the earth. To Sarpi, there was no such thing as the divine right of kings or of popes.

Here was a true man of the Renaissance. He was tough, spiritual, and broad. In the conflict of Bellarmine and Sarpi, of the pope and the doge, of Venice and Rome, lay the classic conflict of church and state.

On the sidelines in Padua, Galileo could not know that this confrontation would have profound implications for him. He stood transfixed, like everyone else in the Venetian republic, when on April 17, 1606, Paul V excommunicated the doge of Venice, the Venetian senate, and all officials of the Venetian state, including Sarpi. These suspects were given only a few days to recant their disobedience to the church and mend their ways. During this famous interdict, all priests in Venetian territory were prohibited from celebrating mass and were instructed to nail the papal bull to their church doors. All of the Venetian republic was cut off from the body of Christ, until the authority of the pope was recognized. No Venetian could receive the saving sacraments of the church. Baptisms and burials were to cease. Marriages were dissolved, and children declared illegitimate. Husbands could desert their wives, and children did not have to obey their parents. Citizens had no obligation to pay their taxes.

With Sarpi as its rock of confidence, Venice replied with grit, as the Venetian republic mobilized its defense. Whenever the basic interests of the republic were threatened, its vaunted libertarianism quickly disappeared, and it became a faceless and brutal tyranny. On May 6, the doge reaffirmed the determination of the republic to maintain its sovereign rights, which "in temporal things acknowledge no superior but God." The priests of Venice were to ignore the papal bull and go about their normal duties to "cure souls and worship God." The churches continued to function, as even the few priests who attempted to nail the bull to the door found it ripped away and themselves arrested.

One influential priest needed a bit of arm-twisting. An official of the state was sent to the wavering priest to inquire whether the priest intended to say mass the following Sunday. The priest replied that he did not know yet, since he had the matter under pious reflection and would do as his conscience and the Spirit moved him. This answer was delivered to the doge's cabinet, known as the Council of Ten. After some serene reflection of its own, the council sent word back to the priest that they respected his position. But they were obliged to inform the priest that if the Spirit prompted him to close the doors of his church on Sunday, the same Spirit would move the council to hang him from his church door that same afternoon.

Only the Jesuits resisted the doge's veto. As the Catholic order principally concerned with matters of ecclesiastical law and doctrine, and with their own brother, Cardinal Bellarmine, acting as the proclaimer of Vatican policy, the Jesuits were torn between their duty to Rome and their duty to their flock. Eventually, their distress reached Paul V himself, and he solved their dilemma. They were either to obey the interdict and suspend operations or they were to leave the cursed Venetian territory forthwith. The great majority chose the latter. They planned to make a heroic departure as long-suffering victims in a sad processional, but the Venetian authorities routed them out of their beds in the middle of the night and herded them onto boats, as the nocturnal crowds taunted them with chants. *"Ande in malora!"* Go with misfortune.

When the spectacle of the Jesuit departure took place, Galileo had been languishing for ten days in Venice on the wearisome business of settling the matter of his university position. (Beyond his increase in salary, he now wanted a year's salary in advance, and he was meeting with resistance.) He wrote about the ejection of the Jesuits to his deadbeat brother, Michelangelo, who was back living in Galileo's house after his latest foreign misadventure. As Galileo told Michelangelo that he hoped to return home in a few days for the celebration of Pentecost, so Galileo naughtily described the ignominious departure of the Jesuits in the middle of the night.

"Last night at 2 a.m., the Jesuit fathers took flight in two barges, which had been brought to take them out of the Republic. They all departed with a crucifix stuck to their necks and holding candles in their hands. I think that they will be leaving Padua and other parts of the state as well, with great weeping and lamentation from their many devoted ladies."

These heady events delayed Galileo's quest for a salary increase, but at last he was able to get what he wanted, after the Tuscan ambassador to Venice paid a call on the harried doge. Eventually, with the doge's approval, the Venetian senate confirmed the reappointment and raised his salary by more than one hundred crowns. Galileo may still have grumbled about the generosity of the senate, for his rival, Cremonini, had just been raised to a yearly salary of one thousand crowns.

For months, Venice and the Vatican had seemed on the verge of war. France and Spain lined up on opposing sides, with their separate motives. Spain sided with the Vatican in the hope of reestablishing its influence over the papacy. France sided with Venice for its Protestant proclivities. (Sarpi was regarded by many, especially in the Vatican, to be a secret Protestant and was suspected of consorting with heretics.) From France, the offers of help were prodigious. The doge was led to believe that an army of fifteen thousand could be mobilized in a few weeks to defend the Serene Republic. But the taste for war soured. Despite the significant Protestant presence in France, King Henry IV, a lapsed Protestant, worried about his standing as a good Catholic, while Philip III of Spain finally came to his senses. He sent word to the pope that he would support the Holy See for good, but not for evil.

As tensions lessened, Pope Paul V summoned Friar Sarpi to Rome to account for his writings. The Vatican representative delivered an oily invitation: "Let the theologian come, and we shall embrace him. He shall be caressed and be well received." Sarpi knew of such caresses. To friends like Galileo, he remarked that the strongest arguments the Vatican employed in cases like his were the rope and the stake. The friar refused, saying he was overwhelmed by the business of the republic. To support Sarpi and to give him solid, earthly ground, the Venetian senate formally vetoed the trip, thus crystallizing the separation between secular and ecclesiastical authority. Unable to get Sarpi in their grasp, the Vatican burned his books. Two weeks later, the Venetian senate doubled his salary in response. This elevated the anger of the pope toward Sarpi to the level of hate.

As the kings of France and Spain and even England offered their diplomatic offices, the worries about war in Venice eventually passed. Accommodations were slowly made between the hostile parties. Venice remained independent of Vatican influence. Its free atmosphere remained intact. The Serene Republic refused to readmit the troublesome Jesuits, but it did hand over the two licentious priests to the ecclesiastical courts for trial.

By the end of the summer in 1606, life for Galileo was returning to its normal frenetic pace. In June he had published his manual on his military compass, dedicated it to the grand duke of Tuscany, and had received a somewhat perfunctory gift as a token of the duke's appreciation: a bolt of fine satin to make an elegant cape. In August Marina Gamba gave birth to their third child, a son, who was given the name of Galileo's father, Vincenzo. With a relaxation of financial pressure, Galileo engaged his mind across a broad front of theoretical problems: mechanics, pulleys, magnets, and temperature, virtual velocity and the motion of heavy bodies, inertia and the principles of free-fall. He and Sagredo were exchanging thoughts about their customary pleasures once again. Together with Sarpi, they were experimenting with magnets, for Sagredo had constructed a large lodestone weighing five pounds, which three years later he would sell to Cosimo de' Medici, the grand duke of Tuscany, for two hundred crowns.

In the late fall Sagredo had taken up residence in the village of Palmanova, east of Venice in Friuli near the Hapsburg border, where he had assumed the position of treasurer in the new fortress. Bored in this remote outpost, he reported to Galileo that the wines of Buri did not have their customary sweetness that season, while those of Rosazzo fell disappointingly between sweet and merely pleasing. For its mellifluous taste and its meager price (five lire for a milk pail), he recommended the Malvasia. Three tubs from the vineyard had been purchased, and he was reserving one for Galileo, one for himself, and one for the salon at Ca' Morosini. Meanwhile, he bubbled about the effervescent wines of Austria, which he was enjoying in quantity in the country and a stock of which he hoped to bring back to his friends in Venice.

In Sagredo's absence, Venice continued to heap honors on her champion and Galileo's mentor, Friar Sarpi. In triumph, he had become even more powerful: The authority of the three councilors of state was concentrated into Sarpi's hands alone. Now that the crisis appeared to be over and the victory of Venice total, Sarpi wished to return to his scholarship. He visualized a monumental work of history on the Council of Trent, the

Catholic council that had begun the Counter-Reformation in 1563 and had reaffirmed the Vatican's global authority over all spiritual and temporal matters. With the republic anxious to grant his every wish, Sarpi requested access to the secret archives of the Venetian state, for they contained the guarded, confidential despatches of the Venetian representatives to the Council of Trent fifty years before. Access to the archives was limited to a precious handful, and even the senators of the republic were prohibited from entering. Now the stacks of incriminating documents were thrown open to a dangerous apostate.

Nothing Venice could do was more threatening for the Vatican. The church's most closely held secrets and its internal dissension were now laid bare to its greatest enemy. By an extraordinary excommunication, Sarpi had been branded anathema, and now he proposed to write a comprehensive attack on the very basis of the Catholic Reformation. By his terse words and compelling thoughts, through his skillful actions, "the terrible friar" had proved himself a formidable opponent, the essence of whose argument was that the church had gone profoundly astray at the Council of Trent by claiming power over temporal matters. The pope's displeasure now escalated into rage.

In the summer of 1607 Venice heard rumors of a plot on Sarpi's life, and Sarpi himself was warned by a writer friend in Rome that the Vatican was determined to "take from Venice its champion at any cost." It was assumed, rightly, that the pope himself was behind the conspiracy. But by good police work, the assassins, including a defrocked priest, were identified, as well as their incentive, a payment of eight thousand crowns. They were arrested as soon as they passed into Venetian territory. The worry seemed to dissipate. Sarpi dismissed these reports, for he had difficulty believing that a pope could be capable of such treachery. Moreover, he thought he would do more damage to the Vatican as a dead martyr than as a live apostate.

"Should a man such as I flee?" he asked rhetorically, a question that later Galileo himself would address. "What man such as I would go into the Temple to save his life? I will not go!" Of this bravery—or foolhardiness—Galileo took note.

Sarpi, however, did acquiesce in accepting a bodyguard. Late every night, the dark, hooded figure left the Ducal Palace with his guard, passed through Saint Mark's Square, proceeded through the zigzags of the Mercerie, past the Rialto Bridge and onto the Strada Nuova behind Sagredo's pink palace, thence along the narrow *calle* to the Campo di Santa Fosca, on to the Ponte della Pugna, and over the bridge of the wrestlers to the Fondamenta dei Servi on the north side of the Rio San Fosca where he entered the Servite monastery and retired to his simple cell. For someone who attended services in the monastery, these routine movements were open and could easily be tracked.

On the night of October 7, a fire broke out in San Lio, the crowded quarter near Santa Maria Formosa, and Sarpi's bodyguard hastened off to witness the spectacle. For a time, Sarpi waited for his guard to return, then he grew impatient and finally set off without him in the company of only his servant and an old patrician. Nearly home, they mounted the stairs of the Ponte della Pugna, over the bridge of the fight, single file, when suddenly, five assailants leapt upon them from the darkness. The old man and the young servant were overpowered immediately, and then the cutthroats fell upon their target, savagely stabbing Sarpi fifteen times and embedding a stiletto in his ear. The instrument passed through the right temple, shattered his upper jaw, and exited from his right cheek. Thus skewered, Sarpi was left in a pool of blood to die, while the assassins retreated, pistols in hand, through the old courtyard of mercy, the Corte Vecchia della Misericordia, and women appeared in the windows to scream the alarm.

As Sarpi was carried to his monastery and friars ran to tell the authorities, word of the assault raced through Venice. A rider was dispatched to Padua for Galileo's doctor, the famous Acquapendente. He hovered over Sarpi for the three weeks that the friar's life hung in the balance. Much attention was paid to the bent murder weapon, for fear that it was poisoned. To find out, the doctors plunged the dagger into a chicken and then into a dog, not the most advanced method of forensic science perhaps, but enough to establish that the instrument was untainted. Through his critical period, Sarpi was miraculously conscious and lucid, so much so that he was able to give a deposition.

"I shall do the enemies of the Republic more harm dead than alive," he observed, as he forgave his attackers.

Though his cloak and cap contained many holes, only three wounds in the head and the neck were life-threatening. When Acquapendente remarked on the "extravagance" of the head wound, Sarpi replied that it bore the "style of the Roman Curia."

This suspicion was accepted uncritically throughout the republic, as a vast dragnet was cast for the murderers. It was clear soon enough that they had escaped into papal territory. Over time, the Venetian ambassador in Rome discovered their identity and that of their boss. The band had included a vagabond priest who had frequented services at the Servite monastery and who had guided the murderers to their quarry. After the attack they had separated, a few going immediately to the palace of the Papal Nuncio, the others taking a gondola to the Lido, where the gang eventually reunited. From there they oared their way to a waiting ship, which set sail and was in the papal port of Ravenna by morning. Once paid and back in Rome, they were shown the courtesy of the pope, who put them on a pension for some years to come. But the pope was disappointed.

Friar Sarpi survived.

The attack on Sarpi had a strange effect on Galileo. He had viewed Venice as a place of earthly pleasures, a safe haven, a convivial paradise of free expression and open experiment. Now it looked like a dangerous place of intrigue and violence, a wide open sewer, a lair for thieves and murderers, an international hot spot. Worse for Galileo personally, he was associated with the radicals of Venice. He was a close friend of Sarpi, the beneficiary of the doge, Leonardo Donà, and the Contarini family, the supplicant of the magistrate and diplomat, Pietro Duodo, and the colleague of Cremonini, whom the Inquisition was accusing of spreading "bad doctrine."

This put Galileo in a difficult position on two fronts, Rome and Florence. With such ideological friends, who were suspected of anti-Roman, anti-Spanish, and anti-Jesuitical sentiments, it might be difficult for him ever to return to Florence (which had fallen again under Spanish influence) or to carry on amiable relations with scientific priests like Christopher Clavius. In the aftermath of the Interdict, Rome was defeated and bitter and unpredictable, while Venice was furious over the attack on Sarpi.

He turned his attention anew to Florence and reopened his line of communication to the court of the grand duke. He seized whatever pretext presented itself to remind the court of his existence abroad and his longing to return home. Upon the death in Pisa of the famous physician Mercuriale, he wrote to the grand duchess, Christine, to suggest that Fabricio d'Acquapendente might be lured from Padua to Florence to serve the Medicis instead of the doges. In talking about Acquapendente, Galileo's real purpose was to focus the attention of the court on himself and his own desires. He found another pretext in the fact that the crown prince—and his former student—Cosimo II was on the verge of taking the reins of power. A medal was to be struck in the prince's honor. Remembering that Cosimo had been especially interested in magnets during their tutorials together in the summer of 1605, Galileo took up his pen to suggest the magnet as the symbol of Medici power and of Cosimo's glory:

> From the lodestone could hang many pieces of iron, and you can add the motto, Love Makes Strength. The allegory is this: the magnet lifts those pieces of iron against their inclination, and the filings are kept *in alto,* almost with violent love. The metal pieces throw themselves avidly, voluntarily against the magnet. In the end, we wonder whether the magnetic attraction between command and obedience keeps the two things together.
>
> In the same way there will be an attraction between the prince and his subjects. The magnet is a round ball, which represents the House of Medici. But a ball also represents the Cosmos. From Cosmos comes the name Cosimo. From this, we appreciate the great Cosimo.

The response from the court was chilly, and that squared with Galileo's winter of 1607–1608. In December it began to snow in Padua, and the snow continued relentlessly into late March. To the unprepared residents, their bleak winter seemed to resemble the climate of Danzig or Riga or some other windswept, forbidding city of the far north. Snow weighted down the tile roofs of the town, and ice covered the streets. It was so cold that the wine froze, a true disaster, and classes at the university were canceled—to Galileo, a benefit. By February the residents were pushing the snow from their overburdened rooftops onto the streets, where it piled up mountainously, making it difficult for the horses to tranverse the byways. The physicians grew worried about the public health. They feared that the plague might break out, as the incidence of pleuresy and lung disease got out of control.

In mid-March the mayor of Padua and Galileo's patron, Tommaso Contarini, ordered the citizens to shovel the snow around their houses into carts, to transport it to the canals and rivers, and to dump it. They were to do this or to face stiff fines. This placed great hardship on those who had neither carts nor money to hire them. As a result, many built huge fires to try to melt the snow, and this caused other dangers, such as making the air unbreathable.

Through the crisis, Galileo grumbled and complained and generally was in bad humor. To him, it seemed as if the forces of superstition had again taken over—many saw the snows as the belated curse of the 1604 comet. The people were returning to their ghosts and their Pavan verses:

> When red the sun goes to bed
> The next day we surely know
> The wind will upset the straw rick;
> And when the moon has its halo
> We are sure that the rain will not come
> From the unnatural sparking of the stars
> And the unusual burning of the Scottanelle
> We forecast drought.
> The creaking doors . . .
> The curled wick of the lamp
> And the singing frogs
> Summon the rain.

Within Galileo's learned societies, the Academy of the Protected Ones, and in his new affiliation, the Accademia della Crusca (the Academy of the Chaff), the public hazard was a continuous topic of conversation, and the elite of Padua felt decidedly vulnerable and besieged. Along with his friendly rival, Cesare Cremonini, Galileo criticized the arduous public measures, partly because of the expansiveness of his own roof, the narrowness of his street, and the expense he was having to bear in the public interest.

With his bent toward hypochrondria and melancholy, he wondered if his fortunes were ever going to turn. His melancholy worsened when Sagredo accepted a diplomatic post in Aleppo, deep in the hinterland of far-off Syria, where for the next three years the Venetian gentleman would deal, uncertainly, with crooked merchants, extortionist Persian emirs, and bloodthirsty pirates. In those days, it took a letter six months to travel from Aleppo to Venice—if the mail-bearing ship was not hijacked on the high seas.

As the seasons changed, so Galileo's fortunes brightened. In the summer he was again summoned to Florence by Grand Duchess Christine, this time for the marriage of young Cosimo. Now the grand duchess wanted his involvement in the engineering discussions for the broad wooden esplanade across the Arno that was to be built for the wedding.

5

THE STONE AND THE
QUARRY

In early 1609 the anxieties of midlife had overtaken Galileo. At forty-five years of age he had become an imposing figure in Padua, with a reputation for unconventional views, an inventive mind, outlandish personality, and extravagant tastes. His contacts in court, both in Venice and in Florence, were broad and warm. He was comfortable in court life, and princes and Venetian senators were comfortable with him. Brilliant though his discourse could be, he was fun-loving in equal measure, with a special ironic and caustic edge that made him an irresistible and intimidating figure.

Beneath the surface, frustration boiled. His salary of five hundred crowns was respectable but by no means handsome, and it was half that of his Aristotelian rival, Cremonini. His financial burdens were many: the generous support for his concubine and their three children, the underpinning of his mansion and Marina's nearby rooms, the salaries of his servants, the dowries for his sisters, the aid for his ungrateful mother, the budget for his private workshop and his instrument maker. He was required to spend long hours with his private students, who now had become various nobles from France and England, Germany and Poland, as well as the king of Sweden, Gustav Adolph, who had come to Padua under the pseudonym Monsieur Le Cat from Geneva. These noblemen sometimes took residence in Galileo's house, along with their servants, and this made Galileo's life all the more taxing.

In the late spring he felt chained to Padua once again, largely because another aristocratic student, Count Alessandro Montalban of Conegliano, who had been living in his house for four years, was about to complete his doctorate and needed his mentor to shepherd him through the final examination.

Like all artists, Galileo resented the time these outside duties took from his own work. Because he was constantly worried about his health, he was terrified that he might suddenly be unable to earn enough to cover his needs. With great projects in his imagination, he more than resented his university duties. He abhorred them. "I'm always at the service of this or that person," he complained. "I have to consume many hours of the day—often the best ones—in the service of others."

The departure of Sagredo for Syria had left a huge gap in his personal life. He missed his friend immensely. Life in Venice was just not the same. Toward the end of April Sagredo had written Galileo a long, wistful letter from Aleppo, full of frustration at not understanding his exotic new surroundings, full of descriptions about devouring one book after another until his mind tired and lost its bearings, and full of annoyance at the insistent demands of his diplomatic duties, which took him away from his study. Sagredo longed for a few months in Padua to "philosophize and to enjoy," but he knew realistically that he would not see the salons of Il Bo for three years.

In his professional life as well, Galileo seemed to be plowing over old material. In February 1609 he had returned to the old trough of military problems. On February 11, he was writing again to Antonio de' Medici in Florence about the trajectory of an artillery shell. He had "finally" found the law of acceleration he trumpeted to Antonio, which established that an artillery shell leaves the cannon barrel with the same velocity with which it eventually strikes the ground. He had been concerned with the problem five years before.

For years he had hoped for one grand invention, that golden brainstorm that would solve all his financial problems. None of his inventions—the medical implements, the military devices, the agricultural patent—had been the breakthrough. He was well known but not famous, comfortable but not wealthy. He looked around at other less talented men and was annoyed that some of their inventions, neither as clever nor as useful as his, had made them rich. He looked at Cremonini and wondered why the university considered this slippery Peripatetic twice as valuable as he. What was he doing wrong?

Among the things he was doing wrong was his constant whining about money. Forever importuning his friends, especially Francesco Sagredo, to lobby the Venetian senate for an increase in his salary, he was never satisfied when the modest increases came through. He was in jeopardy of becoming a genuine pest. After one of Sagredo's early lobbying efforts, the doge, Niccolò Contarini, in whose garden Galileo had installed an irrigation device, complained that he was being pestered on this salary issue not only by Galileo's friends, but also within his own household. "If Galileo is not content with his salary, he can resign," Contarini muttered.

Dispirited, Galileo renewed his overtures to Florence. He longed for an angel and saw his savior in the grand duke of Tuscany. "To serve a Prince! Now that I would like!" he mused. To the grand duke's lieutenant, Belasario Vinta, he wrote a touching appeal, describing the groundwork he had laid in the past sixteen years for great work. "I long for peace and quiet, so that I can complete three great works that I have within my grasp and which I would like to publish. But I need a freedom greater than what I have here. This Republic will never offer me such an ideal situation. These things I can only hope to have from a Prince. Of course, I don't want to appear to be asking unreasonable favors without giving something back in return. It would not be fitting to receive a generous salary from a free state without serving the public for it. To ask something from the public, we have to satisfy the public, not just one person.

"But I have many and diverse inventions, only one of which could be enough to take care of me for the rest of my life . . . if I can only find a grand Prince who would like it. I have always wanted to propose an invention to my Prince before anyone else. Then he could do with this invention and with its inventor whatever he likes. I would hope that he would accept not only the stone but the quarry."

During the first half of 1609, however, Galileo was preoccupied with abstract mathematics, far afield of glittering, useful inventions. It was work he was quite ready to abandon if something more profitable turned up, for the physics of motion was not exactly the best subject to excite a potential benefactor. In late July, idle, he took himself off to Venice for some sport and a well-deserved escape from the insistent Count Montalban.

The day after he arrived in Venice, he heard a riveting rumor. In Holland, among the spectacle-makers in Middelburg, an instrument had been invented that could make distant objects seem near. Through ordinary spectacle lenses fashioned into a tube, a man two miles away could be seen as if he were a few paces away. Apparently, such a device had been presented to Count Maurice of Nassau by a spectacle-maker named Hans Lippershey nine months before, and a patent had been requested. For some reason, the patent had not gone through, but Lippershey had been contracted to make three more instruments for the government and cautioned to keep his methods a secret. All the same, the news of the magical invention was widely reported in diplomatic circles.

In Venice, with his scientific friends, Galileo excitedly discussed the rumor. He knew three things at once. If the rumor was true, the instrument worked upon the principle of perspective. If the instrument worked, it would have immense military value. And, most important, a fortune would go to him who first brought such an instrument to the Venetian state.

This rumor had, it seemed, been slow to make its way south and east. Earlier that spring, three-power spyglasses were being sold as toys in Paris. In May a foreigner turned up with a tube in Milan. In London, as Galileo was hearing about the instrument for the first time, one Thomas Harriot had turned the device skyward and was already mapping the moon. To his surprise, Galileo now learned that the rumor was more widely known than he thought. Sarpi, fully recovered now from his wounds and back at work, knew something. Among his prodigious duties, Sarpi was the adviser to the doge on scientific matters. Now Galileo heard that Sarpi had known of the Flemish developments for months—and had dismissed them as unimportant!

On July 26 Galileo confronted his friend. To Galileo's astonishment, the friar confessed that eight months before, only a month after Lippershey had requested a patent, he had gotten the intelligence through a diplomatic back channel. But the priest had been curiously dense about its possibilities and too harried to bother with the distraction. His mind had been on politics rather than science, he protested to Galileo, as if to excuse his embarrassment. To make things worse, Sarpi's back-channel dispatch had been confirmed by an old pupil of Galileo's, one Jacques Badovere, who had lived with Galileo eleven years before, was now in the French diplomatic service, and who had written Sarpi about the spyglass. Now Sarpi showed Galileo the original report, with a rudimentary explanation of its principles, and a letter he had written in response to Bado-vere six months earlier, dated January 6, 1609:

"I have had word of the new spectacles more than a month and believe the report sufficiently not to investigate further. (Socrates forbids us to speculate about experiences we have not seen ourselves.) When I was young, I thought about such a possibility. It occurred to me that a glass parabolically shaped could produce such an effect. I had a demon-stration, but since these are abstract matters and do not take into account the fractiousness of the matter, I sensed some difficulty. To pursue the matter would have been very tiresome, so I did not experiment. I do not know whether that Flemish artisan has hit upon my idea."

Galileo was aghast. He had good reason to be furious with Sarpi both for his secrecy and his stupidity. After upbraiding his friend, he encour-aged him to be more attentive from now on and enlisted Sarpi's political help for the future. He would soon need it.

On August 1, with Galileo still languishing in Venice, events took a desperate turn. In his own town of Padua, he was shocked to hear that a mysterious Dutchman had arrived and was exhibiting a spyglass to much excited authorities. Suddenly, as he would later quaintly put it, he was "seized with a desire for this beautiful thing." Shoring up his support from Sarpi, Galileo raced home to Padua and there, to his horror, learned that the light-footed Hollander had taken off for Venice, where he was plan-ning to sell the instrument to the Venetian state for a high price.

Frantically, Galileo went to work on the problem in his workshop. Sparing no expense in having the parts made that he imagined he would need, operating on instinct and the scant bits of information about the Flanders telescopes, he took first a lead tube. The device needs either a single glass or more than one, he thought to himself. It can't be only one. A concave lens diminishes objects, and while a convex lens enlarges them, the objects grow more indistinct at a distance. His glassmaker blew various globes of glass and cut from them lenses of different sizes and thicknesses. Galileo began to play with combinations of convex and con-cave lenses. With one fortunate combination, objects were suddenly brought three times closer and made nine times larger. With the results of refraction thus established (without understanding the principle of it), he altered the cut of the lenses and achieved far better results, bringing objects sixty times closer.

By his own account, this trial-and-error experimentation took place in an astonishing twenty-four-hour period.

"The first night after my return (to Padua), I solved it," he wrote fifteen years later in his book *The Assayer*, "and on the following day, I constructed the instrument and sent word of this to those same friends at Venice with whom I had discussed the matter the previous day." It was like him to exaggerate the speed and thereby his genius, but in any event, on August 4, he sent an urgent message to Sarpi in Venice that he had a secret. The message was fraught with meaning; undoubtedly, this was done by prearrangement: Galileo would see if he could realize the potential of the rumors, while Sarpi would block any access to Venetian authorities by foreigners until he heard the results of Galileo's experiments. By his August 4 dispatch, Galileo effectively froze the Dutchman out. Now he could spend another two weeks in a more leisurely attempt to perfect his instrument.

On August 20, he packed up a handsome leather-tooled, ten-power spyglass, paid his instrument maker twenty-one lire, and struck out for Venice. His two-week grace period had allowed him to refine his instrument considerably, so that the spyglass he now took to Venice was of far more excellent quality than the Flemish versions. In size, it was slightly more than an arm's length (*un braccio*), with apertures the size of a Venetian crown, two inches in diameter.

Upon his arrival he was called to the Signoria with great ceremony, for Sarpi, Duodo, and his other influential friends had prepared the doge and the college for a great event. As he ascended the Golden Staircase and swept into the Hall of the Ante-College, he was surrounded by excited gentlemen who plied him with a hundred questions as they reached out to touch the tube. The doge, Leonardo Donà, received him in the Hall of the College, where the Serene Ruler was surrounded by his counselors, by the chiefs of the Council of Ten, and, most importantly, by the Sages of the Order, who commanded the great Venetian navy.

There, amid the furnishings of Palladio, caressed by the art of Veronese and Tintoretto, Galileo presented his magical tube. In time, the assemblage moved from this smaller space into the senate chamber, where, under Tintoretto's monumental painting *Triumph of Venice*, the entire senate pressed around him, as Galileo introduced them to the new age of science.

Their interest was practical at first. The military rather than the scientific value of the instrument was uppermost in their minds. Before long the gathering swept out of the palace, across the piazzetta, to the Tower of Saint Mark's. For centuries the doges of Venice had brought foreign rulers to the tower, to point across the rooftops to the narrow passageway at San Niccolo in the distance, the only navigable entry to the lagoon, and to prate about Venice's impregnable defenses. But in recent decades they had done so with less confidence. Now, one by one, the old men trudged up the steps to this tallest point in Venice to look at distant objects.

The instrument was pointed toward Padua, its source and its inspiration, and there in the eyepiece the shimmering shape of the Tower of Saint Giustina, thirty-five miles away, took shape; then to the distant towns, west to Treviso, south to Chioggia, and even to Conegliano, more than fifty miles away in the northern foothills; then to Murano where the senators were astonished to see the devout entering the church of San Giacomo; then to Collona, at the mouth of the Rio de' Verieri, the river of the glassmakers in Murano, where they watched tiny figures board their gondolas. They turned the tube seaward, out into the Adriatic, and saw galleys on the horizon that would be another two hours under full sail before they could be seen in Venice with the naked eye. The naval high command, hard pressed by pirates on the high seas, knew the importance of this. It was characteristic of Galileo that a few days later, as he described his triumphal moment, he would exaggerate the capability of his instrument to make out a ship fifty miles away as if it were only five.

If this was a triumph of Venice, it was also a triumph of political skill. Somewhere in the shadows of a dank, narrow *calle*, a Flemish adventurer wept. Galileo had turned his presentation into a celebration of Venetian genius, complete with brocaded advance men, distinguished heralds, and secret operatives. Suddenly, the tube represented the flowering of Paduan learning. Where the Flemish entrepreneur savored the fantastic price he would extract from the Venetian authorities, Galileo was smarter. Having seen how fascinated the doge had been at his first demonstration, he returned to Saint Mark's Square several days later, again passed through the loggia and up the Golden Staircase into the presence of the Serene Ruler, where he presented the doge with his spyglass as a gift, for free! Accompanying his present was a pamphlet that described his *cannochiale* and stressed its military uses.

Kneeling before the doge, he proclaimed, "I, Galileo Galilei, the humble servant of Your Highness, who always looks assiduously with all my spirit to perform my duty and always looks to find some utility to benefit Your Highness . . . I now bring this new artifice. Judging that this instrument is worthy of being received by you, I give it to you as a present, putting to your judgment whether more of these instruments should be built or not. This is one of the fruits of science, science which for seventeen years I have conducted in Padua, hoping to be able to present to you even greater inventions, if God wills it and Your Highness wills it, and if you and God want me to spend the rest of my life at your service."

As he was leaving the Hall of the College, exhausted from his ordeal and yet exultant, he was asked to remain in the senate chamber. In due course, the procurator of Saint Mark's and future doge, Antonio Priuli, who was also a governor of Il Bo, emerged to say that the Serene Ruler had made a proposal, if Galileo felt well of it.

Knowing, as he would write a few days later, that "hope has feeble wings and fortune swift ones," Galileo replied graciously and humbly, "I will be content with whatever pleases His Lordship."

The recommendation was to double Galileo's salary, to 1,000 crowns a year, to reappoint him for life, and to present him with an immediate bonus of 480 crowns.

"Since I am chairman this week, and I can command as I please," Priuli said cheerfully, embracing Galileo, "I wish to convene the Pregadi after dinner when your reappointment shall be read and voted upon."

The dinner must be imagined, but not the vote. It was ninety-eight senators for, eleven against, with thirty abstentions. The genius was brought forward and, with appropriate ceremony, befitting the fanfares of Monteverdi, the proclamation of the Council of Ten was read:

> Signor Galileo Galilei, having lectured in Padua for 17 years to the satisfaction of all, having made known to the world diverse discoveries and inventions, but in particular having invented an instrument by which distant things are brought within easy vision, it is proper that this Council do munificently recognize the labors of those who serve the public benefit . . .

At last, it seemed, he had everything in life one could want. The news of his instrument raced across Europe, with the well-endowed military leaders paying particular attention. With instant notoriety and wealth, with illustrious friends and doting potentates, there stretched before him a productive life of grace, ease, and profit as the first citizen of Venice.

His joy should have been boundless, but it was not. Among his first thoughts was not his splendid future life as a Venetian eminence, but that he was a captive of Venice. In his own mind, he was, first and foremost, a gentleman of Florence. In Tuscany lay his roots and his future. For several years the grand duke had been temporizing on his repeated requests for employment. "To serve a Prince! Now that I would like!" Instead of joy and pride and gratitude, he began to scheme about how to escape his generous benefactors, how to use the toasts of Venice to engender the envy of Florence.

On August 29, four days after the doge had taken his extraordinary action, Galileo wrote to his brother-in-law in Florence, Benedetto Landucci, about the epic events on the Adriatic. The letter was strange in the extreme. Landucci, after all, had been badgering Galileo for years to cough up his overdue dowry payments and had even taken him to court. As Galileo's salary rose, his relationship with his brother-in-law had become less adversarial, with a kindness or two exchanged between them. But Landucci was scarcely an intimate friend who would normally be first to receive great news.

Moreover, Landucci held a lowly, ill-paying post in the Tuscan government as a clerk and weigher of silver and therefore had no influence in the Tuscan court. For Galileo to trumpet his fantastic successes to a failed relative, to brag about his fantastic salary to this minor official to whom he still owed dowry money was outrageous and arrogant. Galileo's letter ended curiously, almost in self-pity. "I find myself here, held for life. I shall have to be satisfied to enjoy my native land sometimes during the vacation months."

The salutation carried the request to spread the good news among all Galileo's friends in Florence. So Galileo was shamelessly using his brother-in-law as a messenger of what he hoped would be bad rather than good news to the grand duke of Tuscany, for whom the letter was really intended. (In fact, Galileo was being too clever by half. The court in Tuscany was informed independently of the great events in Venice on the day Galileo wrote to Landucci.)

That grand duke was now his former pupil, Cosimo de' Medici, who had taken over seven months before upon the death of Ferdinand I. The Landucci letter carried the heavy-handed invitation for the new duke to make a counteroffer. As he wrote with mock self-pity, wings of his hope (of returning home) were drooping, since wings of fortune were so swift by comparison. This was meant to pressure Tuscany with his new fortune in Venice.

On August 30 he returned, rejuvenated, to Padua. There could be no letup in activity, for he knew that a legion of imitators would spring into existence. In early September he ordered new lenses to be ground to his specifications in Florence, since while Murano had its wide reputation for decorative crystal, and the work of his poet friend Magagnati had been adequate in the preliminary stages, Florence had more proficient optical craftsmen. Once he had his new lenses in hand, he polished them personally. The result was to enlarge the telescope's power four hundred times, and he had the instrument's stand fashioned to be movable.

One night in the early fall Galileo climbed to the top floor of his house and looked out across his garden and over the wall to the distinctive domes of the San Antonio Basilica to see the new moon. The play of shapes between the cupolas of the exquisite Franciscan church and the crescent moon must have excited him, and he brought his telescope to the window. One imagines it as a mystical, artistic, almost symphonic moment, as the generous spirit of San Antonio hovered over the great church, the pride of Padua, in which Donatello and Giotto and Mantegna had labored. As his gaze was drawn skyward, religion inspired science into an artistic act.

It was also a revolutionary act. In the mind of man then and for several thousand years before was a moon that was smooth, perfectly circular, and polished like a mirror so that it could reflect the sun's rays to the earth for the benefit of man. Into view that night in Padua, though still hazily with his ten-power instrument, came a stunningly different orb. The surface of the moon was not smooth at all, not uniform or precisely spherical but "uneven, rough, full of cavities and prominences." At places there were protuberances that, far from being perfect, seemed to him wartlike. It was, miracle of miracles, not unlike the face of the earth, with mountains and valleys.

Over the next two months he watched, riveted, as the moon transformed itself. First he traced the irregular, wavy boundary between the light and dark sections of the horned moon. He watched how the small spots magically changed in the course of the night, as mountains sprouted before his eyes, and as "seas" (mare) presented themselves. (It would be upon the Sea of Storms that astronauts would land sometime later.) His stare was drawn to a dark gulf in the lower cusp. "When I had observed it for a long time and had seen it completely dark, a bright peak began to emerge, a little below its center, after about two hours. Gradually growing, this presented itself in a triangular shape, completely detached and separated from the lighted surface. Around it three other small points soon began to shine. Finally when the moon was about to set, this trian-gular shape joined with the rest of the illuminated region and suddenly burst into the gulf of shadow like a vast promontory of light, surrounded still by the three bright peaks."

Night after night, he watched, as the moon revealed itself. He noted the small craters, never before seen by human eyes, where their dark cen-ters were turned toward the sun while their bright rims appeared on the side of the spot away from the sun. That part of the moon's surface, he wrote, "is spotted as the tail of a peacock is sprinkled with azure eyes, and resembles those glass vases which, while still hot, have been plunged into cold water and have thus acquired a crackled and wavy surface."

He sketched the half-moon, paying special attention to the large, sealike, circular cavity in the center that seemed to resemble the basin of Bohemia on earth. This was a dangerous opinion. To say it openly, as Galileo would soon do, was to invite the attention of the church. To con-ceive of the moon not as a polished mirror but as a dry, dirty stone with-out water or atmosphere would be a shock to all humankind but a sacri-lege to the church. If the moon had earthlike features, they must exist for human beings, for had not God made the heavens only to please and to benefit man? Was he saying that there were men on the moon? If so, how could they have descended from Adam? Or escaped the Flood?

By August Galileo had become the world's foremost inventor. But it was as a scientist and even as a philosopher that he wanted to be known, not as a mere instrument maker. In these same months, in Germany, Johannes Kepler, the best-known scientist north of the Alps, was formu-lating his laws of planetary motion, the fruit of a rich abstract mind and mystical imagination, harnessed to inductive mathematics. Now Galileo was observing, gathering evidence that would allow him to formulate laws by deductive reasoning. He was measuring the highest mountains on the moon, using his mathematical models and working with the laws of light and shadow, correctly arriving at the conclusion that the altitude of the moon's highest mountains was four miles. He perceived a great work ahead of him, in which he would prove from sensory evidence that the earth was a wandering body, "not the sink of all dull refuse of the uni-verse." If his analogy to Bohemia was dangerous, the notion of a wander-ing earth was explosive.

As Galileo pondered his new heaven, he maintained his thankless attitude toward the munificence of the Venetian republic. When the gen-erous terms of his new arrangement were finalized, he was surprised and disappointed to learn that his big salary was set to begin not immediately but at the beginning of the new year. He seized upon this misunderstanding 'as a pretext to renew his overtures to the Tuscan government. In October he made a brief visit to Florence to dazzle Grand Duke Cosimo, who "to his great surprise and delight was able to see that the moon was a body very similar to the earth." And, just as he had used his Venetian friends to lay the groundwork with the doge, he now set his friends in the Tuscan court to work secretly on the task of bringing the grand duke to make an offer. When Galileo returned home with a gift of eight hundred crowns from the grand duke in his pocket, he protested loudly like a prima donna to the governors of Padua University about a change in his lecturing schedule for the forthcoming academic year.

Galileo was becoming a very difficult man.

Still, by late November, he had made another breakthrough in the strength of his instrument. By manipulating larger lenses, which he could grind with greater exactitude than smaller ones, he had doubled its capability to twenty-power, with the capability to enlarge by four hundred times. On December 1 the new moon appeared. Then and again when it was clear on December 4, he made careful, systematic observations of the lunar surface, improving his earlier sketches and making more exact notes. Meanwhile, his terrestrial observations continued to be directed toward Florence rather than Venice. He made plans to return to Tuscany the following summer after the academic year, to present new wonders to Cosimo.

He would beat his most optimistic projection.

Over the Christmas season he continued to improve the new tool. By the first of the year 1610, he had outfitted his workshop so that he could grind his own lenses, although only a small proportion of them achieved the desired result. Of the hundred telescopes that he would make in the early months of 1610, only ten worked. But those that did were found in modern times to have nearly perfect optics. With his fifth successful telescope, however, the power again doubled, now from four hundred times enlargement to one thousand.

He became a solitary nocturnal traveler. Departing the moon, he visited thousands of stars no human being had ever seen before. At first he traversed the Milky Way. It was, he found, a collection of stars, clustered in large and small groups, in number unfathomable to the human mind. Along the way, he tarried in the Pleiades, the six sister stars near Taurus.

According to myth, one sister, Merope or Electra, was not visible, either because she had married a mortal or had been unable to witness the fall of Troy. Galileo found her and forty other siblings.

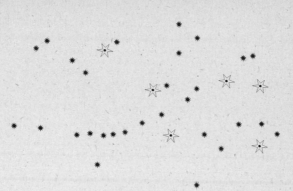

The Pleiades

He then strayed east to the constellation Cancer, and to the nebula Praesepe, to find it not a single star as was believed but again more than forty, arranged like a manger between the two ass colts.

Nebula of Praesepe

Thence to Orion, the hunter who desired the Pleiades and was fated forever to chase them across the sky. There he saw not three stars in the hunter's belt nor six in his sword, but eighty more, and five hundred in all in his constellation.

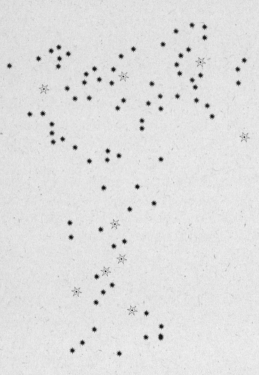

The Belt and Sword of Orion

On January 7, 1610, a day that sparkles in the history of astronomy, he took his seat as usual in front of his window. An hour after darkness, above the cupolas of the basilica, Jupiter rose. The month before he had seen the planet with his inferior tube, but now with this improved artifice, he spied three small but very bright stars near the planet, two to the east and one to the west. Their brilliance, which seemed to exceed that of the other fixed stars nearby of a similar size, interested him, as did their arrangement, for they formed a straight line along the elliptic.

Adi 7. di Gennaio 1610 Giove si vedeua col Cannone co
3. stelle fisse cosi *⊕*. delle quali se ni il cannone
niuna si vedeua cosi:*   à d. 8. affarina cosi ⊕++* era dū g
diretto et nō retrogrado come fsigono i calculatori.
Adi g fu nuglo. a dico. si vedeua cosi _____ *⊕ ciò è cō-
giūti cō la più occidetale si che la scultauag quātā si puo credere.
Adi 11. era in questa guisa ** ⊕. et la stella più vicina
à Giove era la metà minore dell'altra, et vicinistima all'altra
doue che le altre sere erano le dette stelle affarite tutte tre
di egual grandessa et trà di loro egualme lontane; dal che
affare intorno à Giove esser .3. altre stelle errati inuisibili ad
ogni uno sino à questo tēpo.

The following night—led by divine guidance, he would suggest later—he returned to Jupiter and found that the position of the starlets had changed! Now, at equal intervals, all three stars were west of Jupiter.

East   ○ ✳ ✳ ✳   West

Could it be that the planet was not moving eastward, as the charts indicated, but westward? Was it possible that Jupiter had hurtled ahead of the fascinating starlets? He could scarcely wait for the following night, but it was cloudy. On January 10 one starlet had disappeared, and he supposed that the lost star was hiding behind the planet, while the remaining two were now to the east and of equal size. With this "my confusion was transformed to amazement." More so the night after that, when there were still two stars, but one was double the size of the other and much brighter.

"I had now decided beyond all question that three stars were wandering around Jupiter, as do Venus and Mercury around the sun," he wrote, but this opinion changed three nights later, when a fourth starlet appeared.

For the next six weeks he continued to chronicle the mighty movements of Jupiter's swirling system. The implication was clear: The rotation of the satellites around their mother planet represented the Copernican theory in microcosm. It showed that stars could revolve around a planet as that planet itself moved. The parallel to the earth and its own moon was inescapable. With one stroke he had removed the principal objection to the Copernican theory and proved the Aristotelian theory impossible: All the stars were not fixed and rotating around a stationary earth.

Of all the things he had perceived as the first human observer, the moons of Jupiter were the most important, the most newsworthy, the most iconoclastic. He had to publish quickly before someone else happened onto them. As he wrote his narrative, he tried to be generous, inviting all astronomers to turn their attention to these new, revolving stars, now that his priority of discovery was established. To do so, however, they would need to acquire a very accurate telescope, something such as only he could provide.

In two weeks he had written the first draft of the *Sidereus Nuncius,* or *The Starry Messenger.* Still bound to the protocol of his field, he wrote in Latin, the language of scientists. It would be the last time he would do so. As he wrote about the shadowy, spotted surface of the moon, he could not help imagining the earth itself. "I have never doubted that if our globe were seen from afar when it was flooded with sunlight, the land regions would appear brighter and the watery regions darker."

And when it came to his own reputation, it was not a moment for modesty. "I do not doubt that in the course of time, further observations will improve this new science. But this need not diminish the glory of the first observer. My regard for the inventor of the harp is not less by knowing that his instrument was very crudely constructed and still more crudely played. Rather I admire him more than I do hundreds of craftsmen who have brought this art to the highest perfection."

He congratulated his own talents. "To apply oneself to great inventions, starting from the smallest beginnings, is no task for ordinary minds. To divine that wonderful arts lie hidden behind trivial and childish things is a conception of superhuman talents."

On January 30 he returned to Venice and to his small publisher, Tommaso Baglioni. Three years before, when he prepared his defense against the plagiarism charge by Baldassare Capra, he had not wanted to publish the tract in Padua and had asked Sagredo to find him a good publisher in Venice. Baglioni, with its trademark black eagle, had a fine reputation as a typographer, and in 1607 Galileo had been satisfied with the work. Now, at the modest *bottego*, Galileo hovered over the plates as the folios were printed one by one, proofing and correcting the pages as they came off the press. He worked quickly, just as he had written rapidly. Inevitably, his Latin contained mistakes.

Even though he was physically in Venice, his mind belonged to Florence. On that day (January 30), he wrote to the grand duke's secretary, Belasario Vinta, describing his marvelous discoveries and saying with true humility, "I feel an infinite amazement, that is, I render infinite thanks to God, that he has been pleased to make me alone the first observer of amazing things which have been obscured since the beginning of time." He told Vinta of his presence in Venice to publish the discoveries, and gave a capsule of the tract that he would soon be sending to the grand duke along with "an excellent spyglass." Two weeks later, on February 13, he wrote again to Vinta, but now he announced his desire to dedicate the work to the grand duke.

But he had a more attractive proposition, which might please the ruler of Tuscany more than a mere book dedication and might gain Galileo more than a bolt of black satin. He wished the duke's name to live in the stars. Since he was the discoverer and had the duty of naming the new stars, he wished to name them after the prince. But he had a problem and wanted Vinta's advice. Should he call all the satellites Cosimici, after Cosimo? Or should he name them after the four Medici brothers? (Besides Cosimo, there were Francesco, Carlo, and Lorenzo.) Or should he designate them collectively as the Medicean satellites? Six days later Vinta answered that the grand duke preferred Medicean to Cosimici, as Medicean glorified the House of Medici and the city of Florence, whereas Cosimici might be misinterpreted. The names of the duke's brothers did not rate discussion.

And thus Galileo polished his court flattery in the text. A river of praise gushed forth in his dedication. He was reminded of the star that Augustus named for Julius Caesar, only to be mocked by the fleeting honor when the Julian star disappeared as a comet. "But I am able to read Your Highness into the heavens far more accurately," he wrote. "Behold four stars have been reserved to bear your famous name. These bodies belong not to the inconspicuous multitude of fixed stars, but to the bright ranks of the planets. They move above noble Jupiter as children of his own. Jupiter! Benign Star! Next to God, the source of all good things! At the instant of Your Highness's birth, he merged from the turbid mists of the horizon, illuminating the eastern sky from his own royal house. He looked out from that exalted throne upon your auspicious birth, pouring forth all his splendour and majesty, so that your tender body and mind might imbibe that universal influence and power."

In mid-March, 550 copies of the book were published.

The Starry Messenger became the most important book of the seventeenth century. Its fame swept across Europe, as the book, the instrument, and their progenitor were received as miracles of the age. In England, a well-known scientist, Sir William Lower, wrote: "Me thinkes my diligent Galileus hath done more in his three fold discouerie than Magellane in openinge the streightes to the South sea or the dutch men that weare eaten by beares in noua Zembla. I am sure with more ease and saftie to him selfe and more pleasure to mee."

Galileo became the flame for poetry. In diverse languages, styles, and forms, odes and idylls were composed in his honor. He was compared more often to Christopher Columbus than to Magellan, and compared more favorably at that. The Scottish poet Thomas Seggett, who had been with Galileo in Padua, set the tone in a couplet:

> *Columbus gave man lands to conquer by bloodshed,*
> *Galileo new worlds harmful to none.*
> *Which is better?*

Johannes Faber, a mathematician who would soon become associated with Galileo in a scientific society, rhapsodized:

> *Yield Vespucci, and let Columbus yield. Each of them*
> *Holds his way through the unknown sea, it is true.*
> *But you, Galileo, alone gave to the human race the*
> *   sequence of stars,*
> *New constellations in heaven.*
> *O bold deed, to have penetrated the adamantine ramparts of*
> *heaven with such frail aid of crystal.*
> *Happy souls, to whom it is given to survey the citadels*
> *of the gods through your tube, Galileo.*

The most famous poet of the day, Giambattista Marino, was to pick up this favorable comparison to Columbus and bring it to its highest flowering in his epic poem, *L'Adonis*. Making Columbus the argonaut from his native state of Liguria and Galileo into Typhis, the pilot of the ship *Argo* in search of the Golden Fleece, Marino wrote:

> *Cleaving the breast of ocean, vast and deep,*
> *but not without grave peril and bitter strife,*
> *Liguria's Argonaut down on the earth*
> *will yet discover a new land and sky.*
> *Thou, second Typhis, not of sea but heaven,*
> *searching how wide it circles, what it holds,*
> *thyself wilt e'en discover without risk*
> *new stars and lights once hidden to all men*
> *Much dost thou owe to heaven that grants to thee*
> *the invention of the wondrous instrument,*
> *but far more heaven owes to thy superb*
> *device, which makes its beauties manifest.*
> *Full worthy is thy image to be placed*
> *among those stars for fitting ornament,*
> *and those thy frail glass lenses to repose*
> *immortal mid eternal sapphire lights.*

The popular excitement was overwhelming. The sense was everywhere that something tremendous had happened in the world. Sir Henry Wotton, the English ambassador to Venice, reported to the earl of Salisbury on March 13 that all corners of Venice were abuzz with talk of Galileo's discoveries. "The author runneth a fortune to be either exceeding famous or exceeding ridiculous," wrote Sir Henry.

One proud owner carted his new telescope up the bell tower of Saint Mark's in Venice for an early-morning glimpse of distant objects, only to be accosted by the curious hordes who importuned him for a glimpse, detained him for hours, and finally chased him home, until the unhappy man decided he would have to get out of Venice to enjoy the new celestial wonders. Meanwhile, the first edition sold out so quickly that Galileo himself got only six copies rather than the promised twenty. He was already contemplating a second edition in vernacular Italian.

Royalty as well as common folk were caught up in the frenzy, as the requests for telescopes came from everywhere as well as pleas to have stars named after various royal houses. The queen of France, Marie de' Médi-cis, Grand Duke Cosimo's cousin, was so excited to get her first glimpse at the mountains of the moon that she fell to her knees in front of the tele-scope as it was being set up for her at a window—to the shock of the entire French court. Moreover, the queen felt entitled to live alongside her cousins in heaven. When it came from her husband, King Henry IV, the official request changed. "In case you discover any other fine star, call it the Great Star of France, the most brilliant of all," the Gallic demand read. "Or call it by the King's proper name, Henri, rather than by his fam-ily name, Bourbon. Thus, you will not only be doing the right thing, but make you and your family rich and powerful forever."

A comet might have been the right thing for Henry. He was assassi-nated a month after Galileo got this letter.

Galileo enjoyed this royal courtship enormously. He distributed his best telescopes to his best patrons: the dukes of Bavaria and Urbino, the elector of Cologne, and Cardinal Francesco del Monte in Rome, the third brother of his del Monte benefactors. But he reserved his own royal treat-ment for the present grand duke, Cosimo II. Along with an advance copy of his book, he sent his best telescope so that the prince could clearly see his namesakes in the sky. To Vinta on March 19, Galileo suggested that telescopes might be used as a diplomatic tool throughout Europe. Wouldn't the grand duke like to send fine instruments to his best allies? (As historian Richard Westfall points out, this was an ingenious idea that turned the grand duke into Galileo's personal public relations agent.) In case the grand duke was having trouble manipulating his tube, Galileo offered to come to Florence during the Easter recess to instruct His High-ness. It was not education but negotiations that Galileo had in mind.

Predictably, his visit to the Tuscan court at Easter was a happy one. The grand duke, fresh and impressionable at age twenty, had repaired to his beloved Pisa for the holiday, to his palace on the Arno known as the Verga d'Oro, the wand of gold. Together the prince and Galileo climbed to the palace's square tower, across from the steeple of the San Nicola Church, and contemplated the royal stars. Cosimo, his brown eyes sparkling from his thin artistic face, was gripped by excitement. At this moment Galileo might have wished that the great cavalier Giambattista Marino was there to sing both their praises:

> In this same glass thou wilt spy . . .
> Jupiter girt round with other lights,

whence in the sky the Arno's demigods
will leave their names inscribed forevermore.
Then Julius shall yield to Cosimo,
Augustus vanquished by thy Medici.

It would not be long before Galileo himself was openly soliciting celebrated poets to write idylls in his honor. When Andrea Salvadore complied several years later, Galileo improved the final version himself.

At some time during this visit to Pisa, Galileo and Belasario Vinta, the
grand duke's secretary of state, were able to slip away to discuss business. At
least they could discuss the preliminaries of a possible job offer in his native
land. Over Galileo, Vinta was able to wave his own wand of gold. Vinta
offered to meet and better the Venetian salary. The figure mentioned was
an astonishing one thousand crowns per year, the same as the highest paid
court official at the time, three hundred more crowns a year than Vinta
himself made, and three times the salary of any artist or engineer then in
government service. (Galileo's own tutor in 1584, Ostilio Ricci, had earned
a salary of 144 crowns a year as court mathematician, and Cosimo's new
court artist, the brilliant etcher Jacques Callot, made far less.) Galileo
wished to be relieved of any duty to lecture, indeed, of any public duty
whatever, and to devote himself exclusively to his own works. In addition,
he wanted to be relieved of any further claims for overdue dowry payments
by any harassing brother-in-law. "I wish to gain my bread by my writings,
which I would always dedicate to my Serene Master," he said.

He put before Vinta an astonishing array of works in progress or in his
mind: two books on the structure of the universe, "an immense work, full
of philosophy, astronomy and geometry"; three books on motion, "a new
science invented by me from its very first principles"; three books on
mechanics, about which "no one, in quantity or in quality, has done a
quarter of what I have done." He also wanted to write about military science, "giving not only a model of what a soldier ought to be," but also
teaching him valuable mathematics concerning fortification, the movement of troops, sieges, surveying, estimating distances, and artillery
power. As for lesser work, he was contemplating treatises on sound and
speech, light and color, the tides, and the movement of animals. He
wished to complete the time-consuming tabulation of the movement of
the Medician planets and to reprint his tract on the military compass.

Several weeks later, undoubtedly at Vinta's request, Galileo committed
all this to paper in a formal letter. Along with his acceptance of the salary

offer and the list of his projected works, he added one final, revealing request. "To the title of Mathematician," he wrote, "I would be pleased if His Highness would add that of Philosopher." He was no man of mere numbers, of idle measurements, of bloodless formulas, but of physics, natural science, astronomy, metaphysics, military science, and, though he did not mention it, of theology as well. He wanted to be defined and respected as a thinker interested in man's place in the new universe.

While these negotiations were conducted in secret, for Galileo feared the reaction in Venice, the terms were accepted two weeks later, and the deal was struck. On July 10, 1610, Galileo's appointment as chief mathematician and philosopher of the grand duke of Tuscany was officially announced.

As there was rejoicing in Florence, so there was disgust in Venice. The procurator of Saint Mark's, the governor of the University of Padua, and the future doge, Antonio Priuli, who had shepherded Galileo through his Venetian triumph the year before, was especially bitter at this breathtaking act of arrogance. To friends, Priuli remarked that he hoped never again to lay eyes on the ingrate. After all the state honors, the unprecedented salary increase, the various promises on both sides, Galileo had affronted the studio in Padua and offended the Venetian republic. It would not be forgotten. Indeed, the bitterness would increase with time.

Galileo had what he wanted. The praise of a grand duke overcame the pique of a doge. He was above the ire of his colleagues at the university, and beyond shame. Only Sagredo might have succeeded in giving him pause, but he was still far away in Aleppo.

Galileo's move did not destroy every relationship. As he packed up his household, he continued to work and to share his secrets with the fabulous Friar Paolo Sarpi in Venice. With Sarpi and another Servite friar, he made his first observation of the sunspots, evidence of yet another "corruption" in the divine solar system. As they worked together, Sarpi quietly warned Galileo about leaving the protection of the Venetian state. Galileo shrugged the warning off, peering at the grotesque scar that was the visible reminder of the papal attack on Sarpi in the "protected" state of Venice.

In late July he was focused on Saturn, hoping no doubt to find more moons to dedicate to useful potentates or even to assuage the annoyance of a doge. Instead, he was startled to see an olivelike globe, which had ears or handles. After repeated observations he concluded that Saturn was really a triple star. This he announced to his Tuscan benefactor in a brief letter to Vinta on July 30, swearing him to secrecy. To others, he resorted to the anagram to claim priority without revealing the nature of the discovery. Such cryptography was a popular practice of the day. But coming from Galileo at this time, it caused a sensation when Johannes Kepler in Augsburg received this burst:

SMAISMRMILMEPOETALEUMIBVNENUGTTAVIRAS

After repeated requests for a decoding, Galileo finally went public three months later, when he was comfortably settled in Florence; Giuliano de' Medici, then Tuscan ambassador to the Holy Roman Empire in Prague and Galileo's intermediary to Johannes Kepler, had pleaded with Galileo to satisfy the curiosity of the German emperor, Rudolph II, since Kepler himself had misinterpreted the anagram to have something to do with Mars. To emperors, Galileo was always compliant.

"Saturn is not a single star, but three together, which touch each other," he responded. "With a telescope which magnifies 1000 times, the three globes can be seen very distinctly, almost touching, with only a small dark space between them."

At last he decoded his anagram: "*Altissimum Planetam Tergeminum Observavi*" (I have observed the farthest planet as a triple star).

Two years later, however, in December 1612, he was not so sure about his claim of Saturn as a triple star. For he had returned to observing the planet and had been unable to find the secondary satellites that formed the handles. "Looking at Saturn within these last few days, I found it alone, without its accustomed stars, perfectly round and defined like Jupiter, and such it still remains. How can this be? Are the two smaller stars consumed like spots on the sun? Have they suddenly vanished and fled? Or has Saturn devoured his own children? Or was the appearance a fraud and illusion? I cannot resolve so new, so strange, so unexpected a change. The shortness of time, the weakness of my intellect, the terror of being mistaken, have greatly confounded me."

It was a rare spasm of self-doubt.

Part III

FLORENCE

6

THE NASTY SEED

In the early seventeenth century, as Venice went into decline, Florence had entered a period of robust commercial growth. Through the entrepreneurial impulses of the Medici grand dukes, Cosimo, Francis, and Ferdinand, Leghorn had become a vigorous port of call. The warehouses around its harbor and new fortress bustled, and its streets were filled with exotic traders: Greeks and Turks, Persians and Moors. In 1610 Tuscany opened up a commercial mission in Syria. The new markets for Florentine products in the Middle East created an atmosphere of prosperity along the Arno, as capital investment multiplied.

In the new year of 1611, Galileo was once again in poor health. His bouts of real or imagined indispositions increased in frequency, but he had developed a uniquely Florentine antidote. He was nourishing a new friendship with a wealthy young nobleman named Filippo Salviati. Only twenty-eight years old, twenty years younger than Galileo, Salviati doted upon his mentor in the manner of Sagredo. He had Sagredo's wealth and comfortable circumstances as well as his love for good wine and food. Even more than Sagredo, he had a genius for scientific speculation. In his upbringing, the young noble had concentrated more on the cultivation of his body than his mind. He was an accomplished dancer and equestrian, an expert gymnast and marksman, and he had spent much of his youth competing in tournaments and jousts. The courtly society of Florence assumed that this athlete was headed for a military career, but the education of a Renaissance patrician emphasized declamation, mathematics and philosophy, and Latin and Greek; and in the exercises of the mind as well, Salviati proved himself to be quick and intuitive.

He had another quality that was bound to endear him to the new court mathematician: He was disdainful of the self-satisfied Aristotelians and skeptical of authority in general.

During the previous fall, as Galileo took up residence on the Arno, he had instructed Salviati in geometry, and the two had quickly taken to each other. It was, of course, a master-to-disciple relationship. Salviati's villa, fifteen miles west of Florence in Lastra a Signa, became Galileo's new retreat. Called Le Selve ("The Woods"), it was the Florentine equivalent of Sagredo's ark in Venice, where his students came for philosophical exchange, as well as for wine and laughter. High above the Arno Valley, surrounded by ancient olive groves, spiked cedars, and tufted pines, Le Selve was blessed with healthful mountain breezes and clear streams. Galileo thought of it as a sanitorium where he could recuperate and think.

On January 15, 1611, Galileo was in this tranquil retreat, surrounded by the young and faithful, when he wrote to Belasario Vinta, the secretary of state to Grand Duke Cosimo, in Pisa to propose an official trip to Rome. This was to be a triumphal siege of the Holy See, when the wonders of the new science could be spread before the princes of the church, and shame on any who should dare to dispute the evidence! He wanted this to be an official mission of the state. The first mathematician and first philosopher of the grand duke of Tuscany was himself coming to Rome, prepared to demonstrate personally his splendid new discoveries to any holy man with power. He wanted the privileges of a true ambassador of science to be conferred upon him, with the elaborate pomp of diplomatic courtesy. As he would do several times later, Galileo chose the timing for this trip to come after a great discovery, so that he might speak from a position of strength. To Vinta, he wrote that he wished to explain the "great consequences" of his discoveries to those who needed to know (and to approve) them.

His ill health encouraged Galileo to plead for special services from the grand duke. Vinta promptly offered to put a litter, a carriage with a bed, at his disposal and agreed to pick up the expenses of the trip.

His infirmity delayed Galileo's trip for some weeks, but on March 23 he finally set out. It was as if he were an explorer, venturing not to the birthplace of Western civilization but into a hoary wilderness. Besides his collection of telescopes, he took offerings and trinkets for the natives of Rome: among them, fragments of luminous rock, which alchemists in

Bologna had discovered and whose glow in the darkness showed light to be distinct from heat or other sources of illumination. His rocks had a bit of wizardry and even magic to them. Galileo carried them like jewels in a small velveted box, planning to reveal them at just the right moment.

Once in Rome and settled into grand quarters at the Palazzo Firenze, he wasted no time in placing his glories before the church. Among the first whom he sought out was the grand Jesuit mathematician Father Christopher Clavius, who, although he was now very old and had only a year to live, remained a professor of mathematics at the bastion of Jesuit learning, the Collegio Romano. For Clavius, stocky and short, his Italian heavily accented with Germanisms, this must have been a meeting full of emotion. He could recall receiving the brash Galileo twenty-four years earlier, when the ambitious but unemployed young scholar had sought out the Jesuit and had talked brilliantly about his experiments in hydrostatics. In his own work, Clavius clung stoutly to the old cosmology in the face of Galileo's new information.

At first he doubted the authenticity of Galileo's instrument. "To see the satellites of Jupiter, men had to make an instrument which would create them," Clavius had declared. Of Galileo's assertions about the rough, mountainous surface of the moon, Clavius was more creative. If that were true, then the moon's irregularities must be encased by an invisible, transparent crystal to return the moon to its perfect, smooth polish as Scripture demanded. This hypothesis amused and horrified Galileo. "The imagining is beautiful," he would say tartly, "only it is neither demonstrated nor demonstrable."

As Galileo arrived in his presence once again, the pious mathematician was far from hostile to this propagandist for the new science. In the final revision of his master work, Commentary on the Sphere of Sacrobosco, Father Clavius continued to reject Copernican thinking, but he took note admiringly of Galileo's discoveries and insisted that both astronomy and the church had to deal with them. "The whole system of the heavens is broken down and must be mended," Clavius said with a certain wistfulness. Now that young man of 1587 had challenged the church at its roots, especially the church's scientists. Neither he nor his work could be ignored. Clavius himself may have been anointed the "Euclid of the Sixteenth Century," but it was a new century and a new age now, and the fame of this man in his presence was Euclidean as well.

At the Collegio Romano, Clavius and his colleagues had been observing the moons of Jupiter for more than two months. They received

Galileo as a colleague and as an inspiration—they were brothers in the same quest for truth. As pure scientists and mathematicians, these Jesuits were as yet unconcerned with "the great consequences" of these discoveries for Catholic dogma. That was for higher authority.

"We have compared notes," Galileo wrote soon after the meeting, "and have found that our experiments tally in every respect."

Within a few days of his arrival in Rome, Galileo was received by Pope Paul V himself. The pope was an immense man, fleshy and stout with a perfectly triangular goatee and a set of darting, beady eyes. His physical presence alone was intimidating. Still, by lavishing praise on the scientist and even permitting him to speak standing up, rather than on his knees, the pope put Galileo at ease. This honor genuinely flattered Galileo, as he later wrote, almost childlike, to Salviati. More important, the pope promised unwavering support.

This must have been reassuring. For Paul V was an ecclesiastical despot. A Borghese, who had purchased the Villa Borghese, the huge harpsichordlike palace on the bank of the Tiber in the year he was elected pope, Paul V was a lawyer by training. He had been chosen because he was obscure and bookish and had no powerful enemies. Upon his accession—an event he soon ascribed not to men but to the Holy Ghost—he began to exhibit eccentric and tyrannical tendencies, as if he were struggling to overcome his prior obscurity with histrionics. His manner became expansive and grandiloquent, while his thinking remained rigid and literal.

The pope was also suspicious and paranoid. In the first few weeks of his pontificate he had received the news that the statue of the Madonna in Subiaco, the papal retreat thirty miles east of Rome, had perspired! This terrible omen was supposed to presage the death of a pope, and Paul was terrified. He immediately fired his cook on the suspicion of poisoning and put the rest of his retinue under investigation. He feared that any approaching stranger was about to sink a knife into his ample girth. At length, the Roman astrologers saved him. They pondered the heavens and reassured the pope that the danger had passed. The stars were now in a favorable configuration.

Relieved of his anxieties, the pontiff expanded papal authority over secular matters and tried to enforce his overreaching demands to the letter. The number of banned books was vastly expanded, going far beyond the prohibition of dangerous Protestant works to publications that depicted the morals of the clergy and those that departed even slightly from church doctrine.

To herald the new attitude of the Holy See, Paul began his reign with a symbolic act. An obscure scribbler named Piccinardi had been bold and foolish enough to write a secret biography of Clement VIII, Paul's more statesmanlike predecessor, in which the writer suggested an unflattering resemblance between Clement VIII and Tiberius, the deliberate and reclusive Roman emperor during the time of Christ. The writer had not published the work but had made the mistake of whispering of its existence to a pious tattler. For a time he was thrown into a dark, dirt-floored dungeon in the infamous Castel Sant'Angelo. Then, one night, upon the peremptory order of the pope, Piccinardi was dragged from his cell to the bridge of San Angelo and hanged, left to swing full-face toward the dome of Saint Peter's, whose shape must have seemed like a giant squid.

If this was not enough to make Galileo nervous, the chief adviser to Pope Paul was the great intellectual of the church, Cardinal Robert Bellarmine. Galileo could not forget that Bellarmine had been the inquisitor of Giordano Bruno, the brazen, unrepentant Copernican who had been condemned for heresy and burned at the stake only sixteen years before in the Campo dei Fiori. And if neither the Piccinardi nor the Bruno cases were enough to unsettle Galileo, he could always ponder the stilettos of Pope Paul that had been lodged in the skull of his friend Paolo Sarpi.

So indeed, it was with some relief that Galileo received pontifical blessing. He was equally reassured when he heard that Bellarmine had looked through a telescope and was pleased. For it was Bellarmine, more than anyone, who would have to deal with the "great consequences" of Galileo's discoveries.

As Galileo began to captivate Rome, Bellarmine turned his mind to the matter. On April 19, he wrote to Father Clavius and his eminent colleagues at the Collegio Romano for an official position. He had looked through the tube and had seen "some very wonderful things," he wrote, but he had heard "conflicting opinions" about them. He wished his experts to clarify five points.

Was it true, as "the eminent mathematician" asserted, that the Milky Way was merely a collection of "very small stars?"

Was Saturn truly not one star but three stars joined together?

Could it be that the moon had "a rough and unequal surface"?

Or that Venus did change its shape, like the moon?

Lastly, did Jupiter really have four satellites, each with distinct, swift motion?

Five days later the Jesuit mathematicians delivered their sober reply. The tube did indeed reveal vast numbers of stars, especially in the nebulae of Cancer and the Pleiades, and probably had many more still than the multitude that could be seen. Saturn appeared to have a strange oval shape. But they had not perceived an actual separation of two stars at the sides of the planet and therefore could not confirm Galileo's theory of a triple star. As for the moon, its surface was certainly irregular, but Father Clavius personally doubted that these irregularities were mountains and valleys. Perhaps, Clavius suggested, the lunar mass had "more rarified and more solidified" sections accounting for its dapples. On the two points that had the great consequences for church dogma, the phases of Venus* and the moons of Jupiter, Clavius had no qualms whatever. Galileo was correct.

Later, Galileo made sure that this praiseworthy critique was widely distributed. The position of Father Clavius on the moon received undeserved emphasis, from both Galileo's admirers and his detractors. His friend, the artist Cigoli, who was then painting frescoes in the Santa Maria Maggiore basilica in Rome, remarked that old Clavius must not have eyes in his head. "I have an idea for an emblem those pedants could put on their shingle," Cigoli wrote naughtily. "A fireplace with a stuffed flue, and the smoke curling back to fill the house, where people have gathered to whom darkness comes before dusk."

But a buffoon named Ludovico delle Colombe wrote to Father Clavius to praise him for defending an unspotted moon. Galileo was quick to make sport of Colombe's entry, indeed, to appoint Colombe as the official leader of his detractors. In Italian, *Colombe* means "doves," but Galileo debased the word to mean "pigeons." Henceforth, his detractors would be called the Pigeon League.

With the official sanction of Clavius's letter to Bellarmine, the way was cleared for Galileo to be dignified with a visit to the Collegio Romano. Located in the center of Rome, a block from the Pantheon, the college was a pile of heavy stone set around a courtyard. Bellarmine and his student, Gonzaga, lived with the other Jesuits in simple cells on the top floor. A public conference was organized, in which Galileo was installed in a chair of honor before a large gathering. He was not to speak but to listen to a spirited discourse by one Father Odo von Maelcote, in Latin, of course. (Father Maelcote was one of the Jesuit mathematicians who had signed the letter to Bellarmine.) To the intense discomfort of the traditional clerics in

---

*See the discussion of the phases of Venus in chapter 7.

the hall, the students were with Galileo, and they cheered him boisterously.

"We proved clearly," one wrote, "that Venus revolves around the sun, but not without murmuring from the philosophers."

Meanwhile, outside the church, a new patron came forward to embrace Galileo. He was Federico Cesi, the second marquis of Monticelli, a wealthy and influential young nobleman who at twenty-six years of age possessed an enormous curiosity and the courage to break the confines of his aristocratic upbringing. He had a gentle, almost effeminate oval face, with a thin fastidious moustache and goatee, dark brows, and lively, skeptical eyes. As a patron of the arts and sciences, he had the grand ambition to compile an encyclopedia of nature, which he proposed to call "The Natural Theatre." Eight years before, against the wishes of his father, the duke of Acquasparta, the teenage marquis had established a scientific society called the Academy of Lynxes. The members were keen of sight, quick of thought, cunning in strategy, poised to spring upon the weak and the slow. The society's first, romantic statement of principle declared: "The Lincean Academy desires as its members philosophers who are eager for real knowledge, and who will give themselves to the study of nature, and especially to mathematics. At the same time, it will not neglect the ornaments of elegant literature and philology, which like graceful garments, adorn the whole body of science."

At the outset the society had only four members, all nonscientists and all under thirty years of age. Among the first principles agreed on in its inaugural meeting on August 17, 1603, was the promise that each member would instruct the others in some branch of science. Besides Cesi, there was Jean Eck, a Flemish doctor who had been accused of heresy in his own land and who trafficked in black magic. Recently, a new member had been added. He was Giambattista della Porta, whose book on natural magic, published the year Cesi was born, had been widely read and discussed. In his book, della Porta had imagined, along with other sensations, a trick device that could make distant objects appear quite close with the use of optical lenses. To some, della Porta's fantasy must have sounded like diabolical conjuring. In fact, Pope Paul V had summoned della Porta to Rome to face charges as a sorcerer, including the brewing of poisons.

As a secret society, the original members all took a code name and a symbol. Cesi was Il Celivago, the heaven-wanderer, and his symbol was an eagle holding the earth in its claws. Eck was L'Illuminato, the enlightened one, because he was the most learned of the originals, even though he might well have chosen another name. Eck had killed a disgruntled pharmacist who had assaulted him, and he had come to Cesi's attention as he languished in prison. They were joined by *Il Tardigrado* and *L'Eclissato*, the slow one and the eclipsed one.

Thus, until the arrival of Galileo, there hung about the feline academy a certain air of the occult and of pseudoscience, even the taint of scandal. That is certainly how the Catholic church and especially the Collegio Romano viewed the society. They were dangerous young men with dangerous ideas from dangerous books. Through his wide and often incorrect acquaintances all over Europe, it was true that Cesi had amassed an impressive library at his villa on the Via Maschera d'Oro ("mask of gold"). In this urban palace, situated in a warren of narrow cobblestone streets and arched byways not far from the Tiber, the Lynxes met and plotted.

In his palace Cesi also kept a prize collection of fossils, stuffed animals, and astrolabes, and in his library there were many volumes on the new sciences then flourishing throughout Europe, in botany, anatomy, chemistry, natural philosophy, and alchemy. This private library itself became a source of power and influence in Rome, with Cesi doing nothing to hide its dangerous contents. He was too powerful and too friendly with the luminaries of the church to be touched. In fact, as the rebels acquired age and maturity, a healthy competition grew between these independent-minded Lynxes and the traditional intellectuals at the Collegio Romano.

It is easy to see why Galileo would have been drawn to these freethinkers.

Early in 1611 Kepler had written to Cesi about Galileo's book, and undoubtedly Cesi was savoring this chance to have Galileo in his lair. They discovered immediately that they complemented each other perfectly, two spirits with identical interests but contrasting styles. Cesi's philosophical breadth and intellectual curiosity were tempered by a certain Roman prudence and reserve. Galileo's mathematical precision was humanized by his Tuscan impulsiveness and his caustic tongue.

Two weeks after Galileo's arrival in Rome, Cesi put on a fabulous banquet for the guest of honor in a priest's villa on the Janiculum, not far from the Porta San Pancrazio, the gate to Rome named for the Holy Ghost. Among those present were a well-known physician, Johannes Faber, an anti-Aristotelian abbot named Antonio Persio, a Greek mathematician named John Demisiani, and a Swiss naturalist named Johann Schreck, all of whom were soon to become Lynxes. The exception was Giulio Cesare Lagalla, the reigning guru of the Peripatetics in Rome, who was intentionally not invited to join the Lynxes. It would be at this fabulous banquet that Demisiani suggested the name telescope for Galileo's tube.

The gathering began at dusk and lasted into the night. Before dinner the twenty guests huddled around Galileo's instrument, as the inventor dismantled it, showed its lenses, and then put it back together. To demonstrate its powers, he turned it on the great basilica of Saint John Lateran three miles away, and there, amazingly, the inscription of Sixtus V was clearly visible above the entrance to the benediction gallery; then north to the Tuscan hills, where they pinpointed the palace of the Duke Altemps some sixteen miles away and counted all its windows, including the smallest. With that warm-up, they repaired to dinner.

For hours they engaged in excited speculations. Galileo himself was in an expansive mood. To the surprise of some, he lavished praise on the black magician, della Porta, and even gave him credit for inventing the telescope, or at least imagining it, although privately Galileo and his friends considered della Porta to be a charlatan. From Venice, Sagredo would remark acidly about della Porta: "Among the learned, Porta holds the place that the bell holds among true musical instruments."

After the feast of wine and sumptuous food and the learned conversation, the guests climbed to the roof of the villa above Rome where the telescope was set up and fixed upon Jupiter's family and upon the brilliance of Venus. In the days and nights afterward, the men continued their observations with this new human star in their midst. Two weeks after the banquet, Cesi described the joy of Galileo's initiates. "Every serene evening we see new things in the heaven: Jupiter with his four satellites and their distinct periods . . . the mountainous, cavernous, wandering, and aqueous moon, the cuckolded Venus and the triple star of Saturn." And then with the stirrings of a Copernican, the prince wrote, "These observations cause no small difficulty for the old theory that the earth is in the center of the universe."

During the banquet on the Janiculum, Galileo and Cesi fell into a long discussion about the future of the Lynxes, particularly Galileo's own place in that future. Eleven days later Galileo accepted election into the society as its fifth member. Cesi gave him an emerald ring to mark the occasion. Soon after, several foreign-born mathematicians and physicians who had been at the banquet, as well as the anti-Aristotelian abbot, Persio, were also elected, and before Galileo left Rome, he proposed that his young disciple in Florence, Salviati, also be elected. Expressly snubbed were the traditional academics from the established universities who attended the banquet. Instead of them, the Lynxes were soon to induct a friend and disciple of Giordano Bruno. It was purely a symbolic gesture. The society wanted to remain an advance guard.

The banquet above Rome was to be a turning point for the academy. For the next twenty years, until Cesi's death in 1630, it would be a significant force in the intellectual life of the country. Galileo was especially proud of his membership, insisting that his association appear on the frontispiece of his subsequent books. This, of course, dignified and propagated Cesi's enterprise, which could stake a claim as the first authentic scientific academy in history.

Galileo stayed on in Rome through the month of May 1611. In the gardens of the Villa Medici and of the pope's residence at the Quirinal Palace in the city's center, he pleased and amazed a steady procession of dignitaries, including many prelates, who came to experience his "celestial novelties." And during this visit he spent joyful hours in the company of his friend, the Florentine painter Ludovico Cigoli. Cigoli had been commissioned by Pope Paul V to paint the cupola of the great papal basilica, Santa Maria Maggione. Each day the sixty-two-year-old painter climbed—and counted—the 150 steps he had to conquer to reach his work. Cigoli had an artist's appreciation of the sky and a great admiration for what his friend was accomplishing. To the painter, Galileo was an artist and the sky a work of art—"*tante bellezze del cielo.*" The celestial novelties transported him, and he wanted to fold them into his frescoes, for to him they glorified God. Soon enough, mountains and valleys appeared in the crescent moon upon which Cigoli's figure of the Virgin Mary stood. Just as soon, his imperfect, besmudged moon put the painter at the center of a scandal.

In late April, Galileo awed the grand personages of Rome with yet another shocking assertion: He announced that there were spots on the sun. By his own account, Galileo had been observing sunspots for a year, extending back to his time in Padua. There and in Venice he had displayed them to persons of eminence (Paolo Sarpi among them), but Rome was in a different league. With theatrical patience, he had waited for the right moment to reveal his latest shock. To the closed-minded, Galileo was putting forth nothing short of blasphemous witchcraft: Upon the divine sun, there were massive black blemishes! They appeared and dissolved randomly? Altered their shape and seemed to wander about haphazardly like clouds? Then broke up and came back together for no good reason?

Galileo not only spoke this blasphemy but displayed it. To display blemishes on the sun, the source of warmth and light to man, to display them to cardinals in the church—this was to attack a cherished central belief in Christian theology: that the heavens were pure, unchanging, incorruptible. What was a cardinal or an Aristotelian to think? Should he deny the evidence of his own eyes? Was this a trick of optics? If it were true, how could it be explained? Cigoli had no doubts. Excitedly, he wrote to Galileo about the first time he viewed the solar spots, sketching a particularly black and large spot as it appeared in the morning and chronicling where it had ended up at dusk.

On May 12 Galileo wrote to Prince Cesi with the glee of a revolutionary. "I suspect that this new discovery will be the signal for the funeral, or rather for the last judgment, of the pseudophilosophy. The dirge has already been heard in the moon, the Medicean stars, Saturn, and Venus. And I expect now to see the Peripatetics put forth some grand effort to maintain the immutability of the heavens!"

He did not have long to wait. On the same day, from Perugia, he got wind that they were saying his telescope was an optical trick with specks inserted to look like stars. To this Galileo replied that he would pay ten thousand crowns to any genius who could construct a telescope that would make moons go around one planet but not around another. In Bologna, meanwhile, an anti-Galileo cabal was developing at the university. From there came an assault by a young German Lutheran named Martin Horky. Horky was a protégé of Kepler and evidently thought that by attacking Galileo, he could ingratiate himself with his mentor. Horky's work, called A Very Brief Pilgrimage Against the Starry Messenger, was virulent, nasty, and personal. Among other slanders, Horky imputed vanity and the thirst for gold as Galileo's chief motives for inventing Jupiter's satellites. If Horky hoped to drive a wedge between Galileo and Kepler, his tract had the opposite effect. Kepler promptly dumped his student, writing apologetically to Galileo about "this scum of a fellow" and calling Horky's book impertinent and juvenile. He advised Galileo to ignore it.

Then in Florence a young nobleman named Francesco Sizzi, a mathematician of some talent, published a somewhat more serious attack on The Starry Messenger. Sizzi was the first critic to raise theological objections: For Jupiter to have moons would be incompatible with Holy Scripture. This was an overt effort to stir up serious trouble. Lest he be ignored, Sizzi dedicated his work to the one member of the Medici family who despised Galileo. (Giovanni de' Medici, the illegitimate son of the half brother of the grand duke, whose grandiose notion for a monstrous dredging device for the harbor of Lavorno had been debunked by Galileo twenty years earlier.)

But few people did notice—this time. Galileo was being lionized and feted in Rome, favoring the most powerful figures of the church with his teaching. He could afford to be generous and patronizing. To Salviati at Le Selve, he wrote, "I had much rather gain the friendship of Sig. Sizzi by forgiving him all the insults than have him as an enemy through con-

quest. I have managed to apologize for him to the Jesuit fathers, who read
his puerilities with vast amusement."

And in his own copy of Sizzi's book, Galileo copied a stanza from
Ariosto, about the warrior-prince arriving at an easy target:

> The Duke arrived: It would not be honest
> To say that I want the battle tower;
> Which is offered to me so easily
> When it pleases, I shall turn my eyes upon the rampart.

Meanwhile, Ludovico delle Colombe, the head pigeon of Galileo's
Pigeon League, took it upon himself to be the defender of the faith. With
the banner of Psalm 93 held high—"The Lord reigneth. He is clothed
with majesty and with strength; the world also is established that it cannot be moved"—he published a little tract that emphasized the theological incorrectness of Galileo's assertions. "He who would render false all
the belief of mathematics, philosophy, and theology, who dares to demonstrate against all received wisdom and communion, that is a person who
would put an end to Holy Scripture."

Colombe's book consisted largely of biblical texts that Galileo was
supposedly offending with his observations. The Pigeon was convinced
that crystals in the telescope created these fascinating delusions. To such
arguments, which were so contrary to the evidence of the eyes, Galileo
scratched a note in the margin of Colombe's book: "Those who prize the
gift of sight so little deserve to lose it."

Still, if Sizzi was overwrought and Colombe silly, they nevertheless
had planted a nasty seed. From elsewhere came the charge that Galileo's
"pretended discovery vitiates the whole Christian plan of Salvation." A
priest declared that "it cast suspicion on the doctrine of the incarnation."
Another detractor fulminated that if the earth was a planet like the other
planets, the others must be inhabited as well, "since God makes nothing
in vain." "How can their inhabitants be descended from Adam?" he continued. "How can they trace their origin to Noah's ark? How can they
have been redeemed by the Savior?"

Unbeknownst to Galileo, this seed sprouted within the Vatican itself
while he was still in Rome. On May 17, the Congregation of the Holy
Office—the Inquisition—took up the case of Galileo's old Aristotelian
nemesis in Padua, Cesare Cremonini. For Cremonini had just published
his book *Disputatio de Caelo*, which interpreted the lessons of Aristotle

with a naturalistic bent and seemed to question not only the immortality of the soul but the eternity of heaven. It was a classic case of guilt by association. Galileo was a friend of Cremonini. Worse than that, this Galileo was also friendly with the Venetian heretic Paolo Sarpi.

That Galileo should be linked, to his detriment, with his chief opponent in Padua was heavy with irony, and yet it was the beginning for both of trouble with the Inquisition, which would hound them to the end of their lives. Their views were polar opposites, and indeed, Cremonini had been boasting loudly of refusing to look through Galileo's telescope, even as he was writing about Aristotle's view of the heavens. Now they found themselves joined by the one thing they had in common: opinions at variance with accepted Catholic theology. As their names were joined, so they were separated by yet another difference: Cremonini remained protected in the antipapal state of Venice, whereas Galileo was exposed in papal Tuscany.

As he received his final congratulations and prepared to leave Rome, Galileo was unaware of the incipient danger. Flattery insulated him. Upon his departure, an influential cardinal and friend of the House of Medici, Francesco del Monte, wrote a glowing letter to the grand duke of Tuscany about Galileo's Roman triumph. "During his stay here Galileo has given the greatest satisfaction. I truly believe that if we were living under the ancient Roman republic, a column would be erected on the Capitol in his honor."

In July, back in Florence, he received a cautionary letter from an old friend in Padua, who had encountered the estimable Cremonini on the street.

"Mr. Galileo is exceedingly sorry that you wrote a whole great book about heaven, while you refused to see his stars," the friend had teased Cremonini jovially.

"I don't believe that anyone but he saw them," the avuncular Cremonini had postured. "Besides, looking through his lenses makes me dizzy." The man was onstage and knew it.

"What a pity that Mr. Galileo has gotten himself involved in these entertainment tricks," the Aristotelian had continued, driving home his point. "And what a pity that he has forsaken our company and his safe haven in Padua. He may yet come to regret it."

Galileo could only be amused. What could be said about a philosopher who refused to look through the new instrument of science?

"Since he refuses to see my celestial novelties on earth, perhaps he will see them on his way to heaven," Galileo chortled.

7

Black Fire and
Floating Bodies

In more and more of the professionals Galileo encountered, science and religion were intertwined. Scientist-priests seemed to confront him at every turn. Upon his return from Rome, the forces were joined once again, as he was accompanied by a conceited young protégé named Giovanni Ciampoli, who was just beginning to intrude himself into Galileo's life. Ciampoli had studied mathematics with Galileo in Padua and was now studying for the priesthood, and he had great potential for usefulness and later for mischief. For now, Ciampoli was solicitous, but the long journey was tiring, and upon his arrival in Florence, Galileo repaired to his bed for many days.

No sooner was he up again in midsummer than he was drawn into a public dispute that presented new perils. At Salviati's house in Florence he attended a philosophical discussion, where several of his adversaries—men who were looking for an issue to discredit the court mathematician at any turn—were present. On this occasion they happened onto a surprising issue to embroil Galileo in controversy once again. A question arose concerning the properties of bodies floating in water, and a professor from Pisa put forward the opinion that ice was merely condensed water, heavier than its liquid form, and floated only because of its flat and thin shape.

This was no mere philosophical issue. The wider question of floating objects bore upon practical engineering problems such as how much weight floating materials like timber would bear. Four years before, when he was still in Padua but angling to come to Florence, Galileo's opinion had been solicited concerning a wooden esplanade across the Arno that the Medici engineers were designing for the wedding of Cosimo II. By challenging the plans of the court engineers, Galileo had occasioned the dismay of many, including Giovanni de' Medici, the illegitimate prince of the Medici court, himself an amateur engineer, who harbored a real resentment against Galileo for slights in the past.

Still, the hydrostatic problem interested Galileo, and he rose to the challenge. Ice was not condensed water, but rarified water, he replied, not heavier but lighter than its liquid form, whose floating had to do with its physical properties, not its shape. "If it is true that condensation brings about greater heaviness and rarification lightness, then since we see that ice is lighter than water, we must also believe that it is less dense," he said. The Pisan vociferously denied this and clung to his original opinion. In the coming few days he searched for allies.

Eager to step forward was Galileo's avian detractor, Ludovico delle Colombe. Still smarting from Galileo's ridicule of him after their interchange in 1604, when Galileo had twisted his name from dove to pigeon and made him the head of a Pigeon League of opponents, Colombe was perched for attack. As yet, Colombe's effort to plant the nasty seed—that Galileo's celestial opinions flouted Holy Scripture—had not taken root. Now Colombe announced loudly that he would publicly offer proof of his Aristotelian position on floating bodies and triumph over the court mathematician.

"Ever ready to learn from anyone," Galileo replied patronizingly to the Pisa professor, "I should take it as a favor to converse with this friend of yours and reason about the subject."

The announcement of controversy quickly spread all the way to Rome, and a public duel was in the making. The contest had all the trappings of an intellectual joust, with the colors of the Medici streaming from the lance of one side and the colors of ancient Greece from the other. It had a referee, a cleric named Canon Francesco Nori, who was a friend of both contestants, and it had rules about what experiments were proper to offer on either side. It even had a formal challenge, written by Galileo:

Signor Ludovico delle Colombe believes that shape affects solid bodies with regard to their sinking or floating in a given medium such as water. . . . I, Galileo

Galilei, deem this not to be true. I affirm that a solid body of spherical shape which sinks to the bottom will also sink no matter what its shape is. I am content that we proceed to make experiments of it.

The instruments of the duel (that is, the bodies equal in density to water) were to be chosen by Colombe, as well as the shape of the objects. With this concession, Colombe rose to the game enthusiastically, for he was an exhibitionist and a provocateur. Soon he was holding public demonstrations around Florence with small nut-sized balls and heavy, odd-shaped ebony chips, both of which sank like lead to the bottom of his container. Loudly, Colombe boasted of his forthcoming victory over the overrated court philosopher.

The learned of Florence treated the coming contest with rising excitement. Salviati offered his house as a playing field. Upon the appointed day in late August, Colombe showed up with his nuts and chips and his bastard second, Giovanni de' Medici, but Galileo was nowhere to be found. In fact he had received a scolding from the grand duke in the form of a hint that this contest was unseemly and undignified, especially if the court philosopher were to lose. Better for Galileo that he commit his thoughts to paper. "Your praise of the pen" as a method of settling intellectual controversies, Galileo later explained in an apologetic letter to the grand duke, had led him to avoid an appearance at Salviati's house and instead to repair to his writing table. And with the pen, Galileo was at his best. By the tricks of his malicious adversaries, "the mind is bewildered and swatted about from one fantasy to another," he wrote, "just as in a dream, one passes from a palace to a ship to a grotto or a beach, and finally, upon awakening, finds that one has passed the hours without any profit."

Through September, Galileo worked diligently on his essay about floating bodies, for he had lost face in the Medici court as the chief philosopher of the grand duke and was eager to repair the damage. Ironically, as Galileo plied his pen at the grand duke's order, the grand duke abruptly changed his mind about oral debate. The change was occasioned by the visit, in late September, of two distinguished cardinals who enjoyed intellectual discussion. One of them was Maffeo Barberini, the scion of a wealthy Florentine merchant, who was leaving his bishopric in Spoleto for the post of cardinal legate in Bologna, and who was well known as a fancier of scientific and artistic debate. The grand duke was eager to stage an appropriate entertainment for his guests. Galileo was requested to repeat his arguments about floating bodies before this august company and to answer the assertions of an Aristotelian opponent, who was summoned sacrificially from Pisa for the purpose. While Barberini's career in the church was on the rise, Galileo could not know that the benign, animated, fresh-faced figure before whom he would be debating was a future pope who would become known as Urban VIII and who would become the prime adversary of Galileo's life.

On October 2, at the Pitti Palace, the debate was held. Besides the cardinals, the grand duke and the grand duchess Christine were present, and they joined in the argument as various experiments were held. "If you put ebony in water, it will sink to the bottom though you make it thinner than paper," Galileo asserted. When it came to ice, he shoved a heavy plate of it beneath the surface of the water and then released it. As the flat object came bobbing to the surface, there were exclamations and applause. Cardinal Barberini, dressed in his floor-length deep-green bishop's robes and black tiara, immediately took Galileo's side. It was the triumphant side, as Galileo devastated his reluctant foe.

A day later Galileo fell desperately ill once again. He would not regain his strength for two months.

The grand duke, meanwhile, had been well pleased with the debate in court and asked the court mathematician, now restored to good standing, to formalize his argument in a treatise. As he rose from his sickbed, Galileo explained his situation to Prince Cesi: "My infirmities disturbed my mind and made me melancholy, and this made things even worse. Still, haltingly, I have accomplished something. In a few days I will send you a Discourse on a certain dispute with some Peripatetics. That done, I want to spend a few days answering letters. Meanwhile, I will not neglect celestial observations and expect an exquisite addition to my findings."

The exquisite addition was further observations of the sunspots. Through the two years after his first triumphant visit to Rome in the spring of 1611, Galileo's focus alternated between black fire and floating ice.

Galileo had been observing the strange, shifting, terrifying blemishes on the sun for eighteen months. In Venice he had shown the sunspots to Sarpi, and in Rome, with his telescope set up in the garden of the Quirinale, he had shown them to a procession of prelates by placing a paper beneath the eyepiece to reflect the image and protect the eyes, as he conjectured on their origin and nature.

During September 1611, as he prepared to debate over floating ice, he had received two excited letters about sunspots from his friend, the painter Cigoli, who included sketches of his observations. And in the winter months that followed, still in uncertain health, he returned to the apparitions with greater concentration than in the past, for he was intent not only on establishing his priority in discovering them but also on coming to a conclusion about their makeup.

During this period he was spending a good deal of time at Salviati's villa, for he was beset by an array of discomforts including pain in his chest and kidneys, insomnia, and loss of blood. At Le Selve, high above the Arno with its clear view west to the white mountains of Carrara, he imagined the rarefied air to be recuperative. At night, by Salviati's hearth, they read aloud the facetious dialogues of Ruzzante, with whose vulgar barnyard dialect Galileo had a special facility, and the ribald verses of his Venetian friend Girolamo Magagnati, which, according to the poet himself, were "proper enough that even a Cappucine monk could place them beside his breviary at nighttime and still keep laughing."

By day they grew serious. Depending on his energy and the severity of his pain, Galileo worked on his discourse on floating bodies. But his attention was focused more on fire than ice. The correspondence with Cigoli had sparked his curiosity in the sunspots again. Occasionally at dawn and always at dusk during a good sunset, he and Salviati observed the sunspots and diagrammed their position from one day to the next. The spots appeared and decayed, changed their irregular shape, and seemed as if they moved from west to east on a south-north slant, but only within thirty degrees of the sun's equator. When a particularly large spot presented itself, Galileo and Salviati tracked its slanting motion and came to the preliminary conclusion that the sun was tilted upon its axis. By deduction such motion upon its axis might also apply to the earth, thus supporting half of the Copernican theory.

As he and Salviati worked at their fitful pace, they were confronted in late March 1612 with a shock: An unidentified stargazer was observing the sunspots, writing about them, and claiming priority as the first observer. Worse, this interloper was proclaiming the spots to be stars passing across the face of the sun! The observer had chosen the pseudonym of Apelles (a figure who in ancient times had been the court painter to Alexander the Great and who reputedly hid behind his paintings to overhear court gossip). This masked marauder was made more formidable by the fact that he came to Galileo's attention from a respectable source, Mark Welser, who was a banker and the sheriff of Augsburg, a friend of Galileo's and later a member of the Academy of Lynxes. Impressed by the letters, Welser had published them in Germany and sent a copy to Galileo.

In early 1612 Welser had, in the spirit of scientific inquiry, passed on Apelles's letters, requesting a critique from Galileo. "If the solar spots do not come to you as anything really new, as I suppose, nevertheless, I hope you will be pleased to see that on this side of the mountains, estimable men are traveling in your footsteps."

This was not what Galileo wished to hear, since the mysterious Apelles was both promoting error and stealing Galileo's first claim to discovery. According to his own account, Apelles had noticed the sunspots early in 1611 but consigned no scientific importance to them. Then, on October 21, 1611, he realized their importance and focused on them as a scientist. Since Galileo had been corresponding with Cigoli about the blemishes five weeks beforehand and had seen them in Venice two years before that, his priority was clearly established. In his heart, Galileo knew that he was not the first to see the spots on the sun. That probably had happened during the time of Charlemagne, when the people of France had seen a black cloud on the sun for eight days straight. But that could not be considered a scientific discovery.

His paranoia began to contend with his physical ailments and his melancholy. It seemed as if he had to hide every new idea until he had more than proved it. The "enemies of innovation" were out to get him, "making it seem better to remain with the herd in error than to stand alone in reasoning correctly." His safest course was negative: to debunk the false ideas of others, rather than to put forward his ideas like raw meat.

Dispirited and uncertain, he delayed his reply to Welser and Apelles until May, in order to extend his observations and to be certain of his conclusions. Bravely, he tried to suppress his anxieties about his competition. "A man will never become a philosopher by worrying forever about the writings of other men," he wrote.

May 1612 was quite a month for Galileo. His attention was drawn back to earth, as his treatise on floating bodies was finally published. It received broad acclaim and was widely read; a second edition quickly followed. To modern historians of science, the discourse marks Galileo's first entry into experimental physics and forms the basis for his subsequent enduring work in mechanics. Among the first to receive his new book were important cardinals, Robert Bellarmine in Rome and Maffeo Barberini in Bologna. The good impression that Galileo had made the previous October had stayed with Barberini.

"I shall read your treatise with pleasure," His Eminence responded, "both to confirm myself in my opinion which agrees with yours and to enjoy the fruits of your rare intellect."

Predictably, the attacks on the discourse were rushed into print, fanning Galileo's paranoia. One called him "greedy for glory," and another was published by Colombe, who tried to seize a measure of reflected glory by boasting that Galileo's discourse was directed solely at him. Galileo ignored the Pigeon. "There is no point in disputing someone who is so ignorant that it would require a huge volume to refute his stupidities which number more than the lines of his essay."

While his "Treatise on Floating Bodies" triumphed, Galileo turned back to his current fascination with the sunspots. His first letter in reply to the mysterious Apelles, written May 3, was cautious, defensive, and negative. He knew more what the blemishes were not—stars or planets or comets streaming across the face of the sun—than what they were. At first he would say only that the "smokings" behaved like terrestrial clouds. More exact observations were promised. In August 1612 he was ready to be more precise. The spots were definitely a manifestation of the sun's atmosphere and confined to its "tropics." They varied in their density, darkness, and dimensions. And they moved with uniform motion. In his discussion of this, he arrived, almost haphazardly, at a law of physics for which he would forever be remembered, his principle of inertia. "A heavy body on a spherical surface will be indifferent to rest and to movement toward any part of the horizon. It will maintain itself in that state in which it has once been placed. If placed in a state of rest, it will conserve that. If placed in movement toward the west, it will maintain itself in that movement."

His pronouncement upon the value of direct experience over received authority was memorable. "They who depend upon manifest observations will philosophize better than those who persist in opinions repugnant to the senses." Had Aristotle been able to see what he, Galileo Galilei, was able to see, Galileo proclaimed, the wise Greek would certainly have agreed with him.

As he polished his letters on the sunspots, Galileo kept his Roman benefactor, Prince Cesi, abreast of their progress. After the first letter in May, Galileo proclaimed to Cesi that his work had caused the last judgment and funeral of "pseudophilosophy." He anticipated a strong defense of an incorruptible heaven from his opponents, but as yet, he was thinking only of academics. "I expect the tempest over the mountains of the moon will be a joke compared to the lashings I will receive over these clouds."

Before he committed himself to an even more definitive view of the sunspots in his second letter, his cautious side asserted itself. Nervous about the attitude of the church, he wrote to Carlo Cardinal Conti, the prefect of the Inquisition in Rome, to inquire about the dictates of the Bible, especially on the subject of the "corruptibility" of the heavens and on the motion of the earth. Did the Bible insist on a perfect heaven, or was that solely Aristotle's idea?

The grand inquisitor replied obscurely. On the one hand, he seemed to encourage, and on the other, to suppress. Nowhere in the Bible was the perfection of the heavens enunciated, he wrote. In fact, the Bible was averse to Aristotle's view. Nor did it directly address the motion of the earth. But Galileo should be more careful about asserting that until his proof was more compelling. The planets and the stars did "rise and set," the cardinal pronounced, but this language may have been couched in terms that the common people could understand. Galileo should say what he wanted about the sunspots, but just in case he hadn't seen it, the cardinal was sending along a little book that argued that the sunspots were congeries of small stars revolving around the sun.

It was difficult for Galileo to know whether to be relieved or terrified.

After Cesi received Galileo's second, more significant, letter on the sunspots, he pressed his desire to publish the work under the imprint of the Academy of Lynxes, but he worried about the identity of Apelles. Cesi was already sensing a strangely difficult time with the church. That summer there had been a debate on the sunspots at the great Jesuit college in Rome, the Collegio Romano. In it, a peculiar theory had received considerable support: The sunspots were not clouds but clusters of pure stars moving across the sun. Galileo was ready with a reply. In the perfect heaven, the stars were supposed to be fixed and unmoving. Which death knell to the Aristotelian system did they prefer?

To moderate the confusing church resistance, Cesi urged Galileo to write a conciliatory third letter to Apelles, adopting a dignified, nonconfrontational tone and confining himself to strict scientific argument. Galileo tried but failed to contain himself. In his scientific argument, he produced his first and perhaps most dangerous endorsement of the Copernican system. In observing the path of Saturn, he wrote: "I tell you that this planet also, no less than horned Venus agrees admirably with the great Copernican system. Favorable winds are now blowing on that system. Little reason remains to fear crosswinds and shadows on so bright a guide." And when it came to imagining the mysterious Apelles and his other Aristotelian enemies, a vision came into his head of a contemporary painting by Giuseppe Arcimboldo called *Summer*, where a surreal humanoid creature was constructed from a composite of fruits, vegetables, and straw.

Throughout the winter of 1613, unexplainable delay and difficulty bedeviled Prince Cesi in his efforts to gain the approval of the church censors. As Cesi cajoled and lobbied in Rome, Galileo continued his telescopic observations. On December 28, 1612, and again on January 28, 1613, he observed a "fixed star" east of Jupiter and tracked its movement in the constellation Virgo. In recent times astronomers have concluded that Galileo's fixed star was actually Neptune, observed and duly noted 234 years before the planet was actually "discovered." Finally, in March of that year, after some deletions, *Letters on the Sunspots* was published. In the introduction, Galileo was proclaimed the first discoverer of the sunspots. As this was the first of Galileo's works to be published by the Academy of Lynxes, it was prefaced with an adulatory poem, penned by Francesco Stelluti, *Il Tardigrado* ("the Slow One"), one of the four original Lynxes.

> *Your merits, Galileo, are so great*
> *That from the face of darkness*
> *A hundred Olympuses,*
> *Emerge to honor you.*
> *And when you tempt them with your glass,*
> *The great spheres bend to your favor.*
> *To make your valor more luminous*
> *Thousand upon thousand shining bodies are born.*
> *The Sun who brings the day*
> *Also shares its light with you.*
> *Now its pure veil is sprinkled*
> *With spots which you showed us first.*
> *With this art, your grand virtue is adorned*
> *With immortal light.*

Like his previous book, *Letters* was published in the vernacular Italian, which made its vibrant style and devastating arguments all the more powerful propaganda for the new science. Its readership was vastly expanded.

"There are men with horse sense, but because they are unable to read things that are 'Greek to them,' they become convinced that the logic and philosophy are over their heads," Galileo wrote that spring. "Now I want them to see that just as nature has given them eyes with which to see her works, so she has given them brains to penetrate and to understand."

A year after *Letters on the Sunspots* was published, the identity of the mysterious Apelles was revealed. He was Father Christopher Scheiner, a

Jesuit professor of mathematics in the Bavarian town of Ingolstadt. Galileo could take one consolation in his shock: If he, the devout scientist, was meeting resistance from the clergy in his pursuit of the new science, Scheiner's experience showed that a scientific priest had even more formidable problems. When Scheiner notified his superior of his supposed sunspot discovery, the provincial replied that he had read all of Aristotle's writings, and "I can assure you, my son, that I have found nothing similar to what you describe. Go and calm yourself. Your sunspots are the defects of your glasses or your eyes." In the face of such beneficent thickheadedness, Father Scheiner had been forced to publish anonymously, the Jesuit order fearing that if he was wrong, its reputation would suffer. Now he wanted his due.

(Ironically, neither Scheiner nor Galileo had a valid claim to be the first observer. As historian Stillman Drake has pointed out, Charlemagne and even Virgil notwithstanding, the sunspots had been observed during Galileo's time by others: an Englishman called Thomas Harriot, the first cartographer of the moon, and a Hollander named Johann Fabricius, who had published an obscure treatise about them in June of 1611. Thus, the dispute between Galileo and Scheiner was a battle for second place, although there is no evidence that Galileo or Scheiner knew of Fabricius's work.)

With the unmasking of Apelles, it became clear why the Collegio Romano had debated the sunspot issue so heatedly, why it had tilted toward an anti-Galileo position, and why the church censors had given Prince Cesi such a difficult time in granting their formal imprimatur. Moreover, Father Scheiner was not backing down from his claim of first discovery. He meant to fight, and Galileo did not intimidate him.

Thus, in 1614, Galileo found himself in an unresolved dispute over priority with a mean and determined Jesuit. The fight was to grow meaner in subsequent years. It would play a major role in Galileo's Inquisitional trial eighteen years later.

As ever, Galileo would feel himself to be the aggrieved party. Eight years later, he would write in *The Assayer*:

How many men attacked my letters on Sunspots, and under what disguises! The book should have opened the mind's eye for admirable speculation. Instead it met with scorn and derision. Many people disbelieved it or failed to appreciate it. Others, not wanting to agree with my ideas, advanced ridiculous and impossible opinions against me. And some, overwhelmed and convinced by my arguments, attempted to rob me of that Glory which was mine, pretending not to have seen my writings and trying to represent themselves as the original discoverers of these impressive marvels.

Father Scheiner would consider that a personal insult, and his passion for revenge would smolder for twenty years.

If through his vast correspondence Galileo was constantly preoccupied with his enemies and detractors, they were overwhelmed exponentially by his legion of friends and admirers, protectors and disciples. Typical of his support was that of his faithful advocate in Rome, Ludovico Cigoli. After *Letters on the Sunspots* was published, Cigoli wrote to Galileo about the "birds" of the Pigeon League as having popping eyes and stuffed breasts. If he were to draw a figure of ignorance, they would provide the models.

A lesser man might have drowned in the relentless flattery, but Galileo not only had come to expect it, he had come to need it. His genius was on every tongue including his own, as one marvel after another flowed from him.

Occasionally, he had needed to be prodded. That had been the case three years before with a crucial discovery in the strengthening case for Copernicanism. In early December 1610, he had received a letter from yet another disciple-priest, a Benedictine who had studied under him at Padua and assisted in his experiments with the thermometer, who longed more for the scientific than the religious life. His name was Benedetto Castelli. Castelli was a round-faced, balding monk with heavy eyebrows and penetrating eyes, the product of a noble Brescian family, who during his Paduan years had been attached to the monastery at Santa Giustina. Now Castelli had challenged his mentor upon a point of logic.

"If Copernicus's opinion—that Venus revolves around the sun—is true, as I believe it to be, we would see it sometimes horned and sometimes not," Castelli wrote, in an analogy to the phases of the moon. "Have you observed such a phenomenon with your marvelous glasses? If this is so, it would surely convince the most stubborn genius."

In fact, Galileo had been observing Venus for three months and was long since onto Castelli's logic. At first, the Evening Star had been round and full, but distant. Then, as it rose in the sky, it grew in size with each daily viewing until it began to lose its roundness on its eastern side. In November a remarkable conjunction of the moon and Venus had taken place, affording Galileo excellent conditions for observation. As Galileo had received Castelli's letter in mid-December 1610, it had been reduced to a half circle. "In that shape, it has stayed many days, but always growing in size. Now it begins to become sickle-shaped. In the evening, it will continue to thin its little horns until they vanish. But then return in the mornings and be seen with horns thin, turned away from the Sun and will grow toward a half circle until maximum elongation."

These observations were astounding. In their implication for the debate over the two chief systems of the world, they were more important than the discovery of Jupiter's moons. For they proved that Venus revolved around the sun and not around the earth. This made the theories of Aristotle and Ptolemy impossible by definition, even if it did not definitively prove the Copernican theory.

In the fashion of the day, Galileo devised an anagram to establish himself as the first discoverer. Deciphered, it read: *"Cynthiae figuras aemulatur mater amorum."* The Mother of Love imitates Cynthia's shapes. For the prosaic ones who needed a translation, Galileo's metaphor meant that the phases of the moon are imitated by Venus.

Galileo was caught, once again, between two countervailing forces. With this crucial discovery, he had been eager to stake his claim as first observer, for he suspected, correctly, that others were turning their telescopes on this obvious target. Equally, he doubted that the mass of people could be easily convinced, regardless of the power of the evidence. To Galileo and Castelli, the difference was great between knowing the truth oneself and convincing others. "Oh, how many consequences have I deduced, my dear Benedetto, from these observations of mine!" Galileo wrote to Castelli on December 30, 1611. "What of it? Your Reverence made me laugh by saying that even the obstinate would be convinced by these observations. You must know that to convince the reasonable and open-minded man of the truth, these demonstrations would be enough. But to convince the obstinate who care only for vain applause of the stupid herd? . . . The testimony of the stars themselves would not suffice, even if the stars came to Earth and spoke for themselves."

After their collaboration in this most important discovery, Father Castelli had arranged to move to Florence, so that he could assist his mentor in further scientific projects. The monk was frequently at Galileo's side at Le Selve, enjoying the good food and wine with the gusto of a deprived man. Through 1612, he undertook to construct a table of the movements of Jupiter's moons, for Galileo had begun to think that the position of the Medicean satellites could serve as an aid to navigation. When Galileo published his treatise on floating bodies, Castelli took on the unpleasant duty of answering the attack of Colombe and the other Pigeons. And it had been Father Castelli who discovered the method of observing the sunspots by projecting the image of the sun through the telescope onto a blank piece of paper. For these prodigious efforts, Father Castelli was rewarded in the fall of 1613, when he was appointed, no doubt with his mentor's help, to Galileo's old chair of mathematics at the University of Pisa. The post came, however, with a stipulation: He was expressly forbidden from teaching the motion of the earth.

In December 1613, Galileo received a letter from Castelli, rich with gossip and meaning. The monk had been invited for an elegant breakfast at the Verga d'Oro, the Medici palace on the Arno, as the grand duke and his court had begun their winter residence in Pisa. Also present were several academics. As it turned out, Father Castelli had been working on his Jovian tables the night before, and the conversation naturally fell into this interesting area. As the Benedictine told of his activities, Grand Duchess Christine turned to an academic named Boscaglia and asked if he denied the existence of Jupiter's satellites. He did not, but he did deny an analogy of Jupiter's system to the motion of the earth, for that, he said boldly, would contradict Holy Scripture. As a scolding from a layman to a priest, this was an insult, and Father Castelli launched into a peroration in defense and celebration of Galileo, as Boscaglia whispered in the ear of the grand duchess.

After the meal, Father Castelli was leaving when he was hailed by the porter and taken to the private chamber of Grand Duchess Christine. "Her Ladyship began to argue against me by means of the Holy Scripture," Father Castelli wrote to Galileo. "I first expressed the appropriate disclaimers, but then I began to play the theologian with such finesse and authority that you would have been especially pleased to hear." Specifically, the grand duchess was troubled by a passage from Joshua in which the Lord commanded the sun to stand still so that Joshua's soldiers would have a longer day to avenge themselves on the enemies of the Lord. If the sun stood still and lengthened the day, did that not prove by the Word of God that the sun traveled around the earth?

Castelli and Galileo had debated this passage before, and now the monk put forward their arguments without hesitation. In this interrogation of Father Castelli, the grand duke seemed to take the friar's side, as the grand duchess continued to play devil's advocate, "contradicting me in such a way that I thought she was doing it only to hear me defend myself."

Deep as were his trust and affection for Father Castelli, Galileo was disturbed by this report. He could ill afford the opposition of the formidable grand duchess. In a sense, he owed his position in the Medici court to her, for her hiring him as Cosimo's tutor in the summer of 1605 had given him the entry into the Tuscan court he had so coveted. Ever since, this graceful, spirited, and pious lady of Lorraine had been his bene-factor. Now she maintained a power equal to that of her son, the grand duke, retaining the title of grand duchess even after Cosimo's marriage in 1608, when Cosimo gave his wife the lesser title of "archduchess." More-over, Christine had been instrumental in the reform of the Medici court. If this grand dame were to embrace the position of the academicians or, worse, if she were to fall further under the influence of backward priests, Galileo's movement was in jeopardy.

He was on the edge of a fateful step. Until now, the religious argument against the new science had been confined to the ignorant and the power-less. He had been able to ignore the intrusion. If he crossed the line now and entered into the slippery territory of theology, what would be the con-sequence? If he did not enter, would not the theologians intrude themselves further on his territory? He needed to win over the grand duchess to the side of science and to separate her from her backward-looking priests.

On December 21, 1613, his reply to Father Castelli was forceful. He treated the answer as more than a confidential communication—it had the air of a manifesto, even though it began in the avuncular style of the mentor. "What greater fortune can you wish than to see their Highnesses enjoy discussing with you, putting forward doubts, listening to your solu-tions, and in the end, being satisfied with your answers?"

Of course, Holy Scripture could never be in error, he asserted as he moved to the argument, but its interpreters could err, and the greatest error of all was to treat the words of the Bible literally. Those words may have come from the Holy Spirit, but they were crafted loosely to address the ignorance of the common people who were not capable of under-standing higher mysteries. Set against those words was Nature itself, which also flowed from God. Nature too was a truth, and two truths could not contradict each other. When the experience of the senses seemed to contradict the literal meaning of Scripture, "the task of wise interpreters is to find true meanings of scriptural passages that will agree with the evi-dence of sensory experience." What God would give man language, intel-lect, and senses and then expect him to bypass their use?

As for the Joshua passage, it demonstrated not the falsity of the Aris-totelian and Ptolemaic systems, but squared "very well" with the Coperni-can system. Given the motion of the sun and the stars in relation to the earth, he reasoned, the day would be shorter rather than longer if God stopped the motion of the sun alone. "It is absolutely impossible to stop the sun and lengthen the day in the system of Ptolemy and Aristotle. Either the motions must not be arranged as Ptolemy says or we must modify the meaning of the words of the Scripture." For if God stopped only the sun and not the other celestial bodies, he would completely upset and confuse the order of the universe.

The letter to Father Castelli was widely distributed, and at first, Galileo did not seem to mind. Its purpose was to put the religious argument against scientific inquiry on the defensive, to put to shame any who attempted to block his science by brandishing the Bible, to force the theologians to deal with the new evidence. It was also intended to garner support within the Medici court against any interference from Rome. Its effect was the opposite. It alerted churchmen, both humble and powerful, to the arrogance of an impertinent layman. Galileo had dared to trespass on the realm of theology, the queen of all sciences. He had been bold enough to interpret Scripture, to question its reason and its method, to arrogate to himself, a layman, the task of defining the divine purpose of sacred texts and the intention of the Holy Spirit.

This man needed to be watched.

More than a year passed before his challenge was taken up. In the meantime, lest there be any confusion about the confrontation he proposed, he undertook to expand and sharpen his argument against this ill-placed intrusion upon the independence of science. Instead of using his devoted disciple as a messenger, he would write directly to the grand duchess of Tuscany, supposing her to be a friend and the real power in the court and offering her the chance to become the patron saint of the new science.

His letter to Grand Duchess Christine reveals Galileo at the height of his courage. It is a brilliant, passionate document, a masterful disquisition of immense moral power and eloquence. Without artifice, disguise, or qualification, he proclaimed his belief in the Copernican system. "I hold that the sun is located at the center of revolving heavenly orbs and does not change place. And that the earth rotates on itself and moves around the sun." The trend toward that correct view was well advanced and could not be stopped simply by "shutting the mouth of one person," for it would not be sufficient to ban Copernicus's book and all the other books that supported Copernicus. Rather, the whole of astronomy would have to be stamped out. The irony, wrote Galileo, was that Copernicus, a priest and canon and adviser to popes, was highly regarded and his works read in his own time, when the hard evidence supporting his theory was scant. But now his views were under attack, just as daily discoveries made his doctrine "truer and firmer."

Those who seized "the irresistible and fearful weapon" of Scripture to attack the new science were hiding their inadequacy and ignorance in the face of its discoveries. These detractors were incapable of understanding astronomy, and therefore, they were attempting to smother it with religion. As a consequence, the astronomer was required to justify himself in the face of irrelevant assaults and to protect himself against his own observations. The argument was as deft as it was eternal.

Galileo might have escaped his fate if he had left his argument there. So long as he fought for scientific independence against unwarranted and inappropriate intrusion, he was on defensible ground. But in his letter to Christine, he passed over, once again, into the province of theology. There too, his arguments were deft and well conceived, but he had no standing for making them. "The primary purpose of the Holy Writ is to worship God and save souls," he wrote, but who was he to say? "In disputes about natural phenomena, one must not begin with the authority of scriptural passages, but with sensory experience and necessary demonstrations," he proclaimed, but who was he to downplay the authority of Scripture?

He quoted a cardinal: The intention of the Holy Spirit is to teach us how one goes to heaven, not how heaven goes. And he quoted Saint Augustine on the need for Scripture to adapt itself to the new discoveries of man. He even challenged the authority of the pope, the "Infallible One": With regard to scientific propositions, "no one can doubt that the Supreme Pontiff always has the absolute power of permitting or condemning. No human being, however, has the power of making these propositions true or false, contrary to what they are in nature."

He closed his epistle with a stanza from the fifth-century hymn "Caeli Deus sanctissime."

> Most Holy Lord and God of heaven,
> Who to the glowing sky hast given
> The fires that in the east are born
> With gradual splendours of the morn;
> Who on the fourth day, didst reveal
> The sun's enkindled flaming wheel,
> Didst set the moon her ordered ways,
> And stars their ever-winding maze.

The time for debate was over. The question was, What would the church do about Galileo and his new science?

INTERMEZZO

What the Roman Catholic church was to do to Galileo Galilei has been both savored and scorned for nearly four hundred years. What the church did to itself by virtue of its actions has been of equal fascination and avoidance. And what the church did not do, until October 1992, to heal this historical wound remains a vibrant, modern question. The face of Galileo haunts the Holy Roman church.

In 1616 and again in 1633, the church was to step forward into profound error and injustice and thus create for itself the central embarrassment of its modern history. As a result, for centuries the Catholic church has labored under a curse that it is anti-science, even anti-intellectual, that it is an enemy of modern research, suspicious of new frontiers, and antagonistic toward the messengers of scientific breakthroughs.

Perhaps no other charge has so angered popes and prelates over the succeeding centuries after Galileo, for the Catholic church can point to many proud achievements across the wide span of intellectual endeavor. Many of these achievements involve scientific discovery. In 1891, for example, in a time of anticlerical prejudice in Italy, Pope Leo XIII founded the Vatican Observatory, the so-called Specola Vaticana. It was a symbolic act as well as a real one, as if founding a papal observatory could somehow wipe away the stain of Galileo. In his statement at the founding, Leo XIII shook with passionate anger at the accusation that the church was obscurantist. Ironically, it was the same sort of passion with which Galileo had shaken many times when his detractors, many of whom were Catholic priests, had tried to ruin him.

Who are the real obscurantists? Leo XIII asked. The accusers level their charges, he said, "so that they might display their disdain and hatred for the mystical Spouse of Christ who is the true light." In establishing his Specola, the church is "helping to promote a very noble science, which more than any other of the human disciplines raises the spirit of mortals to the contemplation of heavenly events. Now everyone can see that the church and its pastors are not opposed to the true and solid science, whether human or divine, but they embrace it, encourage it, and promote it to the fullest possible dedication."

But the face of Galileo was the church's profane ghost. His case was undigested history, for its essence was ignored. No pope's anger, no amount of pontifical observatories and papal astronomers could obscure the facts. The church had taken 125 years to remove Galileo's works from the Index of Prohibited Works, and it was another hundred years after that before Galileo's works could be published with the church's begrudging sufferance. Two hundred years would pass before Catholic schools were permitted to teach the movement of the earth around the sun. In 1923 the case was rekindled when Galileo's first inquisitor, Cardinal Robert Bellarmine, was beatified after a long and bitter fight. Again in 1943 it was reopened in the secret corridor of the modern inquisition when the church censored a biography of Galileo by one of its own priests. And until as recently as 1984, important documents of the Galileo case remained secret. It is still not known if other important documents in the case lay hidden in the forbidding secret archives of the Holy Office.

In the early 1960s a French priest named Louis-Dominique Dubarle began a campaign to reopen, air, and finally resolve the difficult, awkward, and lasting Galileo question. Dubarle was a Parisian philosopher and a Dominican, and his cause was a kind of personal witness. Undoubtedly, he was animated by the role of his own order, the Order of Preaching Friars, the so-called Hounds of God, in persecuting Galileo. During the Second Vatican Council in 1963, which corresponded to the four hundredth anniversary of Galileo's birth, Father Dubarle and other progressive priests hoped that the church's Galileo problem finally would be resolved. They knew well the value of confession and absolution and wished to apply the remedy to the congregation collectively. But Pope John XXIII died before he could take up the question. His successor, Paul VI, turned a blind eye. The question lay buried in a few obscure documents in the archives of Vatican II.

In 1979, during the second year of his pontificate, Pope John Paul II surprised many when he announced that the church intended formally to reconsider the Galileo case. There was no rising tide of protest, no political requirement to address the issue. The pope's background was partly responsible for his initiative. He was Polish, after all, and like all Poles he had a particular affection for Copernicus (even though Copernicus is only half Polish). In fact, as Karol Wojtyla, the archbishop of Kraków, he had liked to refer to himself as the "Copernican Canon" and had often met with devout scientists who complained of religious censorship over scientific research.

But what did the pope's pronouncement mean? A new trial? A profound apology? Would the secret archives be thrown open? Would the Congregation of the Doctrine of the Faith, the modern-day inquisition, be more open to question about its deliberations?

The pope's statement gave no hint. It emphasized the obvious: Galileo had suffered at the hands of priests. But the pope seemed to consign equal blame on both sides. "In loyal recognition of wrongs from whatever side they come," he said, the church planned to study the case "serenely." Did that portend a stack of impenetrable academic papers? Was the great issue to be laid to rest with a hatchet?

He made no mention of inquisitors, threats of torture or forced exile, or the power of conscience. The apologists in the Vatican spoke openly of how Galileo would still be convicted today, since the essence of the affair was simple disobedience of a church order. This narrow path seemed the escape route. As if to show that the church bore no grudge, the pope invoked the words of Galileo himself. The words he chose were Galileo's flatteries of the holy church. He quoted the letter to Castelli of December 21, 1613. "Holy Scripture and nature proceed equally from the Divine Word"—Galileo's words rolled out in the pope's heavy Polish accent—"the former dictated by the Holy Spirit, the latter as a very faithful executor of God's orders." The modern pope, compatriot of Copernicus, pointed to the fact that Galileo had credited "divine grace" for his telescopic discoveries. And John Paul even quoted Galileo's letter to Grand Duchess Christine, where the scientist wrote, "Holy Scripture can never lie, provided that its real meaning is understood." None of these genuflections to Galileo's greatness seemed to get to the point.

The pope's reopening of the case, announced at a centenary celebration of Albert Einstein's birth, brought into existence a formal commission that included the pope's leading astronomer, the Jesuit Father George Coyne, and the popular and vigorous cardinal of Milan, Carlo Martini (who is a considered *papabile*, a prelate of papal timber). The commission chairman would be Cardinal Paul Poupard, a learned French prelate who was president of the Pontifical Council for Culture and who in times past had been the liaison for the church to the French intellectuals who were demanding the liberation of Galileo from church bondage. The pope asked that the commission answer three questions about the Galileo affair: What happened? How did it happen? Why did it happen?

In the next nine years there would be seven official meetings on Galileo. A book of documents from the secret Galileo file was released, but it was incomplete. An official book of essays was published, under the authorship of Cardinal Poupard, but it was dismissed by the critics as a whitewash. Pope John Paul II touched peripherally on the issue several more times, never by way of admitting error (for he was concerned about the church's moral authority over the brilliant messengers of modern scientific discovery), but by way of trying to promote more "dialogue" between science and faith. "Science can purify religion from error and superstition," he remarked in 1988. "Religion can purify science from idolatry and false absolutes." Purification was the issue.

But what about Galileo?

By the summer of 1991, the wish was that the subject would simply go away. The church had serenely studied it, and now it wished to turn out the lights. The issue was on the verge of being buried alive for another four hundred years.

The church had come up against a question that, in all its wisdom, it could not answer: How does a divine institution confess error?

Part IV

FLORENCE AND ROME

8

O Ye Fools of Galilee!

The Gothic church faced out upon a happy square, where the citizens of the city gathered around a fountain and frolicked near a marble obelisk, which stood nimbly upon bronze tortoises and was topped with a Florentine lily. For more than fifty years this triangular monument had been the finish line for a lusty coach race called the Palio dei Cocchi, which was held every year in late June before the feast of Saint John the Baptist and brought out the most bloodthirsty of crowds. But the *palio* was only one of many boisterous feasts and jousts that made the public space in front of Santa Maria Novella into a continuous carnival.

Its facade was a marvel: an intricate pattern of green-and-white marble, arranged in a complicated play of arch and square and false niche and set around a huge circular window. The window was supposed to be the eye of God. The upper portion of the facing was the most interesting, especially to Galileo. It had been designed by that quintessential man of the age, that perfect combination of art and science, piety and athletics, Leon Battista Alberti, and it presented a large central portal, supported by two massive volutes on either side that were decorated with circular geometric designs. In the tympanum, high above the rose window, the emblem of the Dominican order smiled down upon the passing scene. It was a huge sun with a gentle infant face in the center of its aureole.

Although all this was pleasing to Galileo, at least before 1615, it was the tie of the church to science and learning that drew him. Dante had been educated in its *studium*, and for decades the Academy of Florence had met there to study and purify the Tuscan language, pondering the meter of Petrarch and Dante, once with the help of a brash young scientist. And on either side of Alberti's facade were scientific symbols: on the left, a bronze meridian whose accuracy Galileo would later question, and on the right, a marble astronomical quadrant. These symbols had been designed by a Dominican priest, Friar Ignazio Danti, who had been astronomer and cartographer to the grand duke in Galileo's youth and cosmologist to the pope in Galileo's early manhood. (Danti's quadrant and its associated sundials were attached to the church during Galileo's adolescence to demonstrate the need to reform the Julian calendar.) With his death, Friar Danti vacated the chair of mathematics in Bologna, for which Galileo would compete in 1587, and lose. If Leon Battista Alberti was the perfect icon of the Renaissance man, Father Danti provided the age's perfect marriage of faith and science.

Along the bright and vast nave of crosshatching marble spans, through the corridors of the church and the cloisters of its monastery, Galileo had often wandered. He was there especially when his friend from Rome, Luigi Maraffi, visited and conducted business in the chapter house. Maraffi was the preacher general of the Dominicans, whose job was to promote the teaching and missionary spirit of the order. He was a powerful and progressive priest confident enough to argue for the Copernican theory in sessions at the Collegio Romano with his Jesuit brothers and proud of his friendship with Galileo.

When he came to the chapter house at Santa Maria Novella to counsel his preachers, Maraffi could scarcely avoid the third calling of the Black Friars: to defend the orthodoxy of the Scripture. Like hounds, they trained to hunt down all heretics, who like wolves and foxes threatened the purity of Scripture. On the wall of the chapter house that special duty was graphically portrayed in lovely fresco. Painted the century before, *The Church Militant and Triumphant* portrayed Saint Dominic, the founder of the order, sending forth his black-and-white hounds to catch and rip apart the foxes and the wolves, while the innocent, unsuspecting lambs, the flock of the faithful, slept blissfully unaware, nearby. Maraffi's preachers were proud to be the hounds of God. Even the child of Santa Maria Novella, Dante, had sanctioned their mission.

> Lamb of the holy flock was I, obeying
> Dominic on that road he led us,
> Where those, who do not stray, are nourished.
> "Paradise," X, 94–96

When Maraffi came to Florence again in the late fall of 1614, he expected dissension and even revolt among his hounds. Contention had been brewing for three years, and it spelled trouble for his friend Galileo. In Rome the grumbling about Copernican theory among certain Dominicans at the College of Saint Thomas was serious and stubborn. And Maraffi had learned that in Florence an unholy conspiracy of professors and priests against Galileo was gaining strength. One of his hounds, a professor of ecclesiastical history and a favorite of the Medici, Father Niccolò Lorini, had spoken against the Copernican theory the year before on All Souls' Day. When Galileo heard of it, he complained bitterly, and Lorini had been forced, temporarily, to back off and apologize. It had merely been an idle discussion with fellow priests, Lorini protested in his letter to Galileo, and he had merely offered the view that "the opinion of Ipernicus, or whatever his name is, appears to be against Holy Scripture." Galileo had treated the letter with contempt. "The good man is so well acquainted with the author of these doctrines that he calls him Ipernic," he wrote to Prince Cesi. "You can see how and by whom poor philosophy suffers."

Galileo might have felt that he had put an end to the trouble right there, but Father Maraffi knew that it was more deep-seated. Lorini and another Dominican, Tommaso Caccini, were part of this menacing "league," which fancied itself the counterpart of the Academy of Lynxes, centered around Ludovico delle Colombe, and gathered secretly at the home of the archbishop of Florence. This alliance could lead to something really serious, for Maraffi had been told that Colombe was pressing the priests to denounce Galileo from the pulpit. Galileo himself was no help at all in the face of this budding conspiracy, for to him, pigeons were no match for lynxes, and he scoffed at the cabal. Patronizingly, he thanked Maraffi and Prince Cesi for their sweet concern about those who "are constantly seeking to pick quarrels here. But since the malicious 'league' is few in number, I laugh at it." He would soon cease to laugh.

On December 21, 1614, the fourth Sunday of Advent, Friar Caccini strode in his black cape and white habit to the central pillar of Santa Maria Novella, climbed the circular stairs that coiled upward to the pulpit, and emerged before the multitude of Christmas-season faithful. He was a fine-looking man, the progeny of minor nobility, who had grown up, one of three brothers, in a palace in the Borgo Pinti in Florence and had been marked to be a Florentine banker. Beneath his fine figure lay a restless, resentful nature. He had a visceral, long-standing antipathy toward Galileo and his new ideas, which extended back to Galileo's first arrival in Florence from Padua and was tinged with envy. Moreover, the friar was ambitious and meant to use this sermon to propel himself into a higher station within the Dominican order, after years of frustration.

From the Old Testament, he chose the tenth chapter of Joshua as his text:

> And then Joshua said in the sight of Israel:
> Sun, stand thou still upon Gibeon;
> And thou Moon, in the valley of Ajalon.
> And the sun stood still, and the moon stayed,
> Until the people had avenged themselves
> upon their enemies.
> So the sun stood still in the midst of heaven
> And hastened not to go down about a whole day.
> And there was no day like that before or after it
> That the Lord hearkened unto the voice of man.

And from the New Testament, Father Caccini took his reading from the eleventh verse of the first chapter of the Acts. The words of his reading boomed across the packed nave. "O ye men of Galilee, why stand ye gazing up into heaven?"

The mix was explosive. It combined celestial miracle with power of God over the sun and moon and tossed in a dose of the Holy Spirit. To the unschooled, it might seem that the Holy Ghost was chastising men for trying to understand the mystery of the heavens. To use the eleventh verse of the Acts to attack the new science was a perversion of the verse's meaning, for the biblical words are spoken to the apostles by two angels who appear, as Jesus ascends to heaven after he has told his disciples not to worry about the time when the kingdom of Israel is to be restored. The verse had nothing to do with the position of the stars or the rotation of the planets, or man's curiosity to figure them out. But Caccini was in the grip of passion. He was an agent provocateur, slathering forward like a galloping horse, fulminating about Galileo for spreading an evil doctrine contradictory to Holy Scripture.

Italy's most famous scientist, philosopher to the grand duke of Tuscany, intimate of powerful cardinals in Rome, stood accused publicly of heresy, from an important pulpit, by a vigilante of the faith. Not only he but all mathematicians as a breed were denounced, since their science, according to this beagle of God, was the work of the devil and from them stemmed all wicked heresies. They should be driven collectively from the body of the faithful like germs.

The effect was electric. The streets of Florence were aflame with gossip. Who was behind this accusation? Would the grand duke come to Galileo's defense? Was this an announcement of new Vatican doctrine? Or the mere ravings of a renegade? The sermon accomplished its intent. It created a sensation that polarized opinion between the new science and traditional faith. It induced pleasure and outrage. Not an inconsiderable number were happy to see the arrogant Galileo brought down from his perch, quite apart from the merits. The head of the Pigeon League, delle Colombe, had achieved a level of success with his shadowy agent far in excess of what he had ever been able to achieve with his own writings.

Men of true stature were appalled. From Pisa, Galileo's disciple, Father Castelli, referred to Caccini as a thief and waylayer of mathematicians, but this was neither the first nor the last of such public rebukes, the Benedictine warned. Among the most horrified was Caccini's own blood brother, a cardinal's cupbearer in the Vatican, who imagined himself to be a power broker and had heard the gossip as it quickly reached Rome. "It may come to pass that you'll regret ever having learned to read," the brother said in disgust. "You could have done nothing more annoying to the high authorities here, up to the very highest. It is no use draping yourself with the mantle of religion, because everybody knows how you friars use such cover to indulge your ugly passions. Truly it is a great impertinence. What idiocy is this to set yourself abellowing at the behest of those nasty pigeons! Take it from me, Brother Thomas, reputation rules the world. And just as we were trying to open up a career for you through high protections. Try to think where you would like to go, because you are disliked there and here even more. If you don't find a way to move out, I shall find one for you. You have behaved like a dreadful fool."

Several days later, Galileo heard from Father Maraffi in Rome. The preacher general of the Dominicans was manifestly appalled and embarrassed by the action of one of his brothers. To Maraffi, the issue was the discipline of his own order and the abuse of the pulpit. "At the scandal, I feel infinite disgust, especially since the author is a friar of my Order," Maraffi told Galileo. "To my great regret, I am responsible for all the bestialities which 30,000 brothers have done and can do. I knew this man, Caccini, in his madness and ignorance could be manipulated, but I never would have believed such craziness as this could happen. I must be sure not to open the door, so that in future, any impertinence, which represents the fury of others, can be spoken from the pulpit."

The matter was out of Maraffi's hands. Caccini's denunciation had unleashed a great and terrible power, and it was beyond Maraffi's power and influence to stop it. For two years the warring camps had argued and intrigued, trading theories and slurs. Caccini's public outburst changed the entire picture. Though Galileo could not know it, a formal process was now initiated, one that would continue for another 18 and arguably for another 378 years.

For some time, Galileo and his friends did not appreciate the gravity of what had happened. From Father Maraffi's letter, Galileo might well conclude that the matter would soon disappear. Father Caccini was far out of bounds and would undoubtedly be disciplined by his own order. Such a reprimand might even produce a minor victory for the new science. This happy result was not going to take place of its own accord. Someone would have to make it happen.

Several days after Maraffi's communication, Galileo heard from Prince Cesi, who was becoming the political director of the counterattack. Cesi regretted that he was writing from Acquasparta, since if he were in Rome, he could deal with the crisis immediately and "with dexterity." What were they to do? Cesi saw an opportunity to make Caccini into the example of all "enemies of knowledge," all "perfidious madmen who will never keep quiet" unless they are forcibly silenced. They should work to have the blackguard disgraced and thereby issue a warning to others like him. Perhaps, the prince thought, they could persuade the archbishop of Florence to issue a public rebuke.

Their hopes for the church hierarchy soon sustained a setback, however, when the bishop of Fiesole wound his way down the mountain to Florence and in a public session broke into an angry diatribe against Galileo. The scientist's extravagant and erroneous opinions were causing great anguish among the "supreme Highnesses" in Rome, the bishop fumed, and he should stop. It was clear to Galileo that the overwrought bishop, like many other priests, had not done his scientific homework. The bishop needed to be tactfully informed, Galileo remarked drolly, that the author of this heliocentric opinion was not a living Florentine but a dead German, who printed his book seventy years ago and dedicated it to the pope.

The maneuvers behind the scenes, however, now became more important than what happened in public. The once apologetic professor of ecclesiastical history, old Father Lorini, sprang back into action. After a conclave with his Dominican brothers at the Convent of Saint Mark, he took a fateful step, which was even more significant and damaging than Father Caccini's incendiary sermon.

Lorini put the question formally before the Inquisition. His prime piece of evidence was a copy of Galileo's letter to Father Castelli fourteen months ago, his now well-known manifesto for the Copernican system, in which Galileo showed how the miracle of the sun standing still as recorded in the Book of Joshua could not lengthen the day under the Ptolemaic system but would shorten it. In his covering letter to Rome, Father Lorini denounced these Galileists for their arrogance in attempting to explain the Holy Scriptures "in their own fashion." While the Galileists were "orderly men and good Christians," they were too intent to show how clever they were. "They say a thousand shameless things and scatter them abroad in our city which holds fast to the Catholic faith," the Dominican wrote. As for his own intentions, they were pure. "I am motivated by nothing in this business but zeal for the sacred cause," he told the Inquisition.

Lorini's step was prodigious. By long-standing tradition, the Inquisition was obliged to take up any accusation that was put before it, but in this case the accusation fell on particularly willing ears. Once a charge was leveled, a careful procedure had to be followed. In the following month, both sides jockeyed for position. Through his contacts, Galileo learned of Lorini's action and that his own letter to Father Castelli was the basis of the accusation. He could scarcely be reassured by a letter from his old pupil, Father Ciampoli, that to the best of Ciampoli's knowledge, the "great rumors had not gone farther than to the ears of four or five people at most." His mistake of committing to paper his thoughts about the Joshua story—at least in so loose and casual a fashion—finally dawned on him. "New fields have been opened up to injure me," he groaned.

Belatedly, he realized the folly of allowing his private letter to Castelli to be distributed, and he resolved to rewrite his position carefully for public consumption. He suspected, correctly, that the version of his letter to Castelli that had been sent to the Inquisition had been tampered with, to his disadvantage. And so he sent an accurate copy to a Jesuit mathematician at the Collegio Romano, with the request that it be brought to the attention of his Jesuit brother, Cardinal Robert Bellarmine, still the inquisitor above all inquisitors in Rome. At this point, Galileo seemed to be genuinely dismayed that his Castelli letter was causing problems and saw the Jesuits as his best hope to stop the malice. "If mine eye offend, pluck it out," was his invitation to the Jesuits, an offer that was later accepted.

Within a few days, Galileo was reassured that he had done the right thing in capturing Cardinal Bellarmine's attention. From a separate source, it was reported that Bellarmine did not expect the work of Copernicus to be prohibited, but only to carry a cautionary warning about its hypothetical nature. With that simple caveat, Galileo would be free to discuss the theory whenever he wished.

Independently, the Inquisition was making its own devious effort to procure the original of the Castelli letter. In Pisa, the archbishop received an instruction from Rome, ordering him to obtain the original from Castelli "in a skillful manner." His Eminence immediately summoned Castelli for an audience. Making no effort to conceal his prejudices against the new science, he urged Castelli to renounce his misguided Copernican views. To do so would guarantee his salvation; to persist would ensure his ruin. All creations were made for the enjoyment of man, the archbishop intoned, and therefore, it was a matter of simple logic, as well as profound faith, as taught by the Word of God, that the earth could not be just another ordinary star among millions. Although the archbishop was convinced of his traditional view, he would do both Castelli and Galileo the courtesy of reading Galileo's letter to see if there might be something there that the archbishop had overlooked. Would Castelli kindly give him the original? (Luckily, Castelli had returned the letter to its author.)

If Castelli did not smell a poisoned rat, Galileo did. When Father Castelli conveyed the archbishop's request for the letter, Galileo stalled for time. A few weeks later he complied, but he sent an accurate copy rather than the original, and he instructed the naive Castelli not to let the document out of his hands, no matter what. True to his word, Castelli read the letter aloud to the archbishop, who promptly gave up his quest for the letter itself, having run out of clever strategies.

At this point, the Inquisition had very little to go on. It had a suspect copy of a private letter, several wild and unsubstantiated charges from a doddering traditionalist and fire-eating pastor who was the dupe of academics. But in mid-March, Father Caccini turned up in Rome, pleading as "a matter of conscience" to explain himself before the Inquisition. Until now the friar had appeared to be a scheming, cowering, Uriah Heepish type, ashamed of his controversial sermon, terrified of its implications for his future, ready to be used anew by the papal legates, just as he had been used by the Pigeon League.

Before the cardinals, however, Caccini went on the offensive. Far from retracting his charges against Galileo, he expanded them. With evident gusto, he added innuendo and rumor to his list of accusations. Galileo was alone guilty because he belonged to a certain impious Academy of Lynxes, was intimate with the godless heretic Fra Paolo Sarpi of Venice, and consorted with degenerate Germans (like Kepler?). Asked to explain his sermon at Santa Maria Novella, he said: "After I interpreted the passage concerning the answer to Joshua's prayers, with its special intention for the salvation of souls, I took the opportunity to criticize—with that modesty which befits my office—a certain view originally propounded by Nicolaus Copernicus and nowadays taught by Mr. Galileo Galilei. My charitable warning greatly pleased many educators and devout gentlemen, but it displeased certain disciples of Galileo beyond measure."

"How do you know that Galileo teaches the sun to be motionless and the earth to move?" the inquisitor asked. "Who told you this?"

"I heard this from the bishop of Cortona," Caccini replied. "I also heard this from a certain Florentine gentleman, a follower of Galilei. I do not recall this gentleman's name, but he wears priest's clothes, is about twenty-eight years old, of olive complexion, chestnut beard, average height, and sharply delineated face. He often comes to service at the Santa Maria Novella."

"Has Father Caccini ever talked to this Galileo?"

"I do not even know what he looks like."

"What is the reputation of this Galileo in the city of Florence . . . on matters of faith?"

"He is regarded as a good Catholic by many. But he is suspected by some because he is friendly with a certain Venetian who is famous for his impieties. I have heard that some of his disciples hold the following three propositions:

that God is an accident!

that God is sensuous!

that some miracles of saints are not really miracles!"

"Why is Father Caccini so hostile toward Galileo and his disciples?" the inquisitor wondered, almost out of detached curiosity.

"I have no hostility toward Galileo," Caccini replied. "I don't even know him. Nor do I have any hatred for his disciples. Rather I pray to God for them."

Despite an oath of secrecy, word of Caccini's unctuous deposition filtered back to Florence soon enough. The danger of the Dominican attack had finally registered on Galileo. The danger was not to him alone. His instinct was to head for Rome at once, confident in his connections, sure of his personal powers to persuade. But for nearly eight months, he had been suffering from yet another of his extended illnesses, and he was not fit to travel. Triumphing over this campaign against him would not worry him, he wrote to an influential friend in Rome, if he could but use his tongue instead of his pen. "If I ever get well so that I can come there, I shall do so," he wrote, "to show my great affection for the Holy Church, and my zeal that nothing shall happen from the stings of malign persons who understand nothing."

But for now, his pen was his only recourse. He turned to it with prolixity. In Rome, Cardinal Bellarmine remained the pivotal figure. Once he had seen Galileo's letter to Castelli, the cardinal had seemed to be open to persuasion. For Bellarmine, it was not the Joshua story in the Bible that concerned him but a few lines from Psalm 19:

> In the heavens hath the Lord set a tabernacle for the sun
> Which is like a bridegroom coming out of his chamber
> Rejoicing as a giant in running his course.
> His going forth is from the high heaven,
> And his circuit unto the ends of it;
> And there is nothing hid from the heat thereof.

Let Galileo explain *that* in light of Copernican theory, Bellarmine challenged.

In late March, Galileo attempted to do so. In Psalm 19, God had placed the sun in the noblest place, he replied, imbuing it with the fertilizing power of a bridegroom and the physical power of a giant to move immense distances. The highest part of the sky denoted nothing more than distance from the earth.

On and on, Galileo plunged deeper into the quagmire of biblical interpretation. Unwittingly, he was committing precisely that error of which the Dominican fathers had accused him: interpreting the Bible after his own fashion. The situation had not yet become sinister. For now the cardinal had generous intentions. He was giving Galileo every opportunity to convince him. Not long after his letter on Psalm 19, Galileo waded farther into biblical interpretation, penning his passionate letter to Grand Duchess Christine. This was meant to be his more precise reasoning on the Joshua story than his letter to Castelli, and he sanctioned its wide public distribution (although he refused to publish it). Characteristically, once he began to write, he exercised not care but extravagance. These effusions of his pen were having little effect. More important, they were building a body of evidence that would incriminate him.

With the coming of summer 1615, his health began to improve, and at last he could think about traveling to Rome. It had been four years since he had been there. His arrival, he knew, would cause a considerable stir. Not until the late fall did the preparations grow serious.

In the meantime, the Inquisition continued to take testimony. If Galileo had begun to appreciate the importance of this growing conflict, the church seemed to do so also. But on a matter of such monumental consequence the Inquisition's witnesses were laughable. It sought out no one of stature who knew Galileo well, or what he really believed—not Father Maraffi or Father Castelli or Cardinal Bellarmine, not a score of priestly scientists who had been with Galileo in Padua and Florence and Venice. The Holy Office was afraid that to call hostile witnesses (friendly to Galileo) would compromise the secrecy of its proceeding.

In mid-November the inquisitor of Florence summoned two minor priests who had been mentioned in Caccini's disgraceful testimony. Neither had any relationship with Galileo, nor were they schooled in the fine points of theology. Their sole evidence was their own gossip.

The first was one Father Ferdinando Ximenes, a forty-year-old Dominican living in the monastery of Santa Maria Novella, who instructed his brother friars in, among other things, the casuistry of conscience. Ximenes's sworn testimony began with the admission that he had never laid eyes on Galileo in the two years he had been in Florence, but he had heard that Galileo's beliefs were diametrically opposed to true doctrine. "I have heard some of his students say that God is sensuous, that He laughs and He cries, but I do not know whether this is their own opinion or that of their teacher Galileo." To any but the most conspiratorial soul, this hearsay was lame testimony, but the inquisitors listened intently and pressed on. Who was Ximenes's source of such damaging information? The answer was a minor cleric named Giannozzo Attavanti, the rector of a small parish at Castelfiorentino, southwest of Florence, who claimed to have studied with Galileo and who himself had spouted antibiblical views on the motion of the earth during one of his sessions on conscience with Father Ximenes.

"Is the Rector Attavanti knowledgeable?" the inquisitor asked.

"I know he has no grounding either in theology or in philosophy, but I detected that he has a smattering of both," Ximenes replied. "I think that he was expressing more Galileo's opinion than his own."

"Did the Father rebuke Rector Attavanti?" the inquisitor asked.

"Most instantly."

It might seem that the Inquisition was working its way down the ladder rather than up, but nevertheless it called Rector Attavanti the next day. He turned out to be a thirty-three-year-old Florentine nobleman who began his testimony by admitting never to have been a real pupil of Galileo's at all but merely to have held philosophical discussions with the master "as I ordinarily do with men of letters."

"Has Rector Attavanti ever heard Mr. Galileo say anything, in lecture or in dialogue, which was in conflict with Holy Scripture?"

"I have never heard Mr. Galilei say things that conflict with Holy Scripture or with our holy Catholic faith," the young rector said, but he had heard him argue in favor of the Copernican theory and to say that the sun does not have "progressive motion." The rector had read Galileo's book on sunspots. The inquisitor took a note. The burden of Attavanti's testimony was to recount a dormitory discussion at Santa Maria Novella, where he and Ximenes had debated the Copernican theory and the question of God's human qualities "in the manner of disputation," whereupon they had been overheard by Father Caccini, who rushed in to join the debate. For such insignificant trash, the inquisitor seemed to have an insatiable appetite.

"What has the Rector heard about Galileo's faith?" the inquisitor asked at the end of the pitiful testimony.

"I regard him as a very good Catholic," Attavanti replied generously. "Otherwise he would not be so close to these Most Serene Princes!"

Ten days later the Inquisition decided to widen its probe by examining Galileo's letter on the sunspots for heresy.

On the same day the youthful grand duke of Tuscany, Cosimo II, now twenty-five years old, sat down at his desk in the Pitti Palace to pen several diplomatic dispatches to his ambassador and to friendly members of the Medici court then serving as cardinals at the Vatican.

"Galileo, a mathematician well-known to your illustrious lordship, informs me that he feels himself deeply aggrieved by the calumnies which have been spread by certain jealous persons, to wit, that his writings contain erroneous opinions," the grand duke wrote to Cardinal Francesco del Monte. "He has asked, of his own accord to come to Rome and has asked my permission, for he has a mind to clear himself from such imputations. He wishes to speak the truth, to show his rectitude and his pious intentions." Would the cardinals please smooth the way for the first philosopher and mathematician of Tuscany?

At the same time, the grand duke ordered his ambassador to put two floors of the Villa Medici at the disposal of the ailing scientist. The staff was to respect his privacy and be aware of his indisposition. Moreover, there was to be put at his service a scribe, a servant, and, for his pleasure, a *muletta*. A diligent accounting of the charges was to be kept, since the grand duke, bestirring the banker in his blood, intended to present Galileo with a bill later.

9

THE CARDINAL'S SCOLD

On his last trip to Rome four years before, a pack of fatuous, easily ignored critics yapped at Galileo's heels. Then he had accomplished a noble mission of science: to introduce the new heaven of his telescope to the grand personages of the Eternal City. The grand duke of Tuscany had dispatched him as the flower of Florentine learning, and the Tuscan ambassador, Francesco Niccolini, had received him in Rome as the first citizen of Florence. Now his mission was more dangerous, for the accusatory sword hung over him. Not only did he want the accusation lifted, but he wanted his ecclesiastical accusers chastised. After that, he wanted the method of the new science sanctioned and blessed.

On December 3, 1615, in a mood of foreboding and petulance, Galileo set out for Rome. His reception was bound to be different this time. Niccolini had been replaced by Piero Guicciardini, a diplomat who was not nearly so captivated by Galileo and who considered this trip ill-advised.

"If Galileo stays here any length of time, he is certain to come out with some defense of his opinions," the ambassador wrote nervously. "I do not know whether he has changed his opinions nor whether his temper has improved. But I know for certain that some Dominicans who are very influential with the Holy Office bear him no good will." Then the ambassador issued a warning: "This is not the place to come to dispute about the moon," he wrote, "nor is this the time to defend novelties."

It was not in Galileo's nature, not then, anyway, to listen to nervous ambassadors or to retreat into diplomatic caution. His nature was to confront, to struggle, to overpower. The new science was rich in possibility, and it was under attack. Its very future seemed to be at stake. Religion was trespassing where it had no place, and yet, ironically, it frustrated Galileo as much as anything that his own trespassing upon religious ground had failed to persuade the prelates.

His confidence was extraordinary. He was at the height of his persuasive powers, and he rode from his citadel of enlightenment to hidebound Rome without noticing that the landscape had changed. Rome was not the capital of enlightenment but of the Counter-Reformation. To the powers there, not science but the Catholic faith was under attack. In his selective memory, Galileo remembered the warmth of his reception in Rome four years before and forgot that his honeymoon was over. His high respect and admiration for the cardinals and prelates had not diminished, however. If the priests had traipsed in droves to the Trinità dei Monti and the gardens of the Quirinal to see his novelties before, they would surely listen to his plea for scientific freedom now.

The world of Catholic thought revolved around a diminutive giant, Cardinal Robert Bellarmine. As the guardian of Holy Scripture, Bellarmine was the very soul and nucleus of Catholic theology. A Jesuit who stood no more than five feet tall, to him ultimately would fall the scriptural consequences of Galileo's observations. And Bellarmine seemed to appreciate fully what was at stake in the Galileo problem. Catholic tradition of a thousand years was not to be blithely overturned, certainly not on the basis of conjectures, surmises, or even probabilities.

If Galileo was right, how would the church even begin to reinterpret the biblical passages concerning the centrality of man and his globe? Catholic theologians of the time had virtually no idea of how to go about such a process. The new science of Galileo might require a wholly new "biblical science" for the Catholic church. To accomplish virtually overnight a new way of thinking and proceeding was not easy for a divine institution. For the cardinal, the church should approach any reappraisal of its fundamental beliefs "with great circumspection" and not proceed at all until it was absolutely necessary. A precipitous reinterpretation could undermine the Catholic tradition.

The church would wait for proof, and until it came, even an effort to show how Scripture might square with the Copernican cosmology would be considered heretical. About eight months before Galileo undertook this trip to Rome, a prelate in Calabria named Paul Anthony Foscarini had written a book that attempted to show how the Copernican view might be made compatible with Holy Scripture. Foscarini was an estimable personage. He was the head of the Carmelites in Naples, a professor of theology at the University of Messina, and clearly versed in scientific principles. His book was a well-intentioned effort to protect the church from the scandal of backwardness.

But the church was not grateful, and Bellarmine himself wrote a long and important letter of explanation to the Carmelite. (Eventually, Foscarini's book would be prohibited as erroneous, and it would be placed on the Index.) At the outset, Bellarmine had seemed to be complimentary. He coupled the Carmelite with Galileo and seemed to praise them both for proceeding cautiously. So long as the Copernican view was treated as supposition and hypothesis, Bellarmine declared, it was acceptable to debate the theory and even to write about it. But to argue for its truth in reality was contrary to the precepts of the Council of Trent. Scripture could not be reinterpreted differently from the common belief of the Holy Congregation.

"When there shall be a real demonstration that the Sun stands in the center of the universe, and that the earth revolves around it," Bellarmine had written, "it will then be necessary to proceed with great caution in explaining those passages of Scripture which appear contrary to this." In other words, until there was irrefutable proof of the Copernican system, the biblical view of man's centeredness must prevail. As scientists gazed at the stars with ever-improving instruments, Bellarmine meant to hang on to the Old Testament text of Solomon: "The sun rises and sets and returns to his own place."

Galileo would hear of Bellarmine's letter to Foscarini only through the rumor mill and had to draw his own conclusions. What standard of scientific truth would ever satisfy the Holy Congregation? When did speaking hypothetically amount to advocacy? When did scientific theory ever achieve absolute proof?

There were no answers to these questions. And because there were no answers, the effect was to paralyze Galileo and all practitioners of the new science. If their hypothetical musings went overboard when judged against some standard they could only guess at, the personal consequences were truly terrible.

As a scientist, Galileo could not pursue his work without some operating belief about the system of the stars. His job was to test hypotheses, to argue for his beliefs on the basis of accumulating sensory evidence. Hypotheses were to be accepted or rejected by experiment, and his observations through his telescope had destroyed the Aristotelian, the Ptolemaic, and, for that matter, the biblical hypothesis of the heavens. If he had not yet proven the Copernican view, he knew in his heart to be true. He could achieve a more compelling degree of proof only through further inquiry, debate, and publishing. The very process of scientific inquiry was now in jeopardy.

Counterarguments to well-grounded scientific propositions would always exist, Galileo knew. "If proponents of a proposition were to have no more than ninety percent of the arguments on their side, they would still be rebutted," he remarked.

In Bellarmine, Galileo would be facing a man of firm and secure beliefs, who was quite ready to back up these beliefs with action. To him the Bible had been dictated by God, and this revealed truth was to be taken literally. When in Ecclesiastes it is written, "Alone I encircled the vault of the sky," or when Solomon proclaims, "The sun circles through the meridian," Bellarmine did not see room for interpretation. Thirty years before, in 1586, the Jesuit had published the foremost intellectual attack on the Protestant Reformation, entitled "Disputation Against the Heretics of Our Times," and thereafter, he was often in the front line of theological battle. He had been the cardinal inquisitor in the trial of Giordano Bruno and had sanctioned Bruno's execution. Ten years before, in 1606, when Venice and Paolo Sarpi had challenged the pope's authority, Bellarmine had spearheaded the counterattack. Just as the theologian was ready to celebrate the common belief, so he was ready to punish departures from it. "How great must be God's hatred of crimes and evil deeds committed by men?" he wrote with the burning passion of an inquisitor.

Galileo needed to be wary, but as yet he knew only good things about the cardinal. He remembered how moved Bellarmine had been at the sight of Jupiter's moons and how correct he had been to seek the advice of the Jesuit mathematicians before he lent his support. Here was a man whom Galileo could treat as an equal. As equals, they would surely come to an accommodation.

Moreover, Galileo had heard a story about Bellarmine that pleased him. After Galileo's visit to Rome in 1611, Bellarmine had made it a point to fix a sundial (a faulty one, it turned out) in his garden. Galileo turned this minor episode into a sign that the joys of science had infatuated Bellarmine. Moreover, the cardinal was reportedly becoming quite the amateur astronomer. He was even conducting some simple experiments of his own.

In these quaint stories Galileo saw the harbingers of future good fortune. He would make the great Bellarmine his ally and let him harness the bigots among his brothers in Christ. Indeed, in his letter to Grand Duchess Christine, Galileo had written a passage about the Copernican theory that was a veiled appeal to Bellarmine. "If the opinion is proven to be true, I have no doubt that those theologians, who previously regarded the theory as incapable of being consistent with Scripture, would quickly find new interpretations that would agree very well." Then, with a flourish of wit, he added, "especially if they would add some knowledge of astronomical science to their knowledge of divinity." Such presumption might just anger rather than amuse Bellarmine.

The year before Galileo came to Rome, Cardinal Bellarmine had published a little book entitled *The Mind's Ascent to God by a Ladder of Created Things*. It was, perhaps, not the most catchy title, but the book had achieved a measure of popularity. To Bellarmine, man's ascent to heaven was a series of steps, the seventh of which was the contemplation of the heavens. "Rise thou up a little higher, if thou canst, my soul," he had written. "As thou observest the great splendor of the sun, the beauty of the moon, the number and variety of the other luminaries, the wonderful harmony of the heavens and the delightful movement of the stars, consider this: what it will be to see God above the heavens, as it were a sun, swelling in the light which no man can approach!"

This last reference came from the first book of Timothy, 6:14–16. For the battle with Galileo that was coming, however, the previous verses of Timothy's sixth chapter were more apt. They speak of the duty to teach God's doctrine and not to blaspheme it. "If any man teach otherwise . . . he is proud, knowing nothing but doting about questions and strifes of words, whereof cometh envy, strife, railings, evil surmisings." And then a biblical warning: "Perverse disputings of men of corrupt minds, destitute of truth, supposing that gain is godliness: from such withdraw thyself."

Who in this approaching storm were the men of corrupt minds? Who were engaged in evil surmising? What persons were destitute of truth?

Bellarmine regarded his book as an oblique answer to Galileo's letter to Christine. No evidence exists that Galileo read Bellarmine's book, for he was not much of a reader outside his field. Had he done so, he might have learned about the kind of childlike "scientific experiments" Bellarmine was conducting. With decidedly unusual methodology, the priest was making mathematical calculations about the speed of the sun's revolution around the earth. "At the beginning of the sun's setting, I begin to recite the psalm 'Misere mei Deus,' and I have scarce read it twice through than the whole sun has set," he wrote. "So in that short space of time, the sun must traverse a distance much greater than seven thousand miles. If we say that the body which moves so quickly is a mass greater than the whole earth and accomplishes this swift movement without break or fatigue, certainly a person with any sense at all must admire the infinite power of the Creator."

During his first weeks back in Rome, Galileo installed himself again in the grandeur of the Villa Medici, above the rooftops of the city on the eastern hill. Except for the complaints of the grudging Tuscan ambassador, it seemed like old times for Galileo. Burnishing old friendship, he picked up his relationships with important cardinals. With his wit and his brilliance he once again cast his spell. In the great houses of Rome, he held court, laying before transfixed audiences his concept of the universe. As a general rule, he put forward the Ptolemaic theory first, before he put forward all the arguments about why it could not be true. As an accomplished speaker, he knew how to use humor to keep his audience. "Your Lordship would enjoy Galileo's discourses immensely," Father Antonio Querengo, a friend of Galileo's, wrote to Cardinal Alessandro d'Este at Modena, who greatly venerated Cardinal Bellarmine. "He turns the laugh against all his opponents, answering their objections in such a way as to make them look perfectly ridiculous." Cardinal d'Este might not be laughing.

Just before the new year, Galileo fell into a long conversation about the tides with Cardinal Alessandro Orsini, whom he considered one of his warmest friends in the Roman Curia. Related to the Medicis through his mother, Orsini was a member of a powerful Roman family and had received the cardinal's hat only two weeks before. Orsini was so impressed with Galileo's ideas about the sea's ebb and flow, particularly their relation to the motion of the earth, that he asked the scientist to commit his notions to paper. Ten days later, on January 8, 1616, after diligent work at the Villa Medici, Galileo dispatched his "Discourse on the Tides" to Saint Peter's. He regarded it as a sketch, a preliminary statement of belief that might later be challenged by more exact observations of the tides, for it was clear that he was already contemplating his masterwork. That later work would be a comprehensive treatment of the tides, perhaps even the central point in a passionate advocacy of the Copernican theory. A more complete manifesto, together with a refutation of opposing positions, would have to wait for his *Dialogue Concerning the Two Chief World Systems*.

By the end of January, it began to dawn on Galileo that he was not having such an easy time of it. Gradually, his friends at the Vatican became more circumspect in their dealings with him. News of what was happening in the Holy See became harder to come by. Priests made him aware that by continuing to talk to him, they could run a "grave risk." He recruited third parties to act as intermediaries to the principals. This too proved unsatisfactory. He longed to confront Bellarmine, but Bellarmine was not ready for him. At length, he resorted to putting his position on paper, because, as he wrote to the Tuscan secretary of state, Curzio Picchena, "In many quarters, people are more ready to yield to dead writing than to living speech, for the former permits them to agree or dissent without blushing."

Finally, in early February, there seemed to be a break. He was informed that he had been exonerated of the scurrilous charges brought by the Dominican priest, Caccini. This favorable turn of events elated Galileo, for it accomplished what he needed to accomplish for himself. At last, he was officially innocent of "the devilish malice and injustice" of his persecutors. Even the detestable Caccini himself slithered up to the iron gates of the Villa Medici to protest his goodwill and offer his apology. Galileo's loathing was evident. "In the first half hour in which we were alone, he tried, very humbly, to excuse what he had done, saying he was ready to give me satisfaction," Galileo wrote later to Picchena. "Then he tried to make me believe that he was not the engine behind his acccusation. At last he tried to dissuade me from what I know for sure." Galileo dismissed the worm, declaring him to be ignorant and full of venom.

Had he been concerned only with himself, he might, at that moment, have packed and left. He would have been well advised to do so. But he perceived a larger responsibility to the cause of science. Scientists throughout the Catholic dominion hung on the results of this mission, for they stood ready to declare themselves on the Copernican opinion, if only it were safe to do so. Galileo asserted that, "In the conviction that my assistance may be of use in the investigation of the matter, since I know those truths which are proved by science, I cannot neglect nor should I neglect to offer assistance. I shall follow the dictates of my conscience and Christian zeal." He would stay and confront the issue with the church. It was one of the great mistakes of his life.

As Galileo waited, the Vatican's consideration of the new science ground methodically to a close. For some weeks, eleven "qualifiers" or "consulters" had been meeting about the Copernican problem, which was fast becoming the Galileo problem. The experts possessed many grand titles: the master of the sacred apostolic palace, the commissary of the

Holy Office, the vicar general of the Dominican order. They were skilled in the queen of all science, theology, but untutored in mathematics or astronomy. The panel consisted of six Dominicans, a Jesuit, and an Irish priest. Solemnly, after serene reflection, they put forward their disastrous opinion.

As to whether the sun was the center of the universe, "this proposition is foolish and absurd and formally heretical," since it contradicted the "sense of the Holy Scripture."

As to whether the earth is not the center of the world, nor motionless, but moves with diurnal motion, that proposition is likewise foolish and absurd in philosophy and "erroneous in faith."

For the rigid and dull-witted Pope Paul V, there was no need to question the qualifications or the judgment of his expert panel. Indeed, if the judgment of such a panel was a foregone conclusion, so was its sanction by this narrow-minded pope. The entire machinery of the Vatican had been harnessed behind the effort to snuff out the new science. This meant that no one person, most especially the pope himself, would bear the praise for the moment or the condemnation of history. In the treatment of this monumental embarrassment to the Roman Catholic church, historians over the centuries have overlooked the role of the pope and have concentrated on Cardinal Bellarmine. But the pope had chosen his panel, and now he certified their opinion. He was, therefore, ultimately responsible for this error.

On February 25 the Inquisition met. The minutes of the meeting are clear: Pope Paul V formally ordered Cardinal Robert Bellarmine to call Galileo before him and to warn him about the Copernican opinion. He was not to teach or defend or even discuss it. If he objected to the judgment, he was to be imprisoned. Cardinal Bellarmine became the messenger of this papal order.

One might hope that on the eve of executing this terrible injunction, Cardinal Bellarmine prayed long and deeply. But there is no hint of ambivalence. For him, truth was known. It did not have to be discovered. A proper commission had reaffirmed the truth, and the Holy Father had ratified its finding. Rather, sacred truth needed to be defended against all who were in error. When a famous man was in error, it was all the more important that he be instructed against wickedness that might infect many. The new science had become a pestilence.

Bellarmine took the third vow of his ordination seriously—indeed, he had even written a tract on blind obedience. To him it was a supreme virtue. He also had written about the infallibility of the pope, as the supreme head of the Catholic church and as the direct successor to Saint Peter. His notion was not absolute. A pope could err, even when he consulted with his advisers, as Pope Paul V was doing on Galileo, so long as the issue did not deal directly with doctrine or the collective morality of the faithful. On these questions of dogma and morals, the pope was, according to Bellarmine's credo, always right.

Where did the Galileo case fit into this debate? The Copernican issue was not a question of dogma or morals. The pope could not fall into heresy himself by condemning the Copernican theory, only into a kind of historical disgrace.

For Bellarmine, the matter had become procedural, almost clerical. Even if he believed that the pope and his consulters were wrong about Galileo, he believed as an article of faith that it was his duty to obey. Only one question remained for Bellarmine: How difficult would Galileo be? If he was obstreperous and argumentative, he would have to be sternly reprimanded and warned. But if he was gentle and compliant, a simple explanation of church policy would be sufficient.

On the morning of February 26, 1616, Cardinal Bellarmine received Galileo with formal courtesy. In these two men, representing two distinct and contrary truths, embodying the best of science and the best of faith, the contrast was great even in their physical presence. Virile and in his prime, Galileo was large, stocky, and overpowering, with a round, jovial face and a vaguely unkempt appearance. His voice boomed. His speech was rich and overblown. By nature, he was passionate and theatrical, easily moved to rage and to laughter.

Bellarmine, by contrast, was small and delicate, quiet and reflective. At age seventy-three, twenty years older than Galileo, his life was nearing its end. In his diction he tended toward understatement. Meticulous in his dress, with a sharp, well-groomed brown goatee and a twinkle in his eye, he had an intellectual's appreciation for the scientist and his work. But that did not sway him from his purpose.

They got down to business. Cardinal Bellarmine stated the official position: The Copernican opinion was erroneous, and Galileo was ordered to abandon it—if, indeed, it was true that he held the opinion. Then Bellarmine turned to the inquisitor at his side. As the vicar of punishment, the inquisitor general pronounced upon the consequences of disobedience. If Galileo put up a fuss, the church was ready to treat any obstinacy firmly. The inquisitor was more specific than the cardinal: The opinion that the sun stands still in the center of the universe and that the earth moves must be abandoned. Galileo was "not to hold, teach, or defend it in any way whatever, either orally or in writing." Otherwise, the Holy Office would bring formal charges against him.

Galileo understood what that meant. At the worst, it could be the fires of the Campo dei Fiori or the rope at the Bridge of Sant'Angelo. Somewhere in the middle lay "rigorous examination." Under the circumstances of widespread heresy abroad and agitation in Italy, no light sentence could be imagined. The document with the special injunction reads: "The same Galileo acquiesced and promised to obey."

For more than 350 years that document, the description of the February 26 meeting between Galileo and Bellarmine, has been the subject of a historical dispute. The document was not signed by Bellarmine or by the Dominican vicar general or by any clerk or scribe who had been present. The fact that the document was not witnessed and signed in the proper way has led some modern historians to consider the document a forgery, written later and placed in Galileo's Inquisition file to bolster the church's case against him. This is now largely discounted. The real truth lies in Galileo's demeanor that day: before Bellarmine he was submissive and respectful, and therefore did not have to be formally and sternly reprimanded. The report of the meeting was not so much a legal warning as an internal memorandum for the file.

The questions are twofold: How did Galileo really view his meeting with Bellarmine? And how would he remember it? Unquestionably, however docile he may have appeared to Bellarmine, he emerged from the Holy Office in a petulant mood. He was looking for any excuse to disbelieve or ignore what Bellarmine had told him. He might well have concluded that any such oral warning had to be sanctioned by a formal written edict of the church, before it became truly valid. He would wait to see if that formal written language was as sweeping as Bellarmine's oral presentation.

In the days immediately after the Bellarmine meeting, the salon of the Villa Medici was charged with emotion. Cardinals and princes alike tried to calm Galileo's rage. The Tuscan ambassador, Guicciardini, also sought to quell his anger, even suggesting that if only Galileo would hold his troublesome views secretly "without using so much violence to force others to hold them," he would be free to pursue his science unharried. But Galileo would not be appeased, certainly not by a diplomat. The ambassador was exasperated.

"We all fear that his coming here is going to prove prejudicial and dangerous for him," the ambassador wrote home. "He sets more store by his own opinion than by the advice of his friends. He gets hotly excited about these views of his, and he has an extremely passionate temper, with little patience and prudence to keep it in control. It is this irritability that makes the skies of Rome very dangerous for him."

The ambassador's dispatch indicated that, at least in Galileo's mind, nothing was settled or final. Clearly, Galileo was paying no attention to the diplomat. So Guicciardini had called Cardinal Orsini to the Villa Medici, in the hope that Galileo's best friend in the papal court could talk some sense into his stubborn guest. Orsini, in turn, spoke directly to Pope Paul V, who gave neither Galileo nor his messenger any comfort. Indeed, the pope charged the cardinal with the duty to dissuade Galileo of his views. Immediately afterward, the pope summoned Bellarmine, perhaps to wonder why the cardinal had not put the question to rest. Together, they agreed yet again that Galileo's Copernican view was erroneous and heretical. So why couldn't Galileo get it through his thick head? Nothing was settled, and the process of dissuasion needed to go on.

Meanwhile, the question had finally been put to the General Congregation of Cardinals. On March 3, Bellarmine had reported to them officially that he had admonished Galileo to abandon his opinion and that Galileo had "submitted." In addition, Bellarmine conveyed an order of Pope Paul V to the Congregation: The work of Copernicus was to be placed on the Index of Prohibited Works, and this was to be formally announced by the master of the palace. Once again, the Roman Catholic pontiff, not his underlings, was directing the process.

Two days later, on March 5, the formal edict of the Vatican was published. From Galileo's viewpoint, its most noteworthy aspect was what it did not say. It made no mention of Galileo Galilei, of his published work or his private opinions, while it did prohibit the written works of two churchmen who had advocated the heliocentric view in print and espoused it as truth. Rather, its focus was on Copernicus. "It has come to the knowledge of the Sacred Congregation that the false Pythagorean doctrine, namely concerning the movement of the Earth and immobility of the Sun, taught by Nicolaus Copernicus, and altogether contrary to Holy Scripture, is already spread about and received by many persons. Therefore, lest any opinion of this kind insinuate itself to the detriment of Catholic truth, the Congregation has decreed that the works of Nicolaus Copernicus be suspended until they are corrected."

The March 5 decree is the crucial moment in the whole saga known as the Galileo affair. More than the inconclusive and unclear meeting with Bellarmine the week before, and more than the Galileo trial seventeen years later, this was the act that established the reputation of the Roman Catholic Church as antiscience and anti-intellectual. It is this fatal misstep from which the church has been trying to recover for 378 years.

For Galileo, this became the operative document. It superseded his February 26 meeting with Bellarmine, both in its force and in his own memory. He would remember this edict sixteen years later, as the formal, written, and promulgated action of the church, and he would forget about his meeting with Bellarmine. Not until his trial in 1633 would he see anything written that enjoined him from teaching, holding, or espousing the Copernican view. How could he be privy to secret memoranda about him in the secret files of the Holy Office? He could know only the church's formal published pronouncements. Yet, sixteen years later, he would be tried and convicted on the basis of secret rather than public documents.

From this point forward, Galileo lived under a massive delusion about his situation. From the pope to Bellarmine, the church itself contributed substantially to this delusion. It was as if they had been tough on him for a few sessions, perhaps to scare him a little, and now they were going to be lenient. To Galileo, Copernicus, not he, had become the ultimate target of the church's inquiry. The upshot of all this had been the minor requirement to correct ten lines of Copernicus's masterwork, *De Revolutionibus*. To be sure, Galileo had endured a traumatic and even dangerous month in Rome, but he had escaped formal censure. Or so he thought.

A day after the edict, Galileo's calm satisfaction was evident. As usual, he blamed his enemies for the recent fulminations, but to him the wisdom of the church had finally prevailed. To the grand duke's right-hand man, he wrote dismissively about the minor corrections that would have to be undertaken to the preface of Copernicus's book, where the assertion is made that nothing of the heliocentric view was contrary to Holy Scripture. "I have no interest in the matter and should not have troubled myself about it, had not my enemies drawn me into it," he wrote. To Galileo, the matter had reduced itself to a detail, an annoyance. So minor had been the final result of these discussions that he wrote: "I did not write to you, most revered sir, by the last post, because there was nothing new to report. They were about to come to a decision about this affair as a purely public one, not affecting my personal interests." And then, with a characteristic view of his own noble intentions, he went on: "It may be seen from my writings in what spirit I have always acted, and I shall continue to act, so as to shut the mouth of malice, and to show that a saint could not have shown more reverence for the church nor greater zeal than I have done."

Galileo, the saint? The important point was his grand view of himself. If through this difficult period he equated his conduct with saintly behavior, he had good reason. At no point had he questioned the authority or the wisdom of the church. A lesser man, certainly a less devout one, certainly Giordano Bruno, would easily have slipped into a contempt for church authority. But that was not Galileo.

A few days after the formal edict Pope Paul V received Galileo for nearly an hour. Once again Galileo was obedient and respectful toward this pontiff, for to Galileo, regardless of the pope's limitations, he was the successor to Saint Peter. The audience was "most benign," and the pope was kindly and forbearing. Cardinal Bellarmine may well have suggested and arranged the meeting. Once cautioned, Galileo was now to be assuaged and reassured. For all its gentle purpose, this gentleness only muddled the message of the church and further encouraged Galileo in his grand delusion. In the light of history, it amounted to entrapment. How was Galileo to bear in mind Bellarmine's February 26 verbal admonition in the face of these comforting flatteries?

To the Tuscan secretary of state in Florence, Galileo conveyed the generous compliments the pope had heaped upon him, the praise of his "uprightness and sincerity of mind," the assurances of the pope's "greatest goodwill" and "affection." "When I gave evidence of being still somewhat anxious about the future, owing to my fear of being pursued with implacable hate by my enemies, he consoled me and said that I should put away all care, because I was held in so much esteem both by himself and the whole congregation of cardinals. They would never lend their ears lightly to calumnious reports." As long as he lived, Galileo was safe, Pope Paul assured him . . . as long as he remained submissive.

At this point, Galileo should have gotten out of town. But he hung on in Rome for another three months. Nothing more was to be done to help his own cause or the cause of science. Indeed, only further damage was possible. To be sure, his friends, especially Prince Cesi and his fellow Lynxes, gathered at Cesi's palace on the Via Maschera d'Oro to denounce the church's edict against science and to state publicly their solidarity with Galileo. No one noticed.

* * *

The Counter-Reformation had confronted the Renaissance, and the Counter-Reformation had won a disastrous victory. The new science had been badly harmed, and it would not recover in Italy for several hundred years. Indeed, some mark the decline of Italy in European affairs from this point. The issue was more than historical. Science and faith clashed, and in their terrible conflict, the two were severed, to continue in divergent directions and to lose their common ground. In its insistence on the total victory of theology, the Catholic church branded itself to the modern day as antiscience and obscurantist. It is still struggling to overcome the curse of 1616. And science, fearing the spiritual, became increasingly dry and bloodless, to the point that even the most fantastic discoveries in today's heavens have lost the power to move the soul and the spirit of mortals.

While Galileo tarried in Rome, Cardinal Bellarmine struggled to explain the church's action. The Jesuit theologian had placed himself at the vortex of a historical tragedy and had tainted his personal reputation. His warning to Galileo would forever overshadow anything else in his saintly career. As historian Richard Westfall has pointed out, he was a prisoner not only of his life's work and of his worldview, but also of his age. For so great a mind to have seen the new science as a menace rather than a glory to man and of God was tragic. To Bellarmine, the new science was akin to Protestantism. They had become the two equally insidious and dangerous enemies of his beloved church and to the truth of Scripture as he knew it. They had to be crushed.

Two months after the edict, his lingering presence in Rome had made Galileo a downright annoyance and an outright embarrassment. Ambassador Guicciardini was so fed up with Galileo's provocative actions that he wrote to the grand duke: "Galileo seems disposed to emulate the monks in obstinacy and to contend with personages who cannot be attacked without ruining oneself. We shall soon hear at Florence that he has madly tumbled into some abyss or other."

He had to be ordered out of Rome. On May 23, in a letter from the Tuscan secretary of state who was representing the views of the grand duke, the order was issued. It was couched in elegant and sprightly language, but there was no mistaking its message. The monks were all-powerful. Galileo must not "tease the sleeping dog further," for there were "rumors we do not like."

Reluctantly, Galileo packed his bags. Before he left, however, he insisted on making one thing clear: He had come to Rome voluntarily.

He had not been formally charged with error by the church. He had not been forced to abjure any beliefs whatever. And in no way had he been punished by the church. Galileo's whinings about his malicious enemies could verge on paranoia. But it was true that in Rome and Florence the rumors about what had happened to him at the Vatican were rife.

On May 26, therefore, he paid a call on the only man who could lay these rumors to rest, Cardinal Robert Bellarmine. To the Vatican, Galileo carried with him well-meaning but misinformed letters in which friends sent their condolences at his formal rebuke by church authority. Galileo was horrified at this misimpression and its wide dissemination. Bellarmine was sympathetic and readily agreed to write a letter of reassurance.

It began with the royal "we": "We, Robert Cardinal Bellarmine . . . " After it dismissed all the calumnies that were floating about concerning dire reproaches and punishments, the cardinal stated the truth of the matter: The opinion of the Sacred Congregation had simply been conveyed to Galileo that the Copernican view was contrary to Holy Scripture and could not be defended or held. That, as His Eminence put it, was "all that happened." Bellarmine's declaration was broad and comprehensive. There had been no abjuration in Rome or any other place for Copernican views or any other doctrines. Certain additions and deletions in the original letter showed an intention on Bellarmine's part to make Galileo's absolution as total as plain language could make it.

Later, this letter was of immense value to Galileo. It would become a prime exhibit in his defense sixteen years later. It would be put together with several other letters of support from cardinals of note, who testified to Galileo's "highest reputation" with the College of Cardinals. While Galileo was surely glad for this praise, it did not assuage his bitterness.

"Of all the hatreds," he wrote upon leaving Rome on June 4, "none is greater than that of ignorance against knowledge."

10

GLOOM AT BELLOSGUARDO

In the spring of 1617 Galileo took up residence in a princely palace called Bellosguardo, on a hill west of Florence. As its name suggests, it had a splendid view across the Arno valley to the city of dreams and flowers, of Dante and Boccaccio and Petrarch and now of himself. From its walled grounds, Galileo and his disciples had observed the sky before, and in his hypochondria, he imagined that its rarefied night air would be healthy for his nocturnal vigils. "Don't expose yourself to the night air," Sagredo had warned him about the extremes and the dampness of Florence's weather. "Let Mars and Jupiter go their own ways. Pay attention to your health, and quit wasting your energy answering ignorant philosophers." Affectionately, Galileo ignored the scold.

In choosing to rent Bellosguardo, he was influenced by the closeness of his daughters, Virginia and Livia, who were now sixteen and fifteen years old respectively. As illegitimate children with no chance for respectable marriage, they were entering the Franciscan Convent of Saint Matthew in the hilltop village of Arcetri. This long-awaited admittance of his daughters into the religious life ended four years of finagling, in which Galileo had tried, without success, to get the girls placed in a convent before the "canonial age" and to avoid a doubling of the dowry to the church that such a special dispensation would involve. Since they were at last married to Christ, in the order of the Poor Clares, they were taking the new names of Sister Maria Celeste and Sister Arcangela.

Galileo was particularly fond of his elder daughter, Maria Celeste. As she grew to maturity in the years ahead, she would become more of a support than he could now imagine. Bearing flowers, he would beat a frequent path across the hilltops to their cloister door.

At the price of one hundred crowns per year, he rented Bellosguardo for five years—he would stay fourteen—and he put his mind immediately to its grounds, planting the manor fields with beans, chickpeas, lentils, and an abundance of wheat. His friends celebrated his splendid new circumstance as the just desserts of true genius. From Venice, Sagredo wished him well with a Latin maxim: *Vivere et laetari: Hoc est enim donum Dei* (Live and enjoy: This is a gift from God). The earthy, free-living poet Girolamo Magagnati also wrote from Venice, but more drolly. Of the view from Galileo's "porch," the poet had a certain "dishonest envy" and a "great itch" to come for a visit. By comparison, the view from his modest little porch over the Grand Canal paled perhaps, but still he drank "a toast to the gondoliers who go up and down" and had even "sacrificed a few glasses of fine, cold liquor and spumante in salute to you, which, God willing, has advanced your health a little." Tongue still in cheek, Magagnati reported that his muse was dispirited and ashamed, thinking she was a rogue and a cheat, for one of her ribald verses had been sent to a powerful prince and cardinal in Venice, Don Carlo Cardinal de' Medici, and had been greeted with a disapproving silence.

Galileo was in no mood to enjoy jokes about disheartened muses and stony silence. Through 1617 and most of 1618, he lived in grand isolation, frustrated at being unable to speak out on dangerous subjects, constrained, even in his private correspondence, from addressing his central passion. With the fitful movements of a driven man, he moved to the second rank of his interests. Safe questions could sustain him temporarily: magnets and motion, the condensation of water, the perfection of the microscope, even eventually flood control, the price of horses, and the probabilities in a roll of dice. But not for long.

There was, however, one area of astronomy that fell outside the holy injunction of 1616. For more than three years he had been convinced that the regular movements of his Jovian satellites could serve as an aid to navigators, especially in establishing a ship's longitude. He began to tabulate the movements of his Jovian system and soon came to the conclusion that his method could improve upon the current system of navigation, which could put the navigator within four degrees of his precise location. By mid-1617, he had a complete table and had his instrument maker construct a "jovilabe," a magnificently tooled and decorated brass plate with a 360-degree disc at the top, an armature connected to a smaller disc marked with the divisions of the zodiac, and tables for the positions of the four Medicean satellites.

In tandem, he invented a bizarre helmet with several protruding telescopes, which a mariner was supposed to wear aboard ship, even if it did make him look like a horned Viking. This *celatone* would enable the captain to observe the moons of Jupiter without taking his hands off the wheel. In March 1617 the device was constructed in the Arsenale of Pisa and tested in Leghorn, as Galileo stood on the deck of a warship with a group of captains.

The results were promising. When Galileo presented his findings to his longtime enemy in the Medici court, the soldier Giovanni de' Medici, he stressed its military application, arguing that his spiked helmet would enable a ship captain to spot pirate ships on the high seas sooner or distinguish friendly from enemy ships at great distance. For once the bastard prince was elated, and he sent word to Galileo that his *celatone* was a greater invention than the telescope. The helmet was soon classified as a secret weapon of war.

In the meantime, Galileo was trying to do business with the king of Spain, for Spain remained the dominant naval power in the Mediterranean and had made Tuscany a client state. A contract with the Spanish Navy for his *celatone* was sure to be lucrative. A prickly correspondence passed between the scientist and his agents in Spain about the indecision of the Spanish court. He was aware, Galileo wrote in June of 1617, that a king's ransom had been put behind "inventions" that turned out to have no importance and that the king had decided not to throw his money away again, unless he was assured of success. "I agree with that," Galileo wrote valiantly, "but it is not convenient to my reputation to endure a long and uncomfortable and expensive trip on speculation, in order to present something useful to the King, only to encounter the envy and malignity of the King's counselors." In his beneficence, he even offered to travel to Seville or Lisbon to display his device before the admirals.

There was spirited discussion in the Spanish court about the proposal. But, in the end, Philip III, hounded as he was by many eager and expensive inventors, was unwilling to spend the money on Galileo, who had requested an annual fee of two thousand crowns, twice his annual salary at the court of Tuscany.

In his disappointment, Galileo turned his attention north. For some time he had been cultivating the friendship of yet another regal benefactor, the Hapsburg ruler of the Austrian Tyrol, Archduke Leopold. Leopold was the brother-in-law of the grand duke of Tuscany, a ruler who had held two bishoprics but who would soon renounce them both to marry a Medici himself. In him, Galileo perceived a pliable noble whose scientific fascinations might be useful. In March of 1618, upon a royal visit to Florence, Leopold paid a call on Galileo at Bellosguardo.

The duke did not find Galileo in good shape. To his normal array of afflictions had been added a severe hernia, which required him to wear something akin to an iron jockstrap. Partly because of this burden, Galileo received the archduke stiff and supine in his bed, and listened indulgently as the Austrian prince plied him with eager scientific questions.

Two months later Galileo wrote to Leopold as if he were a prisoner who had been bound and gagged. To predispose the archduke to his message of frustration, a selection of gifts accompanied his letter: the very telescope, he said, with which he had been observing the heavens for the past three years as well as a copper model of his *celatone*, which artisans in Graz were to fashion to the archduke's head size. Additionally, he enclosed copies of his treatises on the tides and on the sunspots. "Since our superiors can discern higher truths where my lowly mind cannot venture, I know I must believe and obey their decisions. . . ." His enclosed letter on the sunspots was to be treated as a poem or a dream rather than an argument for the earth's motion. "Nevertheless, even poets appreciate some of their own images," and so he valued "this conceit of mine." He had placed copies of the treatises with men in high places, he told Leopold. If only, by some chance, other men in high places (someone like an archduke perhaps?) were to embrace "this fancy of mine" and "this chimera I have dreamed up," who knew what might be possible?

The subtext revealed his tortured state of mind.

On the day that Galileo wrote to Leopold in Innsbruck, only a few hundred miles away, in Prague, Protestant nobles tossed two Catholic officers of the Holy Roman Emperor out a high window, sparking a general rebellion of Protestants against Catholics and plunging other Hapsburg dominions, including Austria, into war. With this "defenestration" of Prague, the Thirty Years' War had begun.

In July Archduke Leopold replied to Galileo, thanking him for his gifts and promising to get around to his theories of the sun and the earth, when he could find an idle moment. Protestant armies were massing on his borders, and Protestant agents fomented revolt among his people. The pleasures of science would have to wait for a while.

Despite the magnificence of his surroundings at Bellosguardo, the proximity of his daughters, and the pleasures of the court, Galileo was sick and despondent for most of 1617 and 1618. The weather did not help his state of mind. Winter temperatures had plunged to frigid depths, and this was combined with an unhealthful dampness. When the same thing happened for the third winter running, in 1619, the condition produced a catastrophic crop failure, which depressed the critical Florentine wool trade and the economy in general.

The torment of Galileo's frequent bouts of fever and of groin and arthritic pain was working on his mind as well. Melancholy and hypochondria gripped him. With the approach of spring in 1618, however, his health improved and his spirits lifted. As a reward to himself, he planned a taxing pilgrimage some three hundred miles over the Apennines, through narrow mountain passes and over rough roads to the Holy House of Loreto, fifteen miles south of Ancona.

That this fifty-five-year-old man would undertake such an arduous journey after so long a bout of illness was testimony both to his medieval faith and to his vigor—when he was well. The Holy House at Loreto was supposed to be the Nazareth dwelling where the Virgin Mary had been born and raised. As legend had it, the humble structure had been carried through the air by angels—the reason that later Our Lady of Loreto became the patron saint of aviators—after the infidel Turks threatened it with destruction in the thirteenth century. Miraculous cures were supposed to take place within the simple walls of the shrine, and this, no doubt, was the attraction for Galileo.

The very planning seemed to invigorate him. To Prince Cesi he wrote that he was willing to swing south to Cesi's villa at Acquasparta, another several hundred miles on corduroy roads, if the prince was planning to be there, but this plan did not work. He was, however, able to pay a courteous visit to the archduke of Urbino on his return trip, after the grand duke of Tuscany had written an introduction.

Meanwhile, Prince Cesi had renewed his campaign to get the church to lift its ban on Copernican teaching. To show his openness, Cardinal Bellarmine invited Cesi to address the nature of this new, mobile heaven and to suggest how such a radical departure from accepted doctrine might be reconciled with Scripture. Had such an invitation been offered to

Galileo, it would have been a trap. But Prince Cesi's stature in Rome kept him safe, and the communication was private. When he addressed their enemies, Cesi was instinctively more diplomatic and less contemptuous than Galileo. He appreciated Bellarmine's power and had consistently warned Galileo of Bellarmine's adamancy when it came to the conflict between Copernicus and Scripture. Now, with immense erudition, Prince Cesi argued that more passages in the Bible pointed toward the fluidity of the heavens than to their fixity, especially if one examined the original Hebraic texts of the Old and New Testaments. Among other citations, Cesi relied heavily on the Book of Job, which describes the sky as a "molten looking glass." "He stretcheth out the north over the empty place and hangeth the earth upon nothing," reads the thirty-seventh chapter.

Bellarmine was not persuaded.

In late August 1618 the argument was brought back to science. On August 29, toward the hind legs of the Great Bear, a comet appeared, faintly at first, with its tail pointing south and transversing twelve degrees over the next four days toward the forepaws of the constellation. This event might have escaped popular notice, had not it been followed two months later by the appearance of two more comets. The first was dim, "a sword unfolding itself towards the spirals of Hydra," as one observer put it, moving east to west, and eventually touching the shoulder of the Centaur. Then, ten days later, a third brilliant comet appeared in the neck of the Wolf, moved toward the northern scale of the Libra, growing in intensity, and finally arrived in the constellation of Scorpion. By December 13, it was so bright that it obscured the tenth star of the Herdsman.

This could not be ignored. Like the comets of 1577 and 1604, it occasioned great popular excitement, but unlike those comets, this one could be studied with a telescope. "When three fiery brands were shining in the sky with unusual brilliance," wrote the same observer, "there was no one of such limited intelligence and dull vision that he did not direct his gaze from time to time toward them, and no one who was not amazed at that time by their unusual brilliance."

Despite the many requests for his opinion by those who flocked to his bedside, Galileo was too ill to venture into the night air. Among those who wrote was the hard-pressed Archduke Leopold in Innsbruck. "I heard about your indisposition with the greatest displeasure," Leopold wrote in a postscript. "May God grant you better health in this new year, and everything that you could want in this world." He truly was ill, but he might also have been hiding, for in the past the appearance of comets had brought out the forces of superstition and had put astronomy foursquare in conflict with theology over the fixed perfection of the heavens. Galileo could not afford to become embroiled in that issue now.

Either through indisposition or by design, he left the stage to others. Had he thought about the past, Galileo might have guessed the type of competitor who would fill the void. A powerful and talented Jesuit stepped boldly into the footlights. Father Horatio Grassi was a formidable figure, an adversary who could not easily be dismissed as a "pigeon" or a backward cleric, ossified by Aristotle or theology. Following in the footsteps of Christopher Clavius, Grassi held the chair of mathematics at the esteemed Collegio Romano, but he also was an accomplished architect who would soon be at work on designing the massive Jesuit church to be connected to the Collegio Romano and to be named the Church of Saint Ignatius, after the founder of the Jesuit order. When he was not concerned with celestial events and cathedrals, the Jesuit was at work designing an unsinkable boat.

In his first disputation on the comets of 1618, Father Grassi had appeared before a congregation of his brothers at the Collegio Romano. Reasoning falsely, but with sincerity and civility, there is no evidence that the Jesuit was out to pick a fight with anyone. The comets, he said, had even escaped the understanding of the "lynx-eyes," which was a backhanded compliment to the customary acuity of the Academy of Lynxes.

The comets looked very much like the offspring of Mercury, Grassi proclaimed. The stellar "fetuses" were not located in the upper atmosphere, he was sure, nor were they situated in the cavity below the moon. When he looked at them through his telescope, as had his brothers in Antwerp, Cologne, Paris, and Innsbruck, they had noted that the comet did not grow larger. *Ecco!* The comets were more distant than the moon and lay somewhere betweeen the moon and the sun.

Grassi's lecture at the Collegio was soon published anonymously as a pamphlet, its author being described merely as a member of the Society of Jesus, and it took its place next to a score of other pamphlets proclaiming on the subject. Proudly, the Jesuit concluded his essay with a line from Horace: "With my head exalted, I shall touch the stars."

The gossip surrounding Grassi's "Disputation" (more than its contents) commanded Galileo's attention, for the pamphlet was gaining a wide circulation in influential circles in Rome, and its arguments, particularly about the location of the comets in a Ptolemaic system, were being used to discredit the Copernican view of the universe. As Grassi's paper came under discussion, Galileo was still recovering from his latest illness, but weak and dispirited though he was, he felt an answer was necessary. He was personally in no position to give it, so one of his disciples, the attorney Mario Guiducci, stepped forward to assume the public stance. Guiducci seemed to be a good choice for several reasons. As a youth he had been educated by the Jesuits at the Collegio Romano. Recently, he had been elected as consul to the Academy of Florence. In that capacity, he had a pulpit of science. After long discussions with Galileo about the Jesuitical arguments, Guiducci began to write.

Sick or not, Galileo could not bear to stand by as a spectator in his own fight, on his own field. Soon enough he took over the project, writing the important arguments and marking up Guiducci's introductory remarks with corrections and additions, injecting some vitriol. When Guiducci finally rose before his academy, he did not attempt to disguise the real author of his remarks. His ideas had their origin "in that noble and sublime intellect which adorns the present age no less than this native land by having discovered so many marvels in the sky."

In August 1619, under Guiducci's name, the "Discourse on the Comets" was published. Taken as a whole, it was a learned and dignified scientific paper. It defended the reliability of the telescope and pondered the principles of perspective and refraction; it discoursed on the nature of fire in the universe; and it contained a long historical preamble concerning the ancient Greek view of comets. Its thrust was an attack not on the Jesuits, but on Tycho Brahe, the sixteenth-century Danish astronomer who was famous for the exactness of his pretelescopic observations. Brahe had written about the comet of 1577 in Saggitarius and had attempted a compromise between the Ptolemaic system and the contradictory data his own observations were developing. Since the Jesuits were embracing the cosmology of Brahe, Galileo seemed to understand that, in the radical departure from the old science to the new, this compromiser had to be destroyed.

As a fine literary touch, Guiducci had ended with a line from Dante, where in Purgatory, the Pilgrim was first shown the Garden of Eden. In his discourse and Galileo's, they wished only for full knowledge of that truth "Which rolls away the clouds from all your minds."

The "Discourse on the Comets" ran some forty pages. Had Galileo been able to restrain his sharp tongue, he and Father Grassi might have engaged in a useful dialogue. But he could not, and he would pay for it.

His gratuitous jabs at his opposition, like daggers in a haystack, were remembered, as his overall argument was forgotten. Guiducci had confessed himself an imitator, and Galileo's pen took over: It was better to be an honest imitator than to engage in the deceit of Apelles. Apelles and others had stolen Galileo's ideas, trying to make them their own. "With poorly colored and badly designed pictures, they have aspired to be artists, though they could not compose in skill even the most mediocre pictures." When Apelles heard that line in Vienna, he vowed bitterly to repay Galileo in the same coin. As for Grassi's main arguments, the Jesuit was embracing "mistakes," "absurdities," and "monstrosities."

With these few rapier thrusts, Galileo personalized the debate, alienated the entire Jesuit order, and ensured that a bitter counterthrust would be forthcoming. He may have thought that the Jesuits were fair game, for even within the church brotherhood, they were resented. There were clerics who enjoyed seeing these arrogant intellectuals of the church take a few hits. Galileo assumed that Cardinal Maffeo Barberini, the future Pope Urban VIII, was one of them, and he sent Barberini a copy of the discourse with the note: "Because your illustrious Reverence has frequently shown your liking for things of mine—even though of slight merit—I wanted to send you a copy." Galileo's former student and now fellow Lynx, Monsignor Giovanni Ciampoli, was already associated with Cardinal Barberini, and from Ciampoli, Galileo got his welcome response. "This attack on the Collegio Romano never ceases to please," Ciampoli wrote gleefully. "The Jesuits consider themselves deeply offended."

In Grassi, Galileo provoked a mongoose. The Jesuit was a creative mind, an excellent scholar and expert in optics, a fine writer, and a practiced infighter who set to work immediately to answer the discourse personally and acerbically. Father Grassi chose an interesting artifice: To Galileo's exploitation of Guiducci as his mouthpiece, Grassi answered in the name of "Lothario Sarsi," purportedly a pupil of Father Grassi's with an admiration for his teacher that was equal to Guiducci's admiration for Galileo.

The author turned his ire on Galileo himself. "Galileo indicated that the arguments were his brain-child. Since the lawyer, Guiducci, confessed that he was offering what he had received from the dictation of Galileo, my dispute about these matters is with the dictator, not the consul." That play on words set the tone for what followed. As a further display of literary skill, Grassi adopted a celestial image. Since one of the comets had lodged in the constellation Libra, or the Scales, he called his tract "Libra Astronomica" or "Astronomical Scales" and proposed to weigh Galileo's arguments against the truth. "I recognize the silent dominion of a new light," Grassi wrote. "It orders its light to be weighed on one scale and then the other, and on those scales, its tail is tested."

The "Libra Astronomica" was as strong in its language and as solid in its content as the "Discourse." The issue was drawn starkly between received truth and demonstrated truth. Far from abandoning his embrace of Tycho Brahe, Father Grassi touted the Dane as the only acceptable guide. "Tycho remains the only one whom we may approve as our leader among the unknown courses of stars," he wrote. "It is not safe for a pious man to assert the motion of the earth. . . . He who is dutiful will call everyone away from Copernicus and will reject and spurn his recently condemned hypothesis." When he turned on Galileo personally, he bristled. "Even with his telescope, the lynx-eyed astrologer cannot look into the inner thoughts of the mind." Galileo the astrologer? That could only wound. Grassi flailed at Galileo for "vilifying the good name of the Collegio Romano" and for calling its teachers "unskilled in logic" whose position on the comets was "worthless and supported by false arguments." In the conclusion, "Sarsi" quoted Galileo's "Discourse": "If our conclusions and demonstrations shall be false and defective, then our foundations are weak." "To that remark," Grassi wrote, "nothing need be added."

Father Grassi and the Jesuits had thrown down the gauntlet, and it was now for Galileo to decide whether he dared to pick it up. From many corners he was urged to respond, but his fellow Lynxes were the most persistent provocateurs. From Rome, the physician Johann Faber wrote that the pride of the Jesuits had to be smashed, for the brothers seemed to think that anything of perfection—like the Trojan horse—had to emanate from their school. To Prince Cesi, Faber was more blunt. In the absence of a reply, "it appears that Galileo's adversaries on the Comets are prevailing against him." Another recently initiated Lynx, a brilliant but sickly young man of letters, Virginio Cesarini, "ardently" urged a counterattack on Grassi "to redeem from the ignorant the false title of victory that they award to that composition." Like Mario Guiducci, Duke Cesarini was a product of Jesuit education, and he appreciated how tough the Jesuit fathers could be in a philosophical fight.

In early May 1620, Prince Cesi invited his two fellow Lynxes, Duke Cesarini and Monsignor Ciampoli, to his villa in Acquasparta for a strategy session. For fifteen days they debated what to do about the Jesuits, as if this had become a struggle between the Society of Jesus and the Academy of Lynxes. Finally, they decided on a two-step strategy. The Sarsi letter had to be answered quickly, but it would be better to protect the dignity of Galileo by having another write the immediate response. They should try to avoid a duel between Galileo and Grassi. Guiducci was the obvious choice, but Prince Cesi was of the opinion that Guiducci's first letter had been too acerbic. If Guiducci were to reply, the conspirators thought it wiser that he not respond directly to either the fictitious Sarsi or Father Grassi but to a third party. Since Guiducci had been educated at the Collegio Romano, he chose to write to his old professor of ethics about Sarsi's attack on his honor. This technique had been tried once before in a dispute, when Father Castelli had replied in defense of Galileo to the head of the Pigeon League, Ludovico delle Colombe, on the subject of floating bodies.

The second step of the strategy would be for a formal answer from Galileo himself.

In his letter to Galileo about their strategy session, Monsignor Ciampoli teased, "You should envy our conversation. Here we are, three enemies conspiring against your person, so you can imagine how much we joke about you, talk about your merits which are so little known and respected by me, as I think you know."

In June 1620 Guiducci produced his letter. Regrettably, it was disingenuous, burdened with overwrought anger about how his good name had been stained by Father Grassi. To accept Father Grassi's standard, Guiducci wrote in one of his better parries, was "to govern the world of letters by the rod. To depart is to be considered sinful." Guiducci professed to be hurt that his lecture to the Academy of Florence was now ascribed to Galileo rather than to himself. To show how different were their styles, the world could expect a reply from Galileo himself in the near future, he proclaimed.

For more than two years Galileo vacillated. All around him, epic forces swirled in countervailing directions, adding to his hesitation. Only two weeks after the gathering of the Lynxes at Acquasparta, the Inquisition formally banned Copernicus's *De Revolutionibus* (until it was corrected) and banned Kepler's *Epitome of Copernican Astronomy*. Kepler had worse difficulties closer to home: His aged mother was accused of witchcraft and threatened with the stake. And yet he persisted. In 1619 he completed *Harmony of the World*, a wild, soaring mix of geometry, music, astrology, philosophy, and astronomy in which was buried his

Third Law of Planetary Motion. In the introduction to its Fifth Book, he confessed to have given himself over to "holy raving." "Behold. I have cast the dice," he exclaimed. "I am writing a book either for my contemporaries or for posterity. It is all the same to me. It may wait a hundred years for a reader, since God has also waited six thousand years for a witness."

Galileo could never have written such a thing. Holy raving was precisely what had caused Giordano Bruno to burn. And Galileo did not have a hundred years to wait for his revolution. He wished to write not for posterity but for the here and now. Still, he wavered.

Kepler had finished his *Harmony of the World* amid the cacophony in his streets. The Protestant rebellion in Prague had brought general warfare in Central Europe. Kings, princes, and nobles such as Archduke Leopold, Philip III of Spain, Doge Antonio Priuli of Venice, Maurice of Orange, and the elector of Cologne, with whom at different times and places Galileo had consorted on astronomy, were getting drawn into the conflict.

With the defenders of the true faith under armed attack across Europe and the Vatican taking more and more of an active role, what hope could Galileo have for an openness to new ideas in Rome? As Protestant armies moved successfully on Catholic strongholds, often the first demand of the rebels was for the expulsion of the militant Jesuits. In Prague the great Jesuit cathedral was desecrated, and the Protestant leaders had the Catholic relics burned for firewood. Leopold's older brother, Ferdinand II, the Holy Roman Emperor of Germany, was being derided as that "silly Jesuitized soul." With the Society of Jesus under attack, why should Galileo lunge at an already wounded animal?

But in 1620 the fortunes of the Catholic church, and the Jesuit order, began to improve, as the Protestant forces declined and Catholic armies were mobilized in Bavaria and Flanders. The news of the desecration of Jesuit churches inflamed Catholic fervor. When an army of twenty-five thousand troops of the Catholic League under Ambroglio Spinola crossed the Austrian border from Bavaria in July, with its twelve largest cannons named after the Holy Apostles, Jesuit priests marched in front. The religious war came to a head on November 8, when at the Battle of White Mountain outside Prague the Protestant army was routed. The news of the victory rang church bells throughout the Catholic world, and the choirs sang "Saul hath slain his thousands, and David his ten thousands."

Would a triumphant Catholic church be more open to the new science? Galileo might have asked, or would it lead to a witch-hunt? What would be the attitude of the militant Jesuits in the flush of military victory? And what would be their influence on Pope Paul V? Was this the moment to provoke an intellectual war with the Jesuits? It was prudent to wait and see. Not to miss a chance to ingratiate himself to a new hero, Galileo sent lenses for a telescope to Spinola, so that the Catholic generalissimo might see heretical rebels more clearly at a distance on the holy battlefield.

Early in 1621 the political situation around Galileo changed once again. On January 16, at a celebration for the victory at White Hill, Paul V died abruptly of apoplexy. Galileo could be satisfied that a tyrant was dead. Paul was succeeded by a gentle but ailing old man, Gregory XV, who would consolidate the gains of the Counter-Reformation in southern Germany over the next two years and encourage missionary zeal by establishing the Congregation of the Propaganda. In Gregory's brief pontificate, the standing of the Jesuits rose, as the pope canonized two Jesuit saints, Ignatius Loyola and Francis Xavier. During that celebration an epic opera was staged called *Apotheosis of Saints Ignatius Loyola and Francis Xavier*. The librettist was Father Horatio Grassi.

Two other important figures in Galileo's life passed from the scene during this period. On February 28, 1620, Grand Duke Cosimo II of Tuscany died at the age of thirty, after six years of ill health. His son, the ten-year-old Ferdinand II, succeeded to the throne under the regency of the pious Grand Duchess Christine. As a result, Medici rule was weakened, and this would later have a bad effect on Galileo's fortunes.

As he lost a protector, so Galileo lost a tormentor. In September 1621 Cardinal Bellarmine died. The death of this intimidating intellectual convinced Galileo that he could now undertake an attack on the Jesuits. Perhaps Bellarmine's ban on Copernican teaching would pass away with its author. The great Bellarmine was the embodiment of the Catholic Counter-Reformation, the most powerful of all Jesuits, the personal prosecutor of Bruno and Galileo. In his absence, the artists and intellectuals and scientists could hope for moderation. But Bellarmine's influence lingered.

In late 1621 Galileo began his response to Father Grassi. When his fellow Lynxes heard that he was finally under way, they cheered him on, for they still viewed the Jesuit attack narrowly as an attack on their society and its scientific method. They forgot that Galileo was the man exposed. In a letter to Galileo in May 1622, the ailing Duke Cesarini described the Jesuits as "obstinate worshippers of antiquity" and asserted that in such an unequal contest, the name of the Academy of Lynxes would be saved, just offense would be given to the malevolent ones, and all the world would know the treasure of "your noble speculations."

Galileo rose to his task with relish. Giving full vent to his prodigious sardonic wit, he pronounced Grassi's argument to be "like that of a lacerated and bruised snake, which has no vitality left except at the tip of its tail, but which nevertheless continues to wriggle, pretending that it is still healthy and vigorous." And although he referred to the imperious attitude of his adversary, Grassi's haughtiness was nothing compared to Galileo's. When he thought of himself, an eagle came to mind. "I believe that true philosophers fly, and that they fly alone like eagles." When he thought of Jesuits, he thought of starlings. "Since eagles are rare birds, it is true that they are little seen and less heard, while starlings fill the sky with shrieks and cries, and wherever they settle, they befoul the earth beneath them."

With these barbs and encomiums, Galileo could get on with the contest. More than in any previous work, he was eager to promote himself as a philosopher, as if he were still insecure in his grand title as the first philosopher of the court and had to prove himself. Here he was a philosopher of science, addressing the theoretical foundation of science rather than a practicing scientist with a specific problem that could be weighed, measured, or demonstrated.

The sky needed to be demystified. Suddenly projecting himself as a celestial democrat, he knew no such thing as a pedigree in heaven. "I do not know which of the stars are more or less noble, nor more or less perfect."

If he was intent to be a philosopher, so he would use a philosopher's logic. What would you do, he asked, if a preacher came to you and said, "The number of fools is infinite"? Would you argue with his proposition? "You could prove on Scriptural authority that the world is not eternal. Therefore, there can not be an infinite number of men. Since foolishness reigns only among men, the proposition could never be true, even if all men—past, present, and future—were fools." If that was logic, it was also the statement of a confident man.

And if he would use a philosopher's logic, so he would exhibit a comedian's sense of the absurd. Father Grassi had embraced the ancient Babylonian proposition that centrifugal force created heat, and to prove it the Babylonians had cooked eggs by whirling them in slings. Galileo scoffed at the idea. "Now we do not lack eggs nor slings nor sturdy fellows to whirl them," he wrote. "Yet our eggs do not cook, but merely cool down faster if they happen to be hot. And since nothing is lacking to us except being Babylonians, then being Babylonian is the cause of the hardening of eggs, not the friction of air." Had not the good father felt the coolness on his cheeks when he was riding to post?

Improving on Father Grassi's cold image of the astronomical balance, Galileo called his work *The Assayer*, after the weigher of gold and other precious metals. The book would be treated as a manifesto, a call to arms for a new class of scientists who wished to break the chains of an ancient and ecclesiastical dictatorship. His new class might yet be small, he conceded, but he did not judge the value of a man's opinion by the number of his followers. For the class to grow, a knowledge of mathematics was essential. From that thought and that rallying cry came the sentences that would live in eternity and be remembered as the essence of Galileo: "Philosophy is written in this grand book, the universe which stands continually open to our gaze. But the book cannot be understood unless one first learns to comprehend the language and read the letters in which it is composed. It is written in the language of mathematics, and its characters are triangles, circles, and other geometric figures. Without a knowledge of them, it is humanly impossible to understand a single word of it. Without these, one wanders about in a dark and obscure labyrinth."

In October 1622, a year after it was begun, *The Assayer* was ready for publication. The Lynxes salivated at the coming confrontation. "We want to publish the work and we want to do it in Rome, notwithstanding the power of the adversaries, against whom we will arm ourselves with the shield of truth," Duke Cesarini wrote with the glee of anticipation. Galileo's tract had to come out "in the face of the Church, before the eyes of congregations."

The literary process over, the political process could begin. Since the Academy of Lynxes would publish the work, its six leading members read and approved the contents, checking for any scientific or theological arguments that were at variance with the society's position. After his reading of the manuscript, the doctor Johannes Faber proclaimed that Galileo had illuminated "the happy citadel of the gods." Beyond flattery, this consultation with the lynx-eyed led to some politic suggestions. The book should be presented as a long letter to Duke Virginio Cesarini, the melancholy and dying young Lynx whose support in high aristocratic and ecclesiastical circles was so strong, who was now the secretary to Gregory

XV and would soon assume the title of Lord Chamberlain. To dedicate *The Assayer* to him would be useful in procuring the Vatican's imprimatur for the work.

For months Cesarini and Ciampoli had been preparing the way for Vatican approval. They had arranged for its censor to be Father Niccolò Riccardi, a learned and compliant Dominican and professor of theology at the Dominican College of Saint Thomas (next door to the Collegio Romano) who, conveniently, had recently been involved in a dispute with the Jesuits.

On February 2, 1623, Father Riccardi blessed *The Assayer* with the official Vatican stamp of approval. In it he had found nothing morally offensive or heretical. Indeed, "thanks to the deep and sound reflections of this author," he had found much to glorify their age.

"I count myself fortunate to be born," read Riccardi's imprimatur, "when the gold of truth is no longer weighed in bulk but is assayed with so delicate a balance."

By late May, Monsignor Ciampoli was sending Galileo the first proofs of his book and reporting on a session he had just had with Pope Gregory XV, in which he spent a half hour expostulating on the many qualities of Galileo. Ciampoli was preparing the pro-Jesuit pope for the shock of Galileo's book, but Gregory would not get a chance to read it. A month later, Galileo received a warm letter from another prince of the church. Cardinal Maffeo Barberini, the learned Florentine, thanked Galileo profusely for the help he had given his cousin, Francesco Barberini, in attaining a doctorate at the University of Pisa. Cardinal Barberini assured Galileo of his affection and that of his house. "We are ready to serve you always."

Two weeks later, Gregory XV died. And after a tense backstage drama in the thick of which were the light-footed Lynxes, Duke Cesarini and Monsignor Ciampoli, Cardinal Maffeo Barberini was elected pope.

He took the name Urban VIII.

11

THE HEART OF THE SCORPION

Upon the accession of Cardinal Maffeo Barberini to the papacy in August 1623, Galileo could scarcely contain his joy. Here was a churchman who was the very embodiment of forward-looking vision and deliverance. The new pope hailed from an opulent family of Florentine merchant-princes. A poet himself, Barberini was renowned for his interest in science and the arts. His nephew, Cardinal Francesco Barberini, was a genuinely close friend. Only a few months before Maffeo Barberini's unexpected election, Galileo had assisted in conferring a doctorate upon Francesco at the University of Pisa. A bit later, Galileo would also help Francesco become a member of the Lynxean Academy, thus deepening the debt.

For more than ten years Galileo had been nurturing his relationship with the Barberini family, showering this rising star of the Catholic church with gifts of his books and engaging in a warm correspondence. Their acquaintance had begun in the fall of 1611, when Galileo was putting forward his ideas about floating bodies in water, ideas that were then exciting the court of Tuscany. In late September of that year, Cardinal Barberini had traveled to Florence in the company of another cardinal, and the grand duke had invited Galileo to debate his ideas with an

Aristotelian opponent before the visiting eminences. Predictably, it had been another bravura performance for Galileo, and in the course of it, Cardinal Barberini had heartily taken his side of the question.

With this auspicious beginning, eight months later Galileo had sent to Barberini his tract on floating bodies and received a flattering response. If the good cardinal could understand and appreciate his work on floating bodies, why not his work on orbiting planets? A year later Galileo sent Barberini his *Letters on the Sunspots,* and again the cardinal responded with interest. "I shall read them with pleasure, again and again," he wrote. "This is not a book which will stand idly among the rest. It is the only one which can induce me to withdraw for a few hours from my official duties to devote myself to it, and to the observation of the planets it treats. Meanwhile, thank you for remembering me, and never forget the high opinion I have for a mind so extraordinarily gifted as yours."

Then came the crisis of 1616, when a desperate Galileo needed political support from every corner in the Roman Curia. On the surface, Barberini had seemed friendly. When Caccini's accusation forced the "question" before the Inquisition, Cardinal Barberini had shown a disgust for Galileo's accusers, and said so. Significantly, he did nothing to intercede against the formal admonition of the church, however. This Galileo tended to forget. Indeed, the day after Cardinal Bellarmine had officially warned Galileo not to teach, hold, or discuss the Copernican theory, Cardinal Barberini had underscored Bellarmine's message. Through an intermediary he wrote that Galileo should steer far clear of all theological matters, but so long as he spoke strictly as a mathematician, he had nothing to fear. Characteristically, Galileo remembered the boost and not the caution.

Any hesitation Galileo might have harbored about Barberini was washed away in the gushing praise that the cardinal wrote in a poem about the scientist in 1620. For years, poetry had been Barberini's fancy, and he particularly loved to render passages of the Old and New Testaments into prosaic Horatian meter. Now, in an ode consisting of nineteen stanzas and entitled "In Dangerous Adulation," he portrayed the pursuit of astronomy as a glorious and even moral enterprise:

> *When the moon shines and displays*
> *Its golden procession and its gleaming fires*
> *In its serene orbit*
> *A strange pleasure draws us and rivets our gaze.*
> *This one looks up at the shining evening star*

And the terrible star of Mars
And the track colored with the luster of milk
That one sees your light, O Cynosure.

Or another marvels at either the heart of the Scorpion
Or the torch of the Dog Star
Or the satellites of Jupiter
Or the ears of father Saturn
Discovered by your glass, O learned Galileo . . .

Not always, beyond the radiance that shines
Does it become clear to us:
We notice the black defects on the sun
(Who would believe it?)
By your art, Galileo.

For Galileo, sunk in melancholy for eight years, plagued by sickness real and imagined, the unexpected elevation of Barberini was thrilling. No doubt, he wished that he could have been at the coronation itself, for the glorious procession had been a celebration of Florentine learning. Dressed as a prince, surrounded by princes and musicians, Urban VIII made his way slowly from the Campodoglio, the traditional site of renewal for Roman culture, to an invigorated Vatican, cheered along the way by Roman throngs turned out in velvet and gold. At significant points on the processional route, he paid homage to statues that were to symbolize his coming reign: Glory, Abundance, Public Happiness, Apostolic Doctrine, Zeal, Ecclesiastical Liberty, Magnificence, and Faith. To show his common touch, he stopped to receive the adulation of the crowd before two immense marble lions, out of whose mouths poured a river of wine.

"As the eminence of doctrine was held lofty," wrote a witness to the pomp on the Capitoline, "so the friends of science swelled. All discerned how important was intellect, how necessary it was to know more to sustain learning itself. To show this, the new pontiff paused long at the statue of Humanity."

In the two months after Urban VIII's resplendent coronation, Galileo and his friends wondered how to seize the moment. To the pope's nephew, Cardinal Francesco Barberini, he wrote that "hope is reviving, hope which was once quite buried. We are about to see precious learning recalled from its long exile." Up the hill from Bellosguardo, his cloistered daughter Sister Maria Celeste began a letter to him by saying, "Knowing as I do how greatly the new Pope loves and esteems you, . . . " and then she remembered the pontiff's "many promises" to her father. "May the Lord give you health to fulfill your desire of visiting His Holiness," she wrote, "so that you may enjoy a still greater measure of his favor."

Was it not time for another siege of Rome? In the Eternal City itself, the Lynxes were taxing their brains at how best to take advantage of the situation. To Prince Cesi, Galileo wrote on October 9 that he could never have hoped for such a "marvelous conjunction" of events, which made it possible to resurrect his plans. "I rejoice at such a moment in the republic of letters." Cesi approved of Galileo's plan to come to Rome. Indeed, he insisted on it, especially after an audience with the new pope. "Under the auspices of the most excellent, learned, and benign Pontiff, science must flourish," the prince wrote expansively. "Your arrival will be welcome to His Holiness. He seems to love and esteem you more than ever."

From another source came a similar message. "I swear to you that nothing pleases His Holiness so much as the mention of your name. After I had been speaking of you for some time, I told him that you, esteemed sir, had an ardent desire to come and kiss his toe, if His Holiness would permit it. The Pope replied that it would give him great pleasure, if it was convenient for you, and if the journey would not be bad for your health. Great men like you must spare themselves, so they may live as long as possible."

The pope, it was reported, was having Galileo's *The Assayer* read to him at dinner and throwing his head backward in raucous laughter at its more wicked barbs toward the Jesuits. This was good news, since for political reasons, the Academy of Lynxes had dedicated the book to Urban. Their dedication dripped with flattery. It spoke of this universal jubilee of literature and of virtue "when the whole City and especially the Holy See is more resplendent than ever" after Urban's coronation, and where "every heart is inflamed to praiseworthy studies and worthy actions." They dedicated the work of Galileo to his fellow Florentine who had turned his heroic mind to the highest undertakings in the hope that the patriarch would continue to favor their studies "with the gracious rays and vigorous warmth" of his most benign protection.

The news of the pope's reaction to *The Assayer* was heartening and useful, but Galileo had a genuine inside source in yet another Florentine, Monsignor Giovanni Ciampoli. In 1609 he had heard the scientist lecture at Padua and had hastened to sign up for his course on Euclid. Eventually, they had become close, as mentor and protégé, now as mentor and political informant. Ciampoli was no factotum to the new pope. He had become a confidant who handled intimate papal correspondence.

Ciampoli, however, was a dangerous friend. Arrogant and conceited, verbose and manipulative, he imagined himself to be a great poet whose copious gifts exceeded the mortal talents of Ovid and Virgil. Although he was obedient and fawning on the surface, he wrote satiric verses about the pope behind his back. Appropriately enough, Ciampoli later became a skilled diplomat for the Holy See and handled the papal rapprochement with France and Cardinal Richelieu. He also came to a bad end.

Now, with great eagerness, the monsignor took it upon himself to become the herald of the new age within the Roman Curia. Just as there was a liberal pope who smiled on new ideas, so, to Ciampoli, Galileo had finally crushed the Aristotelian worldview with *The Assayer*. Galileo paid him back. Ciampoli was soon invited to become a member of the keen-sighted Lynxes.

On November 4, 1623, from Rome, Ciampoli wrote to Galileo to urge him to produce an even more pointed and revolutionary work than *The Assayer*. The time was suddenly right. "Here some further new invention of your genius is greatly desired, so that if you should want to publish certain ideas that you have heretofore held back, I am certain that they would also please Our Lord, the Pope, greatly. He does not cease to admire your eminence in all things and to retain all the affection held for you in the past."

Six months would pass before Galileo could make his trip to Rome, for he was feeling poorly again and was unable to travel during the harsh winter months. At last, on April 1, 1624, he set out. Once again he carried fascinating novelties—this time, microscopes. As with the telescope, the invention of the microscope was claimed by a Dutch spectacle-maker, Zacharias Janssen, but Galileo had invented it as an instrument of science in 1610 and as with the telescope, had vastly improved it. Now, instead of stars, he meant to astonish the Roman prelates with gigantic bugs. The journey would be difficult, for between Galileo's uncertain health and the spring floods, he was delayed often along the way.

And sometimes intentionally. He tarried for two comfortable and productive weeks in Acquasparta as the guest of Prince Cesi. Cesi's country palace was an object of great beauty. Nestled in the Apennines, at the base of a high mountain, equidistant from Todi and Spoleto, the palace overlooked a plain of verdant Umbrian fields. Now thirty-nine years old, the proud father of a two-year-old son who was his namesake, Cesi enjoyed long stretches in the country with his family and often entertained guests. With him already as Galileo arrived was Il Tardigrado, the Slow One, Francesco Stelluti, who had been one of the four original Lynxes and who only two years before had written an attack on the Jesuitical view of the 1618 comets, as a kind of skirmish before Galileo's outright war in *The Assayer*.

The Cesi country palace was the most amiable of situations, well suited for extended conversation in front of the fire as the April winds howled outside. The Lynxes plotted strategy for the coming campaign, feasted in the evening, toasted this special moment for the world of letters, and gazed at the stars by night. They were well aware that they were at the forefront of a profound cultural revolution. The joy in one another's company was dampened only briefly by sad news: the untimely death of the young priest and poet, Virginio Cesarini, who had been inducted as a Lynx six years before, and to whom *The Assayer* was dedicated. But this sadness was swept away by the epic events they had to discuss. While Stelluti spent hours riveted by the sight of a bee under Galileo's microscope and sketching it for a book, they agreed that the tide had finally turned in favor of science.

Galileo left Acquasparta on April 22 and arrived in Rome a day later. There he was received as a guest of Mario Guiducci. At once Galileo fell into his customary round of talks with important cardinals. To one, Cardinal von Zollern of Austria, he presented a microscope as a gift to the duke of Bavaria. The good cardinal was utterly petrified by the "horrendous things" he saw swimming around in a drop of water. With the cardinal in that terrified frame of mind, Galileo beseeched him to speak to the pope about the ban on Copernicanism. His fellow Lynx, the physician Johannes Faber, meanwhile peered through the instrument at a fly and was so astonished that he declared Galileo to be another "Creator, since he had things appear that until now were not known to have been created."

Bugs were in high favor in Rome. Three huge, big-bottled bees dominated the coat of arms for the house of Barberini. This fact was not lost on Galileo in bringing his microscopes and Stelluti's detailed sketches of bees to Rome. Immediately upon his arrival, he turned to the Barberinis. Only a day after he settled in, Galileo had his first audience with Urban VIII, the first of six over the coming month. The pope greeted him expansively "with infinite demonstrations of love." Before long, Urban had granted to Galileo's legitimized son, Vincenzo, a handsome pension worth sixty crowns (which the ungrateful son later rejected because it had religious exercises attached to it).

To Galileo's surprise, there stood before him a very different man from the poetic and sensitive prelate of the past. In nine months of his pontificate, Urban VIII had become a warrior pope. The Thirty Years' War was entering its sixth year, as Protestant and Catholic armies jockeyed north of the Alps. Already in Urban's mind, ambitious military plans were taking shape: a daunting, well-munitioned fortress north of Bologna, to be called Forte Urbano, new breastworks for Castel Sant'Angelo, the papal fortress on the Tiber (iron for it was ripped out of the Pantheon), the construction of a huge naval port at Civitavecchio on the western coast, the construction of higher walls around the papal gardens on Monte Cavallo, the vaults of the Vatican Library to be transformed into an arsenal.

To any who might object to these military plans, Urban VIII was dismissive. He listened seldom and talked a great deal, overwhelming his visitors with uninterruptible orations. Arbitrary in his decisions, he had a fondness for taking precisely the opposite course from that which his advisors counseled, as if he felt the need to flaunt his authority. To him, "the judgment of one living pope was worth more than the maxims of a hundred dead ones," and he declared that he knew more than all the cardinals put together. Rarely did he convene the Congregation of the Faith, except, as one commentor remarked, "to cover up certain errors."

Meanwhile, he looked out for the other bees. He soon conferred the cardinal's hat upon a brother and a son, while he made another brother the governor of Borgo, that teeming hotbed of intrigue just outside the Vatican walls.

He was the new autocrat under the tiara, and he was infinitely more dangerous to Galileo than Paul V because Urban and Galileo had a prior bond of friendship.

In their early exchanges about the ban on Copernican thinking, the pope was disappointingly evasive. Galileo was left to picking up his intelligence secondhand wherever he could find it. Cardinal von Zollern, still reeling from the sight of organisms in his drop of water, finally spoke to the pope about the ban. The church must proceed cautiously, the pope had responded, but it had neither "condemned nor ever would condemn the doctrine as heretical, but only as rash." What did that mean? In the days of thumbscrews and pit dungeons, being rash could cover a lot of territory. The question remained muddled.

In a later audience with Urban, however, Galileo was able to have a direct and pointed interchange about the theory. They traded the arguments back and forth about the old and the new thinking. The importance was not that the pope moderated his position—he did not—but that the arguments he used for the old thinking would be remembered. They would be remembered by Galileo himself and inserted into the mouth of a thick-headed character in Galileo's coming masterwork, the *Dialogue Concerning the Two Chief World Systems*. And the pope's arguments would be ridiculed. Urban too would remember the arguments he made. Their rough handling later did not amuse him. In some ways, this is the key to the fate of Galileo. It was a question not of principle but of personality.

Despite the fog that still hovered over the Copernican issue, Galileo was optimistic. As he prepared to leave Rome, he listened to what he wanted to hear. In his mind, he had been not cautioned but encouraged, encouraged to "speak hypothetically" about Copernicus and to write about his conception. In that, he had concluded, there was wide latitude. He would rely on literary artifice that could mask his real views. On June 8 he wrote a gossipy letter to Prince Cesi at Acquasparta. "On the question of Copernicus, His Holiness said that the Holy Church had not condemned, nor would condemn his opinion as heretical, but only as rash. So long as it is not demonstrated as true, it need not be feared." The letter is noteworthy for its upbeat tone.

In a buoyant mood, Galileo felt good enough to poke fun at the censor of *The Assayer*, Father Niccolò Riccardi, who had performed as a real friend. "He sets angels to work at moving heavenly bodies, and these angels make the stars go, as they do go (however that may be) without the slightest difficulty or entanglement! Certainly this ought to be enough for us!"

Before he left, Galileo had one last audience with the pope. Urban praised him and loaded him down with gifts: two medals, one of silver, the other of gold, and the pension for Vincenzo. More valuable was a letter (ghostwritten by Monsignor Ciampoli) that the pope gave him to present to the grand duke of Tuscany.

"We have observed in him not only the literary distinction, but also the love of religion worthy of papal favour," the letter said. "We listened with pleasure to his learned demonstrations which add fresh renown to Florentine eloquence." The pope spoke of his virtues and piety, and of Galileo as his "beloved son." Then, memorably: "His fame will shine on earth so long as Jupiter and his satellites shine in heaven."

The papal praise reflected the lavish sentiments of Giambattista Marino. This most famous poet of the day had rushed back to Rome after the accession of Urban VIII and had counted on the affection of the new pope. In his masterwork, *Adonis*, he had devoted a canto to Galileo.

Much doest thou owe to heaven that grants to thee
the invention of the wondrous instrument,
but far more heaven owes to thy superb
device, which makes its beauties manifest,
Full worthy is thy image to be placed
among those stars for fitting ornament,
and those thy frail glass lenses to repose
immortal mid eternal sapphire lights.

Never until the heaven extinguishes
the gleaming radiance of the stars themselves
should that celestial splendor 'which shall wear
for thee a crown of honor e'er be dimmed.
Brightly will thy glory live with stars,
and thou in flame endure, forever bright,
and with their lovely, burning tongues of light
the stars will tell thy story evermore.

On June 11, the day Galileo left Rome, the Inquisition condemned the work of Marino. The poet fled back into exile in Paris.

Meanwhile, Urban VIII was preparing his decree to excommunicate any Catholic who snorted snuff in church.

The constellation of Rome in 1624 was a confusing place, an aggregation of shifting stars that seemed constantly to alter their brightness and position in the holy firmament and to be animated by no reliable laws of motion, except motion itself. The progressive pope sent out flickering signals, sometimes brilliant, sometimes dark and confusing. Whether Urban VIII was a star or a disappearing comet depended on moment and parallax.

After Galileo left Rome in June, the bizarre case of Archbishop Mark Antony de Dominis preoccupied the church and reflected the confusion. He was a former Jesuit and an intellectual who hailed from the aristocracy and who had briefly touched Galileo's world of science and mathematics before he moved adventurously into the more dangerous jungle of church doctrine. He had been a professor of mathematics at Padua, had written a tract on the nature of the rainbow, and had even speculated on the optics of refraction in Galileo's telescope. Eventually he became the archbishop of Split, the town in Dalmatia where his family of popes and princes reigned as a dynasty.

During the Venice Interdict of 1606, de Dominis had sided with Sarpi and had fallen into the Protestant orbit of the British embassy in Venice, which was operating a fifth column for Calvinism, under the guardianship of the English ambassador, Sir Henry Wotton. Thus began the secret life of the archbishop of Split as a double agent.

In 1617, de Dominis, apparently of his own initiative, attempted to become the courier in a secret mission to smuggle Sarpi's sensational book on the Council of Trent out of Italy to England. But Sarpi did not trust this adventurer and used another channel toward the same purpose. De Dominis slipped out of Italy anyway with a purloined copy of Sarpi's manuscript and made his way along the Rhine and finally to England, where on December 3, 1617, in a showy ceremony at Saint Paul's Cathedral, wearing his purple archbishop's robes, he pronounced himself to be a Calvinist. His mission, he proclaimed to the congregation, was to effect a reconciliation between the Protestant and Catholic churches. James I had made him dean of Windsor in the Anglican church and the master of the Savoy, and de Dominis published Sarpi's book anyway, without the author's permission, appending a dedication to James I.

Within a few years his ecumenical histrionics wore out the English patience, and he was expelled. In Brussels, he appealed to the then-pope, his friend, schoolmate, and relative, Gregory XV, promising a sincere renunciation of his Protestantism if only he could return to Rome. This arranged, on November 24, 1622, he formally renounced his wicked heresies and damned Sarpi's book, whereupon he was welcomed back into the hierarchy of the Curia.

For more than a year his taste for adventure was quiescent, as Gregory XV died and Urban VIII became pope. He returned to scientific speculations and wrote a book about the tides. Galileo disliked the book intensely. "A certain cleric has published a little treatise," Galileo would write in his *Dialogue*, "wherein he says that the moon, wandering to and fro in the heavens, attracts the oceans. The mass of water follows the moon, so that the ocean is full in that part of the world laying under the power of the moon." In the end, the certain cleric could not hold his tongue. With the death of Gregory XV, he lost his protector. Urban VIII doubted the sincerity of his abjuration and put him under more careful watch. De Dominis persisted in boasting indiscreetly about his exploits among the Protestants, and his old opinions were overheard.

He was denounced. And once there was a denunciation, as later would happen with Galileo, a formal process had to be followed. Given the archbishop's power and influence, his friendship with two popes and his eminent family background, his case was treated gingerly at first. He was detained in the papal prison at Castel Sant'Angelo, but in a comfortable apartment attended by two servants.

His interrogation, nonetheless, was ferocious. And de Dominis was equally accommodating. He admitted all he was accused of, recanted yet again, and even sent a breezy thanks to Urban VIII for the comfort of his prison surroundings. But he fell ill during his interrogation and declined rapidly. After a ten-hour interrogation, he died. The Vatican was horrified, fearing an international outcry, and quickly empaneled a board of inquiry to conduct an autopsy. It included the physician Johannes Faber, who was a member of the College of Prosecution Experts but also of the Academy of Lynxes. As a friend, Faber wrote Galileo about the event a few days after the archbishop's sudden demise.

"The Archbishop of Split *ivit ad plures* on the 8th of this month, at 4 in the morning at the Castel Sant'Angelo, after nine days of a bad fever. At seven the same morning, a man came to my house, upon the order of the Pope, asking that I be of assistance, when the body of the archbishop was opened in the presence of a notary of the Holy Office. I believe they were afraid that the world would say the Archbishop was poisoned. We found the intestines to be completely clean, without a trace of poison, although the lungs were a little inflamed. His body had been taken to the Palace of the Apostles where it was deposited—so the cardinal of Saint Susanna told me, when I dined with him.

"The cardinal said that the Archbishop's trial became his sentence, because in reality, he was found dead after the Inquisitor had examined him over the space of ten hours. But he died penitent of his errors and confessing and he received all the sacraments of the Holy Church."

Simply because the culprit had died, the church would not be deterred from completing its examination. More than three months later, on the December feast day of the doubting Saint Thomas, the body of Archbishop de Dominis was exhumed and the casket taken ceremonially to the Dominican basilica of Santa Maria Sopra Minerva in central Rome. There the governor of Rome, the inquisitors and cardinals gathered, the same cardinals who only a few months before had been amazed to peer through Galileo's microscope and see a fly appear as large as a hen. Now the cardinals were dressed in their ceremonial red robes, to signify that they were ready to shed their blood for the church. Before the altar, de Dominis's casket was painted with black pitch, and above it, a portrait of the archbishop was draped in black.

Officially, the culprit was declared a Relapse into Heresy. His soul was formally condemned, his memory declared infamous. Upon the order of the Inquisition, he was stripped posthumously of his ecclesiastical privileges and honors in the See of Dalmatia, his writings banned, and his family property forfeited to the Exchequer of the Inquisition. After the polite applause subsided, the casket was loaded on a cart and taken to the Campo dei Fiori.

There, as the spirit of Giordano Bruno hovered above the square, his decomposed body was raised from the casket briefly to excite the crowd and to impress upon them an abhorrence for the crime of heresy. Then, the bones of this lesser martyr to the purity of Catholic doctrine were burned.

The Roman Curia that burned the archbishop of Split was not the Curia Galileo thought he knew. De Dominis was a daredevil and an opportunist, just as Bruno had been a fanatic and a mystic, and neither man seemed to hold any relevance for the urgent, practical mission of the new science. Galileo basked in the warmth of his recent visits with the forward-looking pope. Urban's welcome and encouragement remained vivid, emboldening him to test the water more pointedly on the Copernican theory. More favorable intelligence bolstered his confidence.

With this reassurance, as well as his own encouraging experience months before in Rome, Galileo turned to a piece of old business. Eight years previously, some months before Cardinal Bellarmine had admonished him about the Copernican theory, Galileo had received a letter from a lawyer-priest named Francesco Ingoli, who was later to become the secretary of the Vatican institution called the Propaganda of the Faith and would oversee the founding of the Vatican printing press. Ingoli was a sincere admirer of Galileo, but he was troubled by the Copernican theory and had presented reasoned and dispassionate arguments against it.

Wisely, after his official warning in 1616, Galileo had refrained from answering. But in Prague Kepler felt no such compunction. He wrote a tract called "Epitome of Copernican Astronomy," which was published in 1618 and promptly placed on the Inquisition's Index of Prohibited Books. Now, bolstered by the fresh enlightenment of Rome, Galileo decided that the time was ripe for his own considered reply.

In the late summer of 1624 he worked diligently on it. His fellow Lynxes heard what he was up to and urged him on, excited by the thought that at last their mentor was prepared to step forward with a well-grounded defense of Copernicus. The warning of Archbishop de Dominis's treatment at the hands of the Inquisition did not shake him. By the end of September the reply was ready, whereupon it was reproduced in manuscript and distributed among the learned in Tuscany and Rome. Running to sixty pages, packed with anecdote and sharp counterpoint, the tract focused on Ingoli's weak scientific arguments and did its best to avoid his theological ones. "I know certain facts," Galileo wrote, "which have been observed by no one else but myself. From them, within the limits of my human wisdom, the correctness of the Copernican system seems incontrovertible." In his entire life, that was as definite a statement of belief in the Copernican theory as Galileo ever made.

Out of caution, however, he refused to have the epistle printed. And he began his sometimes biting commentary with a disclaimer. "From reverence for Holy Scripture and for the Holy Fathers, and from my zeal for our holy faith," he would never hold the Copernican theory to be true, regardless of its probability. He was replying now for several reasons. He wished to show Protestant Germany that not only there, but also in Catholic Italy, a scientist was free to address the compelling scientific basis of the Copernican theory. He was also concerned that his long silence might lead some to think that he was persuaded by Ingoli's arguments.

As the reply to Ingoli was a trial balloon, Galileo anxiously awaited the word from Rome. To float his balloon, he was relying on former students who were attaining stature in both secular and eccelesiastical circles and who had been elected to the Academy of Lynxes. To his protégé Mario Guiducci, he entrusted the mission of presenting his Ingoli letter to Rome. And on the receiving end, he counted on Monsignor Ciampoli, his devoted agent at the throne of Saint Peter.

Several setbacks dampened Galileo's hopes for a speedy vote of confidence from Urban VIII. The situation in Rome was complicated in late 1624, when an obscure cleric raised theological objections to *The Assayer*, denouncing it as heretical on the doctrine of transubstantiation. Galileo's view of atoms and particles in substances seemed to deny the transformation of the consecrated bread and wine into the actual body and blood of Christ, the anonymous priest argued, and thus to deny the divine mystery of the Eucharist. This would violate the central doctrine of the Catholic faith, as espoused by the Council of Trent. The book should be prohibited until it could be corrected. Fortunately for Galileo, the complaint was referred to a friendly cardinal, who read the book and praised it. If it was true that *The Assayer* touched on difficult questions, the cardinal reported to the Congregation of the Index, it nevertheless did not deserve to be condemned.

In light of this nuisance, Galileo's messenger in Rome, Guiducci, thought it best to delay pressing the reply to Ingoli on the Curia, since the Ingoli letter was more dangerous than *The Assayer*. Urban himself was inaccessible, preoccupied by matters of war as the combat in northern Europe with the Protestant forces moved to a new and broader level of violence. Papal forces maneuvered against French, Spanish, and Venetian troops to control the Val Telline, the strategic Catholic valley north of Lake Como that ran thirty miles along the boundary of the Venetian Republic and was the passageway for Spanish troops through the Alps to the Holy Roman Empire. This meant that abstract questions of doctrine were in the unpredictable hands of lesser friars.

In April 1625 Guiducci wrote to Galileo about the delicate situation. After the challenge to *The Assayer* was dispatched, "the matter has quieted down for the time being," he wrote. "Since we lack this support which could guard our flank, it does not seem advisable to run the risk of a beating. The letter to Ingoli explicitly defends the Copernican opinion. Though it is clearly stated that this opinion is found false by a superior light, nevertheless those who are not too sincere will not believe that disclaimer and will be up in arms again. His Holiness is very disturbed by the mess of the war just now, so that one cannot speak to him, and the matter would be left to the discretion of the friars. For these reasons, it seems right to wait and let the matter rest. To keep it alive risks a persecution where one would have to shield oneself from those who can deal blows with impunity. Time may benefit the cause."

At long last, during the Christmas season of 1625, Galileo pressed Ciampoli again for reaction from the pope and finally got his response. Ciampoli had found the right moment to present the Ingoli letter. As with *The Assayer*, the monsignor read the letter to the pontiff at bedtime, as a kind of entertainment. But he apparently read only the witty passages. As with *The Assayer*, there was much in the Ingoli letter to amuse the pope.

In discussing Ingoli's complaint against Copernicus's inaccuracies concerning Venus and Mars, Galileo compared Ingoli to the man who tears down his house when his chimney smokes. Then changing the image, he wrote: "If painters were to bleach a whole canvas whenever they were shown a small imperfection in the finger or eye of a figure, it would take a long time indeed to represent a whole scene."

In speaking of the humanity of Aristotle, Galileo wrote, "Aristotle was a man, saw with his eyes, heard with his ears and reasoned with his brain. I am a man and see with my eyes much more than he did."

And since Ingoli had pointed to Aristotle's many followers over a millennium, Galileo retorted, "A father may have 20 children, but this does not imply that he is more prolific than a son of his who has only one child . . . if the father is 60 and the son 20 years old."

Three days after Christmas, Ciampoli replied to Galileo. The disciple prefaced his letter with dripping flattery. No gift could be more precious than the news of Galileo's good health, Ciampoli wrote, for "parts of your superhuman intellect have stimulated me as if they were treasures of heavenly wisdom."

"I have read your reply to Ingoli," Ciampoli continued, "and have referred a good part of it to the Holy Father who savored greatly the example of the sieve and of heavy bodies in motion."

Friendly though this report was, it was hardly the ringing endorsement that Galileo took it to be. Indeed, it had avoided the issue of Galileo's advocacy of the Copernican theory altogether and had mentioned only a few of Galileo's literary allusions. Galileo was buoyed nevertheless. To him, the lack of rebuke was the essence of the reply. The atmosphere had changed! The gag had been lifted! He was now free to lead the new scientific movement! Indeed, he was being encouraged and even inspired, almost by divine decree, to proceed.

Eight years later, his delusion crushed, he was to speak openly about a divine inspiration of his *Dialogue*. Writing to the brother of Urban VIII, after the pope had become his tormentor, he said that he had begun his *Dialogue* after he heard "almost like the echo of the Holy Spirit, a very short but admirable and most holy assertion suddenly come out of the mouth of a person most eminent in learning and venerable for the holiness of his life."

The voice of the Holy Spirit had been the voice of Urban VIII himself.

Galileo imagined a grand dialogue on the two competing cosmic views. The conception had deep roots in his own life, in his work, and in his culture. This was to be his summing up. His dialogue would connect the high points of his entire scientific life, touch on his many controversies, and put forward his deepest beliefs. Its essence was to be the argument between the conventional and the revolutionary views of the galaxy, between Aristotle and Copernicus, between the Middle Ages and the Renaissance, between him and all his critics over the years. It would be a masterwork that had been promised for fourteen years, ever since he had announced his intention to write a treatise on his system of the world in his *Starry Messenger*.

The literary form of the dialogue was popular and well established in his culture. Its finest flower was considered to be the facetious dialogues of Ruzzante written one hundred years before. His own father had employed the form in his *Dialogue on Ancient and Modern Music*, which had been published when Galileo was fifteen years old and in which, ironically, Vincenzo Galilei had attacked Ptolemy's view of musical composition. And Galileo himself had tried his hand at being a Ruzzante-like rustic with his Cecco dialogue in 1604.

Political reality also influenced the grand design. To thrash out the arguments between Aristotelian and Copernican views as a Socratic dialogue seemed to meet both the encouragement and the caution of Urban VIII. As a dialogue, the issue would be treated suppositionally, theoretically, conditionally. It would not purport to be truth in any absolute or scientific sense but would be seen simply as debate or civilized discussion between sophisticated and well-meaning gentlemen. To the reader was left the decision on which of the disputants was most persuasive.

He was caught between two contradictory purposes: to advocate for the new science and to be able to deny this advocacy at the same time, to cloak his passion in ostensible objectivity. He proceeded, at least in the beginning, as a cautious hero.

His thinking about his *Dialogue* was already well advanced when he received the encouraging letter from Ciampoli. As he sat down to write, the image of old friends and simpler times rushed into his head. His mind rested on the happiest period of life, when he taught in Padua and played in Venice, when Sagredo made him laugh and the liberty of Venice made him soar, when he was still young enough and the world was his, and when the pursuit of pure science was uncomplicated by theological implications.

About Sagredo, he remained infinitely sentimental. No other friendship in his life had been so vibrant, so perfectly joyful in its mixture of inquiry into the unknown and pure fun. From the ark along the Grand Canal to Villa Sagredo along the Brenta, they had discoursed and they had frolicked. No other human being had so stimulated and amused and helped Galileo. And unlike all the other original minds Galileo had known before and since, Sagredo was without self-importance.

Dear Sagredo was dead. He had died four years earlier, on March 5, 1620, in a manner that was sad and predictable. A violent rheumatic cold had shaken his body, and as was his custom, he had disdained medical attention, for he harbored a prejudice against those doctors who practiced by magic and by the stars. (Eight years earlier, in 1612, he had written to Galileo that at last a fever had been cured through a method unknown to the doctors: "I returned to drinking wine without water.") The rheumatic spasm was made worse, Sagredo's brother wrote to Galileo, by the "infinite disorderliness" of his life at the end. Several years after his return from his diplomatic post in Syria, he had moved away from his palace on the Grand Canal to a three-story house near the Arsenale, in the area known as Celestia, where he could look out across the lagoon to the cemetery island and beyond to Murano and feel the sea breezes. There, among his dusty fossils and curious glass inventions, his cats and caged birds, his rare Occidental art objects and disintegrating stuffed animals, his young, beautiful women and empty wine bottles, he had died alone, in squalor. Galileo wished to remember him differently.

Fate had ill-served their friendship. When Sagredo had taken himself off to Syria as the Venetian consul at Aleppo in 1608, he had left a Galileo who was comfortable but forever struggling, accomplished, but one of many accomplished men among the learned of Venice. When Sagredo returned three years later in 1611, Galileo had invented the telescope, had become the most famous man in the world, and had deserted Venice for Tuscany, leaving a great bitterness among his friends in Venice. Sagredo was devastated. Perhaps the Venetian patrician might have prevented Galileo's departure. Certainly, he would have smoothed the leave-taking. Moreover, he worried that Tuscany for Galileo held dangers.

"Where will you find more freedom than in Venice?" Sagredo had written plaintively. "Now you are in your noble native land, but gone from a place where you had many good things. Your prince is full of promise, but here you had command over those who govern. Here you had only to serve yourself, as if you were the king of the universe. The virtue of your young prince may reward you, but who can be sure that the furious winds of flattery in the tempestuous sea of the Court might not submerge you? If not that, at least, trouble you and make you unhappy.

"I do not condemn the youth of your prince. But who knows what the accidents of life can do? Who can guess at the schemes of envious people?

Such people may sow in the prince's mind false and slanderous ideas that can ruin a gallant man. Princes change. Now your prince is amusing himself with your telescope. But what if he enlarges his interests? He may set aside your telescope and forget about you. And who can invent a telescope which can distinguish the crazy person from the sane, the good neighbor from the bad, the intelligent architect from the stubborn surveyor?

"You cannot regain what you have lost. Take good care to hold fast to what you still have."

The extraordinary letter had touched Galileo, but he felt only Sagredo's anguish at lost friendship and had paid no attention to the warning. Perhaps if Sagredo had been there to caution and cajole him in 1610, he would at least have left Venice more gracefully. In his reply, Galileo had tried to assuage the hurt of his old friend. He sought to placate him with jolly words and and sent along a packet of tasty Tuscan truffles. Sagredo replied nostalgically, invoking the memory of their *compagnia antica*, their "ancient company," and their jokes about devout, rich ladies and money-grubbing Jesuits.

From 1611 to Sagredo's death in 1620, their relationship had remained on the level of nostalgia. They had corresponded frequently, typically twice a month and sometimes twice a week, and it is clear from the vast correspondence that Sagredo was living vicariously through Galileo's triumphs and traumas. His letters were tart and chatty, full of eager questions and juicy gossip, redolent with joy in good living. Upon resuming his natural station as a Venetian gentleman of leisure, he acquired his own private glassworks in Murano, where he spent many hours designing and constructing optical and scientific instruments. He wrote to Galileo about thermometers and sunspots, about magnets and Medicean satellites, as he conducted parallel experiments.

Concerning Galileo's intractable opponents, Sagredo was unfailingly sarcastic. "Aristotelians understand nothing of natural causes," he wrote to Galileo, "because they are incapable of understanding. They pursue a profession of being the arbiters of nature, and with this reputation, they pretend to be disinterested in all the senses of man." After Bellarmine's admonition in 1616, Sagredo had renewed his effort to get Galileo to return to the protection of the Venetian Republic and even made inquiries about Galileo resuming his post at the University of Padua.

In an effort to cheer Galileo up after Bellarmine's warning, he had presented his friend with a rare Indian bird that he had brought from Syria and prized immensely. "It does not sing," Sagredo had written playfully, "and has another virtue of living simply on millet and water, without a care. When it finds itself, as often happens, without any food, it makes considerable noise, day or night, with considerable insolence. If you will take it, I would be free of requests of many who keep asking for it. Frankly I would not be too upset if I see him dead due to lack of care. Indeed, I will be obliged to you if you free me of this bird, in the same way I pray God to free you from these awful beasts who torment you. I also pray that by your acceptance, I should be assured that their diabolic nature would not obscure the thoughts of your friend who loves you."

One of their last communications had come during the fall of 1618, when the new comets were blazing through the constellations of the southern sky. Sagredo wrote Galileo not about that exciting apparition but about an outing with their mutual friend, the cavalier Count Bassano. Sagredo and Bassano had ridden into the countryside to paint. For their amusement, the gentlemen were accompanied by their mistresses and even a jester. As lesser nobility, Sagredo was solicitous of the count's frenetic needs, as they stopped to sketch horses and houses, barns and vineyards, and "*i tutti frutti et animali.*"

But they had had several mishaps. In one lurch, the coach had thrown them all out on the ground, and they tumbled onto the grass, laughing, all except the jester, who complained loudly about his bruises and indignities, and when the nobles and their courtesans laughed at him, the jester had the cheek to curse them. At another turn, as Sagredo held the count's freshly painted canvas of a plate of truffles, the coach had lurched again, the door flung open, and Sagredo was thrown into a ditch. But as he landed in a puddle, he held the count's canvas aloft, safe and dry.

"This made me grow in the grace of the *cavaliere*," Sagredo wrote to Galileo, "for I had thought more about preserving one of his works than preserving my own life!"

Upon hearing of Sagredo's death from his brother, Galileo replied: Sagredo had been "his idol."

Filippo Salviati was remembered differently in Galileo's affections. A proud young scientist of great promise, Salviati had been the brilliant disciple whose leaps of intuition could go beyond Galileo's and whose depth and genius were unquestioned. At Salviati's villa west of Florence as well as at his grand house in Florence, they had discovered together the laws of floating bodies and observed the sunspots. It had been to Salviati that Galileo had dedicated his *Letters on the Sunspots*, and to Salviati that Galileo had written about his first triumphant mission to Rome in 1611, entrusting his disciple to spread the news of victory in Florence. Significantly, in that first trip to Rome, Galileo had put Salviati's name (but not Sagredo's) forward for election·to the Academy of Lynxes, and Salviati in turn would recommend other worthy candidates. Others would elect him to the most distinguished cultural society in Florence, the Accademia della Crusca. For that honor, he had been given the name Affidato, "Trusted One."

Salviati too was dead . . . tragically. He had died ten years before at the age of thirty-one under curious circumstances. In the fall of 1613, he quarreled over his station in the Medici court with a minor Medici (Don Bernardetto de' Medici, the nephew of Pope Leo XI) on a point of etiquette: who was to have first claim on an official carriage and who in an official procession should enter a church first. Salviati had been forced to give way. Underlying this competition lay the unsuccessful struggle of his family for several generations to move into the first rank of Florentine society.

Proud and ashamed, he abruptly left Florence in a royal pique and embarked on a long journey. His sojourn evolved into an extended tour of Galileo's friends and enemies. First he went east to Venice where he visited Sagredo, then to Padua, where he saw Galileo's eminent Aristotelian opponent, Cremonini, who assured Salviati of his undying affection for Galileo—outside of philosophical matters. During the early winter Salviati was in Genoa, where he discoursed with a professional contact of Galileo's on the problem of weighing air. And in his last letter to Galileo, Salviati spoke gaily of going next to Spain, requesting recommendations about whom to see there. Two months later, he was dead in Barcelona.

In Salviati, Galileo perceived a romantic image of himself. And in Salviati's memory, he saw the glimmering of literary device. Here had been a young scientist of immense promise, genius, and courage, not unlike the image Galileo had of himself, but more vigorous, more handsome, more athletic, and better born. The memory of Salviati presented an attractive, empty vessel, into which Galileo began to pour his own thoughts and his own genius in an idealized version of himself. Galileo would become Salviati. And Sagredo would become Salviati's foil, the wit who would prod Salviati when his thoughts flagged or became too dense.

But what to do about an opponent for Salviati?

Ever since the publication of *The Starry Messenger* in 1610, Galileo's opponents had been many and varied. They had been both learned and silly, gracious and malicious, pious and heretical, sincere and jealous, dignified and dishonest. No one opponent encompassed the lot. As a foil for the romantic reflection of himself, Salviati, the head of Galileo's Pigeon League and the opponent who first raised the religious issue, Ludovico delle Colombe, was the easiest target. He was Aristotelianism at its worst: conceited, shallow, inflexible, humorless, easily defeated. Colombe might be a useful starting point, for he had laid out his arguments against the motion of the earth in a treatise. But alone he was unworthy of Salviati.

Who could believe that such a rigid fossil would regularly sit in convivial discourse with Salviati and Sagredo?

The *Dialogue* had to be learned and sincere. Cesare Cremonini, the Peripatetic in Padua, and Father Horatio Grassi, the Jesuit in Rome, were certainly learned enough, but they were too formidable and prosy. They were disqualified for opposite reasons: One was a suspected heretic and the other a devout servant of God. Salviati's opponent needed to be genuinely dismayed by the arguments of the new science, armed with some difficult and even compelling arguments of his own, and open to persuasion. He needed to be without malice and genuinely in search of enlightenment, tied to the old arguments for their comfort as well as afraid of the new science for its rootlessness.

In a 1611 letter to the grand duke in connection with his essay on floating bodies, Galileo had put forward a principle about personal attacks. "In my writing, I have thought it would be well not to mention any of my adversaries by name. For whatever the reason, they do not publish their evidence to the world. I do not pretend to conceal my evidence; so I will conceal them. If it happens that I overwhelm their arguments, as I expect, it should not displease them that their names were kept secret. If I do not persuade them, they will have time to name themselves and to rebut my arguments. For I wish not to triumph over my adversaries, so much as to see truth triumph over foolishness."

Salviati's adversary was to be no one in particular, but all of them collectively. Now he gave foolishness a name. It was Simplicio. In the introduction to his *Dialogue*, which he wrote last, he put forward the transparent disguise that the name Simplicio was merely an Italianate translation of Simplicius, the Greek philosopher whose commentaries on Aristotle were a favorite of his Simplicio. This thin protestation fooled no one. *Simplicio* in Italian meant "simpleton."

Sagredo's pink ark in Venice, where Galileo had spent such happy times, was to be the setting for Galileo's dialogue. The location was strategic, as well as aesthetic and literary. It warmed him to remember the discussions that had taken place there, in the "stupendous" city of Venice, that "grand field for philosophizing." And it pleased him more to sharpen the focus of a discourse over the rambling nature of the actual discussions. Given the importance he intended to attach to the tides, Venice was most important of all because of its "marriage to the sea."

In introducing his three characters, he described Sagredo as "a man of noble education and acute mind, Salviati as "a sublime intellect that knew no more exquisite pleasure than elevated speculations," and Simplicio "who seemed to have no greater obstacle in understanding the truth than the fame he had acquired by Aristotelian interpretations." Of all Galileo's enemies, only Cesare Cremonini had ever achieved fame for his commentaries on Aristotle. But the objections and weak arguments of Simplicio were both broader and thinner than those of Cremonini, and so nearly any detractor, even Urban VIII, might see himself in Galileo's simpleton, just as Cremonini could deny that Simplicio was he.

Through 1624 and 1625, as he awaited further encouragement from Urban VIII on his letter to Ingoli, Galileo evolved his concept. He brought his imaginary characters together in a discussion of the central, organizing theme for his dialogue, his theory of tides. His interest in the subject stretched back to his early days of visiting Sagredo in Venice before the turn of the century. In 1597, in his letter to Kepler in which he announced his belief in Copernicanism, his reason was associated with the tides. In 1610 he returned to the subject, after he had discovered the telescope and observed the swirling satellites of Jupiter. In 1616, on the eve of Bellarmine's ban on the Copernican theory, he had written a long letter to his friend Cardinal Orsini in Rome about the problem.

This became his *Discourse on the Ebb and Flow of the Seas*, which he published in 1616. The thrust of his argument was that only the double motion of the earth, upon its axis and around the sun, could explain the tides. The argument was compelling, far more plausible than any explanation the Ptolemaic system could offer. Still, in 1616, Galileo had seemed hesitant about his theory—for good reason, since it is false—as if he expected it to be disproved.

"I hope this sketch does not turn out to be delusive," he had written to Orsini, "like a dream which gives a brief image of truth, followed by an immediate certainty of falsity."

Now he returned to his obsession of the tides, making the working title for the work, "Dialogue on the Ebb and Flow of the Sea." As the book began to take shape, Galileo divided the dialogue into four days, as today an author might divide a book into four parts. At the beginning of the "third day," he cleverly began the interchange of his characters. Salviati and Sagredo sat alone in Sagredo's palace, waiting for Simplicio, who was for some reason late, and reflecting on the discussion of the day before.

"I eagerly awaited your arrival this morning," says Sagredo, the wit, "so that I could hear new ideas concerning the annual revolution of our Globe. Indeed I lay awake much of the night weighing the reasons presented by the two sides, that of Ptolemy and of Copernicus. Some modern Aristotelians put forward opinions which are most childish and ridiculous."

"I have encountered many worse opinions than yours," the protagonist, Salviati, replies. "I blush to repeat them, not so much to spare the shame of their Authors, but because I am ashamed to stain the honor of mankind. In the face of contrary evidence which is both ingenious and compelling, these Aristotelians receive such arguments with disgust and bitter indignation."

"It is not good to get into controversies with such people, for it is not only unpleasant but dangerous," Sagredo replies. "But Simplicio is a man of great candor and altogether devoid of malice. Let us continue our talk with him. Yonder he comes. . . ."

Simplicio enters, out of breath and apologetic.

"You must not blame me but Neptune for my tardiness," says the foil. "In the ebb of this morning's tide, he has drained away the waters under my gondola, after I had entered a certain shallow canal not far from here. Unable to get out of the boat, which had suddenly run aground, I observed a very strange accident: In the water's ebbing, I saw it retreat very fast by several small rivulets, leaving only the ooze. While I sat looking upon this, I saw this motion cease in an instant. Without a minute's interval the same water began to return again. The tide from ebbing became a young flood in the flowing. The water did not stand still for a moment. As long as I have dwelt in Venice, I have never noticed this effect before."

And so the argument on the tides was joined. The characters were defined.

This settled, Galileo marched forward into an ecclesiastical trap.

12

CONVULSION

From his pleasant terrace atop Bellosguardo hill, the city of Florence
lay at Galileo's feet. The spiritual and temporal powers of Italy were
there at his beckoning. His new heaven stretched across the sky
above, and below, his book—a vast canvas of his life and passions—was
taking shape. He reveled in the pleasures of the court and the stimulus of
the salon. A keen sense of what made a worthy banquet had developed
within him. Base and plebeian, he wrote, was the event where food and
drink were inadequate, but the real qualities that made a feast noble were
"the beauty of sumptuous apparel, the splendor of the furnishings, the
sheen of silver and gold, the harmony of song, and the joy of drolleries."
His satisfaction was evident. His world seemed to be in order and his stars
in their proper alignment.

Yet one small and near constellation was not so harmonious and full
of delight. Not far from Bellosguardo, in Arcetri to the east, his daughters, Sister Maria Celeste and Sister Arcangela, lived in poverty and
deprivation. Over the previous five years, Maria Celeste's letters to her
father had described a wretched existence, as if she were quietly beseech-
ing Galileo to do something about her lot. At the Convent of Saint
Matthew where the wind swept through the bare corridors, she and her
sister toiled long hours merely to survive. They made lace to earn a few
farthings, tilled the fields for its tubers and greens, and ministered to
those who were even more poor and afflicted than they. For Maria

212   FLORENCE AND ROME

Celeste, the pleasures of life were simple: the scent of a winter rose, the taste of jam, the bouquet of tomato paste. Her contact with her father was the sole escape from the drudgery and cruelty of her condition.

As she struggled with her own elemental needs, she was forever attentive to his grandiose wants. When he toiled in his vegetable garden at Bellosguardo too long, she worried about his health and scolded him for being too caught up in sensual pleasures. She lived vicariously through his experiences with the rich and powerful, begging him to send her copies of letters he wrote and received from princes and popes, especially Urban VIII, and reassuring him that she shared these important, confidential documents only with her sister. Embarrassed by her limited education and lack of sophistication, she nevertheless cried out to be told about his scientific experiments and his dealings with the famous and powerful. "Your letters come like the footsteps of the friars," she wrote, "not only in pairs but with a lot of noise."

When father and daughter were together, they made jam and mixed medicines, including the powder that was supposed to ward off the plague. When they were apart, they exchanged such delicacies as candied fruits. To amuse the nuns, he sometimes sent little comedies, which he expected them to perform for him when he came to visit. Occasionally, he sent music, a symphony for organ for their Sunday pleasure, for which he was rewarded in return with a simple motet from the convent organist. When the clock on the convent tower broke, he fixed it in an ingenious way. And when he was inattentive, she blamed not him but herself. "I believe it is possible for paternal love to diminish because of a child's ill behavior," she wrote in the late winter of 1628. "Your affection does not seem as cordial as it was. Though you are well now, you never, never write me a line. For more than a month, I have suffered day and night from headaches and can never get relief."

This plea for attention was but one in a long succession of emotional outpourings. With the approach of one winter, she had written that "if we don't receive help from alms, we will run the risk of starvation." Their bread was stale, their wine sour, their meat scarce and tough. "If in your chicken coop, you can find a small hen which is no good at laying eggs, it would be good for our broth." Relentlessly, they were preoccupied with the basic elements that could sustain life. "For the love of God," she wrote, "I wish to be free of the thought which torments me: that we will not have enough money to get through the coming year." She asked of her father not only scraps of food, but of cloth. "With the coming cold, I will be chilled to the bone, if you cannot send me a coverlet, since the one I use now is not mine." At another point she pleaded for a scrap of scarlet cloth that she might tie around her waist, since "I suffer greatly when my stomach is cold and weak."

The bleak existence worked upon the minds of the Poor Clares in strange ways. Some became mystical, longing for a death that would deliver them to a paradise. Their vision of life after death was full of spiced cakes, incense, quince plums, fragrant roses, silver chalices, and crystal as they had seen represented in the frescoes of other convents. Others, like Galileo's second daughter, Arcangela, turned inward and hostile, withdrew from human contact, and exhibited "bizarre" tendencies. Twice the mother superior of the convent sank into such despair that she tried to take her own life. "The first time," wrote Maria Celeste to her father, "she banged her face and head repeatedly against the ground, the second, she cut herself thirteen times in the night." Occasionally, the church sent indifferent priests as confessors to the convent, but, wrote Maria Celeste to Galileo, "they come more to hunt for the hare than to guide the mind."

As a wealthy man, living in luxury, partaking of carnivals and feasts and assorted drolleries, why did Galileo not rescue his daughters from their holy hell? The thought does not appear to have occurred to him, or, given their medieval vow, to them either. Galileo was not inclined to encourage the idea of his daughters' leaving the convent, whatever their condition. He knew of the messiness that could follow a divorce from Christ. His younger sister, Livia, had left a nunnery at the turn of the century, only to burden him with her dowry for years, after his brother, Michelangelo, weaseled out of his share of the duty. And he had had enough of dowries. His oldest sister, Virginia, had allowed her husband, Landucci, to sue him over lagging dowry payments, and once that seemed settled, in 1621 Landucci had abandoned Virginia, forcing her and her children into the care of Galileo. Virginia died in 1623, leaving the children to him, and if that wasn't enough, Landucci reappeared and had the temerity to haul Galileo back into court for the unpaid balance of his widow's dowry. The father was content to see his daughters suffer through their noble service to Christ.

Added to these burdens and annoyances was the fact that his brother Michelangelo was given to dumping his family of seven on Galileo from time to time. On May 5, 1627, Michelangelo proposed to formalize the arrangement by having his wife become Galileo's housekeeper in return for boarding all eight of them, minus himself. Important musical business kept him in Munich. "This arrangement would be good for both of us," Michelangelo wrote breezily. "Your house would be well and faithfully governed, and I should be partly relieved from an expense which I do not know how to meet. Chiara [his wife] will bring some of the children with her, and they will be an amusement for you and a comfort for her. I do not suppose that you would feel the expense of one or two mouths more. At any rate, they will not cost you more than those you have with you already, who are not such close kin, and probably not so much in need of help."

So, Galileo had his fill of penniless wards. He did not want to throw two more innocents upon the world, only to have them eventually end up with him.

The burden of so many mouths and distractions finally wore Galileo out. After ten months, in the spring of 1628, he became ill again. When he recovered slightly, Michelangelo was delighted. "I tremble to think what would have become of poor Chiara if you had died!" he wrote cheerfully. "I think now that with your good leave, I shall have all my family back. For I do not wish them to be in danger of suffering unkind treatment one of these days. Meanwhile, I beg that you see to it that your servants pay Chiara proper respect and obedience, since I could, on no account, suffer her to be mistreated."

In 1624 Galileo had developed a new friend and patron, a gentleman from Bologna named Cesare Marsili, who filled the void in his emotions that had been left by the death of Filippo Salviati. He and Marsili exchanged visits on festivals for foreign dignitaries and at carnival time. For some unspecified reason—perhaps a dread of Lent to follow—carnival seemed to depress Galileo, but Marsili's company alleviated "the feeling of discomfort that has always accompanied the spectacles." And they exchanged frequent letters, full of gossip and scientific chitchat: who was arguing for and against Copernicus, who was in the running to succeed his old nemesis, Giovanni Magini, in the chair of mathematics at Bologna.

The latter question fascinated Galileo. He and Marsili conspired to gain the appointment for a talented priest, Father Buonaventura Cavalier. "I believe that few people since the days of Archimedes, and perhaps no one, have delved so deeply into the understanding of geometry as the Father Mathematician," Galileo wrote to Marsili. (Geometry was to Galileo the mother of all mathematics, and geometrical calculations far more difficult than astronomical problems.)

After Galileo arranged the election of Marsili to the Lynxean

Academy, he personally purveyed to his new friend the huge emerald ring that was the badge of election. It was only one of a number of gifts they exchanged. During Christmas of 1624 Marsili expressed his gratitude for Galileo's attentions by sending four fine Indian chickens to Florence. But this gift went stale. "Your gift arrived," Galileo wrote back. "Unfortunately, the hens were no longer alive, but dead and packed in a small box. Between the restriction of space and the rainy weather, they suffered rather."

Undaunted, Galileo sent Marsili in return the one thing every intellectual in Italy coveted. "In this package, you will find two glass lenses for a telescope. They are the best I have. The rope wrapped around is the length of the tube. I would have sent you a microscope to see things close up, but the metalsmith has not finished the tube yet. As soon as it is ready, I will send it."

During the years 1624 and 1630, Galileo worked fitfully on his *Dialogue*. The first three years, when his health was good and his motivation strong, were the most productive. For several hours each day he worked on the project. To Marsili in December of 1624 Galileo was buoyant about his literary efforts. "I am making progress on my Dialogue, calling into evidence the Copernican system."

Thus, at the outset, his intention was clear. To convince the world of Copernicus's correctness was his cause and his obsession. Again to Marsili, early in 1625, he confided his feeling that he had been cowardly in the past about openly espousing his Copernican intuition, but now, "I feel a rising in my being and want to bring the Dialogue to completion, hoping that Heaven may grant me strength to carry out the work." Learning quickly what all serious writers know, he stated that writing was the mortal enemy of good health.

And what he wrote in that early productive stage did nothing to mask his bold intention. Simplicio took up his burden as the incarnation of all Galileo's enemies, ancient and modern, Aristotelian and clerical, Ptolemaic and pigeonlike. Simplicio constructed the argument of straw for the other two to devour.

"The sun and the moon and the stars are ordained to have no other use than to be of service to the earth," he says. "The earth is corruptible and alterable, while celestial bodies are incorruptible. Therefore the earth is different from celestial bodies. Our senses tell us that the earth is always in the state of being altered, and this has never been detected in the heavens."

Having written this and put it in the mouth of his foil, Galileo pondered how to answer it. To Marsili in Bologna, he wondered aloud about the challenge. "If the Heavens are motionless as they are portrayed by the Peripatetics, I believe that the Heavens would be of no use to themselves nor to us. Our earthly globe would be an inert body and a useless load, so much more ignoble than it really is, just as the cadaver of a dead animal is inferior to the same thing alive."

Sagredo was given the first crack at Simplicio's argument. "What folly it is to say the heavens are inalterable," the wit prates. "Simplicio is confused and perplexed. I can hear him say, 'Who would there be to settle our controversies if Aristotle were deposed? What other author should we follow in our schools, the academies, the universities? What other philosopher has written the whole of natural philosophy, and so well arranged it? Ought we to desert that structure under which so many travelers have found solace and comfort?'" Simplicio reminded Sagredo of the man who climbed up to his cupola to get a view of the city and then demanded that the entire countryside revolve around him, so he would not have to be bothered to turn his head.

Having dismissed Simplicio's arguments with his rhetorical questions, Sagredo could now pity him. Poor Simplicio was like "the fine gentleman who built a magnificent palace, beheld it threatened with ruin because of poor foundations, and to save his paintings and tapestries, tries to prevent the collapse with chains, props, iron bars, and buttresses."

"Please, speak more respectfully of Aristotle," Simplicio protests. "He was the first, the only, and the admirable expounder of all logic. Gentlemen, it would be better first to understand him perfectly, and then see whether you can refute him."

It was for the sage—Salviati (cum Galileo)—to come to Simplicio's rescue. "Logic is the organ with which we philosophize," Salviati says. "A craftsman may excel in making organs and yet not know how to play them."

"But this way of philosophizing tends to subvert all natural philosophy," Simplicio protests. "It disorders and sets into confusion heaven and earth and the whole universe!"

"It is better philosophy to say 'Heaven is inalterable, because Aristotle was so persuaded' than to say 'Heaven is inalterable because Aristotle was so persuaded.'" Then, wryly turning to Sagredo, Salviati says, as if in a stage whisper, "Simplicio has his mind made up with Aristotle on the side of immovability of the earth, whereas I am undecided." And then to Simplicio: "We will need the ingenuity of Sagredo's penetrating wit."

For the sake of good manners, however, the sage proposed to save the foil from the wit's sharp tongue. "Well, Simplicio need not fear a collapse of his mentor yet, Sagredo. There is no danger that such a multitude of great, subtle, and wise philosophers allow themselves to be overcome by one or two like us who bluster a bit. It is vanity to imagine that one can introduce a new philosophy by refuting this or that author. It is necessary first to teach the reform of the human mind and to render it capable of distinguishing truth from falsehood . . . which only God can do." The last phrase seemed tacked on, perhaps much later, perhaps under orders from the Vatican.

In the first three years of its evolution, Galileo's *Dialogue* grew from a narrow tract on the tides to a campaign through his own life and mind. His pen marched past his various crises, tarried in arguments against opponents great and small, as if they were skirmishes before the great, bloody battle. Sometimes sharp, sometimes surprisingly diplomatic, sometimes prophetic and at other times contradictory, always anecdotal and imaginative, human and earthy, bold and sloppy, the book is a perfect reflection of the man himself. His emphasis is more on entertainment than on education, for he seems intent at all costs to avoid pedantry. The exchanges are full of wit and wordplay. Does the number three really denote perfection, as Aristotle would have it? "I do not believe," quips Salviati, "that with respect to legs, the number three is more perfect than four or two."

Between the private man and the committed author, there could be a split. He talked frequently of the thickheadedness of his opponents, and yet fretted about the need to attack an obscure opponent in Bologna. To Marsili he wrote apologetically, "It gives me pain that I have to argue against the cavalier Mr. Chiaramonte in that part where Copernicus is contradicted, and even more unpleasant a task because his arguments are frivolous. He shows that he has not read nor studied nor understood that author. I will do where necessary what I can to protect him. Given his great reputation, this will be possible, since I hold him in very high veneration." In his manuscript, he did not mention Chiaramonte by name.

Yet about Kepler, whom Galileo truly venerated and whose reputation was likewise impervious to attack, he is downright contemptuous in print. "Among all the famous men who have philosophized [about the tides], I wonder more at Kepler than any of the rest," Salviati says. "Though he is a free and acute genius, he has lent his assent to the Moon's dominance over the oceans and to other occult happenings and other such trifles." And to the anti-Copernicans as a group, he is savage. "Silence would be the most appropriate punishment for their worthlessness," Salviati says, "if there were not other reasons which force one to repudiate them. One reason is that we Italians are making ourselves look like idiots. We are becoming the laughingstock for foreigners, especially for those who have broken from our religion."

In his third year of work on his *Dialogue*, Galileo's interest began to flag, and he laid the book aside to pick up science once again. In the summer of 1626 he had returned to the work of William Gilbert and was experimenting with magnets. He constructed a 6-ounce magnet that could capture a weight of 150 ounces, and he was certain that he could improve the proportion. In excitement, he wrote to Marsili that "initially it seemed to me to be a most enormous gain to make the magnet support forty times its innate power, but now an increase of 150 times is not enough for me." He was so consumed with the challenge that "I have almost become a metal worker, and in concentrating on this, I have neglected everything else." This was not good news to intimates like Father Castelli in Rome, who wanted the *Dialogue* brought to fruition.

The following summer he was presented with an amiable dispute between a Florentine gentleman and a parish priest over the proper method to price a horse. Such idle speculation about the value of fine horses was a popular avocation in the parlors of Florence. Galileo welcomed the diversion, setting aside his greater concerns to consider the problem. In judging the value of a horse, one bidder—undoubtedly the priest—had offered ten crowns and the other one thousand. In arriving at the proper value, the equestrians asked Galileo to be their arbiter. Was it better to employ an arithmetic or a geometric proportion in arriving at a fair price between divergent estimates? A geometric proportion was Galileo's answer. The real value of the horse was one hundred. In addressing his response to the gentlemen, he oozed with false humility, apologizing for his "lack of refinement" but hoping that in the manner that bees liberate honey from the austere flower, he could use his pen to extract a similar sweetness from the raw question.

This was far from the only instance when the fanciers of parlor games appealed to Galileo's genius in their disputes. At another point he was sought out on the burning question of why certain numbers turned up more frequently than others in the roll of the dice. Again, Galileo was happy to ponder the question, for the fun of it, but also because one never knew when doing favors for gamblers and horsemen might pay a dividend. It is easy to imagine Galileo lying by his fireplace at Bellosguardo rolling the dice and pondering probabilities. It is just as easy to imagine him making a mark on his political ledger sheet as he finished his answer.

*   *   *

In the Rome of Urban VIII, the real sport of the streets was not dice but astrology. Along the banks of the Tiber and along the Corso, in the warrens of the Borgo and Trastevere, threadbare street vendors hawked sheets called *Avvisi*, which were the equivalent of the present-day tabloid. The sheets purveyed a juicy mix of news, gossip, and prognostication, with a special emphasis on what the stars foretold about events great and small that were soon to happen in the city and in the world. Sensational gossip about the pope and his pious family created especially brisk street sales of the scandal sheets. Fascinating items about the pope's habits and his prodigious eccentricities were rife.

We have learned from Dr. Mancini that Our Father recently lost all his natural color, after he ate some food heavily spiced with pepper. It is known for certain that at Castel Gandolfo he ate only a mouthful of lobster, and this weighed most heavily on his overheated stomach for three days, in which he could digest nothing. The Pope is not well, neither in body nor mind, and this is perfectly clear because through this entire week in the Consistory, he scolded everyone and presented an expression that was both obscure and troubled. Things went so badly after Sunday's dinner that the Court is in turmoil, so much so that cancellation of the coming meetings of the Consistory is under discussion.

An item such as this was particularly sensational, since it dealt with the pope's health. Any glimmer of hope that the current pope might die brought cardinals and their envoys scurrying from the far corners of the Catholic dominion. Spanish cardinals and their surrogates in southern Italy were especially interested, since they were upset by the tilt of Urban toward Richelieu and the French in the Alpine warfare. Swept along in the backwash of the Spanish Inquisition, they felt that Urban was too soft on heresy. The Spaniards, naturally, wished to replace Urban with one of their own.

At the slightest whiff of a fresh pontifical election, the nephews and cousins of papal candidates known as *papabili* scurried about the Vatican corridors with all the vigor and purpose of modern-day lobbyists. Urban himself was partly responsible for this consanguineous vigor, since he had taken papal nepotism to a new level by conferring the cardinal's hat on his brother and two nephews and making a third nephew, Taddeo, the governor of the Borgo. (Meanwhile, he began to construct the vast Barberini palace in central Rome.) The Barberini pope always made sure to orchestrate the ceremonies of their investiture in accordance with favorable signs of the zodiac.

Indeed, Urban VIII was a deep believer in and an avid practitioner of astrology. He had gone to considerable lengths to show that his election to the papacy had come under the most powerful configuration of the stars, nearly as perfect as the position of the heavens at Christ's birth. By the calculations of Urban's personal astrologer, the very moment of Urban's election had occurred when the Sun and Jupiter were in a powerful conjunction, when Virgo had been on the ascendant and Mercury its lord, when the sun was in the constellation of Leo, which was the sign of leadership. With the sun in his horoscope and joined to Jupiter, the Greater Benefic, the zodiacal charts showed that Maffeo Barberini and his family were born to lead the church.

These astrological calculations were all premised on the cosmology of Ptolemy. And the sun became the emblem of the Barberini papacy.

Through the first few years of his papacy, Urban VIII amused himself by demanding to be presented with the horoscopes of his immediate circle and then intimidating his cardinals with the manipulated results. The interest in horoscopes was, of course, widespread in Renaissance culture from princes to paupers, even to scientific geniuses. In 1603 Galileo himself had paid sixty Venetian lire apiece for the horoscopes of his two daughters, Virginia and Livia. And in 1609, undoubtedly as a duty of his office, he had cast a horoscope for Grand Duke Ferdinand I, predicting a long and happy life. But the duke died a few months later. Now in Rome, Urban's obsession elevated a diversion into a popular rage, and the *Avviso* was full of breathtaking prophecies.

An analysis of one's birth in relation to the stars was only half the equation. The horoscope also predicted the time of one's death and other bad news, and this could take a distressing turn. Soon enough, the resentful and the ambitious turned the tables on the pontiff. By 1628, the imminent death of Urban VIII was widely predicted, with solid astrological grounding. Quickly, Urban moved to obliterate any record of the actual time of his birth (April 5, 1568), to make astrological speculations impossible. And he prepared a papal bull outlawing speculations on the death of the pope and even on the death of the pope's family down to his third cousins. Punishment for this crime against divine authority was to be death and the confiscation of property. But this did little to stop the rumors, partly because they were being encouraged by Spanish cardinals.

Urban VIII had fallen prey to his own superstitions and vainglory.

The approach of a solar eclipse in December of 1628 utterly terrified him. Since the sun was the heart and symbol of his papacy, its darkening presaged the death of the Sun Pope himself. What was he to do to counter the evil influences?

In 1628 the pope was lucky. The eclipse fell on Christmas Day, when the blessed power of Christ's birth triumphed over all cosmic evil. The vicar of Christ was protected. The eclipse began over heathen North Africa and proceeded out over the fishes.

Two years later, in June 1630, Urban would not be so lucky. But he would prepare himself better.

In 1629 and 1630, powerful terrestrial forces conspired to alter the course of Galileo's stratospheric orbit. In 1629, Ferdinand II, though he was only nineteen years old, had become the lord of Tuscany, and for a few more critical years as Galileo's fate was determined, the grand duke would be ignored as a weak and callow youth. Among Ferdinand's first actions, however, was to appoint Galileo to the Council of 200, the ruling body of Tuscany, and Galileo responded with promotional zeal.

"Under Ferdinand's happy dominion," he rhapsodized, "no one is troubled by any of the hardships that afflict the rest of the world these days." He would soon be disabused of this notion.

With the Edict of Restitution, vast chunks of Germany had been formally returned to Catholic rule, and this seemed to confirm the positive signs in Urban's horoscope, encouraging the pope into even more grandiose thinking. The king of Spain, Philip IV, was pursuing Galileo to provide him with one of his best telescopes at any price that Galileo would name, and promptly Galileo did so free of charge. In the summer of 1630, brought south from the Po valley and from the Alpine battlefields by deserting soldiers and wayward travelers, the plague broke out in Florence, and the Arno valley below Bellosguardo was filled with the smoke of fumigation and the vapor of witchcraft. Kepler died in the same year, and that left Galileo alone at centerstage.

Early in 1629, after a hiatus of nearly three years, Galileo picked up his *Dialogue Concerning the Two Chief World Systems* once again with the determination of Socrates. And yet he could not be Socrates: He was too committed a propagandist to mask his prejudices with neutral questions. As had happened to him with previous work, the longer he waited to publish, the more reckless he became. His central literary problem had become the character of Simplicio. Should Simplicio change? Should the evidence win him over? Or should he remain inflexible and dense? The more Galileo wrote, the more he became annoyed with his foil, just as he had been annoyed and impatient with those wretches Simplicio represented. As the book developed, Salviati and Sagredo began to gang up on Simplicio.

"If the earth moves, the heavens have order," Salviati says. "If the heavens move, this involves a great difficulty. What force would be needed to carry the innumerable host of fixed stars! I would be unable to understand how the earth, as a body suspended and balanced on its center, indifferent to motion and to rest, would not give in and be made to rotate in the face of such power."

Sagredo fiercely turns on Simplicio. "Why do you reject this explanation?" he snaps. "Why do you resort to such outlandish and labored arguments?"

"I only search for a simple and ready explanation," Simplicio replies lamely.

"This can be found and quite elegantly. Make the earth revolve upon itself in twenty-four hours in the same way as all the other spheres."

"The crucial thing is to move the earth without causing a thousand inconveniences."

"All inconveniences will be removed, as you propound them," Salviati adds.

Surprisingly, Sagredo comes to Simplicio's defense. "But, Salviati, if you wish to persuade one to abandon an opinion which he has imbibed with his mother's milk, you will need powerful reasons. Countless people hold Simplicio's opinion. Your argument appears to be a very great paradox, and all schools of thought deny it."

Salviati is unimpressed. "If you have suffered, Sagredo, as I have so often, from hearing the folly designed to make common people blind to innovation, then your astonishment at finding so few men who hold this Copernican opinion would dwindle considerably. We can have scant regard for imbeciles who believe the earth is motionless, because they think the earth is too heavy to climb up over the sun and then fall headlong back down again.

"There is no need to bother about such men as these," Salviati continues, seeming to avoid the gaze of Simplicio. "We need not take notice of their foolishness. Neither need we try to convert men who can make no distinctions, just to count such fellows in our company in a very subtle and delicate doctrine. With all the proofs in the world, what would you expect to accomplish with people who are too stupid to recognize their own limitations? Nay, I can never sufficiently admire the superior intelligence of those who have taken hold of this Copernican opinion and accept it as true."

Sagredo's time to salve the hurt had arrived. "I consider it great fortune to have met you two," he says. "From your reasonings, all my doubt will be removed."

"You may be mistaken," Simplicio replies ominously. "In the end, you may be more confused than ever."

"That is impossible."

"How so?" Simplicio retorts. "I am good evidence myself. The further our discussion goes, the more confused I become."

"That means you are beginning to change your mind," says Sagredo.

As Galileo picked up his book and sharpened its dramatic conflict, he also resumed his intimate correspondence with Cesare Marsili in Bologna. The correspondence had been interrupted through a misunderstanding. "The truth is that three years have now passed since I heard from a gentleman from Bologna, to my extreme distress, that Your Lordship had been deprived of your life," Galileo wrote in April 1629. "To my joy, I discover that was a lie. Anyway, here we are, alive. So let us return to our philosophical pleasantries."

Among the pleasant distractions to which they returned was Galileo's hope to make a recruit of the priest who had taken over the chair of mathematics in Bologna. To Marsili, he wrote, "I want to encourage Father Buonaventura in the study of astronomy, with the strong hope that he will dedicate himself every bit as diligently as Ptolemy. If he does not reply straightaway to your inquiries, the reason is that he wishes, as suits a master, to put the theory first before practical examination, that is, to comprehend very well the Almagest of Ptolemy and the Revolutions of Copernicus, and then to carry out computations of each doctrine separately."

In Marsili, Galileo had a confidant with whom to discuss old sores as well as pleasantries. A nearly forgotten enemy had cropped up in the rumor mill: the embittered Jesuit who still claimed (under the pseudonym Apelles) to have been the first observer of sunspots, Father Christopher Scheiner. "I hear that the so-called Apelles is printing a long treatise on the sunspots," Galileo wrote to Marsili in April 1629. "That the tract is long makes me suspect that it is full of irrelevancies. Its length can only produce trivial pages, where truth occupies only a small part. If he says anything other than what is contained in my letters on the Sunspots, he will be recording only vanity and lies."

Galileo was caught up dangerously in his own arrogance. The very thought of Father Scheiner preparing his lies infuriated Galileo, and he poured his contempt into his portrayal of Simplicio.

"I ask you, O foolish man," Salviati says scornfully. "Do you imagine some magnitude for the universe, which you judge to be too vast? Why do you pass judgment on things you do not understand?"

"God could have created the heavens even thousands of times larger than it is," Simplicio replies. "But nothing has been created in vain. This beautiful order is for our benefit. Would anything be created that was superfluous? For the use and convenience of whom?"

"Merely taking care of us is adequate work for God, you say?" Salviati responds in exasperation. "We take too much upon ourselves if we believe that, Simplicio. I should not like to tie God's hand so, than that he has no other cares to attend to than those of the human race alone."

Galileo had promised Marsili a look at his manuscript in February 1629, but it was not finished until November. That fall he informed Prince Cesi that he wished to come to Rome to oversee the publication. The prince thought well of the idea. In the first month of the new decade, Galileo's friends gathered regularly at the residence of a Florentine canon, Niccolò Cini, to hear the author read passages from his manuscript. Their enjoyment and their gaiety was evident. An invitation to Galileo for one such session read: "Your Lordship is ordered to appear in the said place at 5 p.m. this evening, under penalty of going without dinner and of being deprived of the olive oil you requested."

By February 1630 the way was being prepared for a speedy approval from the church. Father Castelli was talking to the Dominican, Father Riccardi, who as master of the palace had "censored" The Assayer by praising it without interference. Far from being grateful for the gift of a compliant censor, Galileo had developed a certain contempt for Father Riccardi. Instead of his proper title as "Padre Maestro," Galileo had taken to referring to Riccardi as "Padre Mostro"—"master" perverted to "monster"—which apparently was Galileo's bad joke about Riccardi's immense girth. Whereas Riccardi did not seem to present a problem, Castelli had received a cautionary signal from the pope's brother, Cardinal Antonio Barberini. If the earth revolves around the sun, His Eminence had said, it must be a star, and this would convulse church doctrine. Adopting the role of the family doctor, Father Castelli thought the condition treatable.

A month later, Castelli wrote again with better news. From Tommaso Campanella, the eccentric Dominican and ex-convict turned papal astrologer, word came of a conversation in which Campanella had complained to the pope about the difficulty of converting progressive German nobles to the Catholic faith because of the 1616 admonition to Galileo. To this lament, the pope had replied, "It was never our intention and had the matter been left to us, that decree would never have been passed."

Galileo seized upon this intelligence, but for once he was cautious. He had reason to doubt the word of the volatile and unpredictable Campanella, for the report had the odor of a trap. About this news, Galileo wrote to Prince Cesi and interjected a condescending note about the portly censor for his book, Father Riccardi.

"Whether the report is true or false, the Father Monster adheres neither to Ptolemy nor to Copernicus, but is content in his own way to imagine the angels moving the celestial bodies without difficulty or intrigue, however they go, and that to him is quite enough."

On May 3 Galileo arrived in Rome with his manuscript. He was full of hope and anticipation, but his buoyancy quickly drained when he was greeted with a scandalous mention in the *Avviso*:

Galileo, the famous mathematician and astrologer, is here, and he hopes to publish a book in which are impugned many opinions upheld by the Jesuits. He has let it be known that Donna Anna will give birth to a male child, that at the end of June we will have peace in Italy, and that shortly thereafter, Don Taddeo and the pope will die.

The item had been planted, and it was brilliant. How any more damaging references could have been packed into the two sentences is hard to imagine. Galileo was no astrologer, but a serious scientist who had contempt for traffickers in the occult. The Jesuit order was put on notice, falsely, that Galileo was about to attack it frontally. The innuendo scarcely described the essence of the *Dialogue*. To foretell the end of hostilities in Italy (after the sixth year of what turned out to be the Thirty Years' War) was an international sensation, and when the prediction did not come true, its author would certainly be excoriated. Taddeo Barberini was the pope's nephew and the powerful governor of the Borgo. The birth of a male son to his wife, Anna, would excite public gossip, but the death of Taddeo would constitute a major event in Roman politics.

That was nothing, however, compared to the prediction of a pope's death. If Galileo had really predicted Urban's death, he would not only be encouraging the crash of a papacy but violating the explicit order of Urban VIII not to speculate on his death or that of his family. That the solar eclipse was less than one month away gave the item both timeliness and plausibility.

If the paranoid pope, himself a slave to astrology, saw the libel and took it seriously, he gave no indication of it when Galileo was ushered into his presence at about the same time. Instead, science and faith engaged in a long colloquy. In Galileo's eternally rosy view, the audience confirmed the ease of the approval process ahead, for he wrote to Florence that "His Holiness has begun to treat my affairs in a way that I can expect a favorable result." Since the pope had not read Galileo's manuscript, he could scarcely be more than polite, but Galileo did not easily distinguish between diplomacy and approval.

Galileo also met with Father Riccardi, who was for the moment the pivotal figure. In an abundance of caution, Father Riccardi had recruited a Dominican father and professor of mathematics, Father Raphael Visconti, to study the work. Visconti's mission was to ensure that in Galileo's book the argument for the Copernican theory was entirely hypothetical.

During his visit to Rome in the spring of 1630, Galileo's relationship with his censors was friendly. The Dominicans were obliging. They suggested corrections here and there, which Galileo readily accepted, and they gave no hint that the work was in danger.

By early June the heat of the Roman summer became oppressive, and worries that the plague in Milan might spread south to Florence made Galileo impatient to leave. He was sure that his affairs were basically in order. He was, he wrote, "completely satisfied about the prospects" for publication, and Urban VIII had made him all the more so by funding two ecclesiastical pensions, adding a bonus of forty crowns to one for special merit. Because of the plague, Galileo simply could not wait for every last detail to be wrapped up.

The church seemed to understand. Since the author had to leave, Father Riccardi presented him with a conditional imprimatur. The book was provisionally approved, but a correct preface and conclusion still needed to be written. There would be time to consider this later, Riccardi felt. A second review would be necessary, and this unprecedented step was strong evidence of the church's ambivalence. As the folios were readied for printing, Riccardi was prepared to hover over the process page by page.

So far, Galileo received no hint of this ambivalence. On June 16, in a letter to Galileo, Father Visconti minimized the outstanding problems. "The Master kisses your hands and says your work is pleasing to him. Tomorrow, he will speak with the Pope about a foreword for the work. Of the rest, a few small things still need to be taken care of, and then the work will be ready."

The author took heart and climbed into his carriage.

In the days before Galileo's departure, the Barberini pope was unable to focus, because his mind was far away in the zodiac. On June 10 a solar eclipse, more sinister even than the one of December 1628, occurred. For months Urban VIII had been obsessed with his preparations for this darkening of his astral symbol. In the papal apartments at the Vatican, Agostino Tassi had been commissioned to paint a mural whose centerpiece was a brilliant sun, so that each morning the pontiff could awaken to the warmth of his impresa regardless of the meteorology. More important, the pope had released the master of the occult, Friar Tommaso Campanella, from a prison in Naples. Campanella was a Dominican who had been implicated in the Spanish-inspired conspiracy against Urban's papacy in Calabria and had been sentenced, after torture, to thirty years in prison.

To Campanella's credit, however, were two accomplishments. Twenty-six years earlier he had written his masterwork entitled *The City of the Sun*, in which he imagined a great Catholic victory over the Protestant heresies and the establishment of a global Catholic utopia, presided over by a philosopher-pope and smiled upon by the sun itself. That squared with good astrological thinking, for under Ptolemy, Italy was the geographic region of the world under the sway of the sun. In Urban VIII, Campanella had conveniently perceived the incarnation of his perfect global theocracy. Such a true believer was more useful at the pope's side than in a distant prison.

Campanella's chief utility to Urban, however, was his magical astrological gifts. In the year of his liberation from prison, Campanella had published his tome on astrological practices, called the *Astrologica*. For months before the solar eclipse, the eccentric friar staged occult rituals to soothe the pontiff's fears of death. The smoky ceremonies were held in the Quirinal Palace, at the Barberini palace in Castel Gandolfo, and in the papal apartments in the Vatican. In a magical chamber, white silk cloth was hung and rose vinegar sprinkled on the floor. Urban and Campanella donned white robes and shut themselves into their dark chamber, as incense of myrtle and laurel was burned. Soft music dedicated to the beneficent planets Jupiter and Venus was played, while the prelates drank astrologically distilled liquors to disperse the evil influences of Mars and Saturn. As the terrified pope huddled in a corner, Campanella created an artificial universe of crystal and candles and moved them about to represent the favorable configuration of the planets and the stars in Urban's horoscope.

When the dreaded day finally arrived, Campanella's ministrations proved successful. The eclipse did not darken the Roman sky at all, but began at sunrise over Corsica, touched only a small patch of northern Italy.

Thereafter, Urban rewarded Campanella with a monthly stipend of fifteen crowns.

In Florence, a month after Galileo's return, ominous signs began to present themselves. The first two seemed to be unrelated. On August 1 Galileo's patron and dear friend, the Lynx of all Lynxes, Prince Federico Cesi, died. The magnitude of this loss would become apparent only in the ensuing months. The Academy of Lynxes was to publish Galileo's work, but the academy depended on a strong center. If trouble were to arise, who could be Galileo's advocate and protector in Rome? Later that month, an inscrutable letter arrived from Father Castelli, urging Galileo "for the most weighty of reasons," which he dared not commit to paper, to publish the *Dialogue* in Florence rather than Rome, and "as soon as possible."

What could it mean?

For the moment, Galileo ignored Castelli's alarm, for he too was eager to have his work published in Florence. The plague was a good pretext to accomplish his goal. The scourge reached Tuscany that summer and was rising toward its virulent climax in November. Communications among the Italian states were breaking down, making normal business impossible. To publish in Florence seemed to be in everyone's interest, so long as the Vatican could exert sufficient control with its local inquisitor. In late September, permission was received. A month later, Father Riccardi sent word that Galileo would not be asked to send the entire revised work back to Rome for certification. The master of the palace suggested that the book might be made acceptable with a proper preface and conclusion.

The process moved forward as best it could in a city that was now in the full grip of terror. With the uncontrollable epidemic, blackened and bloated corpses began to pile up in the streets, filling the air with the stench of decomposition. Quarantine and stringent sanitary regulations interfered with commerce. Mass graves were dug, and gravediggers became aggressive entrepreneurs. Stealing from the quarantined and afflicted was rampant. Any bruise, cut, or blister, however innocent, could cause horror and occasion arrest and interrogation. Suspected plague carriers were hunted down, and Jews were seized at the gate of San Frediano and deodorized. The crowded town squares were filled with the malnourished as well as the diseased and were given over to ceremonies of witchcraft and rituals of superstition. Masses were held in the streets, so that they could be witnessed from the surrounding windows. Payment was tendered to merchants by dropping coins into vats of vinegar.

The authorities worked feverishly to contain the uncontainable. A number of magical remedies were proposed, which overtaxed the herbalist shops. Lily oil, cedar syrup, and a brew of bran flakes and figs were thought to be salubrious. Traditional antidotes for snakebite (usually containing arsenic crystals) were embraced as the cure for bubonic poisoning. The base for another potion was snake meat from an eggless female. Some gravitated to the thought that a sack of precious stones over the heart would ward off infection. The most common medicine was a powder called theriaca, which Galileo and Sister Maria Celeste had mixed in their quiet times together. It was a confection of sulphur and arsenic, myrrh and gingerroot, peony leaves and Palestinian incense. After its preparation, theriaca was to be put in a sack of red damask and dangled over the heart, but outside one's clothing in winter, for sweat was believed to dilute its power.

Doctors were impressed into public service and treated the afflicted, regardless of class, at two fortresses that were made into state hospitals. The physicians were overwhelmed, and their burden was made all the more dangerous when the rumor spread that they were poisoning the infected. Other physicians were criticized for being terrified of their patients. They were said to conduct their examinations of the sick at such a distance that they needed the "glasses of Galileo." Authorities looked to the work of the great doctors of Padua for wisdom, and the recommendations of Galileo's personal physicians, Girolamo Mercuriale and Fabricio d'Acquapendente, became the standard treatment. Acquapendente had recommended that barbers burn the nape of a child's neck to guard against infantile infections. When a bubo actually presented itself in a patient, Mercuriale had suggested this procedure: "Insert a large cutting glass below the bubo and suck the blood. When there is no more blood, apply three leeches and cover the wound with a pigeon whose chest has been cut open. A plucked rooster can also be used, applying its soapy gray entrails directly onto the wound."

A contemporary poet wrote:

> *Behold your country,*
> *See how pestilence has covered her with wounds!*
> *Her blood-stained breast is bereft of her citizens,*
> *And has become a trench for bones and corpses.*
> *Her streets are horrid, turbid torrents*
> *Of Death and Lamentation.*

Under the circumstances, to venture into the oppressive city center was a dangerous enterprise indeed. Once there, it was hard to find intelligent and competent professionals, since most had fled to the countryside. Nevertheless, Galileo navigated the hazards and found a printer by the name of Landini whose reputation was high and whose emblem was three bearded fish. By January, Landini's press was turning out the folios. For the next two months, the author hovered over the presses, carefully correcting the sheets as they came off the blocks. From Bologna, his friend Cesare Marsili had ordered thirty copies, and Galileo was able to send these, unbound, in late February. This was a private action, for the book still lacked the church's imprimatur.

By the spring of 1631, approval was still withheld for unexplained reasons, and the author was becoming angry and paranoid over the delay. Unable to fathom what the problem was, Galileo finally blew off his frustration to several close associates. In March he persuaded the grand duke of Tuscany to intervene, hoping that the Medici prince could force the matter to a head, so that he could enjoy the labor of fifty years before he was dead. In a letter to Marsili, Galileo threw caution windward. "Malignity, envy, and ignorance are untamed animals," he wrote in fury. "I see them in what I experience every day. Even though my enemies be convinced by a hundred proofs and accept my new opinions, which they first denied, they do not cease to oppose other new opinions with the hope of proving me false on some other front. They hope to find just one slight error, so that all the other true doctrines of mine might be canceled."

A month later Galileo heard that further delay could be expected as Father Riccardi reopened yet another round of discussion with the pope. "To my great vexation, I learn that after keeping me in suspense for nearly a year without a resolution, the Father Master of the Palace means to pursue the same course with His Holiness, namely, to delay and spin out everything with empty words," he said to the grand duke's secretary.

"This is not easy to endure. My affairs are afloat on a vast and boundless ocean." To the Medicis, he wondered if a personal audience with the pope might bring his ship to port. He could demonstrate how trivial the alterations were and how submissively he had acquiesced in the church's suggestions. "Those present will then know how true and just my doctrines are," he said to the grand duke, "and that I have never entertained other views than those held by the most venerable and holy fathers of the church." This was disingenuous.

In late May, as the fury of the pestilence began to abate, so the plague on the house of Galileo also seemed to slacken. Father Riccardi finally produced his guidelines for the inquisitor of Florence. The truth of the Copernican system was, on no account, to be conceded. Its mention was occasioned solely because it was well known and under public discussion, but reference to it had always to be in a hypothetical vein. Never, never could it be discussed with reference to Holy Scripture, and the admonition of 1616 could, under no circumstances, be ascribed to ignorance in Rome. The preface and conclusion were to agree with these precepts.

In that regard, Riccardi seemed to be writing guidelines for himself. As for the preface and the conclusion, "I will send them from here," he wrote the inquisitor.

Thus, the pious censors wrote the first and last words of Galileo's book. Five weeks later Riccardi sent his insertions. "I send you the preface. The author may alter or embellish the wording, so long as the substance is preserved. The end must be treated in the same way."

The preface was tortured and contradictory, an apparently hypocritical genuflection to the admonition of 1616. It was confusing to any reader who did not know that the language was the pope's and not Galileo's. When the book was eventually published, Galileo had the preface printed in different type, as if to separate the Vatican gibberish from his elegant text. But the conclusion was clear.

At the end of the book, after four intense days of discourse the three interlocutors are exhausted but serene and well satisfied. Salviati turns his vision heavenward.

"When I consider what marvelous things men have understood, what he has inquired into and contrived, I know only too clearly that the human mind is a work of God, and one of the most excellent."

Sagredo is more earthbound. "I count myself little better than miserable, when I ponder the many, marvelous inventions of men," he says. "I feel stupid and confused, and I am plagued by despair. If I look at some excellent stone, I say to myself, 'When will you be able to remove the excess from the block and reveal so lovely a figure hidden therein? When will you know how to mix different colors and spread them over a canvas like a Michelangelo or a Titian?' And music . . . and architecture . . . and poetry. How sublime is the mind of man!

"But now, since the hottest hours of the day are past, I think we should enjoy our cool hours in a gondola."

They rise, and Salviati turns to Sagredo in an aside. "I must say to you, Sagredo, that in acting the part of Copernicus in our arguments, I wear a mask. Be guided not by what I say when we are acting out our play, but by what I do after I have put off the costume. For perhaps then you will find me different from what you saw on the stage."

Down the monumental staircase of Sagredo's pink palace they descend. One imagines Salviati and Sagredo arm-in-arm, jolly and expansive, while slightly behind, silent and spent, Simplicio follows.

At Sagredo's dock, the patrician's gondola waits. Salviati turns to mollify Simplicio. "I hope I have not offended you with my heated opinions, Simplicio. I have no ulterior motive. I wanted only to give you every opportunity to introduce lofty thoughts, so that I might be better informed."

The lines can be read as a confession of insincerity or as dripping with contempt. The gondola moves off in the twilight, and Simplicio remains on the quay, watching the compadres drift away.

"You need not make excuses, Salviati," he says to himself. He has become the voice of the Roman Catholic church. "They are irrelevant, especially to me, who is accustomed to public debate. I have heard antagonists grow angry with one another countless times, even break out into insulting speech, and sometimes even come very close to blows. Of the debates we have held, I can only say I remain unpersuaded. From such feeble ideas of the matter as I have formed, I admit that your thoughts are ingenious. But I do not consider them true or convincing. It is excessive boldness for a human being to restrict Divine Power with some special fancy of his own."

The established church, thus, had the last word. It was as if with its seal of approval the Vatican had provided a curse rather than a blessing.

13

THE TRIAL OF GALILEO

1

By the end of May 1632, the first copies of the *Dialogue Concerning the Two Chief World Systems* arrived in Rome. As always, Galileo made sure that the grand, the powerful, and the pious got complimentary copies. Cardinal Francesco Barberini, the pope's nephew, was the first to receive the book.

The initial reception was favorable. The genius and literary skill of its author were praised, and his characters were touted as clever inventions. Salviati was received as a grand Socratic, Sagredo as a free and witty genius, while Simplicio was seen as a good sport in a philosophical comedy. From Venice, Friar Fulgenzio Micanzio, Sarpi's protégé and biographer, who had loved Sagredo as much as Galileo did, wrote of Galileo's portrayal of the Venetian eccentric. "My God, what dignity you have imparted to the worthy personality of Sagredo! I can almost hear him talking." And another reader treated the book as a Renaissance thriller. "It is full of wonderful, new things, explained in such a way that anyone can understand it perfectly," he wrote. "Wherever I start reading, I can't put it down."

But the voice of caution also was heard. A former student of Galileo's, now a canon in the cathedral at Treviso near Venice, wondered if it wouldn't be better to forgo publication of these radical doctrines and simply deposit a few manuscripts in selected libraries abroad so as "to avoid strange things that could happen" if the book were published. This advice was as naïve as it was belated.

A month after the first copy of his book arrived in Rome, Galileo heard that his old adversary, Father Christopher Scheiner, the Jesuit who still doggedly claimed to have been the first to observe the sunspots twenty-two years before, also had acquired a copy in a Roman bookshop and was livid. Before the very eyes of the bookseller, Scheiner had turned red with rage. His hands shaking as he read the passages about himself, he complained to the proprietor that he had had to pay ten crowns of pure gold for the privilege of suffering slander and humiliation.

That Scheiner would take violent exception was entirely predictable, for Galileo, in the Third Day of the *Dialogue*, had wagged his wicked tongue at Scheiner, yet again calling the Jesuit "vain" and ill-advised, and treating his competitor as a benighted amateur. The reference was gratuitous, and it aggravated an old wound for no good reason.

"In this Dialogue, the author has made null all my mathematical researches and has laid violent hands on my 'Rosa Ursina,' and on my discovery of the annual movement of the Sunspots," Scheiner exclaimed. "I am preparing to defend myself and the truth!"

Not content to suffer his indignities alone this time, he appealed to the fellowship and solidarity of his entire order, which in the days of Father Clavius had been cautiously favorable toward Galileo and had remained neutral in 1616. In Scheiner's effort to enlist his brothers, he had an eager listener in the reigning genius of the Jesuits, the estimable Father Horatio Grassi. Grassi, of course, had been equally bloodied by Galileo's savage pen, although not in the *Dialogue*, and even though he was absorbed in his daunting architectural duties with the construction of the Saint Ignatius Church, he was delighted with the notion of revenge, however belated. So long as the bitter and single-minded Scheiner did the dirty work, Grassi was happy to lend his weight. With evident satisfaction after the Jesuitical revenge was complete, Grassi ascribed Galileo's problems not to his science but to his arrogance. "He has been ruined by himself," Grassi would write. "He is too infatuated by his own genius, as he disdains the genius of others. It is not surprising that everyone conspires to injure him."

Behind the scenes, the Jesuit opposition soon had its effect. The censor of the book, Father Riccardi, was already feeling the heat from the Jesuits, as they wondered loudly how this heretical book could have been passed for publication. Urgently, Father Riccardi wrote to the inquisitor in Florence (with whom he had worked to approve the book for publication the year before) to try now to seize all copies of the book before they were shipped outside of Tuscany. He made no secret of the fact that the pope had ordered the seizure, although only Riccardi's, not the pope's, authority was invoked. "There are many things which are not liked and which the masters want in every way to correct," Riccardi—the "master" who was supposed to have corrected everything—wrote urgently. The inquisitor was to act "with caution" and avoid a scandal. But it was too late. The books had already been sent out.

Riccardi was in trouble. His mistake had finally dawned on him: He thought a diplomatic preface and conclusion would be enough to defang the *Dialogue*. Frantically, he looked for help wherever he might find it. Among those he sought out was a Florentine nobleman who was a friend of Galileo's and a distant cousin of Urban VIII. The Florentine wanted to know what the tempest was about, and Riccardi replied that the holy fathers were now questioning whether the end of the *Dialogue* had sufficiently put faith above scientific theory. "This is the pretext," Riccardi said frankly, "but the reality is that the Jesuit Fathers are working behind the scene with all their strength to have the book banned. The Jesuits will prosecute him with the utmost bitterness."

In mid-August, Galileo's publisher in Florence, Landini, received the inquisitional injunction against the further sale of the *Dialogue*. (It was even being said in Rome that Landini's logo of three fishes was a scurrilous satire on Urban VIII's three nephews who had been promoted to the church hierarchy.) This was Galileo's first indication of how serious his postpublication problems were. A few days later he learned that a special commission had been appointed by the pope under the leadership of his nephew, Cardinal Francesco Barberini, to examine the book for error. On the commission there were no mathematicians, but only "irate theologians" who harbored antipathy toward Galileo. They included the pope's personal theologian and one convinced anti-Copernican Jesuit.

At the news of this stacked deck, Galileo appealed to the young grand duke of Tuscany, only to get his first glimpse into how powerless his benefactor would be in the face of the church's fury. To protestations of concern by the Tuscan ambassador in Rome about the commission, the Vatican replied with a certain tired forbearance that out of deference and "kindness" to the grand duke himself, the matter had been referred to this special commission rather than immediately placed in the hands of the dreaded Inquisition, where it belonged.

Behind the formal and amorphous responses of the official church lay the white rage of Urban VIII. This would not become clear until September 4, when the Tuscan ambassador, Francesco Niccolini, went to see the pope. The diplomat carried with him a formal diplomatic protest from the grand duke of Tuscany, which complained that Galileo's book had been formally approved for publication in Florence by church authority. Now it was suspected of heresy and was being brought before a papal commission! How could this be?

The audience began routinely enough, with the normal delicate business between diplomat and pontiff, until the first mention of Galileo's name. Then, with terrifying suddenness, the volatile pontiff exploded in anger, charging Galileo with inserting himself into the most serious and dangerous topics that could possibly be imagined at this troubled period of church history. He presented himself as a pure victim and an innocent man of God who had been tricked by conniving advisers like Father Ciampoli and Father Riccardi and ridiculed by Galileo himself.

"But Mr. Galilei published his book with the expressed approval of your ministers," Niccolini protested. "I myself obtained the approved preface and sent it to Florence."

"I have been deceived by Galileo and Ciampoli!" Urban cried out. "Ciampoli dared to tell me that Mr. Galilei was ready to do all I ordered, that everything was fine, and this without ever having seen, much less read, the work! And the Master of the Palace! He allowed the book to be pulled out of his hands with beautiful words, to be printed in Florence without complying with the proper form of the Inquisitor."

"Your Holiness has appointed a Commission," Niccolini said. "I humbly beg Your Holiness to give Mr. Galilei the opportunity to justify himself."

"In matters before the Holy Office, the procedure is to arrive at censure and then call upon the defendant to recant."

"Does it not seem to Your Holiness that Galileo should know in advance the objections which are being raised against his work? What is the Holy Office worried about?"

"The Holy Office does not proceed in this way," the pope hissed. "Such things are never given in advance to anyone. Besides, he knows very well where the difficulties lay. We have discussed them with him."

"I beseech Your Holiness to consider that the book is explicitly dedicated to our Most Serene Patron, the Grand Duke of Tuscany, and that Mr. Galilei is one of the Grand Duke's present employees," Niccolini pleaded.

The pope dismissed this remark with a wave of the hand. "I have prohibited works before which had my pontifical name on the front and which were dedicated to me. Besides, in matters involving great harm to religion—the worst harm that can be conceived—His Highness, the Grand Duke, as a Christian prince, should do his part to prevent such harm. The Grand Duke should be careful not to get involved, because he would not emerge honorably."

"I must repeat," Niccolini persisted. "I cannot believe Your Holiness would bring about the prohibition of an already approved book without at least hearing Mr. Galilei first."

"This is the least ill which could be done to him," Urban snapped. "He should take care not to be summoned by the Holy Office."

Stunned at the pope's irrationality and very glad that he had not presented the grand duke's formal written protest, the ambassador glumly left the Vatican. Niccolini had restrained himself when the pope referred to his kangaroo commission as a collection of serious and holy men, well versed in the sciences. He had withheld a retort when the pope referred, more than once, to Copernicus's theory as "perverse." In a report to Florence about this ugly audience, he had concluded that "the sky was about to fall." The best strategy under the circumstances, he concluded, was to delay. The prudent course was quiet and skillful diplomacy. To make a public uproar could only cause a break between the Tuscan state and the Vatican, and ruin Galileo in the process. They should try to work through more rational underlings for the time being because, "when the Pope gets something into his head, that is the end of the matter . . . especially if one is opposing, threatening or denying him. At that, he hardens and shows no respect to anyone."

In the September 4 conversation, only a glimmer of what was generating the pope's fury broke through. It was not that Galileo had introduced perverse doctrine or overstepped his bounds as a layman or was disobedient to church edict. Those did not evoke rage; they called only for judicious correction. Rage came from ridicule. One remark by Pope Urban VIII explains the entire Galileo affair: "He did not fear to make sport of me."

Therein lay the insidious cleverness of the Jesuit campaign to ruin Galileo. As if Scheiner and Grassi were Iagos to his Othello, they had convinced the pope that he was Simplicio in Galileo's dialogue! The Holy Father was meant to be the fool, the simpleton, the butt of jokes. By contrast, the genius of the piece was meant to be the Copernican, Salviati, who was really Galileo. It was as if the Barberini pope had been stung by one of his own killer bees. His rage had simmered for eight months. Had he not once doted on Galileo? Had he not prided himself in his literary and scientific enlightenment? Had he not talked with Galileo intimately from the heart? Now he felt deeply and personally betrayed. To confide in an admired friend and then to be ridiculed publicly with a distorted version of one's own confidential words—that was difficult for anyone. For a pope and a Barberini! Charged with the protection of the faith! This was too much.

This spin on the *Dialogue* was made overt when the papal commission rendered its conclusions in mid-September. Among its eight indictments was that sacred doctrine had been placed *in bocca di un sciocco*—in the mouth of a silly fellow.

The cunning of the Jesuits was as mean as it was false. It may be that in drawing the character of Simplicio and in writing his lines, some tie to Urban VIII had lodged in Galileo's subconscious. But the conscious model for Simplicio was not Urban but Ludovico delle Colombe, the president of Galileo's Pigeon League, the Aristotelian who had challenged Galileo's first telescopic observations and charged that they were contrary to Holy Scripture. The objections of all his enemies collectively had been grafted onto the Pigeon.

Something else of importance emerged from the commission's work. In the Galileo file in the Vatican's secret archives, the unsigned minutes of Cardinal Bellarmine's 1616 admonition of Galileo had been discovered. If the pope's fury was now driving the process, this document now became the bloody stiletto. By placing its emphasis on this suspect document and ignoring the formal edict the Vatican had issued ten days later (in which the Copernican theory had been condemned but Galileo had not been mentioned by name), the commission jubilantly concluded that it had the one document that "alone is enough to ruin him completely."

On September 15, after receiving the commission's report, the pope sent word to Niccolini that the Galileo case had been turned over to the Inquisition. The pope was taking the unusual step of informing the ambassador out of the "paternal affection His Holiness feels towards His Most Serene Highness, the Grand Duke. . . . His Highness should put aside all respect and affection towards his Mathematician and be glad to participate in shielding Catholicism from any danger." Both the ambassador and the grand duke were sworn to secrecy.

Three days later Niccolini made one last appeal to the pope in person, but to no avail. To the ambassador, it became clear that another factor was operating in the background. Certain Spanish cardinals were charging Urban VIII with being soft toward heretics. This added a political motivation for Urban to use the Galileo case to prove his opponents wrong. Through Galileo, the pope would show how tough he could be.

They went over the same old arguments, until the pope, cold and dispassionate now, finally called a halt. "Enough! Enough!" he held up his hand. There was nothing more to say.

But Niccolini persisted. The ambassador hoped that the inquisitional process would change—and harm—Galileo's great work as little as possible. At this, the pope's face broke into a patronizing smile, and he answered obliquely with a story. A virtuoso had once sent his book to a cardinal for the imprimatur. The manuscript was so beautifully transcribed with such a lovely hand that its author made a request: If any page required amendment, could it be marked with a drop of wax? In time, the manuscript was returned, spotless, without a single mark, and the author rejoiced at the approval of the church. But the cardinal corrected him. The prelate had not used any wax because, said Urban the storyteller, "he would have had to go to a store, ask for a vase where the liquified wax was kept, and throw the whole book in to censure it."

The pope was so pleased with his joke that Niccolini felt compelled to twitter.

Toward the end of September, the wheels of the Inquisition began to turn. The inquisitor in Florence received his official instruction to order Galileo to Rome, where he was to report to the commissary general of the Holy Office. On October 1 Galileo was presented with his summons and agreed to comply. His shock at this news was evident. For weeks he had been sunk in disbelief and denial. Now there could be no further doubt.

On October 13 he wrote a desperate, heartrending letter to his supposed friend, Cardinal Francesco Barberini. The letter was a howl from the lower depths. "This vexes me so much that it makes me curse the time I devoted to these studies in which I strove and hoped to deviate somewhat from the beaten track generally pursued by learned men. Not only do I repent having given the world a portion of my writings, but now I feel inclined to suppress those still in hand, to consign them to the flames and thus to satisfy the longing desire of my enemies to whom my ideas are so inconvenient."

This letter is among the most touching and anguished epistles that Galileo ever wrote. Besides the suggestion that he had put the torch to his papers, it also contains the startling claim that his *Dialogue* had been divinely inspired. He had heard, "almost like an echo of the Holy Spirit, a very short but admirable and most holy assertion suddenly come out of the mouth of a person, eminent in learning and venerable for the holiness of his life. It was an assertion which, in no more than ten words cleverly and beautifully combined, summarizes what one can gather from lengthy discussions scattered in the books of the sacred doctors."

He did not identify this holy voice. Who might it have been? Cardinal Bellarmine? He had died in 1621. His angel? Perhaps it was Cardinal Maffeo Barberini, now Pope Urban VIII. His nephew chose to ignore this claim of angelic inspiration. It smacked too much of witchcraft and madness. The assertion would never be repeated.

Finally, in his October 13 letter, he appealed to Cardinal Barberini to delay the trial, or at least to have its venue shifted to Florence. "If neither my great age, nor my many body infirmities, nor the deep concern I feel, nor the weariness of a journey under the present most unfavorable circumstances, are considered sufficient reason by the high and sacred tribunal for granting this dispensation, or at least a delay, I will undertake the journey, esteeming obedience more than life."

A month later, in the presence of the pope, the Inquisition formally heard Galileo's requests for delay and change of venue. They were denied. Two days afterward, the ever diligent Niccolini made a personal appeal to the pope. "Your Holiness incurs the danger, considering Galileo's great age and his high anxiety that he may be tried neither in Rome nor in Florence," the ambassador said. "He may well die along the way."

"He can come, with every comfort, very slowly in a litter," Urban replied, and then using the royal We, he said, "May God forgive him for being so deluded as to involve himself in these difficulties, from which We had relieved him when We were cardinal."

Whether from true illness or from artifice, Galileo took himself to his bed. This purchased him another month's delay, until finally, just before Christmas, a suspicious vicar from the Inquisition visited him to determine the severity of his condition. From his bed, Galileo professed again his readiness to come devoutly to Rome, but at present he had no heart (or stomach) for it, especially now that he had been attacked by sudden illness. Blithely, he handed the vicar a medical certificate from his physicans. They had found his vital powers much diminished. His weakness was due to frequent attacks of giddiness, to melancholy, indigestion, insomnia, and a lingering hernia. These things taken together, a journey to Rome was dangerous to his life.

The patience of the Vatican was running out. On Christmas Day, his own disciple, Castelli, urged him to make the journey before the ill will toward him grew even worse. Just before the new year, the pope issued an order to the inquisitor in Florence: Neither His Holiness nor the Holy Office would tolerate further evasions. Galileo was to come voluntarily or be brought in chains. Now even the grand duke of Tuscany wrote to him, pitifully confessing his powerlessness to block the journey.

Galileo girded himself for an arduous trip. To a celebrated jurist in Paris, he wrote his final parting shot. "If to say the earth moves is heresy, while demonstrations and observations show it does move, in what predicament will the Holy Church have placed itself?" More to the point, from well-informed sources he had heard what the Jesuit fathers were whispering about him in the highest quarters: "My book is more dangerous and injurious to the Church than the writings of Luther and Calvin."

2

On January 20, 1633, with all his strategies for delay exhausted, Galileo finally climbed laboriously and reluctantly into a litter and set out for Rome. The scourge of plague again gripped northern Italy, and he knew the journey would be slow. The pestilence had resumed its terrible cycle of death the year before, and the bloated bodies once again were stacked up in the streets. Officials adopted stringent measures, ordering a strict quarantine, forbidding citizens to enter the houses of their friends, even barring women and children from going out of doors for long stretches. Among the measures adopted to halt the spread of pestilence was to interrupt the free flow of travel.

In the end, no human strategy had any impact, and Florence fell back on faith and magic. From Impruneta, six miles south of the city, where, by legend, the Holy Virgin had appeared in a small woods to offer comfort some centuries before, the icon of the Madonna was taken to Florence in a solemn procession. In a ritual that was followed only in times of great natural catastrophe, the Madonna was greeted at the Porta Romana by the archbishop of Florence and a delegation of secular officials on horseback and paraded to the churches of Santa Maria Novella and the Duomo of Santa Maria del Fiore, then taken to Santa Croce, before slowly wending its way back to Impruneta, passing by the convent of

Galileo's daughters in Arcetri. But the magical Madonna had little effect.

Galileo had other problems. For five days before his departure, he was tormented with pain in his legs, and he was suffering from indigestion and insomnia.

A few days into the journey, his litter was halted and detained on the border between Tuscany and Latium, in the unhealthy valley of the Paglia River. There, at the Ponte a Centino, he was stuck in quarantine for twenty days. Little could be done about it. In Rome Ambassador Niccolini tried to shorten the quarantine, knowing how it would further sap Galileo's strength. To no avail. The ambassador sped the release by only two days.

At last, on February 13, the first Sunday in Lent, Galileo's dusty carriage pulled up before the stone entrance of the Villa Medici, where he fell into the care of Niccolini. The ambassador found him tired but in reasonable health. After a day's rest, the traveler had regained enough strength to pay a call on Cardinal Francesco Barberini. The pope's nephew received Galileo cordially but correctly at the Vatican, and Galileo, in turn, humbly reaffirmed his obedience as a good Catholic. His first request was to be allowed to remain at the Tuscan embassy on the Trinità dei Monti as he awaited trial, rather than be thrown in the prison of the Holy Office. Cardinal Barberini granted this request provisionally. Then Galileo inquired how he should comport himself in the coming weeks. The answer, rendered "as a friend, ex officio," was that he should not socialize nor even talk to anyone who might come to visit him, for "this could cause harm and prejudice." The Vatican had no intention of allowing the prisoner to preside over his salon of admirers and to build a base of trouble.

During the next two months, as Galileo awaited his summons to judgment, his mood swung wildly between hope and despair. The pain in his legs had persisted for over forty days, as well as his indigestion. Only good diet could relieve his distress. At first he misread the silence of the Vatican as a good sign: "The big storm is tranquil now, and there is no fear of a new storm," he wrote to the Tuscan secretary of state. "The situation is dangerous, but we should not despair that our little boat will make it to port. Though I have little strength, to borrow from Ariosto, I make sail with modesty against the raging billows."

For many days the Vatican did not even acknowledge his presence in Rome. Niccolini sailed around the becalmed waters of the Holy See, lobbying Galileo's case and trying to pick up bits of intelligence. Six days after his arrival, the Inquisition sent an emissary to speak with the prisoner. They chose a sheepish priest whom Galileo regarded as an old friend. His mission was to gauge Galileo's state of mind and to draw the culprit out, for the church feared most of all that the scientist might be girding himself for a dialectical battle. Naively, Galileo interpreted the visit as an expression of good intentions and a harbinger of leniency. "I take these visits to mean the beginning of a mild and kindly treatment by the Inquisition," he wrote, "very different from the threats of cords, chains, and dungeons."

On February 25 the ambassador heard that the many and sundry charges had been reduced to one: disobedience. This sent Galileo soaring. "Of that one charge, I shall be able to clear myself without much trouble when the grounds of my defense are known," he wrote home. "In the end a favorable issue may be hoped for." As Galileo was writing this, Niccolini was writing to his home office with greater specificity and less optimism. "The main difficulty consists in this: These gentlemen maintain that in 1616 he was commanded neither to discuss the question of the earth's motion nor to converse about it. He says, to the contrary, that these were not the terms of the injunction, which were that that doctrine was not to be held or defended. He considers that he has the means of justifying himself since it does not appear at all from his book that he holds or defends the doctrine . . . or that he regards it as a settled question."

On February 27 Niccolini had his first audience with Pope Urban since Galileo's arrival and found the pope's fury unabated. The ambassador filled the room with blandishments about Galileo's deep faith and assurances about his submissive and obedient frame of mind. But the pope cut him off. The church had accorded Galileo the singular favor of not clapping him in irons and throwing him in the dungeons of Castel Sant'Angelo, the pope said. Niccolini pleaded for speed in the proceeding, since the prisoner was old and sick. The Holy Office moved slowly, the pope replied. It would not be hurried. Galileo had been unwise to publish heretical opinions, the pope went on to say, for it introduced an "imaginary" dogma into the world that was especially dangerous in Florence, "where the intellects are very subtle and curious." This backhanded compliment was matched only by his sop to Galileo as an "exceptional man."

As his elegant imprisonment moved into its second month, Galileo fretted at the silence of the Vatican. The control over him was such that Niccolini had to request permission of the Vatican for the old man to exercise his aching legs in the adjoining garden of the Trinità dei Monti church. From his buff-colored, frescoed chamber above the salon of the Villa Medici, he looked across the rooftops of Rome to Saint Peter's, from which he had received "not one syllable" for days. Increasingly, the dome appeared like some gigantic, sinister octopus in the distance. Wanly, he held on to hope. "If one can judge by rare signs, the accusations have lost much of their gravity," he surmised. "Some charges have been dropped entirely for their evident insignificance, which bodes well for those that remain. One can hope that the remaining charges will end up in the same way. I cannot think any other way if I am to believe that truth will always win over falsity."

Urban VIII, however, saw it as an issue not of truth or falsity, but of obedience or disobedience. On March 13 Niccolini again went to see the pontiff and found him more livid than ever. A torrent of invective rolled out of him uncontrolled, and Niccolini had to be careful that he did not aggravate the situation with an ill-chosen word. The Holy Office would have to try Galileo formally, Niccolini was informed. During the trial, the prisoner would have to be held in the Vatican.

"May God forgive Mr. Galilei for meddling with these subjects," Urban exclaimed. "We are dealing with new doctrines in relation to Holy Scripture. The best course is to follow the common opinion. Mr. Galilei has been my friend. We had conversed and dined together intimately in the past. So I am sorry to displease him. But the interests of the faith are involved."

"If he is heard, he will give every satisfaction, with the proper reverence due to the Holy Office," the ambassador assured the pope.

"Mr. Galilei will be examined in due course," the pope responded, as if he were not listening. "But there is an argument which no one has ever been able to answer. That is, God is omnipotent and can do anything. But if he is omnipotent, why do we want to bind him?"

"I am not competent to discuss these subjects," Niccolini said diplomatically. "But I have heard Mr. Galilei himself say that he did not hold the opinion of the earth's motion as true. Since God could make the universe in innumerable ways, one cannot deny that he might have made it as Copernicus suggests."

At this, the pope once more flew into a rage. "One must not impose necessity on the blessed God," he said frigidly.

Niccolini saw that he should back off. "He is here to obey, Your Holiness, and to retract everything for which he can be blamed. I do not know about this new science, and I do not want to utter some heresy. . . . But I beg Your Holiness to have compassion. Make him the beneficiary of your mercy. I beseech you to allow him to remain at Villa Medici."

"I will arrange for Mr. Galilei to have the best and most comfortable rooms in the Vatican," the pope said, closing the subject.

Back at Villa Medici, Niccolini had the heart to tell Galileo about only part of his conversation with the pope, for he began to worry about depressing him. From this point forward, the ambassador quietly but firmly argued that Galileo should acquiesce in every demand of the church. He should give up his scientific opinions, at least for the purpose of this trial and in the interest of a quick resolution.

Niccolini's campaign to engineer Galileo's collapse culminated on April 8 after the ambassador had his last audience with the pope and before the trial began. Upon this occasion, the pope was distant, unmoved to the billows of rage he had exhibited on prior occasions, but also unmoved to sympathy for a sick and aged prisoner. He announced flatly that Galileo must soon report to the Holy Office. The prisoner would be retained, not in a dungeon as was customary, but in comfortable rooms that might even be unlocked. The Vatican was making an exception in this case, the pope said, out of regard for the good relations between himself and the grand duke of Tuscany.

Niccolini made a pass at requesting that Galileo be allowed to return to the Villa Medici at night to sleep. The pope refused. His resolve was evident. Niccolini painted Galileo as a man in great pain. In fact, for the previous nights, the stone hallways and the circular staircase of the Villa Medici had been filled with the moans and even screams of Galileo, as he continued to suffer terrible arthritic pain in his legs. Who was to say that his pain was not partly psychological, partly spiritual?

Upon returning from the Vatican, Niccolini found Galileo still argumentative. It was time, the ambassador decided, that the old man hear the unvarnished truth. After conveying the news that Galileo would be locked up in the Vatican, Niccolini told him not to bother further to defend his opinions. The scientist should submit to whatever the prelates wanted from him. Otherwise, the consequences were too terrible to imagine.

Galileo was shaken at the news that he was about to become a real prisoner. The ambassador was his only contact with the outside world. Now it was as if he had lost his last friend. He fell into deep despair. The following day, in a dispatch to the grand duke, Niccolini reported his conversation with the pope and his hard advice to Galileo. Of the latter, he wrote with sorrow, "He was extremely distressed by this. Since yesterday, he looks so depressed that I fear greatly for his life."

3

On the morning of April 12, 1633, the prisoner was summoned to the Vatican for his first interrogation. False hope still clouded his vision, as he expected to be back in the comfort of the Villa Medici by evening. His ecclesiastical jailers had other comfort in mind, however, and he was soon disabused of this fantasy. His address would be the Vatican itself until his trial was over.

This straightened out, he was ushered through the Arch of Bells to the Palace of the Holy Office, the mysterious and secretive domed sacristy on the south side of Saint Peter's. Down its long, magnificent hallways decorated with the severe portraits of cardinals, past the dark Hall of General Audiences, he walked at last into a spare room of white plastered walls, whose only adornment was a large crucifix upon which hung the bloody body of Christ.

Behind a simple oak table sat the inquisitor. On his left was the prosecuting attorney of the Holy Office, aptly named Father Carlo Sincero. Both were dressed in the vestments of the Dominican order—a white floor-length, hooded tunic, covered with a black mantle. To the right of the inquisitor sat a Dominican nun, the scribe, whose face was hidden in shadow by her huge white-and-black habit. With a flat voice, Father Sincero administered the oath, admonishing the suspect "to tell the truth" fully and openly.

"Do you know . . . or can you guess . . . why you were ordered to Rome?" the inquisitor began, impersonally, speaking not to Galileo but to the historical record.

He was Cardinal Vincenzo Maculano. Maculano was a tall, thin man, fifty-five years old, whose wrinkled, leathery visage was marked by a large, bulbous nose, a small mouth, drooping ears, and piercing, deep-set eyes. He hailed from Firenzuola, a small town in the north of Tuscany. His family history was festooned with a few flowers of minor nobility, but his father was of humble origin, a tax collector and stonemason. For years after Maculano assumed the robes of a Dominican, he did not seem to be destined for high office. He had labored in the backwater, quietly developing a proficiency in applied mathematics and cultivating an unusual specialty, for a priest, in military architecture. Ten years before Galileo's trial, Maculano finally had been able to employ this skill, when he was ordered to Genoa to consult on the stupendous project of reinforcing and strengthening the walls and defenses of the city. This had a holy purpose: The Thirty Years' War was entering its tenth year, and Pope Urban VIII had become a huge military spender. Only toward the end of 1632, with the walls of Genoa's harbor near completion and with the Galileo affair already preoccupying the Holy Office, had Maculano been elected as the commissary general of the Inquisition.

"I imagine that the reason I was ordered to Rome is to account to the Holy Office for my recently published book," Galileo replied.

"Can you explain the character of the book on account of which you think you were ordered to Rome?"

"The book is written in dialogue and treats the construction of the Universe."

"If you were shown this book, could you identify it as yours?"

"I hope so."

The inquisitor shoved the book forward on the table toward Galileo with evident distaste. The author picked it up and leafed through it for a long moment before he replaced it on the table.

"I know this book very well," he said.

The inquisitor could not have been pleased by the tone of these early exchanges. This was not a contrite man who stood before him. Not shame but pride marked his demeanor. It was time to join the issue.

"Were you in Rome in 1616?" the inquisitor asked.

"Yes."

"For what occasion?"

"I had heard objections to the opinion of Nicolaus Copernicus: that the earth moved and the sun was fixed in the sky. I came to hear what was proper to believe."

The last sentence was a taunt. The inquisitor ignored it. "Did you come voluntarily or were you summoned?"

"Of my own accord. I discussed this matter with some cardinals."

"What specifically?"

"The cardinals wanted to be informed about Copernicus's doctrine, for his book was very difficult to understand by those who are not professional mathematicians and astronomers."

That was an even sharper provocation. Cardinals were ignorant of science and needed elementary instruction like schoolchildren. Again the inquisitor ignored it. "Since you say you came to Rome to find the truth regarding Copernicus's opinion, what then was decided?"

"The Holy Congregation of the Index determined that this opinion—of the sun's stability and the earth's motion—is repugnant to Holy Scripture, when it is taken absolutely. It could be treated as hypothesis only, in the way that Copernicus himself treated it."

"Were you notified of the Church's decision?"

"Yes . . . by Cardinal Bellarmine."

"And what did the Most Eminent Bellarmine tell you?"

"That Copernicus's opinion could be held as supposition. The opinion could not be held nor defended as absolute truth."

"Were others present when you were notified?"

"There were some Dominican fathers present, but I did not know them, nor have I seen them since."

"Were you given any injunction?"

"As I remember it the affair took place in the following manner. One morning, Lord Cardinal Bellarmine sent for me. At first, he told me a certain detail that I should like to speak only to the ear of His Holiness, the Pope, before telling others."

This was an impertinence. He stood before a tribunal of the Holy Office under the sanction of the pope and under oath to tell the complete truth, and here he was saying brazenly that he was withholding part of the truth, a truth so sensitive that only the ears of the pontiff could bear to hear it. Again, the inquisitor indulged the provocation. He could afford to be patient.

"At the end, Lord Cardinal Bellarmine instructed me. It may be that I was given an injunction not to hold or defend the Copernican opinion. It was many years ago. I do not recall it."

"If one were to read to you what you were told, then would you remember it?"

"I do not know whether I would remember what was told to me then, even if it were read to me."

The trap was no surprise to the witness. Niccolini had been told of this document, which the church had been so pleased to find in Galileo's file and regarded as enough in itself to convict the scientist. Galileo had not been unduly upset when Niccolini informed him of its existence. He had other documents in his possession that superseded this piece of evidence, which after all had never been given to him.

The inquisitor nodded to the prosecutor, Father Sincero, who stood and read the February 26, 1616, injunction slowly and importantly.

At the palace of the Most Illustrious Lord Cardinal Bellarmine and fully in the presence of the Commissary General of the Holy Office, the Most Illustrious Lord Cardinal warned Galileo that the said opinion of Nicolaus Copernicus was erroneous. In the Name of His Holiness the Pope, the aforementioned Galileo was ordered and enjoined to abandon completely this opinion. He is not to hold, to teach or to defend it in any way whatever, either orally or in writing. Otherwise, the Holy Office would start proceedings against him. The same Galileo acquiesced in this injunction and promised to obey. Done in Rome—

Galileo broke in passionately. "I do not recall that Lord Cardinal Bellarmine gave me this injunction any way, except orally. Perhaps the injunction was that I could not hold or defend. Maybe even that I could not teach. I do not recall the phrase *in any way whatever* but maybe there was such a phrase."

It was time to spring his own trap. For he had his own letter from Cardinal Bellarmine, and there was nothing suspect about it. Unlike the purported record of the injunction, which was unsigned and unstamped with any official mark, Galileo's letter bore the small, scholarly, unmistakable signature of Bellarmine. Dated May 26, 1616, it stated flatly that the doctrine of Copernicus was considered contrary to Holy Scripture and "therefore cannot be defended or held." Galileo had been so informed. Just as flatly, it declared that Galileo had not received any penances, "salutary or otherwise," nor had he been forced to abjure any opinion. As the two documents were put side by side, Galileo's was clearly the more authentic.

"The truth is I did not think about it, because the letter of May 26 explained the order. Regarding the two phrases in this injunction which are not mentioned, named 'not to teach' and 'in any way whatever,' I do not remember them. They were not in Bellarmine's May 26 letter. And it was upon this letter to me that I relied. This was my reminder."

The inquisitor was not pleased. Was his case to boil down to an argument between two contrasting documents? A quibble over a phrase that may or may not have been uttered seventeen years before? A dispute over the failing memory of an old man? He changed his tack.

"After the injunction, did you obtain any permission to write your book?"

Galileo's head swam at the question. Should he mention all the encouragements to write his masterwork? Should he invoke the conversations he had had with Urban VIII himself nine years before when the new pope had invited further examination of the Copernican hypothesis? Should he mention the divine inspiration? Should he remind them of his letter to Ingoli in 1624, which treated the same subject openly as an advocate and had received no rebuke from the church then? Why now?

"No. By writing this book, I do not think that I was contradicting any injunction," he said blandly.

The inquisitor waded further through a mire of procedural detail concerning the publication of the book. Galileo's answers were unrepentant. If the book was published in Florence rather than Rome ... if he had dealt with the church's censor by mail rather than in person ... the plague, not he, was to blame. He had sought, and he had received, the necessary permissions.

"When you asked the Master of the Sacred Palace for permission to print the book, did you reveal to the Most Reverend Father anything about the injuction of the Holy Congregation previously given to you?"

"I did not say anything to the Father Master of the Sacred Palace, because I did not judge it necessary to say anything," Galileo replied. "I had no such scruples, since the book neither held nor defended the opinion of the earth's motion and the sun's stability. To the contrary, I showed Copernicus's reasons for his opinion to be invalid and inconclusive."

With that excessive claim, the first interrogation ended in a wash.

4

Galileo's prison at the Vatican was a luxurious suite of three rooms, normally occupied by his very own prosecutor, Father Carlo Sincero. The rooms were appointed with priceless icons and outfitted for every comfort. The prisoner had the run of the spacious corridors outside his suite, as well as the Vatican gardens in which to walk and ponder his situation. Special meals were sent over daily from the pantry of the Tuscan ambassador. A servant stayed with the prisoner to look after his every need. Repeatedly, the Vatican, including the pope himself, had reminded the ambassador that such gentle treatment was unique in the four-hundred-year history of the Inquisition. The customary quarters for a culprit were the dirt-floored dungeons of Castel Sant'Angelo, which had been provided within recent times for a knight of the House of Gonzaga who had been charged with moral error.

At the church's beneficence, Galileo was not grateful but miserable. He bridled at the "harshness" of his treatment.

His lifeline to the outside world was Niccolini, to whom he wrote daily. In the days after the first interrogation, Niccolini himself got caught up in Galileo's delusional thinking. The proceeding, the ambassador wrote to his home office, was moving in agreeable ways. With so much talk in the first round about how the imprimatur for the book had been earnestly sought and improperly granted, it seemed that the church officials, not Galileo, had made the real mistakes. Niccolini was "beginning to think that this party will end with someone else being blamed." Moreover, he had appealed to the pope's brother, Cardinal Antonio Barberini, who was an inquisitor general and susceptible to court flattery. "This Cardinal takes things seriously when one goes to him for help since he likes to be esteemed," Niccolini wrote. He was sure that this contact with the pope's brother had benefited Galileo more than anything else the ambassador had done.

Meanwhile, the pope himself had gone to the high country of Castel Gandolfo to celebrate Easter and was not due back until after the feast of the Ascension forty days later. There, at the Barberini palace high above Lake Albano, caught up in the spirit of Easter, the pope was likely to return to Rome in a forgiving mood, Niccolini surmised. "I believe they will free Galileo immediately after His Holiness returns from Castel Gandolfo."

The diplomat's brief lapse into fantasy ignored the fact that an ongoing, grinding process had been under way for four months and could not now be waved away by the changing mood of a volatile pope. Indeed, Urban VIII was deliberately distancing himself from the process. He tarried at Castel Gandolfo while the cardinals of the Holy Congregation took up the Galileo case upon his specific order. There were ten of them, including the pope's family representatives, Antonio and Francesco Barberini, who had been commissioned by the Holy Apostolic See as inquisitors general "against heretical depravity in all of Christendom" and who were watching nervously over Maculano's prosecution.

The first interrogation had not pleased the inquisitors general. They now had in hand the reports of three experts, that is, the formal analysis by Vatican theologians. Without qualification and with specific citations, these reports asserted that Galileo's Dialogue had in fact taught the Copernican view, and, therefore, that he had violated the injunction of 1616. Predictably enough, the harshest report had been written by a Jesuit, Father Melchior Inchofer, a professor of mathematics and theology in Sicily. Among the points he had made were these:

Those committed to the "common scriptural interpretation" of the sun's motion were presented as small-minded, dense, half-witted, and idiotic.

As for Galileo's expressed reason for writing the *Dialogue*—that foreigners were criticizing the Roman Catholic church for being antiscience, and his work was to straighten them out—no good Catholic would have dared.

He wrote in Italian rather than Latin for the sinister purpose of enticing common people, in whom errors like Copernicanism easily take root.

He expressed high praise for one William Gilbert (an Englishman, the personal physician to Queen Elizabeth I, who had written a very good book on magnetism), who was "a perverse heretic, a quarrelsome and sophistical defender of Copernicus."

In his interrogation, Maculano had scored on no point of substance. In fact, he had not scored at all. What lay ahead was a protracted fencing duel with a demonstrable genius, not only of science, but of rhetorical debate. If Galileo continued in the petulant vein of the first round, as seemed likely, the process would make the Vatican look ridiculous. Put another way, the way that Maculano now expressed it to his board of directors: "It would become necessary to apply greater rigor in the administration of justice and less regard for the ramifications of this business."

In this banal way, the ugly subject of torture first arose. "Rigor" had always been in the background. It was fully accepted as part of the justice system. It was applied routinely. It was nothing to be ashamed of on the part of those who administered it. Indeed, the law required that each stage of torture be chronicled, including each scream and twitch from the culprit. If torture was going to be inflicted on Galileo, now was the time to do it. As the cardinals discussed it, however, they preferred to succeed with a "voluntary confession."

What was to be done?

Maculano had an idea. He proposed that he interview the culprit privately, using persuasion tempered with threat to try to bring him to a recognition of his error.

At first, the cardinals expressed skepticism, even animosity toward the proposal. It seemed too bold, with little chance of success if the inquisitor were merely to employ reason and intellectual argument. But Maculano was a master of motivation. In Galileo, he had a deep believer, one who respected and admired and wanted to obey the authority of the church, and who was terrified of the place reserved for heretics in a Dante-esque inferno. Moreover, he was a hypochondriac. He was terrified of sickness and physical pain and well aware of the church's readiness to inflict them. The prisoner was worldly, a reasonable man with whom one could discuss practical and political realities. He was no Bruno, contemptuous of the Holy Church, stubborn in his beliefs, martyr to the end.

With nervous reservation, the cardinals finally assented to the extra-judicial contact.

Wasting no time, the inquisitor went to see Galileo that very afternoon. For four days Galileo had been confined to his bed, besieged again with sharp pain in his loins and bedeviled by intense anxiety. Adding to his mental distress was his concern about his beloved daughter, Sister Maria Celeste, and his shame over what she was thinking. She had written him after hearing of his imprisonment by the Holy Office. The conflict between her vibrant love for her father and her faith was painfully evident. "[Your imprisonment] grieves me greatly, because I'm sure that you are anxious and uneasy and perhaps without bodily comfort. On the other hand, it had to come to this before the business could be terminated. I am confident about the righteousness of your cause and your innocence in this matter. I hope for a happy ending with the help of Almighty God, to Whom I cry without ceasing, recommending you to His care. Only be of good cheer. Do not give way to grief. Fear can affect your health. Turn your thoughts to God and put your trust in Him who like a loving Father never forsakes those who trust in Him unceasingly."

Between faith in God and prosecution by His apostles on earth, even a genius could get confused.

Amid the fragrance of Easter flowers in the Vatican gardens, Maculano and Galileo huddled for hours. Galileo picked up where he had left off in his formal interrogation, and they went over the familiar arguments. The inquisitor put forward practical and political points as well as moral and scriptural ones. The pope would not be assuaged, no matter what the scientific evidence. That was a fact.

At the right moment, with ecclesiastical euphemism and without elaboration, the inquisitor let Galileo know that he was in immediate danger of the rack. This interview was in itself the first stage of torture. It was the first step of any interrogation, ancient or modern. Galileo was a subtle man. He did not have to be shown the instruments of torture or introduced to the hangman to be convinced of the church's determination. The interrogator would work on his extraordinary mind and his fertile imagination. Undoubtedly, Maculano expected that only a brief, veiled mention of the heretic's fork or Bruno's iron gag would be sufficient. He hoped that he would not have to go through the unpleasant ritual of actually showing the prisoner the heretic's fork with its sharp prongs on either end, to be stuck into the heretic's chin and the chest, secured with a collar on the neck, and its stem embossed with the word *abiuro*, "I recant." And the mention of torture would be dropped into a larger positive context: For the good of the church and for the good of his own soul, the great scientist needed to see his error and to confess it publicly.

In time, the persistent inquisitor began to wear his subject down. Then abruptly, surprisingly, "by the grace of God," Galileo collapsed. Perhaps he *had* gone too far in his book. Perhaps he *had not* followed the proper procedure for approval. Perhaps he *had* violated Bellarmine's injunction. Suddenly, Maculano became a psychologist rather than a priest, the confessor rather than the interrogator. In the contrite, heartfelt words that poured out of Galileo, the inquisitor perceived a sense of relief. Finally, the culprit had seen the light. He would confess voluntarily. He asked only for time to think about how his confession could be honest.

Had cowardice or expedience triumphed? To have the courage of his convictions was to become a martyr of science. To give in was to survive, perhaps still to fight another day. It is an eternal dilemma.

Full of self-congratulation, Maculano rushed back to the Holy Office to spread the divine news of the church's victory. "I hope His Holiness will be satisfied. In this manner, the case can now be brought to a speedy conclusion," he wrote to Cardinal Francesco Barberini. "The Tribunal will maintain its reputation. The culprit can be treated with mercy. Whatever the final outcome, he will be thankful for the favor which has been given him. Tomorrow, I will obtain his confession. After that, I will question him about his intention and allow him to present a defense. That done, he can be granted imprisonment in his own house, as Your Eminence has suggested." To this cheerful report, the inquisitor signed his name, "Your Humblest Servant, Fra Vincenzo da Firenzuola."

5

A day after the inquisitor wrote this, Galileo was again escorted to the Holy Office. When the prisoner was before him, Maculano spoke with dry impatience. "He may state whatever he wishes to say."

From his sleeve, Galileo pulled his confession and began to read haltingly. In the two days since he had met privately with the inquisitor, he had obtained a copy of his *Dialogue* and had earnestly reread it, checking the work against his "purest" intention. He had not opened the book for three years. To his utter surprise, he now professed, it appeared as if a strange author had written a completely new and almost unrecognizable

book. It had dawned upon him finally how the book could be misinterpreted. He had been careless in weighting his arguments "on the false
side," not to make the counterargument equally strong. Occasionally, his
counterarguments had been "made of straw," he now said, and that was
misleading, especially when one was using the dialogue form. He had
been carried away, he now thought, with pride in his own subtlety and
cleverness, as well as by his vanity and desire for glory.

"My error then was one of vain ambition, pure ignorance, and inad-
vertence," he said.

Maculano was stunned. If, after this epic prosecution, he were to present such an insipid "confession" to the Holy Office, the irate pope, and
the inquisitors general, he would be laughed out of the Vatican. The
statement was inadequate and unacceptable. There had been no direct
reference to the Copernican theory, no appreciation of his heresy against
Catholic dogma, no remorse for the harm he had done to the faithful, no
admission of flagrant disobedience. The statement was a confession of literary conceit. In the corridors outside the witness room, the inquisitor
confronted the culprit with his veiled anger. Soon after, Galileo returned
to his interrogation chamber to add something else for the record.

What he added only made things worse. He proposed to go back to
work on the book, not to correct the offending passages, but to add
another entire day to the dialogue, a hundred more pages, in which he
would show that he did not really subscribe to the Copernican view. In
this addendum he promised "to confute the Copernican arguments in the
most effective way that the blessed God will enable me." He begged the
holy tribunal to allow this "good resolution."

For so brilliant a man, this was a breathtakingly dense proposal. The
suspect did not appreciate what was going on. The statement did demonstrate, however, a flickering spark of resistance in one who was being
steamrollered.

To everyone's surprise, the day after his second appearance at the
Holy Office, Galileo was permitted to return to the Tuscan embassy. The
reason given for his release from his Vatican "prison" was to assist his
recovery from his nagging infirmities. The real reason was to reward his
expressions of vanity and excess, to encourage even greater honesty and
remorse, and to hold over him the possible return to holy austerities,
should he not continue down the correct path. Galileo regarded his liberation as an answer to the prayers of himself and his daughter. To Sister
Maria Celeste, he wrote, "All mercies come from Him."

From where, then, were these harshnesses coming?

On May 10 he was called again to the Holy Office. The matter was proceeding by the steps Maculano had outlined: first, the confession, now the opportunity for a defense, later the rigorous examination about motive. Even to Galileo, there was no longer any mystery about these steps. To save time, he came prepared. Standing before "His Paternity," he was informed that he had eight days to present his defense. The delay would not be necessary, he replied, and pulled a statement from his sleeve, laying it upon the bare oak table. It was meant to show his sincerity and the purity of his intention, without excusing his transgressions. Maculano said nothing in reply. He would get to the question of intention later. Without ceremony, the cardinal took the statement without reading it and dismissed his subject back into the care of the Tuscan ambassador.

Galileo's defense is a poignant, indeed pathetic, document. It restated his position that as a reminder of the church's position he had relied on Bellarmine's personal letter of May 26, 1616, which contained the church's admonition not to hold or defend the Copernican theory, but not the words "teach," or "in any way whatever." In the publication of his book, given its official stamp of approval, he had obeyed the injunction of the church, he protested again.

The pitiable section came in the statement's conclusion, which some regard as unworthy of a great man, evidence of profound cowardice, and proof of his guilt. (Others, with less taste for martyrdom, see Galileo's acquiescence as yet another example of his modernness: his instinct to survive in order to struggle later.) In it, the sick old man threw himself on the mercy of his judges. After ten months of constant mental distress, not to mention the arduous journey to Rome, he feared that his life had been shortened by this ordeal. That was punishment enough. He had suffered horribly, and he begged them not to add to his suffering, not to join his legion of enemies who so hated him and would rejoice in their further censure.

If this was humiliation, he had more steps to go before he reached rock bottom.

In the days after this "defense," Galileo's health miraculously improved. His confinement at the Villa Medici was less restrictive than at the Vatican, although the ambassador had to sue for leniency at every turn. Through his persistence, Niccolini got permission for Galileo not only to enjoy the gardens at Villa Medici but also to travel to the Barberini Palace thirty miles south of Rome. There in the mile-long gardens of Castel Gandolfo he could exercise his pained legs as long as he wished.

He was conveyed to Castel Gandolfo in a half-closed carriage, for the suspected heretic was not to be seen in public.

With his gasps of fresh air, Galileo's delusions returned. He wrote to friends that the proceeding was moving speedily toward a happy end and received many congratulations in reply. "His Holiness has begun to treat my affairs in a way that permits me to hope for a favorable result," he wrote to Florence on May 18.

On May 22, to Niccolini, the pope promised a conclusion to the unpleasantness the following week, but the weeks dragged on without any word. Even the grand duke of Tuscany was getting impatient at the delay—and its expense. He suggested to his ambassador that Galileo start paying a bill at the Villa Medici. The suggestion horrified Niccolini. "I am not about to discuss this matter with him while he is my guest. I would rather assume the burden myself."

This time Niccolini was not caught up in Galileo's optimism. In his dispatch to the home office about his audience with the pope on May 22, he conveyed his impression that Galileo's *Dialogue* was on the verge of being placed on the Index of Prohibited Books. To head off this dire consequence, Niccolini had proposed to the pope that Galileo write a formal apology for his transgressions, but the pope was cold to the idea.

"I have not told [Galileo] everything," Niccolini wrote, pleading with the home office to keep his communiqué secret, lest word reach Galileo through other informants. "I plan to prepare him slowly, so as not to distress him."

6

On June 16 the tribunal of cardinals held a private meeting with Pope Urban VIII. The moment for judgment had arrived, with the next step to be an examination of Galileo's "intention." The examination would be "rigorous." Through the previous four months, the prisoner had repeatedly spoken of the purity of his motives, of his obedience and faith and respect for church authority, and of the sincerity of his intention as a devout Catholic. Such loftiness was impossible in a heretic, and the church did not believe it for a minute. This motive could not be allowed to stand on the record.

Galileo's guilt or innocence had long since ceased to be an issue. This was now an exercise of preparing the record for history. That record needed to include a confession from the culprit's own forked tongue that he possessed the black heart of a heretic. In the decree that emerged from this meeting of the Holy Office, the next steps were laid out: to prove the wicked intention under the threat of torture. Torture was unashamedly mentioned in the Latin of the holy decree: *etiam comminata ei tortura* ("and also having threatened him with torture"). He was to recant before a full session of the Congregation of the Holy Office. Then he was to be condemned to prison for life. In the future, he was not to utter a single word about cosmology, or to discuss the Copernican theory, or even to teach its opposite, the Ptolemaic. This showed how much the Holy Office feared his semantic brilliance: The man had a way of debunking accepted belief with clever words of support.

Moreover, *The Dialogue Concerning the Two Chief World Systems* was prohibited and placed on the Index. As if that weren't enough, the book was to be publicly burned as trash. Finally, his sentence was to be distributed to papal nuncios and inquisitors throughout Italy and read publicly to professors of mathematics and science.

Niccolini learned some details of this judgment three days later in an audience with Urban VIII. Some personal punishment for Galileo was going to be necessary, the pope told him; on this the cardinals were united. (That was a lie. Among the dissenters was the pope's nephew, Cardinal Francesco Barberini.) Leniency might be possible, but only out of regard for the good relations between the Holy See and the grand duke of Tuscany. Should that happen, it must be clearly understood as an extraordinary favor, not to be expected by others, for the holy fathers meant to discourage other brainy heretics by Galileo's example.

On June 21, for the last time, Galileo's carriage set out for the Vatican. Down the hill from the Church of the Trinità dei Monti, it passed into the historic center of the city, not far from the Campo dei Fiori, where in that year of 1633, three conspirators against Urban VIII were burned together upon a single pyre, consuming with it the memory of Giordano Bruno. The litter moved on, crossing the Tiber on the Ponte San Angelo, from which past heretics were hanged, past Castel Sant'Angelo, where religious prisoners faced the most unspeakable "austerities" every day. Galileo knew full well how this day could end. The most common beggar understood the meaning of "rigorous examination." He was tired, broken, and resigned.

In the now-familiar star chamber, Maculano wasted no breath. "Do you have anything to say?"

"I have nothing to say," Galileo mumbled.

To Maculano, that was neither acceptable nor true. "Do you hold or have you held that the sun, not the earth, is the center of the universe?"

The witness was silent. Finally, with effort, he began his answer. "A long time ago, I was undecided between the two opinions, of Ptolemy and of Copernicus. Either opinion could be true in nature. . . . it was debatable. But after the decision of the Holy Congregation of the Index and since I was assured by the prudence of the authorities, all my uncertainty vanished. I held and still hold Ptolemy's opinion to be very true and undoubted."

What more did the church need? Like a pit bull, Maculano pressed on. "From the manner in which you defend the opinion of Copernicus in your book, you are presumed to have held that opinion. You are asked again to tell the truth!"

Again, Galileo tried to be reflective. "I did not write the *Dialogue* because I held Copernicus's opinion to be true. I thought I was doing a beneficial service by explaining the astronomical reasons for both opinions. I tried to show that neither had the strength of conclusive proof. After the determination of the Superiors, I have not held the condemned opinion."

"I repeat. From the nature of the book, you are believed to have held the opinion of the earth's movement and the sun's stability. Unless you tell the truth, the Holy Church will resort to the remedies of the law against you. We will take appropriate steps against you!"

"I do not hold this opinion of Copernicus," Galileo said with a super-human effort, as fatigue drowned him. "For the rest I am in your hands. Do with me as you please."

This resignation, this despair seemed to excite rather than satisfy the inquisitor. "Tell the truth!" he shouted. "Otherwise, we will have no recourse but torture!"

"I am here to obey."

Mercifully, Maculano called a halt. The terrified and crushed old man was led away.

It remained only to make a public example of him. To announce so important a sentence against so famous a person, to trumpet so complete a victory for the church, required a suitably grandiose setting. The Dominican basilica in central Rome, the Santa Maria Sopra Minerva, was the site for such a public spectacle. Located immediately behind the Pantheon, in a cramped space of twisting cobblestone streets next to the Collegio Romano, the medieval basilica was unremarkable from the out-side. Its flat, stucco facade was adorned with only simple circular windows and wooden doors, which seemed to accentuate the studious quality of its order. But inside, like the interior life of a pious scholar, it was majestic and luminous, with imposing ribs and vaults and trusses surrounding its central choir, which contained the tombs of the two Medici popes of the previous century. This emphasized the Dominican authority over the written word and its place in the real world. The basilica had been built over the Roman temple of Minerva, the Etruscan goddess of arts and letters, where in ancient Rome writers had gathered for literary events.

On the morning of June 22 a large number of cardinals joined with the black friars, and they moved through the transcept of the Santa Maria Sopra Minerva, down the adjoining cloister (which, two centuries before, Torquemada had had painted with biblical scenes), and into the great hall of the adjoining Dominican convent.

As this sea of red and black arranged itself in the pews on either side of the great hall, the culprit was brought in. At a simple prayer stand, upon which lay the Holy Bible, he knelt to receive his judgment.

Maculano rose and spoke for the tribunal and for the church. For nearly a half hour his voice droned on with a narrative of the case and an explication of Galileo's crime. As the cardinal read from his parchment, Galileo waited for the announcement of his punishment, only half listening to these overwrought words and important phrases. "We deemed it necessary to proceed against you by a rigorous examination," he heard Maculano say. And then piously, "Here you answered in a Catholic manner." Given the interest of the grand duke of Tuscany, the prisoner expected a light punishment, certain salutary penances perhaps, a ban on further cosmological speculations certainly. "You are vehemently suspected of heresy," the inquisitor was saying. "We are willing to absolve you, provided that . . ." What further did they want? Had he not done everything asked of him? Had he not confessed to every crime? Now he was about to acquiesce in the public spectacle they wanted most of all. Was this not enough?

By public edict, the *Dialogue* was to be prohibited, as an example to others to abstain from similar crimes. He had expected that. And then, "We condemn you to formal imprisonment in this Holy Office at our pleasure. As a salutary penance we impose on you to recite the seven penitential Psalms once a week for the next three years."

The betrayal by his church was complete. Despite assurances to the contrary, he was, after all, to be a prisoner of the Inquisition, with an indefinite sentence. He was a figure in disgrace, to be held up as an example to any scientist whose experiments were suspected of challenging ancient biblical thought. At seventy years of age, he would probably be imprisoned for the rest of his life. If there was any mercy in this maximum sentence, it was that his soul was not in jeopardy. He had escaped excommunication and therefore was not yet condemned to everlasting damnation.

If he was shocked, he was too tired, too dejected, too much in pain to feel it. His anger would be slow to rise.

Maculano took his seat and nodded to the condemned man. It was this—the professions of the culprit—that the throng of priests had come to hear. How complete was his humiliation? How thorough had been the inquisitor's work? Would there be even the smallest hint of disobedience or disrespect left in him?

His opening lines reassured them. The words were categorical and sounded sincere enough. He presented the picture of a chastened and contrite man, crushed not by the church but by the weight of his own conceit and vanity. The picture gave satisfaction. He did now believe . . . he had always believed . . . he would in the future continue to believe all that was taught by the Holy Catholic and Apostolic Roman church. He acknowledged that, against church command, he had propounded arguments of great cogency for a wicked opinion and was therefore an outlaw of the church.

"I desire to remove from the minds of Your Eminences and of all faithful Christians this strong suspicion of heresy. With sincere heart and unfeigned faith, I abjure, curse and detest my errors. I swear that in future, I will never again say or assert, verbally or in writing, anything to encourage this suspicion."

Then, as if he wished to please them with a gratuity, he offered himself now as an agent of the old system against the new science. "Should I know any heretic or person suspected of heresy, I shall denounce him to this Holy Office."

He laid his hands upon the Holy Scripture. "In the event that I should contravene any of these, my promises—which God forbid—I submit myself to all the pains and penalties that might be imposed in the sacred canons."

The sentence of a lapsed heretic was fire in the field of flowers. And the field was aflame with the vapors of righteous indignation. Within months of Galileo's abjuration, the Campo dei Fiori hosted a triple burning: a cardinal and two monks who had tried to assassinate Urban VIII with black magic. Before a wax effigy of the pope, the conspirators had held a black mass in the hope of bringing Urban VIII to an abrupt end and installing the cardinal in his place.

Part v

SIENA AND ARCETRI

14

BLIND OBEDIENCE

Most Pious Father,

    Galileo Galilei begs most humbly that Your Holiness commute his long confinement in Rome to something similar in Florence, for reasons of his infirmity and also because he expects a sister-in-law with eight children to arrive soon from Germany, to whom no one can offer help and protection so well as himself. He will receive any consideration of Your Holiness as a great favor.

    With this pathetic and partly insincere supplication—insincere, for he cared little about his brother Michelangelo's oversized family—the broken man made his last direct appeal to the pope. But Urban was not to be moved. "We must proceed gently," the pope remarked. "We must rehabilitate him only by degrees." Urban was, however, prepared to take a small step. He released Galileo from the languor of the Roman summer. The culprit would be permitted to take up a new imprisonment in the palace of the archbishop in Siena.

    In early July 1633 Galileo left Rome for the last time. For a moment along the way, his spirits seemed to lift, as he dismounted in Viterbo and walked, as a vigorous seventy-year-old man, for four miles, only to reenter his coach and crumple once again into despair. Three days after his journey began, he was welcomed in Siena by his most congenial jailer, Archbishop Ascanio Piccolomini. For generations, the Piccolomini family of Siena had been well known for its learning and cultivation. It had produced a pope and many humanists; Ascanio's father had been a cavalry commander and master of the Medici court. When Galileo had come from Padua to Florence in the summer of 1605 to teach mathematics to Cosimo II, Ascanio Piccolomini, then a young noble of the court, had joined in the lessons. With strong ties to the Florentine Barberinis, he became a priest after Urban VIII became pope and five years later was the archbishop of Siena.

An elegant and slender man in his late thirties, the handsome archbishop had openly solicited this charge from the church. He greatly admired the convicted heretic. As he received his formal Latin instruction from the Vatican and promised his superiors that the commands of the church would be followed in every way, so he had written to Galileo of his "extraordinary happiness" at the "honor" of having him in his house. In the episcopal palace, attached to the green-and-white-striped duomo of Siena, the archbishop prepared sumptuous rooms for his guest.

Not far away in Arcetri, Galileo's daughters were beside themselves at the news of the church's sentence and distraught at their father's silence. They knew nothing of his fate, whether he had been consigned to a pit in the papal prison at Castel Sant'Angelo or to something more gruesome. "The news of your fresh trouble has pierced my soul with grief," Sister Maria Celeste wrote on July 2 in a state of shock. "Dearest Lord and Father, now is the time for the exercise of that wisdom [with] which God has endowed you. Bear these blows with the fortitude of soul which your religion, your age, and your profession demand." The absence of any word from her father drove her to fear as well as anxiety. She appreciated the church's potential for vengeance, and thus she opened her father's house in Arcetri to two friends, so that they could sweep through his private papers and spirit away anything that might be incriminating before the priests got hold of it.

On July 13, with Galileo already settled in Siena, Maria Celeste wrote to her father about their precaution. "They feared you were in trouble," she wrote of his friends. "Seeing how anxious they were on your account, it seemed to me right and necessary to prevent any accident. So I gave them the keys and the permission to do as they saw fit."

No doubt this added to Galileo's sense of himself as a moral outcast and a criminal before man and God. During his first weeks in the archbishop's care, he aimlessly wandered the halls. He could not sleep, and his nocturnal screams filled the corridors of the palace. The situation became so desperate that his athletic caretaker considered binding his arms at night, for fear that in his flailing, Galileo might injure himself.

Six months of captivity had taken a tremendous toll. Ennui oppressed him, he readily confessed, a condition in which his shame, anxiety, and anger were made worse by his relentless physical pain. Two weeks into his stay in Siena, he wrote plaintively to the secretary of the grand duke to renew a campaign for his release. He may have been ashamed, but he was also incensed. His abjuration had been the price of freedom, he had been led to believe, and this subsequent imprisonment was a breach of his agreement with the Inquisition.

"I beg you to move His Highness to solicit the favor of my liberty from His Holiness," he wrote. "You might point out that the house of the Grand Duke has been deprived of my services for a long time." But the weakness of Ferdinand II was all too apparent. Still only twenty-three years old in 1633, he was a prince without power, a young man still under the thumb of his pious mother, a figurehead intimidated by both Spain and the Vatican. What power the grand duke did have was focused on the plague, which still held Tuscany in its grip. While his ambassador in Rome made an effort, he was told that it was far too soon to think about leniency.

Meanwhile, the Vatican was busy informing its inquisitors throughout Italy about the disposition of the Galileo affair. Notice of the sentence and Galileo's abjuration was distributed formally, with the implication that the dogs of Christ were to be vigilant in rooting out any lesser Galileos who lurked under their protectorate. The inquisitor of Venice received the standard accompanying letter, which explained that the documents were sent "to you so that you may make it known to your vicars and that all professors of philosophy and mathematics may know of it; that they may know why the Church proceeded against the said Galileo and recognize the gravity of his error in order that they may avoid it and thus not incur the penalties which they would have to suffer in case they fell into the same." With these decrees, the decline of Italy began.

The suppression did not cease with the wide dissemination of the Galileo sentence and the warning to all devout scientists. Actively the church encouraged reactionary academics to write against Copernicus and Kepler, but most of all against Galileo. A flurry of backward-looking treatises flooded the market. One, dedicated to Urban VIII, was entitled "Against the Author of *The Two Chief World Systems*" and contained the following logical propositions: "Animals which move have limbs and muscles. The earth has no limbs or muscles, therefore, it does not move. Angels make Saturn, Jupiter and the sun turn around. If the earth revolves, it must also have an angel in the centre to set it in motion. But only devils live here, so it would therefore be a devil who would input motion to the earth. . . . it seems, therefore, to be a grievous wrong to place the earth, which is a sink of impurity, among the heavenly bodies, which are pure and divine things."

In addition to sweeping actions, there were also petty ones. Those priests who had had a hand in the Galileo affair were disgraced. Father Riccardi, who had censored and approved Galileo's *Dialogue* for publication, was fired as master of the sacred palace. The inquisitor of Florence who had allowed the book to be published there was reprimanded. Father Castelli fled from Rome, afraid that he would be compromised, and did not return for months. For Monsignor Ciampoli, an intimate of the pope and an agent of Galileo, Urban VIII reserved special anger at betrayal within his inner circle. "May God help Ciampoli, for when it comes to these opinions, he is a friend of the new philosophy." Ciampoli was exiled from Rome to endure minor church posts for the rest of his life.

As the weeks passed in Siena, Archbishop Piccolomini set about to lift Galileo out of his dejection. Among his first acts was to order lenses to be sent from Florence, so that they might construct a telescope together and conduct celestial observations. Instead of the solitary confinement that the Vatican intended for the prisoner, Piccolomini created a virtual salon of poets, scientists, and musicians who filled the palace with laughter and good conversation as they paid homage to Galileo. Outside his windows, the streets of Siena were equally happy. A corner of the Piccolomini family palace afforded a view of the Piazza del Campo, where that summer the colorful *palio*, the most famous horse race in Italy, was run in July as it had been run for centuries. Music from the great organ of the duomo swelled over the piazza outside his rooms.

Among those whom Piccolomini brought into Galileo's presence was a local professor of philosophy named Alessandro Marsili. In discussions with him, Galileo's interest in mechanics and physics was rekindled, specifically investigations into the structure of matter, the strength of materials, and the properties of fluids. By September, Galileo was writing again, sending mathematical propositions to his correspondents and considering the problem of casting bells.

Another guest to Piccolomini's salon did not have quite as good an effect on Galileo. This was a certain benighted priest named Francesco Pelagi, who made the unfortunate mistake of preaching a sermon in the duomo on the question of whether a whirlpool had the action of impulsion or attraction. Galileo took violent exception to the priest's remarks, loudly rebuking him, and they fell into a shouting match. The arch-bishop's solution was to bar Father Pelagi from the episcopal palace.

In the late fall Galileo was confident and bold enough secretly to send a copy of his condemned *Dialogue* to Paris (where the Vatican's grip was looser), so that it could be translated into Latin and widely circu-lated. With the archbishop's encouragement, he was even contemplating a new dialogue, one safely removed from the thicket of theology, to be called *Discourses on Two New Sciences.*

In his new dialogue, Simplicio would be made over into a more attractive character. The archbishop influenced this positive approach, for no doubt he saw himself in the role of Simplicio in his own house. He was the prod to genius. When the French poet Saint-Amant came to call on Galileo, he found the scientist in a room lined with silk tapestry, appointed with the most sumptuous carved furniture, with scientific papers spread about, and locked in a spirited discussion with the arch-bishop on a mathematical problem. After observing the broad, powerful figure of the elderly Galileo and the tall, vigorous figure of the youthful archbishop in a sleek black cassock with red piping, the poet wrote, "I could not but admire these two venerable men."

Not everyone admired the spectacle. Was Galileo an honored guest to be praised and pampered? Or was he a dangerous heretic to be con-demned and ostracized? To the complainers and the papal spies, Arch-bishop Piccolomini had lost his bearings. His deference before this heretic offended pious men. Soon enough, a denunciation was lodged with the Vatican. Galileo was sowing un-Catholic opinions and encouraged this prelate of the church. That prelate was even suggesting that Galileo had been unjustly and severely treated by the church and was rightly impeni-tent of the charges against him. To Piccolomini, read the anonymous accusation, Galileo was the first man of the world. Out of such opinions could stem evil fruit.

As Archbishop Piccolomini worked to restore Galileo's confidence, Sister Maria Celeste kindled his longing to return to Florence. In the fall of 1633 Galileo had renewed his request to the Vatican through the Tus-can ambassador to be released from his frescoed prison. The request lan-guished in Rome.

As it did, Maria Celeste wrote him about the simple things of Arcetri, and this even more fired his desire to return home. In October the plague had finally lifted in Florence, and once again there was a procession from Impruneta, this time of thanks. Led by Grand Duke Ferdinand himself, the happy procession of the Holy Madonna had passed by the door of Sister Maria Celeste's convent, to the great excitement of the Poor Clares. She spoke of how the wine casks had to be disassembled and the timbers bared to the sun, lest the casks sour the wine, of how hail had injured the vines and wind had blown away the pears, of how thieves had invaded the convent's garden, of her lace embroidery, and of the stubbornness of "my lady mule." She told of buying wheat and selling lemons, and with the proceeds (two lire) of purchasing three holy masses to be said for him.

"There are two pigeons in the dovecot waiting for you to come and eat them," she wrote. "The beans in the garden wait for you to gather them. Your tower is lamenting your long absence. When you were in Rome, I said to myself, If he were but at Siena! Now that you are at Siena, I say, Would that he were at Arcetri! But God's will be done."

When she finally received the text of his sentence, she was mortified, and yet she found a bright side. "I was glad to have read it, because I found a way of being some slight use to you. I shall take upon myself that part of the sentence which orders you to recite the seven Penitential Psalms once a week."

Her anguish, her conflict, her deep love and longing finally overcame her, and she became ill. Her illness gave fresh urgency to his appeals for liberation, and at last the pope relented, more from the reports of Galileo's lavish confinement than from charity for Sister Maria Celeste. On December 1, 1633, the edict was issued: Galileo would be permitted to return to Arcetri, there to live in solitude under the strictest control of the local priests, to entertain no one, nor to allow his friends to gather in number.

When Sister Maria Celeste heard the news of his imminent arrival, she wrote mournfully from her sickbed, "I do not think that I shall live to see that hour. Yet may God grant it, for it be for the best."

But she did see the hour. Galileo took up residence in a small villa called the "Little Jewel" on the narrow cobblestone street that ran through the hilltop village. A wall barred his view of the street, but the rear of the house opened onto a grand vista, across a grove of olive trees and an enormous holm oak to the Convent of Saint Matthew and beyond to the far western hills of Tuscany. His rooms were spartan, but there was an open loggia with a ribbed wooden ceiling where he could spend time in contemplation and where he could train his telescope on the sky.

Among his first actions was to write an obsequious letter of thanks to Cardinal Francesco Barberini, the pope's nephew, for his new circumstance. "For this and a thousand other favors which I have received from your benign hand, I am obliged always to serve and venerate Your Eminence." Among his first callers was the grand duke of Tuscany, Ferdinand II himself.

In the first four months of his house arrest, his faith rather than his science was taxed. Maria Celeste could not recover her strength. Galileo was constantly on the simple street or along the path through the olive trees, to her bedside. In the walled cloister of the Convent of Saint Matthew the roses bloomed that winter, as if for her. On the first day of spring, she contracted a violent dysentery. Six days later, at the age of thirty-three, she died.

On her last day of life, Galileo returned home to his villa in the company of a doctor who had just told him that his daughter's condition was desperate. When he entered the courtyard, the vicar of the Inquisition stood before him. Waving aside Galileo's personal matters, the vicar delivered a stark message from Rome: The prisoner was to cease these repeated requests to return to Florence, for medical treatment or any other reason. If he needed medical attention, his doctors could come to him. If he persisted in these annoyances, he would be returned to Rome and placed in the prison of the Holy Office.

"From this answer," Galileo remarked, "it seems to me that, in all probability, my present prison will be exchanged only for that narrow and long enduring one which awaits us all."

But there was another face of the church on this sad occasion. In Siena, upon hearing of the loss of Sister Maria Celeste, Galileo's last jailer, Archbishop Piccolomini, sat down to convey his sorrow. "I would like to be free with myself, to be there with you to console you," he wrote. "But upon this subject, I would not be able to find the proper words. . . . I would hope that such a daughter, now in the presence of God, could intercede in your behalf, and that God will make it possible for a change of your fortune and grant to you peace of mind." Once again, the archbishop was the subtle voice of apology for the severe actions of his church.

Four weeks after his daughter's death, Galileo reached the bottom of his despair. After fifteen months of exile and humiliation, sickness and tragedy, he seemed close to losing his mind. His blood pressure vacillated, his heart rate surged, his hernia distressed him more than ever, and he had no appetite.

"I feel myself perpetually called by my beloved daughter," he wrote on April 27. "I loathe myself."

The seasons changed. Letters poured in from around Europe. Gradually, Galileo began to work again. There were simple pleasures: his garden, his lute, his surviving daughter, Sister Arcangela, there still at the Convent of Saint Matthew. Arcangela was no equal to Sister Maria Celeste, for her nature was resentful, brooding, and dry. Still, his self-loathing did not last.

In Paris, far from the lash of the church, Galileo had a new friend. Elia Diodati was a parliamentary lawyer who had visited him over the years and with whom he carried on a learned correspondence. Diodati wanted a portrait of Galileo. The grand duke thought well of the idea and detailed his court painter, Justus Sustermans, to the task. As a leading portraitist in Europe, the Flemish artist was in important company. He had been influenced by Rubens and Van Dyck, who were both painting at the end of their lives. Rembrandt was just beginning, and Velasquez was in his prime.

Sustermans lived on Galileo's side of the Arno, halfway up the hill from the town, not far from San Miniato, where a small, walled lane called Via Giramonte merged with the thoroughfares named for Michelangelo and Leonardo, Petrarch and Machiavelli. From July to September, during the hottest weeks of that summer, Galileo ventured from his seclusion to Sustermans's modest studio. It was as far down the hill toward his beloved city as he dared to go, for the studio represented the outer limit of his quarantine. When he arrived at the low-slung stucco cottage, he could look over a vine-covered wall to see the dome of Florence, close enough to touch, it seemed, and perfectly framed, like forbidden fruit.

Sustermans placed his subject at the window, in the pale north light, and allowed him to talk. For in talking, his vitality sprang forth, his eyes grew lively, and his skin became luminous. The glint in his eye was part bemusement, part contemplation, part impatience at the slowness of the sun to set and bring on, once again, the night.

Sustermans captured the universal man. The figure is unadorned: a simple black sack shirt with a floppy white collar, as if the shirt had been thrown on haphazardly. The face turns toward the soft light, light that painters call celestial or spiritual, and the visage has an air of being startled by something unexpected, an effect produced by the mouth being slightly open and the sidelong glance of the eyes being especially acute.

The eyes are the focus. In the figure's age, in its depth of character, in its expression of wonder, it is saintly and reminiscent of Saint Peter.

As Sustermans painted, so Galileo's son, Vincenzo, painted a verbal picture of his father in old age. "He had a jovial face, especially in old age, a stature that was stocky and upright, with a robust and vigorous complexion which was well suited to the hard work of Atlas, and enabled him to endure long observations of the heavens. His discourse was rich in its sentences and serious in conception. In light conversation, he had great wit and humor. He was easily moved to rage, but more easily placated. His memory was exquisite, so much so that he could recite great quantities of poetry, especially a great part of *Orlando Furioso*, which among all poems was his favorite, and who he put ahead of all Latin or Tuscan poets. He found lies detestable, perhaps because, preoccupying himself with mathematical science, he knew the beauty of truth."

Upon its arrival in Paris in 1636, the Sustermans portrait was put beside Diodati's other treasures. In the accompanying letter, Galileo poured out his sentiments about his misfortune to his foreign correspondent. Not long after Maria Celeste's death, he passed on to Diodati the report of a "revelation" as if it were a headline. An important Jesuit mathematician at the Collegio Romano in Rome had remarked to one of Galileo's friends: "If Galileo had only known how to retain the favor of the fathers of this college, he would have stood in renown before the world; he would have been spared all his misfortunes, and could have written about everything, even about the motion of the earth."

Self-serving though this remark was, Galileo took it at face value. Not his opinions, but his disgrace before the Jesuits had sacked him. As Diodati received this "revelation," he was busy managing the Latin translation of the *Dialogue* and arranging for its publication in Holland. Additionally, the lawyer was secretly making arrangements to publish Galileo's overtly Copernican *Letter to Christine*, written twenty years earlier. With a certain private joy, Galileo savored the thought that these translations would increase the anger of his enemies.

Through these last years of reflection about his fate, his best correspondence, for obvious reasons, was sent abroad. He had been fairly warned that any indiscretion that came into the hands of the Vatican would land him in the dungeon of the Holy Office. To another Frenchman, Nicolas Fabri de Peiresc (who had attended Galileo's lectures in the Paduan period, had become a learned man of Aix, and was lobbying in Paris with an important cardinal for Galileo's liberation), he wrote about his inability to speak out about his injustice. "It is advisable for me to succumb. I must remain silent about the attacks that have rained down on me in such number, in order to suppress the [Copernican] doctrine and publicize my ignorance. It is also advisable that I swallow the sneers, the sarcasms, the insults."

But he seethed with bitter rage over suffering this injustice committed "under the lying mask of religion" and even more over this requirement to remain silent. "I do not hope for any relief, and that is because I have committed no crime," he wrote to Peiresc on February 22, 1635, to thank him for his efforts in his behalf. "I might hope for a pardon if I had erred. With the guilty a prince can show forebearance, but against one wrongfully sentenced when he is innocent, it is expedient to uphold rigor, so as to put up a show of strict lawfulness."

One specific sneer wounded him: that his model for Simplicio in the *Dialogue* had been Urban VIII himself. This especially nasty idea had been planted in the pope's head by Father Christopher Scheiner, Galileo's most bitter enemy among the Jesuits, and Scheiner's effectiveness had been akin to Iago's in whispering to Othello about Desdemona's infidelity. Galileo had pleaded with many personages of influence, even the pope's own brother, to disabuse the pope of this horrendous delusion. One of the *grande signori* was the French ambassador to Rome, François de Noailles. Yet another student of Galileo's from his Paduan days—indeed, he had been a private student who studied military calibrations and the theory of fortification—Count de Noailles became a constant voice for the pardon of his former teacher.

Galileo kept a keen eye on these efforts in his behalf. He mentioned them in a letter to a monastic brother of Friar Sarpi's: "I have it from Rome that His Eminence Cardinal Antonio Barberini and the French ambassador have seen His Holiness and tried to convince him that I never had the least idea of making game of His Holiness. I would never intend so sacrilegious an act, as my malicious foes have persuaded him. This was the primary cause of all my troubles." But fury still gripped the pope, and he remained evasive about the possibilities for clemency.

Thus, in old age, Galileo had boiled his troubles down to two: his disgrace before the Jesuits and this unforgiving, delusional wrath of Urban VIII. Only with bitterness could Galileo remember that this man had once written a poem in his honor called "In Dangerous Adulation."

Still, he worked. By mid-1636 he had completed his *Discourses on Two New Sciences*. It was a work of pure science, unalloyed with the dangerous elements of theology. More precisely, it was a work of physics, and it advanced his "new science of motion," in which his view of time and space was radical and fresh and in which he discovered the first law of motion. In the "Third Day" of the *Discourses*, he describes his experiment of rolling spheres down an inclined plane. From this he develops a formal mathematical argument leading from the definition of natural motion to the law of free fall for heavy bodies. "I imagine a movable body projected on a horizontal plane, all impediments to motion being removed. It is then manifest that the body's motion will be uniform and perpetual upon a plane, if the plane be extended to infinity." Thus, in the physical world, motion was just as natural as rest. Isaac Newton would extend and perfect Galileo's principle fifty years later in his first law of motion.

As in the *Dialogue Concerning the Two Chief World Systems*, Salviati, Sagredo, and Simplicio again took the stage, but they were all older and wiser, less confrontational and more gracious. Salviati had mellowed considerably, and Simplicio had learned more mathematics. Instead of ignorant or silly questions emanating "from the mouth of a fool," the new Simplicio became the young Galileo, asking the informed questions about mechanics that Galileo had asked as a youth.

Galileo's sentimentality about Sagredo and about Venice remained constant, as the dialogues began with a poetic bow to the floating city. "Your famous arsenal, my Venetian friend, is very familiar to me," Salviati begins, "and it seems to provide a large field for philosophizing, particularly in that area known as mechanics. Every sort of instrument and machine is continually in operation there. And among its many artisans, who have been taught by their fathers, some reason splendidly."

"You're right," Sagredo replies. "By Nature, I'm a curious man, and so I frequent the place for my own diversion." The real Sagredo could hardly have avoided the place, since he lived but a half block from the wall of the arsenal in the last years of his life. "I watch the activity of those called 'the key men,' and I talk with them about the effects which are not only remarkable, but also difficult to comprehend."

And so in the opening to this masterwork, less controversial but often called his most enduring scientific work—the telescope notwithstanding—Galileo is drawn to the practical doer, the artisan, rather than the thinker.

The Discourses on the Two New Sciences represents the final triumph of Galileo's life. In the wake of his gigantic defeat at the hands of the church and the wrenching death of Maria Celeste, with his old age and his creeping blindness, there was good reason to quit. He could easily have receded into melancholy, self-pity, and paralysis, withering away pathetically. Instead, he picked up old problems that had confused him in his youth, solved them, polished the work, and produced his most enduring scientific legacy. His effort was gargantuan and heroic.

Where was he to publish his masterwork? Sentimentally, he longed for Venice, but the inquisitor was too powerful there. Vienna seemed a possibility, until he learned that his archenemy, the Jesuit Christopher Scheiner, was there. And so he was thrown back on his Paris cabal. In a communication from the count of Noailles, he learned that the French ambassador was completing his tour in Rome and would be returning to Paris via Tuscany. The count wanted to bypass Florence, however, for he did not have time for the necessary diplomatic courtesies to the grand duke.

Of the church, Galileo requested permission to leave Arcetri and meet the count in Poggibonsi, a tiny way station on the post road to Pisa, twenty-five miles south of Florence. Astonishingly, the church, unaware of Galileo's purpose, consented, and Galileo left Arcetri for the only time in his eight-year confinement. In Poggibonsi, he met his French advocate for the first time in person and handed him a copy of the manuscript. In a letter of instruction to Diodati, he explained it. "The work which you will publish contains two totally new sciences which demonstrate first principles and mathematical equations and open the door to a vast field of infinite conclusions. Here my world is presented in comparison to that which remains to be seen."

For his trouble at accepting this clandestine literary mission, the count of Noailles was to be favored with the book's dedication, when it was published nearly two years later in Leyden. The book showed the world, Galileo wrote wryly in his dedication, that while he might remain silent, he was not passing his life in idleness. Heaping superlatives upon the count, he also charged him with a grave responsibility: "If I may be permitted to say so, you are now obliged to defend my reputation against anyone who attacks it."

As the publisher in Leyden went to work on his new book, Holland threw itself open to Galileo. Through Diodati, he learned that the court in Amsterdam was offering a vast sum of money, about thirty thousand crowns, to any scientist who could devise a method of determining longitude at sea. This news made Galileo's blood rush, and he quickly dusted off his old notes on his *celatone*.

With Diodati acting as his agent, his proposal was well received. The Dutch offered a necklace of gold worth five hundred crowns and promised another two thousand crowns for the expenses of designing and constructing any models of his invention. Word reached Italy that Galileo would be offered a distinguished chair at the Athenaeum of Amsterdam.

Within the Roman Curia, this blizzard of news evoked high anxiety and deep embarrassment. How unseemly that a condemned heretic be gathering in this foreign lucre from his prison! And yet, how could the church maintain its moral authority in the face of such international praise? How could Galileo be a moral leper and an international hero at the same time? The ambivalence of the church was manifest in an ironic letter that Cardinal Francesco Barberini wrote to the inquisitor in Florence about the Dutch overtures. The church would be most displeased if the great Italian scientist were to put his new invention in foreign hands and "deprive Italy of the glory of having established, before others, so noble a discovery."

To discourage Galileo from engaging in so unpatriotic an act, the church forbade him to accept the foreign gold.

During heady flirtations with wealthy Dutchmen, his various supplications and self-justifications to the church, and his secret efforts to encourage the wide circulation of his entire oeuvre throughout Europe, Galileo felt the stirrings of a degenerative disease. In the spring of 1636 he developed an infection in his right eye, and by May he had to give up his nocturnal observations. Since he was barred from traveling down the hill to Florence for proper medical treatment, the condition worsened, so that more than a year later he wrote to Diodati that he had experienced "the total loss of my right eye which has seen such glorious things." The left eye was also failing, as it too had become infected and was clouded by a constant profusion of tears. Three months later, he could no longer look through his telescope.

Darkness was descending.

By Christmas of 1637, the process was complete. On January 2, 1638, he wrote to Diodati, " Alas, my good sir, your dear friend and servant Galileo is hopelessly blind. You may imagine the distress this causes me. By my remarkable observations, the sky . . . the world . . . the universe . . . was opened a hundred or a thousand times wider than anything seen by the learned of all the past centuries. Now, that sky is diminished for me to a space no greater than that which is occupied by my own body."

Once again a campaign was launched for his liberation. Leading the effort this time was his old disciple, Father Castelli, who was restored in the good graces of the pope and doing important public service on Rome's waterworks. Castelli's efforts raised the alarm, and the inquisitor of Florence paid a visit to Galileo. On February 13 he reported to Rome that he found the culprit totally blind, with a cataract condition that had gone unattended for six months and was now incurable.

"With this and his other ailments," the inquisitor wrote, "he has the appearance more of a cadaver than a living person."

He was blind but not idle. As he waited for a Vatican reprieve, he gave definition to the last of his celestial discoveries. During the many months it took the dark film gradually to form over his eyes, he had returned to the most human form in the heavens. With his glazed vision, he had gazed at the face of the moon and wondered if the visage looked down upon the earth always with the same expression. He found that it did not. Sometimes the man in the moon showed his "full face," then he turned a bit to the right, then a bit to the left, now raising his chin up slightly and then down. The variations were daily, monthly, annual, and that seemed to explain the equivalent movements of the oceans, "of which by common agreement of everyone, the moon is arbiter and superintendent."

For a believer and a scientist, contemplating his blindness, his relation to his church and his God, his death, these speculations suited. The face in the moon was alive and speaking to him. But what was it saying? Was it the face of God or of Satan? He wrote his observations on the inscrutable and changing face of the moon to an unusual correspondent, a military officer of the Venetian Republic, an icon for his age who was practiced not only in the military arts but in poetry, mathematics, and astronomy. Galileo signed his letter: "From my prison in Arcetri."

Six days after he wrote the letter, the matter of his "indisposition" was put before the Congregation of the Holy Office. Four years later, Urban VIII was still proceeding "gently," rigid in his opposition to clemency, obsessed as ever with his Ptolemy-based astrology. (A year after, according to lore, a chicken laid an egg bearing the outlines of a bee and the sun, the symbols of the Barberini papacy. The hen immediately dropped dead, but the egg was rushed to Urban VIII, who declared it the sign of heavenly approval.) The Inquisition agreed that the liberation of the culprit was still too dangerous a course. Now that Galileo's sight was beyond saving, however, the cardinals did grant to the blind man permission to visit his doctor in Florence "to cure his indispositions." He would be allowed to stay at the house of his son on the steep street near the Ponte·Vecchio called Costa San Giorgio. While he was there, he was not to venture into the city "upon the pain of formal imprisonment for life, and of excommunication from the Beatitude of believers." He was not to converse with anyone "upon your condemned opinion of the motion of the earth."

As a special dispensation, the Vatican gave him permission to hear mass that Easter in the local church.

His prison in Arcetri—his "low hut," as he had come to call it—was minimum security. He was watched, but not too closely. No hooded figure stood sentry at his gate. With discretion, unauthorized visitors could slip in to see him. The English philosopher Thomas Hobbes came, bearing the good news that his "unfortunate Dialogues," as Galileo now referred to his book, had been translated into English. No doubt they discussed the choice that Galileo had faced before the Inquisition: to confess his true beliefs and to die, or to renounce them insincerely and to live. The young English poet John Milton also came to visit, and he was appalled at what the Dominican "licensers of thought" had done to the famous man.

What would their conversation have been? The question has fascinated writers for centuries, especially since Milton later went blind himself, and in his epic poems about heaven and hell he would make the steep slopes of Tuscany into the precinct of the devil. In the nineteenth century the English writer Walter Savage Landor imagined their conversation and made Milton the voice of outrage. Landor's Milton is startled as he suddenly notices the scars of torture.

"Let us talk of something else," Galileo mumbles.

"Italy! Italy! Italy!" Milton cries. "Drive thy poets into exile, into prison, into madness. Spare thy one philosopher! What track can the mind pursue, in her elevations or her plains or her recesses, without the dogging and prowling of the priesthood?"

During the final three years of his life, Galileo was attended by assistants who read to him and conducted his correspondence. A constant low-grade fever visited him, and back pain was added to his list of infirmities. In January 1639, on account of his poor health, the Inquisition permitted a seventeen-year-old youth named Vincenzo Viviani to come to live at the little villa in Arcetri. As he cared for the master, Viviani encouraged Galileo to recount the incidents of his life. This stimulated the old man to revisit old mathematical problems and to ponder his lingering controversies. Viviani's questions kept Galileo vital and alert, probing, questioning, wondering.

His mind remained a wonder of invention and intuition. Once in 1641, when his daughter Maria Celeste came into his mind, he remembered her annoyance at the convent clock, which could never seem to strike on time and was always falling behind. He had fixed that clock for the sisters of Saint Matthew, and now his thoughts returned to the art of clockmaking. "He hoped that the even, natural motions of the pendulum would correct all the defects," Viviani wrote of the occasion. But he could not sketch and thus had to talk about his ideas for the design for a clock to his son, Vincenzo, who had come to visit. These discussions led to a sketch of a new clock, which would test the prevailing theories of clockmakers.

When the copies of his *Discourses on Two New Sciences* became available, he dispensed them like jewels to his correspondents and patrons, as he had always done with his works. The questions and the responses the book generated enlivened his last correspondence and even brought some surprises. Through 1640 and into 1641, now seventy-six years old, he corresponded with an Aristotelian opponent from Bologna named Fortunio Liceti, who had challenged some of his positions and seemed to be writing now in the hope that their exchange might be publishable. In his letters, Galileo toyed with his adversary. "Against all the reasons of the world, I am criticized for having impugned the Peripatetic doctrine. But I profess that I have observed the Aristotelian teachings more religiously than many others who try to pass me off as hostile to the good Aristotelian philosophy."

Liceti was flabbergasted. "That you, Esteemed Sir, profess not to contradict Aristotelian doctrine is good to hear, and speaking frankly, very new to me," he wrote. "From your writings I would tend to gather the contrary."

To another equally distant acquaintance, Tuscany's representative in Venice, he wrote an even more surprising letter, after the diplomat passed along certain astronomical observations that had seemed to confirm the Copernican theory. "The falsity of the Copernican system must not on any account be doubted, especially by us Catholics, who have the supreme authority of Holy Scripture interpreted by the greatest masters in theology. These masters assure us of the fixity of the earth and the movement of the sun around it. That most sound argument, taken from the omnipotence of God, renders false the conjectures of Copernicus."

To take seriously this last, insincere statement of Galileo, one would need to have heard the tone of voice in which he dictated it to Viviani. In its isolation and its violence to all his other work, except his abjuration after rigorous examination, it was scarcely the renunciation that it has been taken to be.

The letter is a joke on history.

At the end, he fell in love. The object of his affections was a lady of nearby Prato, Alessandra Bocchineri Buonamici, who was thirty years younger and married to Geri Buonamici, a Tuscan diplomat and her third husband, who had written a long account of Galileo's trial. Galileo and Alessandra had met ten years before, when Galileo had just completed his *Dialogue Concerning the Two Chief World Systems* and was entering the horror of trying to secure the church's license to publish.

Meeting Alessandra had been something of an epiphany for Galileo. That a man of his eminence and a woman of her refinement could converse at such length with such evident pleasure as emotional and intellectual equals seemed to come as an enormous surprise to him. "I realized how much value you were," Galileo wrote to her after their first encounters in the summer of 1630. "Nothing I wanted more than to see you again, and that was the real reason that I sped my return. How deprived of your conversation I feel!"

But he would be deprived of it for ten years, as she returned with her husband to Germany. When it resumed again, he was old and blind and lonely. He reveled in the sound of her voice and pined for her letters. "I long to talk to you," he wrote in the spring of 1640, "for it is so rare to find women who can speak so sensibly as you." She brought him gifts he could touch and feel, wool and linen. "I have been trying to find the way to come there and stay for a day of conversation with you, without creating scandal," she wrote in March 1641, and she imagined how she could slip a small carriage into Arcetri and bring him to Prato for several days. "Patience!" she wrote of their separation, for she would try to find a way for them to be private.

"I have never doubted your affection for me," he wrote in the spring, hoping she and her husband would come to stay for four days in Arcetri, "secure that you, in this short time which I may have left, know how much affection flows in me for you."

Then on December 20, 1641, with a certain finality, he responded to Alessandra's latest expression of concern. "Your letter found me in bed gravely indisposed for some weeks now. Many, many thanks for the courtesy which you have always shown to my person and for your condolences which visit me now in my misery and my misfortune."

It was his last letter. He died two weeks later.

Apology

On October 31, 1992, in the ornate royal hall of the Apostolic Palace in the Vatican, Pope John Paul II gathered the Pontifical Academy of Sciences before him to resolve the Galileo affair for the Roman Catholic church once and for all time. It fell to Cardinal Paul Poupard of France, the chairman of Galileo's modern pardon board, to make the initial presentation. Dressed in his floor-length black gown and his red cardinal's hat and speaking in elegant French, the cardinal addressed the assemblage solemnly. The pontiff, a figure of pristine white, slumped in his commodious chair, listened with his chin supported by his fist.

The theologians who attacked Galileo, Poupard declared, failed to understand that the Scripture was not literal when it came to a description of the physical world. Galileo had suffered greatly from their errors of judgment. "These errors must be frankly recognized," the cardinal exclaimed. Then, in his most surprising statement, he accorded Galileo the compliment of being "more perceptive" in his interpretation of Scripture than the theologians who opposed him, even though it had been forbidden by the Council of Trent for any layman to interpret Scripture.

The pope formally received and accepted the findings of his commission, and then he turned to his own formal declaration. Hunching over the sheets without lifting his eyes to his audience, he read without emotion. His discourse was general. He focused on the historic uneasiness between science and the Catholic faith over the years and lamented the "tragic mutual incomprehension" that had marked the relationship. Little was new or specific in his statement; the symbolism of the occasion sufficed. The pope did not mention the eccentricities of his predecessor, Urban VIII, nor did he directly criticize the behavior of the Inquisition. The lessons of the "Galileo affair," he said, remain valid and could be relevant in the future, especially in the area of biogenetics. For technology now made possible morally abhorrent human engineering.

The following morning, the Vatican newspaper, *L'Osservatore Romano*, carried the decision on its front page under the headline FAITH CAN NEVER CONFLICT WITH REASON. Inside, the text of Cardinal Poupard's statement was reprinted with the headline "Galileo Case Is Resolved."

Elsewhere in the world, the headlines were not so dignified. On the front page of *The New York Times*, the headline read: AFTER 350 YEARS, VATICAN SAYS GALILEO WAS RIGHT: IT MOVES. The lead in the *Los Angeles Times* read: "It's Official! The Earth Revolves Around the Sun, Even for the Vatican." Inevitably, the editorial cartoonists feasted. In Milan's national newspaper, *La Repubblica*, under the headline GALILEO, EXCUSE ME, the irrepressible and irreverent cartoonist Fortini depicted the pope opening his papal robes and exposing himself like some dirty old man, as he uttered Galileo's legendary line, *"Eppur si muove."*

Several months later, in April 1993, I went to see Cardinal Poupard. His office is in Trastevere, downstream from the Vatican, in a functional modern complex known as Palazzo San Calisto. His Eminence had invited me to see him in his private apartments on the top floor of the palace. My questions were to be submitted in advance, ostensibly for translation reasons. I conceded the point in return for permission to film the audience.

When the time came, I was ushered into an expansive suite of rooms that had the feel of Park Avenue, full of books from floor to ceiling, oriental rugs, fine paintings and sculpture that the cardinal had collected in his life and travels. From behind the desk of his study, he greeted me sternly, for I was ten minutes late, and I had submitted difficult questions. Why had it taken the church thirteen years to come to grips with the Galileo case? Was the pope's statement of the previous October 31 a formal apology? Was the church embarrassed by the worldwide derision of the pontiff's statement? When I had faxed the questions to the cardinal, the hotel concierge looked at me in astonishment, as if he expected me to be burned at Campo dei Fiori at dusk.

At my request, Cardinal Poupard was dressed in full regalia. Red piping trimmed the borders of his long black robe; red buttons festooned its front, and its waist was cinched with a red silk cummerbund. A heavy silver cross hung around his neck, and his red cap covered the back of his graying head. He cut an imposing figure. About him hung the air of authority.

It was not long before I realized that I was dealing with a politician as much as a priest. Once he arranged himself in his chair, he held up a copy of his own book on Galileo, making sure that the camera zoomed in on the title.

After this moment of ecclesiastical self-promotion, I began softly. Why had the church taken so long to resolve this issue? I asked. An "interdisciplinary" exercise such as theirs took time, he replied, as his translator, a nervous American nun named Sister Anne Clare, read his prepared answer from a printed page on her lap. Was the pontiff's statement of October 31, 1992, a formal apology? Not at all, the cardinal said with a wave of his hand. It was merely a "formal recognition" of error. I did not quite understand the difference but pressed on.

Could he imagine the church ever having to say anything further about the case? Why? he replied rhetorically. It is done. *Finito.* Why, then, did the official statements contain no specific criticism of Urban VIII's bizarre behavior or of the excesses of the inquisitors? Because his commission's study was not about personalities—extraordinary as both Urban VIII and Galileo were—but about events, he replied. Galileo's judges, not the pope himself, were to blame. I thought Urban VIII was one of his judges.

To listen to Cardinal Poupard was to conclude that the church had experienced no anguish whatever in the Galileo reconsideration. The conflict between science and faith was a myth, he said dismissively. Without missing a beat or appreciating the contradiction, he repeated again the standard church line about Galileo that I had heard often in three years of writing: Galileo had been condemned because he insisted on treating his Copernican theory as truth rather than hypothesis, and he could not prove it. This position deflected attention from a simple fact: The Copernican theory *was* true, and the church had used extreme and rigorous methods to crush that truth and protect its falsehood.

The cardinal was talking about the pope as a fancier of science. As a man with a great capacity for trust, John Paul had merely asked toward the end of the commission's work, "At what point are we?"

"I don't think we can take the matter any further," the cardinal had replied.

"Good," the pope said. "Let's get on with it."

But wasn't the church embarrassed at the coverage in the newspapers? *Au contraire*. The coverage was ample, precise, positive, and responsible. To prove it, the cardinal proudly unfolded magazines from France and from Spain with massive and well-illustrated spreads on the Galileo pronouncement, several of which contained pictures of himself. He gave me a copy of his own article on the Galileo resolution that had been printed in the Parisian newspaper *Le Figaro* and which began with a description of how the pope, "*avec une belle intrépidité*," had instituted this reconsideration.

The cover story of the French monthly *Nostre Histoire* had carried a headline about Galileo as an effort to "purify" Catholic history. And so before I rose to leave his lovely apartment, I asked Cardinal Poupard, "Who is next?" Giordano Bruno?

He smiled indulgently. There are many fascinating personalities, he said, but the case of John Huss, the Bohemian reformer who railed against forged miracles and ecclesiastical greed in the Middle Ages and who burned at the stake in 1415, would be his next "intervention." But, said the cardinal wistfully, his real interest lay with Joan of Arc. She had been condemned by an archbishop and burned, before she was made a saint and became the patron of France.

Biographer's Notes

1: The Wrangler

Vallombrosa: John Milton, *Paradise Lost*, Book I, lines 301–304; D. M. Ercolani, "Galileo Galilei Novizio Vallombrosano," library, monastery at Vallombrosa; *Vallombrosa e I Suoi Dintorni*; William Wetmore Story, *Vallombrosa*; Nello Puccioni, *La Vallombrosa*; Virginia Wales Johnson, *Summer Days at Vallombrosa*; interviews with P. Pierdamiano Spotorno, Vallombrosan monk.

Pisa: Michel de Montaigne, *Journey Through Italy*; Janet Ross and Nelly Erichsen, *The Story of Pisa*, pp. 88–385; Col. George Frederick Young, *The Medici*.

Birth of Galileo: Antonio Favaro, "Sul Giorno Nascita di Galileo," Reale Memorie, Istituto dell Scienze, Arte e Lettere, 1887; Galileo Galilei Speciale, *Il Tirreno*, Pisa, May 1992; G. del Guerra, "Opuscolo sulla casa natale di Galilei," 1964; "Sulla Case ove nacque Galileo Galilei," courtesy of R. Sonini, Pisa.

Vincenzo Galilei: Fabio Fano, "Notizie della vita di Vincenzo Galilei," La camerata Fiorentina, Istituzione Monumentale dell Arte de Musicale Italiana; Stillman Drake, "Vincenzo Galilei and Galileo," *Galileo Studies*; Claude Palisca, "Camerata Fiorentina: A Reappraisal," Studi musicali, 1972; Nino Pirrotta, "Temperaments and Tendencies in the Florentine Camerata," *Musical Quarterly*, April 1954.

Vincenzo's music: Strunk, "Dialogo."

Vincenzo and Girolamo Mei: C. V. Palisca, "Girolamo Mei: Mentor to the Florentine Camerata," *Music Quarterly*, January 1954.

Count Ugolino's lament: Dante's "Inferno," *The Divine Comedy*, XXXIII, lines 79–84.

Vincenzo and the Tuscan court: Alfred Einstein, *The Italian Madrigal*, vol. 2, pp. 131–32.

Vincenzo on the weight of authority: J. J. Fahie, *Galileo*, p. 13.

St. John Gualberto and Vallombrosa: Story, *Vallombrosa*, pp. 22–35; Johnson, *Summer Days*, 57–71; "Horatio Morandi," Dizionario storico biografico di scrittori, letterati ed artisti dell'ordine di Vallombrosa.

Scandal at St. Francis: Montaigne, *Journey*, p. 148.

Galileo as a Pisan student: Thomas B. Settle, "Ostilio Ricci, A Bridge Between Alberti and Galileo," *Actes*, 12th International Congress on the History of Sciences, Paris, 1971; Charles B. Schmitt, "The Faculty of Arts at Pisa at the Time of Galileo," *Physis*, 1972.

Horace on the young and the old: *Epistles* II, 1, 85.

The lamp in the cathedral: Vincenzo Viviani, *Racconto*, in *Works*, vol. 14, p. 603; Stillman Drake, *Galileo at Work*, p. 21; Fahie, *Galileo*; William K. Shea, "The Significance of Experiments in the Writings of the Young Galileo," *Revue de l'Université d'Ottawa*, 1971.

2: LUCIFER'S ARM

Christopher Clavius: *Catholic Encyclopedia*; Augustus De Morgan, *A Budget of Paradoxes*, p. 26.

Tower of Winds: Author visit; film, *People with Long Eyes*, Vatican Observatory.

Galileo and Clavius correspondence: Galileo Galilei, *Le Opere di Galileo Galilei* (hereafter cited as *Works*), vol. 10, pp. 22–24, 27–29.

Francis I and Bianca Capello: Col. George Frederick Young, *The Medici*, pp. 600–624.

Poggia a Caiano: Author visit; Young, *Medici*, p. 619.

Bardi's camarata: Fano, "Notizie della vita di Vincenzo Galilei"; Stillman Drake, "Vincenzo Galilei and Galileo," *Galileo Studies*; Palisca, "Camerata Fiorentina: A Reappraisal," Studi musicali, 1972; Pirrotta, "Temperaments and Tendencies in the Florentine Camerata," *Musical Quarterly*, April 1954.

Galileo on music: Galileo Galilei, *Discourses on Two New Sciences*, pp. 101–2.

Academy of Florence: Eric Cochrane, *Florence in the Forgotten Centuries*, p. 84; Eric Cochrane, *Tradition and Enlightenment in the Tuscan Academies*, pp. 69–73, 112–14.

Dante lecture: *Works*, vol. 9, pp. 7–10, 29–57.

Del Monte to Galileo, Dec. 30, 1588: *Works*, vol. 10, p. 39.

"In Bologna, lovers; . . . in Pisa, friars": Schmitt, "The Faculty of Arts at Pisa at the Time of Galileo."

Watermelons in the grass: Lelio Torelli to Cosimo I, 1560, quoted in ibid.

Girolamo Borro: Ibid.

Montaigne on Borro: *Essays* I: 26, p. 111; Michel de Montaigne, *Journey Through Italy*, p. 147.

Mazzoni: Frederick Purnell, Jr., "Jacopo Mazzoni and Galileo," *Physis*, 1972.

Tower of Pisa experiment: Viviani, *Racconto*, in *Works*, vol. 19, p. 606; Galileo, "De Motu," *Works*, vol. 1, p. 249; Ernest A. Moody, "Galileo and Avempace: The Dynamics of the Leaning Tower Experiment," *Journal of the History of Ideas*, 1951; Lane Cooper, *Aristotle, Galileo, and the Tower of Pisa*; W. R. Shea, "The Significance of Experiments in the Writings of the Young Galileo," *Revue de l'Université d'Ottawa*, 1971.

Galileo on grand personages: "Capitolo contro il portar la toga," *Works*, vol. 9, pp. 21–24, 213–23.

Galileo on motion: "De Motu," *Works*, vol. 1, pp. 243–419; Raymond Fredette, "Galileo's De Motu Antiquiora," Istituto di Storia della Scienza, 1971; I. E. Drabkin, *Galileo: On Motion*.

Sensitivity to criticism: Drabkin, transl., "Memoranda on Motion," *Galileo*.

Galileo's literary sensibility: Erwin Panofsky, *Galileo As a Critic of the Arts*, pp. 18–19; and *Works*, vol. 9, p. 69.

Galileo on bottles: "Capitolo. . ." *Works*, vol. 9, pp. 21–24, 213–23.

3: THE GOLDEN OX

University of Padua: Antonio Favaro, *Lo Studio di Padova*, vol. 1, pp. 51–164; Scandaletti, *Galileo Privato*, pp. 74–83.

Moletti: Favaro, *Studio*, vol. 1, pp. 104–5.

Pinelli: Ibid., vol. 1, pp. 40–43; author interview with Bellinati.

Senate resolution: *Works*, vol. 19, p. 111.

Grand dukes, Francis and Ferdinand: Col. George Frederick Young, *The Medici*, pp. 600–648.

Galileo's inaugural lecture: *Works*, vol. 19, p. 43; Favaro, *Studio*, pp. 106–8; author interview with Prof. Luigi Olivieri, University of Padua.

Tycho Brahe and inaugural lecture: Fahie, *Galileo*, p. 36.

Pinelli's salon: Favaro, *Studio*, pp. 40–43; Scandaletti, *Galileo Privato*, p. 76; interview with Bellinati.

Gesuiti e Bovisti: Favaro, *Studio*, vol. 1, pp. 59–68.

Galileo's acceptance of traditional cosmology: *La Sphaera*, quoted in Favaro, *Studio*, vol. 1, pp. 125–26, 162.

Falling ill in Costozza: *Works*, vol. 2, p. 37.

Giordano Bruno in Padua: J. Lewis McIntyre, *Giordano Bruno*, pp. 12, 69.

Galileo's device to raise water: Favaro, "Galileo e Venezia," *Studio*, vol. 2; *Works*, vol. 14, p. 126.

On fortification: *Works*, vol. 2, pp. 7–142.

Dante on the tar of the Arsenale: Dante, "Inferno," *The Divine Comedy*, XXI, lines 7–18.

On thermometer: Galileo, *La sensata esperienza*, pp. 39–40; Favaro, *Studio*, vol. 2, pp. 193–212; *Works*, vol. 11, p. 506, vol. 12, pp. 139–40, 157–58, 167–68.

Dialogue on device to raise water: Patent application, *Works*, vol. 14, p. 126.

Sagredo: Antonio Favaro, *Amici e corrispondenti di Galileo*, vol. 1, pp. 199–322; *Il Carteggio Linceo della vecchia accademia di Federico Cesi*.

Sagredo's self-portrait: *Works*, vol. 12, pp. 45–46.

Sagredo's summer house on Brenta: Author visit.

Galileo-Sagredo pranks: Gaetano Cozzi, *Paolo Sarpi tra Venezia e L'Europa*, p. 175; Scandaletti, *Galileo Privato*, p. 93.

Venice as a place of pleasure: Galileo Galilei, *Discourses on Two New Sciences*, *Works*, vol. 8, p. 49.

Schini shop in Venice: Favaro, "Galileo e Venezia," *Studio*, p. 87.

Venice in seventeenth century: U. Tucci, "Vita economica a Venezia nel primo 600," paper given at conference entitled "Galileo e la cultura Veneziana," Venice, June 1992.

Telephone reference: Galileo, *La sensata esperienza*, pp. 139–40 and *Dialogue Concerning the Two Chief World Systems*, p. 106.

Magagnati letter: *Works*, vol. 10, pp. 182–83.

Flap over Jesuits in Padua: Cozzi, *Paolo Sarpi*, pp. 151–52.

Twenty ducats for being boring: McIntyre, *Giordano Bruno*, p. 70.

Acquapendente: L. Premuta, "La filosofia sperimentale di Galileo 'padovano' e le concezioni meccanicistiche in biologia e in medicina," paper given at conference, "Galileo e la cultura Padovana," Feb. 13–15, 1992; author interview with Luigi Olivieri.

Mazzoni letter: *Works*, vol. 2, pp. 195–202.

Galileo's letter to Kepler and Kepler's response: *Works*, vol. 10, pp. 67, 69.

Galileo timidity: Libero Sosio, "Galileo Galilei e Paolo Sarpi," paper given at conference entitled "Galileo e la cultura Veneziana," June 19, 1992.
Military compass: Works, vol. 2, pp. 337–414; Favaro, Studio, vol. 1, pp. 165–92.
Galileo's accounts for compass sales: Works, vol. 14, p. 166.
Capra plagiarism charge: Favaro, Studio, vol. 1, pp. 182–91; Works, vol. 2, pp. 513–600.
Alvise Cornaro: Marisa Milani, "Galileo Galilei e la letteratura pavana," paper given at conference at Accademia Patavana, Feb. 1992.

4: FROGS AND MICE

Year of the Jubilee: Ludwig Von Pastor, The History of the Popes, vol. 24, pp. 269–80.
Execution of Bruno: J. Lewis McIntyre, Giordano Bruno; A. Paterson, Infinite Worlds of Giordano Bruno; Dorothea Waley Singer, Giordano Bruno, pp. 171–80; Paul Eugene Memmo, Heroic Frenzies, Studies in Romance Languages series; Bruno, Works, pp. 340 and 401–2; "In Occasione del Monumento a Giordano Bruno," Vatican Library.
Michelangelo Galilei: Fahie, Galileo, p. 68.
Marina Gamba: Scandaletti, Galileo Privato, pp. 103–9; Favaro, Studio, vol. 2, pp. 47–48, 157–59; Galileo, La sensata esperienza, pp. 246, 251.
Giulia visit of 1604 and her espionage on her son: Letters in Favaro, Studio, vol. 2, pp. 225, 226, 228.
Galileo and the duke of Mantua: Favaro, chronology and "Galileo e Venezia."
Comet of 1604: Works, vol. 2, pp. 275–85.
Altobelli letter: Works, vol. 10, pp. 116–17.
Cremonini: Dizionario biografico degli Italiani; "Cesare Cremonini: Il suo pensiero e il suo tempo," conference in Ferrara, April 7, 1984. Author interview with Luigi Olivieri.
Cecco dialogue and background: Marisa Milani, "Il Dialogo in perpuosito de la Stella Nuova di Cecco di Ronchitti da Brugine, 1605," Giornale storico della letteratura Italiana; Stillman Drake, Galileo Against the Philosophers, pp. 1–53.
Galileo's legal entanglements, spring 1605: Favaro chronology, Galileo a Padova.
Venice interdict: J. Norwich, History of Venice, pp. 506–17; Leopold Ranke, The Ecclesiastical and Political History of the Popes of Rome, vol. 2, pp. 224–41; Rev. Alexander Robertson, Fra Paolo Sarpi; Horatio Brown, The Venetian Printing Press, 1469–1800, pp. 158–73.
Bellarmine: James Brodrick, Robert Bellarmine.
Sarpi: Gaetano Cozzi, Paolo Sarpi tra Venezia e L'Europa; Fulgenzio Micanzio, La vita di Padre Paolo; Libero Sosio, "Galileo Galilei e Paolo Sarpi,"paper given at conference "Galileo e la cultura Veniziana, June 1992"; The Catholic Encyclopedia.
Sarpi on Index: Luigi Barzini, The Italians, p. 316.
Sarpi on the true Christianity: Brown, Venetian Printing Press, p. 160.
Sarpi on Jesuits: Barzini, Italians, p. 319.
Galileo on Jesuit departure: Works, vol. 10, pp. 157–58.
Sagredo letter from Friuli: Works, vol. 10, pp. 163–64.
Sarpi's extraordinary powers: Cozzi, Paolo Sarpi.
Attack on Sarpi: Micanzio, Padre Paolo; Cozzi, Paolo Sarpi; Robertson, Fra Paolo Sarpi.
Galileo's letter to Christine re Acquapendente: Works, vol. 10, pp. 164–65.
Galileo's letter to Christine re coat of arms, September 1608: Works, vol. 10, p. 221; Mario Biagioli, "Galileo the Emblem Maker," Isis, June 1990.
The snows of 1607–8: Milani, "Galileo e la letteratura."

The Pavan verse: Il "faelamento" of Rovigio Bon Magon e Tuogno Regono a Galileo Galilei, "GSLI," CLXV, translated by Marisa Milani for the author.

5: THE STONE AND THE QUARRY

The king of Sweden as Galileo's student: Favaro, Studio, vol. 1, p. 158; Favaro, Galileo Galilei a Padova, pp. 223–71.

Galileo correspondence with Vincenzo Renieri, 1633: Works, vol. 15, p. 361; Favaro, Amici e Corrispondenti di Galileo, vol. 1, pp. 475–76;

Letter to Antonio de' Medici re artillery: Works, vol. 10, p. 228.

"To serve a prince!": Works, vol. 10, p. 233.

Sagredo's wistful letter from Aleppo: Works, vol. 20, pp. 242–43.

On chronology about telescope discovery: Stillman Drake, "Galileo's First Telescopes at Padua and Venice," Isis, 1959; A. Van Helden, "The Invention of the Telescope," American Philosophical Society, June 1977; Edward Rosen, "When Did Galileo Make His First Telescope," Centaurus, 1951.

The precision of Galileo's lenses: Greco, Molesini, and Quercioli, "Optical tests of Galileo's lenses," Nature, July 9, 1992.

On Sarpi knowledge of earlier spyglasses: Gaetano Cozzi, Paolo Sarpi tra Venezia e L'Europa, p. 180.

Dispatch to Venice, August 4, 1609: Drake, "Galileo's First Telescopes at Padua and Venice."

Galileo's own account: The Assayer, Works, vol. 6, pp. 257–59.

Dignitaries awed in the Tower of St. Mark's: Drake, "Galileo's First Telescopes at Padua and Venice."

Galileo's gift of telescope to doge: Works, vol. 10, pp. 250–51.

On his salary hike, Galileo's letter to Landucci, August 29, 1609: Works, vol. 10, 253.

First vision of the moon: Galileo Galilei, The Starry Messenger, pp. 15–38.

His publisher, Baglioni: Dizionario biografico degli Italiani; Brown, Venetian Printing Press, pp. 263, 265.

Letters to Vinta: Works, vol. 10, pp. 280, 283, 288, 297.

Sir William Lower poem: Francis R. Johnson, Astronomical Thought in Renaissance England, p. 228.

Faber, Seggett poems: Marjorie Nicolson, "The Telescope and Imagination," Modern Philology, 1935.

Marino tribute: Giambattista Marino, Adonis.

Demand of the French court: Fahie, Galileo, p. 99.

Grand duke as Galileo's PR agent: Richard S. Westfall, "Galileo and the Accademia dei Lincei," Novita celesti e crisi del sapere, Florence, 1984.

Marino and Cosimo: Marino, Adonis, canto 10, verse 44.

Letter to Vinta: Works, vol. 10, p. 348.

Priuli's bitterness: Ibid., vol. 11, p. 503.

Sarpi's discouragement to leave Venice: Letter to author from Libero Sosio, Sarpi scholar.

Observations of Saturn as a triple star: Nov. 13, 1610, letter to Emperor Rudolph II, through Giuliano de' Medici, Tuscan ambassador at the German court, in Works, vol. 10, p. 474; Fahie, Galileo, pp. 108–9.

Doubts about Saturn as triple star: Letter to Welser, Dec. 1, 1612, in Works, vol. 5, pp. 186–239.

6: THE NASTY SEED

Le Selve: Author visit.

Galileo to Vinta re visit to Rome: *Works*, vol. 11, pp. 26–27.

Galileo's magical box: Pietro Redondi, *Galileo Heretic*, p. 9.

Galileo at Palazzo Firenze: Walter J. Miller, S.J., "Galileo's Visits to Rome," *Sky and Telescope*, vol. 11, 1952.

Pope Paul V: Leopold Ranke, *The Ecclesiastical and Political History of the Popes of Rome*, vol. 2, pp. 220–309.

Piccinardi: Ibid., pp.222–23.

Bellarmine correspondence: James Brodrick, *Robert Bellarmine, Saint and Scholar*.

Colombe and the Pigeon League: Karl von Gebler, *Galileo and the Roman Curia*.

Prince Cesi and the Academy of the Lynxes: Domenico Carutti, *Breve storia della Accademia dei Lincei*, pp. 1–38; *Il Carteggio Linceo*; Drake, *Galileo at Work*; Redondi, *Heretic*, p. 29; Westfall, "Accademia dei Lincei," *Novita Celesti e Crisi del Sapere*, 1984.

Banquet at the Janiculum: Edward Rosen, *The Naming of the Telescope*, pp. 30–35; Gabrieli, "Galileo in Acquasparta," *Atti della Reale Accademia d'Italia*. Memorie della Classe di Scienze Morale e Storiche, Rome, 1943.

Sagredo on Giambattista della Porta: *Works*, vol. 11, p. 398.

Galileo on those who refused to look through the telescope: *Works*, vol. 10, p. 484. He was referring to Giulio Libri, a professor at Pisa and Padua, who like Cremonini had refused to look through the telescope.

Galileo detractors: Andrew Dickson White, *A History of the Warfare of Science with Theology*, pp. 130–57.

7: BLACK FIRE AND FLOATING BODIES

Galileo on floating bodies: Thomas Salusbury, trans. *Discourse on Floating Bodies*; letter to grand duke, *Works*, vol. 4, pp. 49–51; Stillman Drake, "The Origin of Galileo's Book on Floating Bodies and the Question of the Unknown Academician," *Isis*, 1960.

Galileo challenge to Colombe: Salusbury, *Discourse*.

Galileo's complaints to Cesi about his health: *Works*, vol. 11, p. 247.

Cigoli letters on sunspots: *Works*, vol. 11, pp. 208 and 211.

Magagnati and his ribald poems: *Amici e corrispondenti di Galileo*, vol. 1, pp. 65–92.

Background on sunspot letters: Stillman Drake, *Discoveries and Opinions of Galileo*, pp. 59–84.

Neptune: Charles T. Kowal and Stillman Drake, "Galileo's Observations of Neptune," *Nature*, Sept. 25, 1980; Francesco Bertola, 11Le Osservazione di Galileo del Planeta Nettuno," in *Galileo e la Cultura Padovana*, edited by G. Santinello.

Reaction to discourse: Stillman Drake, Introduction to *Discourses on Two New Sciences*; F. R. Wegg-Prosser, *Galileo and His Judges*, p. 16.

Bellarmine to Galileo on Discourse: *Works*, vol. 11, pp. 337ff.

Galileo on Colombe: *Works*, vol. 20, p. 422.

Conti letters: Ibid., vol. 11, pp. 354–555 and 376.

Stelluti poem: Ibid., vol. 5, p. 13.

Galileo on the "horse sense" of the common man: Ibid., XI, p. 326ff.

Provincial to Scheiner: J. J. Fahie, *Galileo*, pp. 130ff.

Drake on sunspot claims: Drake, *Discoveries*, p. 83.

Cigoli letters on ignorance: Giorgio de Santillana, *The Crime of Galileo*, pp. 21ff.

On Venus: Stillman Drake, "Galileo, Kepler, and Phases of Venus," *Journal for History of Astronomy (JHA)*, Oct. 1984; Owen Gingerich, "Phases of Venus in 1610," *JHA*, Oct. 1984; Richard S. Westfall, "Science and Patronage," *Isis*, 1985.

Castelli letter to Galileo re Venus: *Works*, vol. 10, p. 482.

Galileo to Castelli: *Works*, vol. 10, pp. 502–4.

Letter to Grand Duchess Christine: Maurice A. Finocchiaro, ed., *The Galileo Affair*, p. 87.

8: O Ye Fools of Galilee!

Santa Maria Novella: Author visits; Orlandi and Grossi, *Historical-Artistic Guide of Santa Maria Novella and Her Monumental Cloisters*; T. B. Settle and M. L. R. Bonelli, "Egnatio Danti's Great Astronomical Quadrant," Annali dell'Istituto e museo di storia della scienza di Firenze, 1979.

Lorini first denunciation: Folio 342, Vat MS.

Lorini apology to Galileo: *Works*, vol. 11, p. 427.

Galileo to Cesi re Lorini: Ibid., *Works*, Albèri, vol. 8, pp. 241–42.

Tommaso Caccini: Antonio Ricci-Riccardi, *Galileo Galilei e fra Tommaso Caccini*.

Blast from Caccini's brother: Giorgio de Santillana, *The Crime of Galileo*, pp. 104–5; Ricci-Riccardi, *Galileo and Caccini*, pp. 69–70.

Father Maraffi apology: *Works*, vol. 12, pp. 127–28.

Cesi to Galileo re Caccini: Gabrieli, "Galileo in Acquasparta."

Bishop of Fiesole: Galileo to Piero Dini, Feb. 16, 1615, in *Works*, vol. 12, pp. 142–43.

Lorini to the Inquisition: Ibid., vol. 19, p. 297.

Ciampoli attempt to salve Galileo's feelings: Ibid., vol. 12, p. 145.

"New fields of injury": Galileo to Dini, ibid., pp. 142–43.

"If mine eye offend": Postscript, ibid.

Efforts of archbishop of Pisa: Mellini to archbishop, Feb. 27, *Works*, vol. 19, p. 306.

Caccini before Inquisition: Testimony in Maurice A. Finocchiaro, *The Galileo Affair*, p. 136.

9: The Cardinal's Scold

Ambassador Guicciardini's dismay about Galileo visit: *Works*, vol. 12, pp. 206–7.

Foscarini-Bellarmine interchange: Richard J. Blackwell, *Galileo, Bellarmine, and the Bible*, Appendices 6, 7, and 8.

Clash of two world views: Andrew Dickson White, *A History of the Warfare of Science with Theology*, pp. 130–57.

Bellarmine: James Brodrick, *Robert Bellarmine, Saint and Scholar*, pp. 332–78; E. McMullin, "Bellarmine," *Dictionary of Scientific Biography*, vol. l, pp. 587–90; Richard S. Westfall, "Bellarmino, Galileo, and the Clash of Two World Views"; Blackwell, *Galileo, Bellarmine*.

Caccini's visit to Galileo: Galileo to Picchena, Feb. 20, 1616, in *Works*, vol. 12, p. 238.

Report of the Inquisition: Sergio Pagano, *I Documenti*, pp. 99–100.

Bellarmine on infallibility: Jacobo J. Corboy, S.J., "The Doctrine of Infallibility of the Pope in Bellarmine and His Influence on the Definition in the Vatican Council."

The special injunction of February 26, 1616: Maurice A. Finocchiaro, *The Galileo Affair*, p. 147.

Guicciardini to Cosimo II re Galileo's admonition: March 4, 1616: *Works*, vol. 12, pp. 241–42.

Decree of the Index, March 5, 1616: Finocchiaro, *Galileo Affair*, pp. 148–50.

Galileo to grand duke, through Picchena, March 6, 1616: *Works*, vol. 12, pp. 243–44.

Westfall on Bellarmine: Westfall, "Bellarmine, Galileo."

May 26 Bellarmine letter: Finocchiaro, *Galileo Affair*, p. 153.

10: GLOOM AT BELLOSGUARDO

Bellosguardo's air: Stelluti, in *Works*, vol. 13, p. 347; Sagredo, ibid., vol. 11, p. 553.

Sagredo on Bellosguardo: *Works*, vol. 13, pp. 349–50.

Magagnati on Bellosguardo: Ibid., p. 348.

Celatone: Ibid., pp. 311–14, 344.

Giovanni de' Medici on celatone: Ibid., vol. XII, pp. 370, 372–73.

On king of Spain: Ibid., pp. 321–23.

Galileo to Archduke Leopold: Ibid., p. 389.

Archduke Leopold to Galileo: Ibid., p. 397.

Cesi campaign: Gabrieli, "Galileo at Acquasparta."

Cesi warning about Bellarmine: *Il Carteggio Linceo*, p. 477.

Cesi appeal to Bellarmine: Ibid., p. 648.

Description of comets: Grassi, "Astronomical Disputation of the Three Comets," in Stillman Drake and C. D. O'Malley, *The Controversy on the Comets*, pp. 6–7.

On Grassi: Pietro Redondi, *Galileo Heretic*; pp. 29ff.; introduction of Drake and O'Malley, *Controversy*.

Grassi's "Disputation": Ibid., pp. vii–xxv.

Guiducci's "Discourse on the Comets": Ibid., pp. 21–66.

Ciampoli's pleasure at Jesuit offense: *Works*, vol. 12, p. 465.

Grassi's Libra: Drake and O'Malley, *Controversy*, pp. 69–132.

Faber on Jesuit pride: *Works*, vol. 13, p. 23.

Cesarini ardent plea: Ibid., p. 89.

Strategy at Acquasparta: Gabrieli, "Acquasparta"; Redondi, *Heretic*, pp. 44–46; *Works*, vol. 13, pp. 38ff and 46ff.

Guiducci's letter to Tarquinio Galluzzi: Drake and O'Malley, *Controversy*, pp. 133–50.

Kepler's Harmony: Arthur Koestler, *The Sleepwalkers*, pp. 388–98.

Thirty Years' War: C. V. Wedgwood, *The Thirty Years War*, pp. 141–266.

Galileo gift to General Spinola: *Works*, vol. 13, p. 66.

Cesarini on "obstinate worshippers": Ibid., p. 89.

The Assayer: Stillman Drake, ed., *Discoveries and Opinions of Galileo*, pp. 270–80.

Cesarini on the church's face: *Works*, vol. 13, p. 106.

Ciampoli on Gregory XV attitude: Ibid., vol. 11, p. 30.

Riccardi imprimatur for The Assayer: Drake and O'Malley, *Controversy*, p. 152.

11: THE HEART OF THE SCORPION

Mark Antony de Dominis: Pietro Redondi, *Galileo Heretic*, pp. 107–11; Chandler, *History of Persecution*, pp. 269–71; Galileo Galilei, *Dialogue Concerning the Two Chief World*

Systems, 4th Day, p. 428; *The New Catholic Encyclopedia*; H. Newland, *The Life and Contemporaneous Church History of Antonio de Dominis*, Oxford, 1859.

Faber letter on de Dominis: *Works*, vol. 13, p. 207.

Letter to Ingoli: trans. Maurice A. Finocchiaro, *The Galileo Affair*, pp. 154–97.

Anonymous denunciation of *The Assayer***:** Finocchiaro, *Galileo Affair*, p. 202.

The coronation of Urban VIII: Mascardi, "Le pompe del Campidoglio . . . per Urbano VIII quando piglio il possesso . . . ," a contemporary description, Vatican Library.

Guiducci letter: *Works*, vol. 13, pp. 160–61.

Ciampoli letter: Ibid., pp. 146–47.

Characters in the Dialogue: "Degl' interrlocutori nei dialoghi Galileiani e in particolare di Filippo Salviati Linceo," *Il Carteggio Linceo*; Biagi, Maria Luisa, "L'incipit del Dialogo sopra i Massimi sistemi," paper given at conference, "Galileo e La Cultura Veneziana," June 20, 1992.

On Sagredo: Gaetano Cozzi, *Sarpi tra Venezia e L'Europa*, pp. 155–59, 165–67, 175–79, 196–205.

Sagredo letter to Galileo re freedom in Venice: *Works*, vol. 11, pp. 170–72.

Sagredo on Aristotelians: Ibid., p. 379.

Sagredo and the rare Indian bird: Ibid., pp. 257, 270, 278.

Sagredo's method of getting well: Ibid., p. 371.

Galileo's letter upon Sagredo's death: Albèri, *Works*, vol. 7, p. 62.

On Salviati: "Contributi alla storia della Accademia dei Lincei," p. 966, Biblioteca dei Lincei, Rome.

Salviati letters to Galileo: *Works*, vol. 11, pp. 290, 595, 610.

Galileo on his enemies: Letter to the grand duke, in *Works*, vol. 4, pp. 30–35.

12: CONVULSION

Maria Celeste: Mary Allan-Olney, *The Private Life of Galileo*; Giuliana Morandini, introduction to *Lettere al Padre*; Antonio Favaro, "Galileo Galilei e Suor Maria Celeste"; Letters, in *Works*, vol. 13, pp. 398, 399, 400, 402, 404 et seq.

Michelangelo letters: *Works*, vol. 13, pp. 394 et seq.

Cesare Marsili: Letters released at Venice symposium, "Galileo Rediscovered," under auspices of United Nations Educational, Scientific, and Cultural Organization, Sep. 1991.

Galileo on dead hens: Ibid., Galileo to Marsili, Dec. 17, 1624.

Sagredo in Dialogue, "What folly. . . .": Galileo Galilei, *Dialogue Concerning the Two Chief World Systems*, p. 50.

Sagredo, "Simplicio is confused . . . ": Ibid., pp. 56–57.

Simplicio, "If Aristotle is to be abandoned": Ibid., p. 112.

Simplicio, "Please, speak more respectfully . . . ": Ibid., p. 35.

Salviati, "Logic is the organ": Ibid., p. 35.

Salviati, "It is better philosophy": Ibid., p. 56.

Sagredo on man in cupola: Ibid., p. 56.

Galileo on writing as bad for health: Galileo to Marsili, Jan. 17, 1625, Venice symposium.

Galileo's intention in Dialogues: Galileo to Marsili, Nov. 22, 1625, Venice symposium.

Galileo's criticism of Kepler: Galileo, *Dialogue*, p. 462.

Galileo's work on magnets: Galileo to Marsili, June 27, 1626, Venice symposium.

Galileo on horses: *Works*, vol. 6, pp. 563–612.

Galileo on dice: Ibid., vol. 8, pp. 591–92.

Urban VIII and astrology: D. P. Walker, *Spiritual and Demonic Magic*; Luigi Amabile, *Fra Tommaso Campanella*.

Avviso on pope's health: Amabile, *Tommaso Campanella*, vol. 2, p. 149.

Papabili and cousins: John Beldon Scott, *Images of Nepotism*, p. 73.

Solar eclipse, Dec. 25, 1628: Theodor Oppolzer, *Canon of Eclipses*, pp. 27–71.

Salviati, "If the earth moves": Galileo, *Dialogue*, p. 120.

Sagredo, "Why do you reject this explanation?": Ibid., p. 122.

Salviati, "If you have suffered, sagredo": Ibid., p. 327.

Marsili alive!: Galileo to Marsili, April 7, 1629, Venice symposium.

Galileo's slur against Scheiner: Galileo to Marsili, April 21, 1629, Venice symposium.

Salviati, "I ask you, O foolish man . . .": Galileo, *Dialogue*, p. 367.

Ominous signs: Castelli to Galileo, Albèri, *Works*, vol. 9, p. 201.

Galileo's frustration at delay: Galileo to Cioli, *Works*, vol. 14, pp. 215, 258.

Avviso against Galileo, May 18, 1630: Amabile, *Tommaso Campanella*, vol. 2, p. 149.

Visconti to Galileo, June 10, 1630: *Works*, vol. 14, p. 120.

Eclipse, June 10, 1630: Oppolzer, *Canon*, pp. 270–71.

Urban's preparations: Amabile, *Tommaso Campanella*.

Urban's occult obsessions: Scott, *Images*; Walker, *Magic*; Amabile, *Tommaso Campanella*.

Campanella: Amabile, *Tommaso Campanella*.

Plague in Florence: G. Calvi, *Histories of a Plague Year*, pp. 63–70.

Mercuriale and Acquapendente on plague remedies: Ibid., pp. 68–69.

Galileo's fury: Galileo to Marsili, April 5, 1631, Venice symposium.

Proposal for meeting pope: Galileo to Cioli, May 3, in *Works*, vol. 14, p. 258.

Riccardi to inquisitor, May 24: *Works*, vol. 14, p. 266.

13: The Trial of Galileo

The high praise of Micanzio: *Works*, vol. 14, pp. 349–50, 362–63.

Cautionary note: Paolo Aproino to Galileo, March 13, 1632, in Fahie, *Galileo*, p. 264.

Scheiner as foolish and vain: Galileo Galilei, *Dialogue Concerning the Two Chief World Systems*, p. 346.

Scheiner's rage: *Works*, vol. 14, p. 360.

Ambassador Niccolini audience with Urban VIII, Sep. 4, 1632: Maurice A. Finocchiaro, ed., *The Galileo Affair*, pp. 229–32.

Indictments of papal commission: Finocchiaro, *Galileo Affair*, pp. 218–22.

Howl from the lower depths: Galileo to Cardinal Francesco Barberini, Oct. 13, 1632, in *Works*, vol. 14, pp. 406–10.

Galileo's request for delay: Pagano, *I documenti*, p. 17.

Vicar's visit to a sick Galileo: Ibid., p. 120.

Castelli to Galileo, Dec. 25, 1632: *Works*, vol. 14, p. 442.

Galileo's parting shot: Galileo to Diodati, Jan. 15, 1633, in Finocchiaro, *Galileo Affair*, pp. 223–26.

Galileo to grand duke of Tuscany through Cioli (the pretrial letters): Feb. 19, March 12, 19, in *Works*, vol. 15, pp. 43, 63, 69.

Niccolini on Feb. 27 audience with Urban VIII: Finocchiaro, *Galileo Affair*, pp. 245–46.

Niccolini on Urban, March 13: Ibid., pp. 246–48.

Niccolini and pope, April 8: Ibid., pp. 248–49.

Galileo's first interrogation: Ibid., p. 256.

Inchofer report: Ibid., pp. 261–71.

Maculano: Giuseppe Galli, O.P., *Il Card. Vincenzo Maculano al processo di Galileo*.

On torture: Author consultations with John Tedeschi, Tom Cohen, and Marisa Milani; Karl von Gebler, *Galileo Galilei and the Roman Curia*, pp. 253–63.

Maculano's self-congratulatory letter to Holy Office: April 28, 1633, in *Works*, vol. 15, pp. 106–7.

Second deposition: Finocchiaro, *Galileo Affair*, pp. 277–79.

Maria Celeste to her father, "Put your trust in Him": April 20, 1633, in *Works*, vol. 15, p. 98.

Niccolini dispatch, May 22, 1633: Finocchiaro, *Galileo Affair*, pp. 253–54.

Niccolini audience with Urban VIII, June 19: Ibid., pp. 286–87.

Final interrogation: Ibid.

Abjuration: Ibid., pp. 292–97.

14: BLIND OBEDIENCE

Galileo to Urban before leaving Rome: *Works*, vol. 19, p. 362.

Galileo and Piccolomini: C. Ururgieri della Berendenga, *Pio Il Piccolomini*.

Maria Celeste letters: *Lettere al Padre*; *Works*, vols. XV and XVI.

Vatican letter to Venice inquisitor: Karl von Gebler, *Galileo Galilei and the Roman Curia*, p. 269.

Galileo to secretary of grand duke: *Works*, vol. 15, p. 187.

Anti-Galileo treatise: Gebler, *Roman Curia*, p. 271.

Alessandro Marsili in Siena: Stillman Drake, *Galileo at Work*, p. 355.

Father Pelagi: "Rassegna Bibliografica," Marchesini, Archivio di Stato, Siena.

Saint-Amant: Ibid.

Simplicio as the young Galileo: Stillman Drake, Introduction to Galileo, *Discourses on Two New Sciences*.

Anonymous accusation against Piccolomini: *I documenti del processo di Galileo*, Vatican, p. 207.

Maria Celeste: Mary Allan-Olney, *The Private Life of Galileo*.

Little Jewel in Arcetri: "L'Ultima dimora di Galileo," Antonio Godoli and Paolo Paoli, Instituto e Museo di Storia della Scienza, 1979. Author visit.

Vicar of the Inquisition: Galileo to Diodati, in *Works*, vol. 16, p. 116.

Sustermans portrait: Sustermans retrospective and author interview of Charles Cecil, an American painter in Florence.

Urban as Simplicio: Galileo to Micanzio, July 26, 1636, in *Works*, vol. 16, pp. 454–55.

Rendezvous in Poggibonsi: Drake, *Galileo at Work*, p. 375, and dedication of *Two New Sciences*.

On Galileo's Dutch dealings: *Works*, vol. 17, p. 356.

Milton and Galileo: Neil Harris, "Galileo as Symbol: 'The Tuscan Artist' in *Paradise Lost*," Annali dell'Istituto e Museo di Storia della Scienza, 1985.

Imaginary conversation: Walter Savage Landor, *Imaginary Conversations*, New York, AMS Press, 1983, vol. 2.

Liceti correspondence: *Works*, vol. 18, pp. 232–37, 244–45.

Tuscany's man in Venice: Exchange of letters between Galileo and Francesco Rinoccini, *Works*, vol. 18, pp. 311, 314–16.

Vincenzo Viviani: Michael Segre, "Viviani's Life of Galileo," *Isis*, 1989.

Alessandra love letters: *Works*, vol. 18, pp. 194, 311, 319, 374.

SELECTED BIBLIOGRAPHY

Albion, Gordon. *Charles I and the Court of Rome*. Louvain: Sureaux du Recueil, 1935.

Allan-Olney, Mary. *The Private Life of Galileo*. London: Macmillan, 1870.

Amabile, Luigi. *Fra Tommaso Campanella*, 3 vols. Naples: C. A. Morano, 1882.

Armitage, Angus. *The World of Copernicus*. New York: New American Library, 1951.

Barzini, Luigi. *The Italians*. New York, Atheneum, 1964.

Berendenga, C. Ururgieri della. *Pio Il Piccolomini*. Florence: Olschiki Editore, 1973.

Blackwell, Richard J. *Galileo, Bellarmine, and the Bible: Including a translation of Foscarini's letters on the Motion of the Earth*. Notre Dame: University of Notre Dame Press, 1991.

Bowsma, William J. *Venice and the Defense of Republican Liberty: Renaissance Values in the Age of the Counter Reformation*. Berkeley and Los Angeles: University of California Press, 1968.

Brodrick, James. *Robert Bellarmine, Saint and Scholar*. Westminster, Md.: Newman Press, 1961.

Brown, Horatio. *The Venetian Printing Press, 1469–1800*. Amsterdam: Gerard Th. van Heusden, 1969.

Burckhardt, Jacob. *The Civilization of the Renaissance in Italy*. New York: Penguin Books, 1990 (original, 1855).

Campanella, Tommaso. *La Citta del Sole*. Ed. Edmondo Solmi. Modena: 1904.

Il Carteggio Linceo della vecchia accademia di Federico Cesi, 2 vols. Rome: 1938–1941.

Carutti, Domenico. *Breve storia della Accademia dei Lincei*. Rome: Salviucci, 1883.

Chandler, Samuel. *The History of Persecution*. London: J. Gray, 1736.

Cochrane, Eric. *Florence in the Forgotten Centuries, 1527–1800*. Chicago: University of Chicago Press, 1973.

———.*Tradition and Enlightenment in the Tuscan Academies, 1690–1800*. Rome: Edizioni di storia e letteratura, 1961.

Cooper, Lane. *Aristotle, Galileo, and the Tower of Pisa*. Ithaca, N.Y.: Cornell University Press, 1935.

Corboy, Jacobo J., S.J. "The Doctrine of Infallibility of the Pope in Bellarmine and His Influence on the Definition in the Vatican Council." Ph.D. dissertation, Gregorian University, Rome, 1961.

Coyne, G. V., ed. *The Galileo Affair, A Meeting of Faith and Science: Proceedings of the Cracow Conference, May 24–27, 1984*. Citta del Vaticano: Specola Vaticana, 1985.

Cozzi, Gaetano. *Paolo Sarpi tra Venezia e L'Europa*. Turin: Einaudi, 1979.

De Morgan, Augustus. *A Budget of Paradoxes*, 2 vols. New York: Dover Publications, 1954.

De Sanctis, Francesco. *Storia della letteratura Italiana*. Milan: Feltrinelli Editore, 1956.

de Santillana, Giorgio. *The Crime of Galileo*. Chicago: University of Chicago Press, 1955.

Drake, Stillman, ed. *Discoveries and Opinions of Galileo*. Garden City, N.Y.: Doubleday, 1957.

———. *Galileo at Work: His Scientific Biography*. Chicago: University of Chicago Press, 1978.

———. *Galileo Studies: Personality, Tradition, and Revolution*. Ann Arbor: University of Michigan Press, 1970.

———. *Mechanics in Sixteenth Century Italy*. Madison: University of Wisconsin Press, 1969.

Drake, Stillman, trans., with introduction and notes, *Galileo Against the Philosophers*. Los Angeles: Zeitlin & Ver Brugge, 1976.

Drake, Stillman, and O'Malley, C. D., trans., *The Controversy on the Comets of 1618*. Philadelphia: University of Pennsylvania Press, 1960.

Einstein, Alfred. *The Italian Madrigal*, vol. 1. Princeton, N.J.: Princeton University Press, 1949.

Fahie, J. J. *Galileo: His Life and Work*. London: John Murray, 1903.

Favaro, Antonio. *Amici e corrispondenti di Galileo*, vols. 1–3. Firenze: Libreria Editrice Salimbeni, 1983.

———. *Galilei a Padova*. Padua: Antenore, 1968.

———. "Galileo Galilei e suor Maria Celeste." Florence: G. Barbèra, 1935.

———. *Lo Studio di Padova*. 2 vols. Padua: Antenore, 1968.

Finocchiaro, Maurice A., ed. *The Galileo Affair: A Documentary History*. Berkeley: University of California Press, 1989.

Galilei, Galileo. *Dialogue Concerning the Two Chief World Systems, Ptolemaic and Coperni-*

can. Trans. Stillman Drake, with foreword by Albert Einstein. Berkeley: University of California Press, 1953.

———. *Discoveries and Opinions of Galileo*. Trans. with introduction and notes by Stillman Drake. Garden City, N.Y.: Doubleday, 1957.

———. *Galileo's Early Notebooks: The Physical Questions*. Trans. with commentary by William A. Wallace. Notre Dame: University of Notre Dame Press, 1977.

———. "Letter to the Grand Duchess." In *Man and the Universe*. Compiled and edited by the faculty of Lynchburg College. Washington, D.C.: University Press of America, 1982.

———. *On Motion and On Mechanics*. Trans. with introduction and notes by I. E. Drabkin and Stillman Drake. Madison: University of Wisconsin Press, 1960.

———. *Le Opere di Galileo Galilei: Edizione Nazionale* [Works], 20 vols. Florence: Tip. di G. Barbèra, 1890–1909. Directed by Antonio Favaro; also *Prima edizione completa*, vols. 1–16, ed. Eugenio Albèri. Florence: Societa editrice fiorentina, 1842–1856.

———. *The Starry Messenger* (*Sidereus Nuncius* or *The Sidereal Messenger*). Trans. Edward Stafford Carlos, M.A. London: Dawsons of Pall Mall, 1880.

———. *Discourses on Two New Sciences*. Trans. with introduction and notes by Stillman Drake. Madison: University of Wisconsin Press, 1974.

Galilei, Vincenzo. "Dialogo della musica antica et della moderna." In *Source Readings in Music History*, ed. Oliver Strunk. New York: Norton, 1950.

Galli, Giuseppe, O.P. *Il Card. Vincenzo Maculano al processo di Galileo*. Estratto dalla rivista memorie domenicane, 1965.

Galluzzi, Paolo, et al. *Galileo: La Sensata Esperienza*. Milan: Amìlcare Pizzi, 1988.

Galluzzi, P., ed. *Novita celesti e crisi del sapere*. Florence: Giunti Barbèra, 1984.

Gebler, Karl von. *Galileo Galilei and the Roman Curia*. Merrick, N.Y.: Richwood Publishing Co., 1977.

Geymonat, Ludovico. *Galileo Galilei*. Trans. Stillman Drake. New York: McGraw-Hill, 1965.

Gingerich, Owen. *The Great Copernican Chase and Other Adventures in Astronomical History*. Cambridge, Mass.: Sky Publishing Corp., 1992.

Golino, Carlo, ed. *Galileo Reappraised*. Berkeley: University of California Press, 1966.

Horace. *The Poems of Horace: Consisting of Odes, Satires, and Epistles*. New York: AMS Press, 1978.

James, Henry. *Italian Hours*. New York: Ecco Press, 1987.

Johnson, Francis R. *Astronomical Thought in Renaissance England*. Baltimore: Johns Hopkins Press, 1937.

Johnson, Virginia Wales. *Summer Days at Vallombrosa*. New York: A.S. Barnes Co., 1911.

Koestler, Arthur. *The Sleepwalkers: A History of Man's Changing Vision of the Universe*. New York: Macmillan, 1959.

Koyre, Alexandre. *Galileo Studies*. Trans. John Mepham. Atlantic Highlands, N.J.: Humanities Press, 1978.

———. *Metaphysics and Measurement. Essays in Scientific Revolution*. Cambridge, Mass.: Harvard University Press, 1968.

Marino, Giambattista. *L'Adone*. 1623. Reprint. Trans. Harold Martin Priest. Ithaca, N.Y.: Cornell University Press, 1967 (first published in 1623).

McCarthy, Mary. *Venice Observed*. London: Heinemann, 1961.

McIntyre, J. Lewis. *Giordano Bruno*. London: Macmillan & Co., 1903.

Memmo, Paul Eugene. *Heroic Frenzies*. Studies in Romance Languages series, no. 50. Chapel Hill, N.C.: University of North Carolina Press, 1965.

Micanzio, Fulgenzio. *La vita del Padre Paolo*. English trans. London: Moseley & Marriott, 1651.

Milton, John. *Paradise Lost*. 1667, Reprint. New York: Collier Books, 1962.

———.*Paradise Regained*. 1671. Reprint. New York: Collier Books, 1962.

———.*Samson Agonistes*. 1671. Reprint. New York: Collier Books, 1962.

Montaigne, Michel de. *Journey Through Italy: 1580–1581*. New York: Harcourt, Brace, 1929.

Norwich, John Julius. *A History of Venice*. New York: Alfred A. Knopf, 1982.

Oppolzer, Theodor. *Canon of Eclipses*. Trans. Owen Gingerich. New York: Dover Press, 1962.

Panofsky, Erwin. *Galileo As a Critic of the Arts*. The Hague: Martinus Nijhoff, 1954.

Paschini, Pio. Vita e opere di Galileo Galilei. Rome: Herder, 1965.

Pastor, Ludwig von. *The History of the Popes, from the Close of the Middle Ages*. 2nd ed., vols. 23–24. Ed. by F. I. Antrobus and R. F. Kerr. Trans. from German. St. Louis: B. Herder, 1902–1910.

Paterson, Antoinette Mann. *The Infinite Worlds of Giordano Bruno*. Springfield, Ill.: Thomas, 1970.

Pedersen, Olaf. *Galileo and the Council of Trent*. Vatican.

Pieralisi. *Urbano VIII e Galileo Galilei*. Rome: 1875.

Poupard, Paul. *Galileo Galilei: Towards a Resolution of 350 Years of Debate, 1633–1983*. Pittsburgh: Duquesne University Press, 1987.

Puccioni, Nello. *La Vallombrosa e la Val di Sieve inferiore*. Bergamo: Istituto italiano d'arti grafiche 1916.

Ranke, Leopold. *The Ecclesiastical and Political History of the Popes of Rome*. London, John Murray, 1840.

Redondi, Pietro. *Galileo Heretic*. Princeton, N.J.: Princeton University Press, 1987.

Ricci-Riccardi, Antonio. *Galileo Galilei e Fra Tommaso Caccini*. Florence: Successori Le Monnier, 1902.

Righini-Bonelli, M. L., and Shea, William R., eds. *Reason, Experiment, and Mysticism in the Scientific Revolution*. New York: Science History Publications, 1975.

Robertson, Rev. Alexander. *Fra Paolo Sarpi: The Greatest of the Venetions*. London: Sampson Low, Marston & Co., 1894.

Rosen, Edward. *The Naming of the Telescope*. New York: Henry Schuman, 1947.

Ross, Janet, and Erichsen, Nelly. *The Story of Pisa*. Neudeln-Liechtenstein: Krauss Reprint, 1970.

Santinello, Giovanni, ed. *Galileo e la Cultura Padovana*. Padua: Antonio Milani, 1992.

Scott, John Beldon. *Images of Nepotism: The Painted Ceilings of Palazzo Barberini*. Princeton, N.J.: Princeton University Press, 1991.

Shapere, Dudley. *Galileo: A Philosophical Study*. Chicago: University of Chicago Press, 1974.

Shea, William R. *Galileo's Intellectual Revolution: Middle Period, 1610–1632*. New York: Science History Publications, 1972.

Singer, Dorothea Waley. *Giordano Bruno: His Life and Thought*. New York: Henry Schuman, 1950.

Smith, Logan Pearsall. *The Life and Letters of Sir Henry Wotton*. 2 vols. Oxford: Clarendon Press, 1907.

Story, William Wetmore. *Vallombrosa*. Edinburgh: W. Blackwood & Sons, 1881.

Taub, Liba. *Ptolemy's Universe: The Natural Philosophical and Ethical Foundations of Ptolemy's Astronomy*. Chicago: Open Court, 1993.

Tedeschi, John. *The Prosecution of Heresy: Collected Studies on the Inquisition in Early Modern Italy*. Binghamton, N.Y.: Medieval and Renaissance Texts and Studies, 1991.

Viviani, Vincenzo. "Racconto istorico della vita di Galileo Galilei." In *Works*, vol. 19, pp. 597–632.

Walker, D. P. *Spiritual and Demonic Magic*. Notre Dame: University of Notre Dame Press, 1975.

Wallace, William A. *Prelude to Galileo: Essay on Medieval and 16th-Century Sources of Galileo's Thought*. Boston: Reidel Publishing Co., 1981.

———. *Reinterpreting Galileo*. Princeton, N.J.: Princeton University Press, 1984.

Wedgwood, C. V. *The Thirty Years War*. Garden City, N.Y.: Doubleday, 1961.

Wegg-Prosser, F. R. *Galileo and His Judges*. London: Chapman and Hall, 1889.

Westfall, Richard S. *Essays on the Trial of Galileo*. Vatican City and Notre Dame: University of Notre Dame Press, 1989.

White, Andrew Dickson. *A History of the Warfare of Science with Theology*. 2 vols. London: Macmillan, 1900.

Wootton, David. *Paolo Sarpi Between Renaissance and Enlightenment*. Cambridge, 1983.

Young, Col. George Frederick. *The Medici*. New York: Modern Library, 1933.

ACKNOWLEDGMENTS

In the three years it has taken me to complete this book, I've benefited from the help of many institutions and people on two continents and in two and sometimes three languages. In this country my research home was the U.S. Naval Observatory Library, a remote and difficult-to-reach facility behind electronic sensors and secret service guards, lying as it does about a hundred yards from the vice president's mansion in Washington. Its inaccessibility was a great boon to this book, for I had no difficulty in capturing the full attention of the fine librarians, Brenda Corbin and Gregory Shelton. Meanwhile, Silvana de Luca, my neighbor in Bethesda, built my command of the Italian language with exuberance and good cheer as she prepared me for my research trips to Italy and helped with translations. Wallace Ragan, the Latin teacher at St. Albans School, helped with Latin translation, especially Galileo's lectures on the nova of 1604.

To my delight, I was to find that the Italians were truly curious about an American writer who dared to take on the life of so great an Italian, even though they recognized, in their minds if not in their hearts, that Galileo belongs to the world. What if an Italian dared to write the life of George Washington, they would ask drolly. In this most Catholic of countries where Galileo is often in the news and where his face peers out at them from their constantly devaluating two-thousand-lire note, they welcomed an outside perspective.

During my first research trip abroad, in the summer of 1991, I met the writer Idanna Pucci, whose noble lineage traces back to the eleventh century when her family competed with the Medici. From the outset, as she became a friend and colleague, Idanna was unfailing in her enthusiasm, partly, she said, because after her long sojourns to far corners of the earth, my Galileo project brought her back to her Tuscan roots. Through her, I developed my friendship with Cosimo Mazzoni and Antonella Berardi. From their gracious and lively estate in Fiesole, not far from the precipice where Leonardo da Vinci is supposed to have tested his flying machines by pushing winged slaves off the ledges, they helped in countless ways. While in Florence, I benefited greatly from the ideas of Dr. Franco Pacini, the director of the Arcetri Astrophysical Observatory, Paolo Galluzzi, the director of the History of Science Museum, John Spike, the art historian, and Charles Cecil, the American painter.

I began to refer to my Italian trips as making my swing around the Galileo circle. Normally, the circuit started in Rome, and indeed, the writing of the book began there, when I spent a month at the American Academy in Rome in January and February 1992. Under the guidance of the then-director, Joseph Connors, and in the spirited company of my fellow writers, musicians, and scholars, like Alexander Stille, Sarah McPhee, and Stephen Hartke, I got my Roman bearings and my introductions.

At the Vatican, Archbishop John Foley, the communications director for the Holy See (whose formal title is president of the Pontifical Council for Social Communications and who is a graduate of the Columbia School of Journalism), was welcoming. For his cooperation, he asked only two things in return: that I be accurate and fair. In turn, Father Leonard Boyle, the spry Irish priest who is the director of the Vatican Library and expert in all things from Torquemada to the Toronto Blue Jays, was a pleasure to know. I treasure my memory of walking the long corridors of the stacks and drinking cappuccino with him in Bramante's sixteenth-century grotto, which serves as the library's cafe. Father Josef Metzler, the exacting director of the Vatican Archives, was also unfailingly responsive to my requests, including my desire to see the heavily guarded original record of Galileo's trial. This cordial openness, along with the splendor of the frescoed reading rooms, made my research at the Vatican one of the most memorable experiences of my writing life.

At the Vatican Observatory at Castelgandolfo, south of Rome, I spent many interesting hours in conversation with the pope's Jesuit astronomers,

George Coyne and Martin McCarthy. Father Coyne had been central to the thirteen-year reconsideration of the Galileo case, and I appreciated his honesty about that process. At a bishops' conference on Galileo in Castel Gandolfo, I met Richard Westfall, the Galileo specialist from Indiana, who had come to instruct the Catholic bishops about Galileo, even though he is an elder in his Protestant church in Bloomington. His insights both in conversation and in writing have informed this work.

From Rome, I would travel to Florence to spend days in the National Library and at the Institute for the History of Science, and from there make my side trips to Pisa. In Pisa, Roberto Sonnini, a journalist at *Il Terreno,* was my guide and companion. He made it possible for me to be on top of the Tower of Pisa in April 1993 when physicists re-created Galileo's gravity experiments by dropping balls of various weights and densities.

The third matrix for Galileo study is, of course, Padua and Venice. In the summer of 1992 I spent three weeks in these splendid cities as the guest of Paolo Palmeri, an anthropologist at the University of Padua, who along with Alberto Pizzati, an architect and restaurateur, looked out for my needs. I am grateful to three individuals for their research assistance there: Father Claudio Bellinati, a true Galileo expert and the archivist of the Episcopal Curia, Professor Marisa Milani, a professor of literature at the University of Padua, and Giampaolo Seguso, whose father, Archimede Seguso, is the most famous glassmaker in Murano. It was also in Padua that I met Dr. Thomas B. Settle, who has spent thirty years studying Galileo and who is now engaged in re-creating some of Galileo's early experiments.

Toward the end of the writing, I was fortunate to have the perspectives of a distinguished and diverse group of scholars. These are my advisors for the forthcoming PBS television series on Galileo: Owen Gingerich, Ernan McMullin, Anthony Grafton, Liba Taub, Kenneth Manning, Berrien Moore III, Paul Knappenberger, Jr., Riccardo Giacconi, and Jehane Kuhn. I am grateful for their thoughts and encouragement.

Like many books before it, this book has its North Carolina connection. My long-time colleague and dear friend Alfreda Kaplan once again polished my syntax, as she has done for twenty years.

Finally, I thank James Devereaux, S.J., My former colleague at the University of North Carolina, a Shakespearean scholar, and a former provincial of the Jesuit order. He read the manuscript and provided me with many helpful comments.

INDEX